The Circulation of Agency in E-Justice

Law, Governance and Technology Series

VOLUME 13

Series Editors:

POMPEU CASANOVAS, *Institute of Law and Technology, UAB, Spain*

GIOVANNI SARTOR, *University of Bologna (Faculty of Law – CIRSFID) and European, University Institute of Florence, Italy*

For further volumes:
http://www.springer.com/series/8808

Francesco Contini • Giovan Francesco Lanzara
Editors

The Circulation of Agency in E-Justice

Interoperability and Infrastructures for European Transborder Judicial Proceedings

Springer

Editors
Francesco Contini
Research Institute on Judicial Systems
National Research Council of Italy
Bologna, Italy

Giovan Francesco Lanzara
Department of Political and Social Sciences
University of Bologna
Bologna, Italy

ISBN 978-94-007-7524-4 ISBN 978-94-007-7525-1 (eBook)
DOI 10.1007/978-94-007-7525-1
Springer Dordrecht Heidelberg New York London

Library of Congress Control Number: 2013953929

Printed on acid-free paper

Springer is part of Springer Science+Business Media (www.springer.com)

Contents

Abbreviations

ADR	Alternative Dispute Resolution
AI	Artificial Intelligence
APC	Insolvency CMS
AS4 Profile	AS4 is a Conformance Profile of the OASIS ebMS 3.0 specification
ASiC	Associated Signature Container, published by ETSI as TS 102 918
ASiC-S	Simple form of ASiC
BAILII	British and Irish Legal Information System
BIECPO	Building Interoperability for European Civil Proceedings On line
BNI	National Desk for Payment Order Procedures
C-SIS	Technical support function of the Schengen Information System. Central site containing SIS reference database
CCBC	County Court Bulk Centre
CCITT	International Telegraph and Telephone Consultative Committee
CEM	Certified Email
CG	Central Gateway
CIF	Centre for Informatics (Slovenia)
CITIUS	Third generation Procedural Management Program
Citius Payment Order Procedure	Computer application for civil small claims procedure
Citius Plus	Fourth generation Procedural Management Program
Citius-H@bilus	Computer application for court staff
Citius-Judges	Computer application for judges
Citius-Public Prosecution	Computer application for public prosecutors
Citius-Web	Computer application for lawyers and solicitors
CMS	Case Management System

COVL	Central Department for Enforcement on the Basis of Authentic Documents
CPA	Collaboration Protocol Agreement
CPC	Claim Production Centre
CPEPT	TOL dedicated email
CPR	Civil Procedure Rules
CRA	Constitutional Reform Act
DCA	Department of Constitutional Affairs
DCE	Data Circuit-terminating Equipment
DG Market	European Commission Internal Market and Services Directorate General
DGAJ	Directorate-General of Justice Administration
DGPJ	Directorate-General of Justice Policies
DMZ	De-Militarized Zone in informatics
DSS	Digital Signature Services
DTD	Document Type Definition
DTE	Data Terminal Equipment
E-CODEX	e-Justice Communication via Online Data Exchange
e-GMS	Government Metadata Standards
EAW	European Arrest Warrant
EAW FD	European Arrest Warrant Framework Decision
ebMS	ebXML Message Service
ebXML	Electronic Business using eXtensible Markup Language
EC	European Community
ECC	European Consumer Centre
ECC-Net	European Consumer Centre Network
EIF	European Interoperability Framework for European public services
EPO	European Payment Order
ESCP	European Small Claims Procedure
ETSI	European Telecommunications Standards Institute
EU	European Union
EUI	External Users Interface
Eurojust	European Union's Judicial Cooperation Unit
Europol	European Police Office
FAQ	Frequently Asked Questions
FD	Framework Decision
FTP	File Transfer Protocol
GCL	Government Category List
GIF	Government Interoperability Framework
GNU/Linux	GNU's Not Unix!; GNU/Linux Operative system
GPCível	First generation Civil Procedural Management Program
H@bilus	Second generation Procedural Management Program

HMCS	Her Majesty Court Service
HMCTS	Her Majesty Court and Tribunals Service
ICANN	Internet Corporation for Assigned Names and Numbers
ICT	Information and Communication Technology
ID	Identity Document
IDT-UAB	Institute of Law and Technology at the Universitat Autònoma de Barcelona
IETF	Internet Engineering Task Force
iFAQ	Intelligent Frequently Asked Questions system
II	Information Infrastructure
INA	Institutional Interface Architecture
Interpol	International Criminal Police Organization
IRSIG-CNR	Research Institute on Judicial Systems, National Research Council of Italy
ISO	International standardization organization
IT	Information Technology
ITIJ	Institute of Information Technologies in Justice
ITU-T	International Telecommunication Union (ITU) Telecommunication Standardization Sector
IUI	Internal Users Interface
JBPM	Java Business Process Management (workflow management system)
JSA	Schengen Convention Joint Supervisory Authority
JWD	Judges' Work Desk
KZ-1	Penal Code (Slovenia)
LDAP	Lightweight Directory Access Protocol
LEAs	Law Enforcement Agencies
LG	Local Gateway
LOFTJ	Act on the organization and functioning of judicial courts
Log4j	Apache log4j is a Java-based logging utility
LSP	Large Scale Pilot
MCOL	Money Claim OnLine
MJU	Ministry of Public Administration (Slovenia)
MoJ	Ministry of Justice
MS	Member State
N-SIS	National section of the Schengen Information System
NIF	National Interoperability Framework
NLP	Natural Language Processing techniques
OA	Bar Association
OASIS	Europol Analysis System
OASIS	Europol Analysis System (Overall Analysis System for Investigation Support)

OASIS	Organization for the Advancement of Structured Information Standards
OBIE	Ontology Based Information Extraction
OCR	Optical Character Recognition
ODR	Online Dispute Resolution
OECD	Organization for Economic Cooperation and Development
OPJK	Ontology of Professional Judicial Knowledge
OSI	Open Systems Interconnection
OSI	Open Systems Interconnection (OSI) model
OWL	Web Ontology Language
PCOL	Possession Claim OnLine
PdA	Access Point
PKI	Public-Key Infrastructure (digital signature)
POLIS	Office automation tool for judge and for sharing judicial decisions.
PolisWeb	Web-based application for remote accessing to CMS and judgements databases (POLIS).
POS	tagging Part-of-speech tagging
RDF	Resource Description Framework
RDSC	Registry Department of the Supreme Court (Slovenia)
RUG	Justice Network Infrastructure
RUPA	Public Administration Network Infrastructure (before SPC)
s-TESTA	Secured Trans-European Services for Telematics between Administrations
SC	Supreme Court (Slovenia)
SEI	Software Engineering Institute
SEKT	Semantically Enabled Knowledge Technologies
SGBD	Management system databse
SHA-512	Secure Hashing Algorithm, 512-Bits
SI	Semantic Interoperability
SICC	Litigation CMS
SICID	New Litigation CMS
SIEC	Enforcement CMS
SIL	Labour CMS
SIRENE	Supplementary Information Request at the National Entry
SIS	Schengen Information System
SIS I+	Updated version of the Schengen Information System
SIS I+RE	Schengen Information SystemI+ Renewal and Evolution
SIS II	Second Generation Schengen Information System

SIS one4All	Modified version of SIS I+ offered by Portugal to new member states to allow the enlargement of the Schengen area over the SIS I+ limits
SISNET	SIS virtual private network
SITAF	Procedural Management Program for Administrative and Tax Courts
SML/SMP	Service Metadata Locator/Service Metadata Publisher
SOA	Service Oriented Architecture
SOAP	Simple Object Access Protocol
SPA	Service Provider Architecture
SPC	Public Administration Network Infrastructure
SSL	Secure Sockets Layer
SSL/TLS	Secure Sockets Layer/Transport Layer Security
START	PEPPOL Transport Infrastructure Secure Trusted Asynchronous Reliable Transport
TECS	Europol Information System
TOL	Trial Online
TOL PolisWeb	Web-based application for remote accessing to CMS, court databases, and statistics (TOL)
TribNet	Complementary application for access to the general public
TSL	Trust-service Status List
UK	United Kingdom
ULS	Ultra Large Scale Systems
VIS	Visa Information System
W3C	World Wide Web Consortium
WS-RM	WS-Reliable Messaging
WSMO	Web Service Modeling Ontology
WSS	Web Services Security
X.25	Is a packet-switched service
XAdES signature	XML Advanced Electronic Signatures, published by ETSI as TS 101 903
XML	eXtensible Markup Language
ZEPEP	Law on E-Commerce and E-Signature (Slovenia)
ZIZ	Law on Enforcement and Securing of Claims (Slovenia)
ZPP	Civil Procedure Law (Slovenia)
ZS	Court's Law (Slovenia)
XSL	Extensible Stylesheet Language
XSL-FO	Extensible Stylesheet Language Formatting Objects
XSLT	XSL Transformations

Introduction: The Challenge of Interoperability and Complexity in European Civil Proceedings Online

Francesco Contini and Giovan Francesco Lanzara

This book contributes to an understanding of the complexity involved in the design of systems and infrastructures supporting online transborder judicial proceedings in Europe. It deals with critical questions that have both practical and theoretical relevance in building pan-European e-government systems: How should online transborder judicial systems be designed in order to deliver effective and timely judicial services to the citizens, businesses and public agencies of the European Union? What are the major technological, legal and institutional challenges involved in building interoperability of systems and services across national jurisdictions?

During the last decade, the Commission of the European Communities has made a strong commitment towards the development of European e-government services, namely, public services that the administrations of the member states are to deliver to any European citizen, administration or company issuing a request, application or claim, without distinction of territory or nationality. The development of European Public Services is seen as a necessary component of the making of the common market and the empowerment of European democracy. Full support for the common market requires that member states develop e-government services that must be open and seamlessly accessible throughout all Europe, so that European citizens and businesses are enabled to carry out transactions with public administrations other than their own. The broad effort at creating a pan-European e-justice area has also been supported by the European Union justice sector effort through the establishment of a European e-Justice Strategy.[1] According to European e-government policy, the implementation of transborder public services will require that member states' public administrations and nation-based technical and legal systems be made

[1]http://europa.eu/legislation_summaries/justice_freedom_security/judicial_cooperation_in_civil_matters/jl0007_en.htm. Last visited 3 January 2013.

F. Contini (✉) • G.F. Lanzara
Research Institute on Judicial Systems, National Research Council of Italy (IRSIG-CNR), Bologna, Italy
e-mail: francesco.contini@irsig.cnr.it

'interoperable', that is, able to communicate and exchange data, documents and information with one another (see IDABC, European Interoperability Framework, version 1.0 and version 2.0, Commission of the European Communities).[2] Such transactions must be given a legal form, that is, in order to be effective, they should meet the legal requirements established at European and national levels. In addition, they should be made intelligible from a semantic point of view. At a more general level, the effective implementation of European e-government policy requires that both the European Union and the member states support the circulation of agency across national borders and public sectors, that is, the capacity of a subject to act and produce administrative effects in transborder transactions. This raises the question of how such requirements can be fulfilled, that is, which alternative technical and institutional architectures should be built in order to support pan-European interoperability. In order to support the transborder circulation of administrative and legal agency, European Public Services and Information Systems must rely on a common infrastructure, both technical and institutional, no matter which architectural solutions are envisaged or which software applications and systems are developed. The design of technical and institutional architectures that may enable and support the circulation of agency is at the core of the concerns of this book.

The book offers both a conceptual discussion and an empirically driven analysis of the emerging entanglements between technology, law and bureaucracy in the contemporary restructuring of public service delivery systems. Specifically, it investigates the transformations of the legal and institutional frameworks of the judiciary that are brought about by two major factors: ICT-based innovation and the creation of new pan-European judicial proceedings (such as the European Payment Order and the European Small Claim Procedure that we examine in the book). We focus on how *information technology*, legal frameworks and institutional arrangements can be connected and integrated so as to provide a shared platform (or multiple platforms) that may host and support a variety of e-government services for the broader European public. Building upon our previous work (Contini and Lanzara 2009), we complement current approaches to the making of e-government, most of which tend to emphasise the technology and the management dimension, by stressing the critical role of institutional frameworks and rules in fostering technical and institutional innovation. 'Service digitisation' and 'managerial rationalisation', we claim, must be replaced by 'institutional reconfiguration' and 'architectural design' in order to understand how innovation is shaped and how new forms of agency can be sustained by the new systems.

Our main purpose is to help increase awareness of the institutional complexities involved in the development of judicial e-services and open up a window on a range of viable design criteria and scenarios. We build upon leading-edge research in the

[2]The European Interoperability Framework 1.0 is downloadable at:http://ec.europa.eu/idabc/en/document/2319/5938.html; the 2.0 at http://blog.webwereld.nl/wp-content/uploads/2009/11/European-Interoperability-Framework-for-European-Public-Services-draft.pdf. Last visited 30 December 2012.

fields of e-government, information infrastructures and institutional innovation, and at the same time we aim to offer a contribution that goes beyond current approaches. An approach in good currency focuses on the performance of e-government systems, being mainly interested in operational efficiency, performance measures, cost reduction, applications, rational procedures, etc., but shows little interest in the design dimension, that is, in how technical architectures and institutional infrastructures are to be built. The innovation potential and added value of e-service systems are assessed in close connection with management functions, requirements and objectives of the public sector, and in the perspective of bureaucratic innovation (Dunleavy et al. 2006; West 2007).

A second research approach privileges instead the architectural dimension of e-government systems, stressing the critical importance of the technical infrastructure and the existing installed base in the development of complex e-government systems (Ciborra 2000; Hanseth and Monteiro 1997; Star and Ruhleder 1996). This body of literature has produced relevant insights into the dynamics of infrastructures and has led to a design methodology suited to handling the complexity of information infrastructures and technical platforms upon which systems and applications for public services can run (Hanseth and Lyytinen 2010). From this perspective, an information infrastructure is defined as a large-scale assemblage of heterogeneous components, such as standards, protocols, gateways, converters, linkages and other devices that enable and support electronic data interchange and system operation and communication (Lanzara 2009; Monteiro et al. 2012). This approach, though, has mainly focused on the technical and the information aspects of infrastructure, putting relevant phenomena such as agency, organisational dynamics and institutional frameworks into the background of analysis—phenomena that we want to bring to the forefront of our research.

The theme of the book is the idea of circulation of legal agency across national borders, media and functional domains, that is, the capability for citizens, legal practitioners, private companies and public administrations to enact actions with transborder legal effects by using different media and connecting different functional domains. More specifically, we focus on the agency that agents must enact in order to issue claims to and obtain justice from jurisdictions other than their own. As we shall see, such a capability impinges on a complex array of technical, legal and organisational arrangements that enable, support and complement human agency in legal affairs and without which legal agency would not be able to circulate.

We have been driven to see the circulation of agency as a relevant phenomenon by keeping track of the recent implementation of two cross-border judicial remedies at the EU level: the European Small Claims Procedure (ESCP) (Regulation (EC) No. 861/2007) and the European Payment Order (EPO) (Regulation (EC) No. 1896/2006). The first was introduced with the purpose of simplifying and streamlining cross-border small claims litigation; the second is a simplified procedure for uncontested cross-border monetary claims. As stated by the EU Justice Commissioner: 'They offer citizens and businesses across EU the means for quicker, more efficient resolution of cross-border cases, by making it easier to enforce a claim against a defendant in another member state' (Reading 2011: 2). Inasmuch as they are cross-border procedures directly accessible to citizens and businesses without the involvement of lawyers, they provide a challenging test bed for e-justice developments, as well as a rich and innovative case for e-justice and e-government studies.

These two procedures, together with the country-based and additional European cases presented in the book, were the study object of the research project 'Building Interoperability for European Civil Proceedings Online', co-financed by the EU Commission (JLS/2009/JCIV/AG/0035). The project was coordinated by the Research Institute on Judicial Systems of the Italian National Research Council and conducted with the partnership of the Law Faculty of the Central European University in Budapest, the Institute of Law and Technology of the Autonomous University of Barcelona, the Centre for Social Studies of the University of Coimbra, the ICT Department of the Italian Ministry of Justice and the University of Bologna's Department of Political and Social Sciences and Centre on EU Law. The results of the project are available at www.irsig.cnr.it/biecpo.

The national and European case studies that we have analysed in depth provide a rich and unique empirical background to map out the circulation of agency in ICT-enabled proceedings and the technical, legal, institutional and semantic conditions that may enhance or hamper it. Cases comprise leading national e-justice applications developed in England and Wales, Portugal, Slovenia and Italy. Two European e-justice applications currently online are also analysed: e-Curia (at the European Court of Justice) and the European Arrest Warrant. Moreover, the book presents the approach and the preliminary results of e-Codex, the European large-scale project in which nineteen Ministries of Justice, the EU Commission and other technical partners are collaborating to develop pan-European e-justice services. The goal is to facilitate the cross-border access of citizens and businesses to legal procedures in Europe and to improve the interoperability between legal authorities within the European Union.[3]

The materials presented are grounded on theoretical inquiry and extensive case study research. Case studies have been developed according to a common methodology, which envisaged, among other things, a thick description of the strategies adopted to develop the system under examination, the system's developmental history, the architectural configuration, the growth of the infrastructure supporting ICT-enabled procedures and the current functioning of the system.[4] Data are analysed by developing a theoretical framework that takes account of the opposing requirements of system interoperability and evolvability. Because of the growing interdependencies of law, technology, languages and institutions between European member states, a rise in the level of dynamic and interactive complexity is predictable in transborder judicial procedures, particularly when they are carried out in a multimedia environment. Such complexity, though, must be harnessed so that

---

[3]See http://www.e-codex.eu.

[4]The outline of the research method is available at http://www.irsig.cnr.it/BIEPCO/documents/case_studies/Interoperability_Guidelines_May 2011.pdf. Last visited 4 January 2013.

it does not overwhelm the capabilities of professional users and ordinary citizens to carry out their judicial transactions with ease and at low cost.

The book aims to offer a broader perspective on the interoperability problems arising from the interaction of national judicial systems and from the widespread adoption of ICT-based systems. We point out the critical relevance of developing a European technical and institutional infrastructure in order to support the transborder circulation of legal agency. Effective circulation of legal agency requires multilayer interoperability, a shared and carefully designed infrastructure and strategies to reduce and handle interactive and dynamic complexity. The design challenge is to develop systems that balance the requirements of procedural simplicity and minimal complexity on the one hand and the requirements of functionality, usability and legal fairness on the other, while at the same time being capable of evolving and adapting to changing circumstances. While functional and procedural simplification is required to implement and sustain effective judicial e-services, technical and legal solutions must be designed that deliver substantial value to the users, and adaptable configurations must be granted to meet ever-changing technical and social conditions.

We do not intend to offer easy managerial recipes or ready-made solutions for handling the manifold complexity involved in developing e-justice applications that support transborder judicial proceedings. Rather, both in the empirical and theoretical contributions, we put our emphasis on the critical role of the existing technical and institutional infrastructure, which we call the 'installed base'. Originally, the installed base was defined as 'a shared, open (and unbounded), heterogeneous and evolving socio-technical system consisting of a set of ICT-based and institutional capabilities and their user, operations and design communities' (Hanseth and Lyytinen 2010: 4). We extend this definition to the legal and institutional domains: there is not just a technological installed base, but also a legal and an institutional one, and they are so deeply intertwined that it is often impossible to disentangle them or act on one without affecting the other (Contini and Lanzara 2009; Kallinikos 2009). We submit that the 'cultivation' of the installed base is a viable and cost-effective design strategy for developing e-government systems. Indeed, building upon the installed base facilitates system bootstrapping and keeps complexity in check. In dealing with complex and large-scale systems and infrastructures, no blueprint design is possible, no Faustian design is likely to be successful starting from scratch; instead, one should rely on the patient assembling and the careful cultivation of old and new components, and on the smart conversion or enhancement of existing technical and institutional capabilities into new ones.

Outline of the Book

The book is structured in three parts and fourteen chapters. Part 1, 'Beyond Interoperability', introduces and discusses the key concepts and the theoretical framework developed in the course of the 'Building Interoperability' project (2010–2013).

In Chap. 1, Giovan Francesco Lanzara articulates the idea of the circulation of agency and stresses its relevance for the development of transborder e-services in the European judiciary. He spells out the multiple sources of interactive and dynamic complexity that hinder the circulation of legal agency across borders, functional domains and media and proposes the dual and complementary requirements of Maximum Feasible Simplicity and Maximum Manageable Complexity that should guide the design of systems and architectures supporting the circulation of legal agency. E-government solutions for judicial services should fall in the design space limited by such upper and lower thresholds, which in turn depend on technological and human characteristics.

In Chap. 2, Ole Hanseth deals with a number of conceptual and practical issues that emerge when designing ultra-large-scale systems such as the kind of ICT and institutional infrastructures supporting pan-European e-government systems and services. He makes the point that the requirement for more interoperability brings about more complexity and, consequently, less flexibility, thus generating a design dilemma. Hanseth persuasively argues that interoperability criteria and requirements must be complemented by a design focus on system flexibility and evolvability, and that the design of e-government systems and architectures must also address the problem of their evolution and adaptation, a problem which is apparently underplayed in the EU interoperability strategy.

The question of how the law 'can make it simple' for users and enable the circulation of agency is the topic of Francesco Contini and Rick Mohr's Chap. 3. Based on evidence from the case studies, they show how small but smart changes in the legal infrastructure can create favourable conditions for the development of e-justice or, in other words, how functional simplification can be produced by law. Conversely, they analyse the outcomes of development processes in which rigid legal constraints introduce complexity, first into the development process itself and then into the daily use of the systems. To prevent the growth of complexity, they suggest approaches to decouple law and technology as much as possible while assuring the performativity of the utterances exchanged through digital channels.

Part 2 presents national and European experiences of e-justice and discusses their implications for interoperability and the circulation of agency. Case studies follow a common methodology and are structured according to a common template, although with some variations that depend on their specificity. They describe the development and the deployment process of the applications and discuss the findings in light of the concepts presented in the first part of the book. National cases are arranged from the simplest to the most complex. Transborder procedures add further layers of complexity because they must comply with different languages and jurisdictions and, in the case of the European Arrest Warrant, with different legal frameworks and technological infrastructures.

Chapter 4, by Giampiero Lupo, illustrates England and Wales's Money Claim OnLine (MCOL) and Possession Claim OnLine (PCOL), comparing their different architectures and performances. MCOL features here as the most prominent illustration of how an effective e-service can be implemented through the smart exploitation of the technological and organisational installed base and of how a strategy of functional simplification can support the circulation of agency.

Gregor Strojin's Chap. 5 deals with Slovenia's COVL, a money claim e-service in which Maximum Feasible Simplicity is pursued through a combination of legal, organisational and technological changes. The establishment of a national jurisdiction for injunctive orders, coupled with changes to the pre-existing procedural rules, created an institutional environment favourable to procedural digitisation. This has been carried out mostly with internal resources granting a strong control of the judiciary over the entire system.

In Chap. 6, Coimbra's Conceição Gomes, Paula Fernando and Diana Fernandes discuss Portugal's CITIUS, an electronic payment order procedure developed through the years in a piecemeal fashion by cultivating the legal and technological installed base. System complexity has been controlled through the joint introduction of legal and technological changes so as to adapt law and technology to each other in a stepwise fashion. The mutual and recursive adaptation has been possible because, as in Slovenia, technological development has been carried out with limited outsourcing, thus securing greater flexibility in system development.

Davide Carnevali and Andrea Resca discuss Italy's Trial OnLine in Chap. 7, undoubtedly the most complex and problematic national case of e-service implementation that we have encountered in our research work. The case illustrates the legal, technical and institutional factors that hamper e-justice development and the circulation of legal agency in digitally enabled civil proceedings, turning technological innovation into an almost impossible mission. The case also shows how the take-off of the system was possible only after a dramatic downsizing of the originally ambitious, comprehensive plan and a radical simplification of the proceedings.

Problems of system interoperability and evolvability are the subject of Marco Velicogna's Chap. 8 on the European Arrest Warrant (EAW) and the Schengen Information System (SIS). The chapter illustrates how the pre-existing information infrastructure and organisational units put in place to grant the interoperability levels required by the Schengen agreement contributed to the implementation of the EAW. At the same time, it shows how, at the present stage of development, the entanglements between technological and organisational components are hindering the evolution of the system in unexpected ways.

Chapter 9, concluding this part, written by Francesco Contini, examines e-Curia, the e-justice application developed by the European Court of Justice. E-Curia is a case in which smart regulation of technological components, unconventional solutions to the problems of identification and transmission of procedural documents, and an effective black-boxing of procedural complexity carried out by the registries of the Court have led to a smooth and successful development of the first e-justice application supporting transborder litigation.

The contributions in Part 3 assess the legal, organisational and semantic conditions for the circulation of agency in transborder civil proceedings. The focus is on the procedures made available to European citizens and businesses to facilitate an 'uncontested pecuniary claim' (EPO) and cross-border claims of a limited amount (ESCP). Such procedures are first considered from legal, practical and semantic perspectives so as to obtain a comprehensive view of key factors that may affect the circulation of legal agency. The final chapter discusses how technology and institutional changes can support the implementation of e-justice procedures, foster a broader use of them and facilitate the overall circulation of legal agency. It is at this final stage of the research and of the book that the theoretical and empirical findings of the research areas find a final synthesis.

Marco Mellone in Chap. 10 describes the EU legal framework for transborder civil proceedings and discusses the critical legal issues affecting the regulations of the EPO and the ESCP. Particularly he focuses on the mechanisms of legal interoperability and assesses the problems which at the present state prevent a fast and effective communication between courts and case parties situated in different member states.

The legal assessment is supplemented by Gar Yein Ng's analysis presented in Chap. 11. She reports on the simulation experiments conducted to test the practical use of the EPO and ESCP. The findings point to the micro-sources of complexity that make the circulation of transborder legal agency difficult in practice for both claimants and courts and provide inputs for empowering the circulation of agency.

The question of semantic interoperability is the topic of Chap. 12, by the Barcelona team comprising Marta Poblet, Josep Suquet, Antoni Roig and Jorge González-Conejero. They explore problems of communication and interpretation of meaning in the EPO and ESCP. The chapter discusses the opportunities offered by contemporary semantic technologies to mitigate semantic frictions in the circulation of legal agency and to identify a set of specific semantic tools to face some of the key problems affecting the circulation of agency.

In Chap. 13, Marco Velicogna examines the e-Codex project, the first e-justice pilot developed to support the electronic exchange of data and documents required to handle the EPO and the ESCP. The chapter discusses the architectural choices, how the platform will support the circulation of agency and the problems faced at the implementation stage.

Finally, to bring Part 3 to a close and complete the book, Francesco Contini in Chap. 14 makes an overall assessment of the case study materials and findings. Based on the assessment, he spells out a number of practical design principles and the key institutional and technological architectures. He then evaluates their implications for the circulation of legal agency in transborder proceedings in terms of the dual requirements of Maximum Feasible Simplicity and Maximum Manageable Complexity.

Acknowledgements The making and publication of this book have been made possible by the European Commission's grant JLS/2009/JCIV/09-1AG (Directorate-General Justice, Freedom and Security) for the project 'Building Interoperability for European Civil Proceedings Online' (2010–2013), for which the authors wish to express their gratitude.

The book has benefited in various ways from the e-Codex project, co-financed by the European Commission through the Information and Communication Technologies Policy Support Programme (CIP-ICT-PSP.2010.5.2 ref. 270968), in which some of the authors are currently engaged.

Giovan Francesco Lanzara wishes to thank the London School of Economics and Political Science and his colleagues of the Innovation and Information Systems Group at the LSE Department of Management for the fertile intellectual exchanges that throughout the years have nurtured some of the ideas and research work that fed into this book. He is also grateful to the Department of Political and Social Sciences of the University of Bologna for relieving him of part of the teaching load in the academic year 2012–2013, which greatly facilitated project-related work and the completion of the book.

Francesco Contini feels deeply indebted to the Research Institute on Judicial Systems of the Italian National Research Council for the support and encouragement during the 30-month-long project and the drafting of the book. In addition, he wants to thank Richard Mohr because some of the key concepts used in the book have been developed and refined during discussions and previous work carried out together. Finally, he expresses his gratitude to Claudia, Emma and Laura for having been so patient and understanding (perhaps too much), especially during the holiday time he spent writing and editing the book.

References

Ciborra, C. U., ed. 2000. *From control to drift: The dynamics of corporate information infrastructures*. Oxford: Oxford University Press.

Contini, F., and G. F. Lanzara, eds. 2009. *ICT and innovation in the public sector: European studies in the making of e-government*. Basingstoke: Palgrave Macmillan.

Dunleavy, P., H. Margetts, S. Bastow, and J. Tinkler. 2006. *Digital era governance: IT corporations, the state, and e-government*. Oxford: Oxford University Press.

Hanseth, O., and K. Lyytinen. 2010. Design theory for dynamic complexity in information infrastructures: The case of building Internet. *Journal of Information Technology* 25(1): 1–19.

Hanseth. O., and E. Monteiro. 1997. Inscribing behaviour in information infrastructure standards. *Accounting, Management and Information Technologies* 7(4): 183—211.

IDABC. 2004. Documentation on the European Interoperability Framework version 1.0 (November 2004) and draft version of 2.0 (2010). http://ec.europa.eu/idabc/en/document/.\kern\fontdimen3\font.\kern\fontdimen3\font.\kern\fontdimen3\font/5938.html. Accessed 4 Jan 2012.

Kallinikos, J. 2009. The regulative regime of technology. In *ICT and innovation in the public sector: European studies in the making of e-government*, eds. F. Contini and G. F. Lanzara, 66–87. Basingstoke: Palgrave Macmillan.

Lanzara, G. F. 2009. Building digital institutions: ICT and the rise of assemblages in government. In *ICT and innovation in the public sector: European studies in the making of e-government*, eds. F. Contini and G. F. Lanzara. Basingstoke: Palgrave Macmillan.

Monteiro, E., N. Pollock, O. Hanseth, and R. Williams. 2012. From Artefacts to Infrastructures. *Computer Supported Cooperative Work* 14(4): 1–33. Published online 6 June 2012.

Reading, V. 2011. Foreword. In *A citizens' guide to cross-border civil litigation in the European union*, ed. European Judicial Network in Civil and Commercial Matter. Bruxelles: European Commission.

Star, S. L., and K. Ruhleder. 1996. Steps toward an ecology of infrastructure: Design and access for large information spaces. *Information Systems Research* 7(1): 111—134.

West, D. 2007. *Digital government: Technology and public sector performance*. Princeton: Princeton University Press.

Part I
Beyond Interoperability

Chapter 1
The Circulation of Agency in Judicial Proceedings: Designing for Interoperability and Complexity

Giovan Francesco Lanzara

Abstract The central concern of this chapter is the assessment of the technical and institutional conditions that support or hinder the circulation of legal agency, i.e. the capability for agents to produce legal and administrative effects across national borders, media, and functional domains. Dynamic and interactive complexity is acknowledged as a critical factor that hinders the circulation of agency and the effective delivery of judicial e-services across Europe. I spell out the multiple sources of complexity that arise in the design of e-services in the domain of civil justice, both at the national and the pan-European level. I set my analysis within the broader issue of the design of large-scale systems and infrastructures and argue that interoperability requirements must be complemented by the equally critical requirements of system adaptability and evolvability. Finally I propose the twin design principles of maximum feasible simplicity and maximum manageable complexity that should be followed when developing e-government services and systems.

1.1 The Challenge: Enabling the Circulation of Agency

All efforts at building e-government systems must confront the following critical questions:

- How should e-government systems be designed so that they may deliver timely and cost-effective public services to users?
- How can systems create value for citizens and businesses, and for the society as a whole?

G.F. Lanzara (✉)
Department of Political and Social Sciences, University of Bologna, Bologna, Italy
e-mail: giovan.lanzara@unibo.it

F. Contini and G.F. Lanzara (eds.), *The Circulation of Agency in E-Justice*, Law, Governance and Technology Series 13, DOI 10.1007/978-94-007-7525-1_1,

After a 20-year-long history of e-government development efforts, these questions remain at the core of public officials' and designers' concerns, and very much the focus of leading-edge research in the field of ICT-based innovation in the public sector (Contini and Lanzara 2009; Dunleavy et al. 2006; Hanseth 1996; Hanseth and Lyytinen 2010). Since its early times, ICT has been looked at as a powerful means of rationalisation and innovation for government and the public sector. In the eyes of policy makers and ICT people, e-government was viewed, and in many instances still is viewed, as 'putting services online'. That means straight 'service digitisation', with little regard for whether the users will indeed use the services and with a considerable underestimation of the institutional complexity involved in ICT-based innovation in the public sector. Even today, 'government goes online' or 'digital governance' are pervasive and recurrent buzzwords, but little effort has been put into understanding which parts of government go online, what turns digital and what is actually involved in the process. Moreover, only occasional and superficial inquiry has been conducted into the reasons why ambitious, comprehensive and expensive e-government development programs have been of little consequence for broad user adoption and social diffusion.

In more recent times, though, both practical experience and theory-based empirical research have shown that putting government online entails substantial institutional reconfiguration at all levels of government. The making of e-government involves building a new kind of technical and institutional infrastructure and setting up institutionally embedded communication systems. Effective e-service delivery will not happen without a deep restructuring of the organisational structures and routines of the public sector (Henman 2010). We have become more aware that ICT calls for normative and institutional innovation in the ways government operates and induces changes in the government/user relationship. Without a deeper understanding of how innovation is shaped between the rules of technology and law and between the organising principles of bureaucracies and markets, it will be difficult to develop online public systems that work properly and serve people.

Although the questions opening this chapter may be considered too wide-ranging, they have a practical relevance inasmuch as the value of such public systems, and the increasing returns to investment they generate, depend very much on the number of people who actually adopt them. Without reaching a critical mass of users, the system will not take off and the flow of positive externalities will be thin, as we have learned from leading evolutionary economists and economic historians (Arthur 1994; David 1985). Even though in recent times designers' and government's concerns have shifted from a government-centric to a more user-centric approach (OECD 2009), e-services have been growing at a slower pace than expected. Among the many explanations aired for this (a lack of user-friendliness, ingrained habits and practices, resistance to change, the digital divide, mistrust in ICT or in government, fear of privacy violation, etc.), one could well be that designers and policy makers have failed to implement systems that deliver the value they promise. In other words, with notable exceptions, they have failed to develop systems that can be powerful attractors of people right from their initial stages.

They have failed to strike the right balance between complexity and simplicity, that is, developing systems that provide users with value and at the same time are simple enough to facilitate smooth adoption and use. Systems are often too complex for the layperson. System complexity is an obstacle to user take-up of the system, and the strategy of designing functionally complex systems right at the outset and handing them to users is self-defeating, even if in principle the systems may be well engineered, technically sound and based on a robust legal framework.

In this chapter, and throughout the whole book, we explore the complexities that arise in the design of e-services in the domain of civil justice, both at the national and the pan-European level. In the process, we shift our focus from public service delivery to the idea of 'circulation of agency'. This shift entails a reframing of the notion of the user as a passive recipient of services provided by the government machinery to the idea of an 'active agent' who is enabled to act and pursue her goals or rights with and through the system.

Our central theoretical concern has been to explore the technical and institutional conditions that support or hinder the circulation of legal agency. Agency is broadly defined here as the capacity of an entity—human or nonhuman, material or symbolic—to produce effects upon a state of affairs. By 'circulation of agency', we mean the possibility for such capacity to be transmitted across multiple media, national borders and functional domains. For example, a firm's or a public office's agency is said to be able to circulate when purposeful actions initiated in a specific place, time and functional domain are carried across a sequence of multiple enchainments without that agency losing its effectiveness, its meaning and its capability to produce effects in a different place, time and functional domain. The question of the circulation (or transmission) of legal agency has emerged as the ordering leitmotif in the course of our research work and plays a key role in this chapter and in the entire book.

Complexity hinders the circulation of agency through the system and the effective delivery of e-services. Dynamic and interactive complexity emerges from the multiple interactions and interdependencies between the different domains of technology, law and organisation. When online public services are developed, multiple functional domains are brought to bear on one another and complex entanglements emerge through which agency is supposed to circulate.

Therefore, the questions formulated at the outset may be reframed as the following:

- How can we design e-government systems that support the circulation of legal agency in the EU?

In trying to provide an answer to this question, we build upon both the achievements and the limitations of current approaches and upon independent, extensive field research. The research project 'Building interoperability for European civil justice', co-financed by the European Commission, has been an opportunity as well as a playground to develop and test our ideas through a number of case studies dealing with the development of judicial e-services at the national and European level. Here we lay out our line of argument in a nutshell:

> In order to enable the circulation of legal agency, interoperability is a critical requirement, but in order to build interoperability, an underlying infrastructure is needed. However, infrastructural (architectural) and procedural complexity stand in the way of the circulation of agency; moreover, interoperability is not the only critical requirement, as adaptability and evolvability are also important. Thus, design criteria must be developed to tackle the interactive and dynamic complexity involved in developing systems and infrastructures that enable and support the circulation of agency.

We set our analysis within the broader issue of the design of large-scale systems and infrastructures. Although our research has been conducted within a specific public domain, the judiciary, we claim that our findings can provide useful insights into the design of e-government systems in all domains of the public sector in which the delivery of public services to citizens is the critical mission. Indeed, due to its unique normative thickness and heavy regulative status, the judiciary is quite recalcitrant to innovation and often presents greater problems of re-design and adaptation than other domains of the public sector.

The remainder of the chapter is structured as follows. In the next section, we briefly refer to the European context within which we carried out our research work, namely, the EU policies of building European integration in the field of public services. In Sect. 1.3 we discuss the idea of the circulation of legal agency and in Sect. 1.4 we illustrate the problems of the circulation of agency based on our empirical work. In Sect. 1.5 we discuss the concepts of interoperability and adaptability and we argue for the critical role of infrastructure in enabling and supporting the circulation of agency. In Sect. 1.6 we articulate the major sources of complexity arising from interdependencies between functional domains, national jurisdictions and multiple media. In Sect. 1.7 we argue for the need to search a dynamic balance between procedural and infrastructural complexity. Finally, in Sect. 1.8 we propose general design strategies that should be enacted when developing e-government systems, both at the level of the infrastructure and at the level of the procedure.

1.2 The Research Context: Building Interoperability for European Civil Justice

In a wide variety of policy documents the European Commission has put the emphasis on building interoperability as the key requirement for achieving judicial cooperation among member states (MSs): transborder delivery of e-services will require that MSs' public administrations and nation-based technical and legal systems be made interoperable, that is, able to communicate and exchange data, documents and information with one another with the aim of extending judicial services across the European Union. In the judiciary, as in many other public domains, such transactions must be given a legal form, that is, in order to be effective, they must meet the legal requirements established at European and national levels. In addition, transactions and procedures must be comprehensible from a semantic point of view, that is, executable in multiple languages. At a more general level, the effective implementation of the European e-government policy requires that both the EU and the MSs support the circulation of agency across national borders and public sectors. This raises the question of how such requirements may be fulfilled, that is, which alternative technical and institutional architectures should be designed in order to support pan-European interoperability and the circulation of agency.

For example, in the case of civil justice, national courts and Ministries of Justice are responsible for delivering judicial services online across European borders when they receive and process transborder claims. In order to do that they should adapt or update their technology, language, legal rules, administrative procedures and organisational structures according to the guidelines of the European Interoperability Framework (EIF). As will be illustrated later, this is not an easy goal to attain, due to a variety of reasons. Transborder interoperability puts immense pressure on national administrations and, most critically, inflates the overall procedural and architectural complexity. Furthermore, it is highly unlikely that an interoperable connection with EIF could be attained with the same ease, speed and timeliness by all MSs. Even if the principles and guidelines of the EIF do not have a mandatory character and do not replace national frameworks, the conditions and requirements for transborder interoperability are very demanding for most national governments. Previous studies have shown that national justice systems in the EU MSs are very heterogeneous (Fabri and Contini 2001; Contini and Lanzara 2009), and for most of them, in their present state, the attainment of an effective transborder circulation of agency will require a great deal of redesigning and restructuring.

Due to differences in the MSs' conditions, it is likely that the interactions between the EIF and each National Interoperability Framework (NIF) will generate a broad range of different solutions and configurations, thus amplifying complexity, for a number of reasons:

- Firstly, NIFs start out at different stages of development. Some countries, such as the UK and Finland, have already established and tested their NIF, which is already operating; some are still in the process of building it, but lag behind.
- Secondly, NIFs sit upon different existing infrastructures (installed bases and legacy systems), each with its own specific structural and functional features that will most likely generate path-dependence with further development. This amounts to saying that some developments and adaptations to harmonise the NIF with the EIF may be costly and difficult to realise.
- Thirdly, NIFs respond to different bureaucratic and legal requirements in each MS. It is likely that in some countries, such as Italy, the linkage and harmonisation of the NIF with the EIF will be accomplished through further legislation, thus injecting further legal complexity into the system.

All these elements will influence the patterns of transformation of the NIFs and most likely will increase the level of complexity of the whole system. In other words, we may be confronting the paradoxical outcome that the pressure to convergence and conformity to the EIF guidelines by the MSs will also generate heterogeneity, because it is likely that each single national administration or jurisdiction will take its own distinctive path to align its procedures and systems to the EIF principles, possibly leading to different outcomes.

At the same time, MSs with an already well-developed infrastructure and interoperability framework will lobby to extend their solutions to other countries. All this amounts to saying that the adoption and implementation of EIF guidelines by the MSs will most likely generate processes of change in the national jurisdictions (in the legal codes, in the administrative procedures, in the technical solutions, etc.). These processes are critical; hence, it is important to monitor them carefully, because whether a smooth and swift circulation of legal agency will effectively be enabled across trans-national borders will ultimately depend on their outcomes.

1.3 The Circulation of Agency in Judicial Proceedings

A major goal of the EU e-government policy is to improve transborder accessibility of public services across the European Union. Such a goal requires each MS to develop e-government services that must be open and seamlessly accessible throughout the EU, so that European citizens and businesses are able to carry out online transactions with public administrations other than their own. For such transactions to be effected, systems must let agency flow throughout national borders, media and functional domains.

In our context, legal agency is the capacity of a citizen or business firm to claim and obtain money from a debtor, the capacity of an online procedure to swiftly produce the identification of a claimant or applicant, the capacity of an electronic document to travel across multiple jurisdictions in the EU without losing its legal validity and meaning or, at a larger scale, the capacity of a national case management system to exchange selected data across large public and private databases in order to fulfil its institutional mission. Agency is enabled, channelled or hindered by technical, procedural and institutional arrangements that may influence the capacity to act in various ways, enhancing, guiding or limiting it. Whoever engages in developing transborder ICT-based judicial proceedings must necessarily aim at enabling some kind of legal agency, empowering individuals, businesses and administrations to produce legal effects through their actions.

The sketchy examples just made show that the term 'agency', as we use it here, does not exclusively refer to the purposeful activities of human agents but is attributed to anything (actor, object, document, system, code, device, tool) that may produce effects, to anything that makes something happen, thereby changing the state of affairs. Indeed, in complex technical and institutional environments it might often be difficult or even impossible to locate agency exclusively with the human agent or with a group of human agents. It is often more rewarding to attribute it to systems, networks or assemblages constituted by human and nonhuman components, which are both called ‘actants’ (Callon 1992; Latour 1992, 2000). In other words, the human agent as such is not or needs not be the only locus of agency in a complex system. Agency is also shaped and channelled by a variety of nonhuman actants. To select some examples from the judiciary, even the courtroom, through its spatial and procedural arrangements, is an ‘active’ component of the agency carried out in oral proceedings, because its procedures and decisions effect changes in the state of things and even produce new realities; at the smaller scale of single artefacts, the transcript or the video of a hearing work as ‘actants’ inasmuch as they ‘make do’, enabling the circulation of agency within a complex web of humans and artefacts. To illustrate further how different technical or legal arrangements can enable or hinder agency in judicial systems, we can take the case of digital signatures and identification. Legal procedures require them in order to bestow upon an actor some form of legal agency. Depending on the means of identification, which can be more or less constrictive, technically feasible or legally acceptable, the actor’s capacity to act legally can be greatly enhanced or severely limited (Mohr and Contini 2011). Following from these considerations, it is important to stress here that legal agency does not only amount to the exchange of bits and information but also produces changes of status, and in order to be effective must itself be made ‘legal’. Interoperability, therefore, must not only enable or facilitate exchange of bits and flows of data across systems but must also support the production and transmission of legal effects across different systems, domains and territories.

In the design of European civil proceedings online, agency must be able to travel across different national jurisdictions (legal, administrative and contractual environments), different functional domains (legal, technological, organisational, economic) and different media (oral, paper, digital) (Mohr and Contini 2011). In the two specific cases of European Small Claims Procedure and European Order for Payment, which were the object of our study, the kind of agency that must circulate online is mainly, although not exclusively, legal. In order to effect smooth circulation of agency, the interoperability framework must allow for a number of things: the transborder transmission of data; the recognition of the data’s and documents’ legal validity; the constancy of the meaning of data, documents and specific legal actions; and the administrative effectuality or performativity of judicial decisions across national jurisdictions. In the ‘conventional configuration’ of judicial systems impinging on a local or national jurisdiction (Mohr and Contini 2011), the circulation of agency is traditionally effected through long-established paper-based procedures and supported by material artefacts such as application forms, case folders, printed documents, dockets, counters, etc., or, as we have just mentioned, the spatial layout of the hearing room. The development of e-justice entails the reconfiguration of agency across multiple media. This ‘complexity leap’ originates from the new mediation of agency brought in by the digital environment. In the making of European e-services, however, a second major ‘leap’ is occasioned by the ‘boundary crossing’ across different national jurisdictions (see Fig. 1.1).

Agency in transborder judicial proceedings cannot be carried by (and ‘housed’ within) the traditional configuration within a national jurisdiction; it must be

		Jurisdiction	
		National →	Transborder
Media	Conventional	Conventional Paper-based procedure	EPO and ESCP at present
	Digital ↓	National ejustice case studies	EPO and ESCP digitally enabled

Fig. 1.1 Complexity leaps

extended across national borders and across different media through sequences and networks of multiple assemblages (*agencements*), which connect pre-existing and new components in emerging techno-institutional configurations (Deleuze and Guattari 1980; Contini and Lanzara 2009). To this purpose, national legal and administrative systems must learn to communicate with one another and engage in cooperative action; they must also learn to operate in a new multi-media environment, where the digital media 'remediates' the legal practices, the procedures, the familiar tools and the meanings, that is, it remediates agency and the channels through which agency circulates. The outcome of this reconfiguring process is an emerging assemblage (*agencement*) of heterogeneous components—multimedia, multi-functional and multinational—across which judicial and administrative agency should presumably be able to circulate through the channels, linkages and gateways that provide for systems interoperability.

1.4 Problems with the Circulation of Agency: The Experiments with EPO and ESCP

In order to explore how complexity may hinder the circulation of agency in pan-European justice, we have run a practical experiment designed to test the extent to which two recently designed European procedures, namely, the European Payment Order (EPO) and the European Small Claim Procedure (ESCP) could meet the European objectives. A UK correspondent filed an EPO and an ESCP to an Italian court by following the instructions provided by the e-justice portal (http://e-justice.europa.eu) and by the European Judicial Atlas in Civil Matters (http://ec.europa.eu/justice_home/judicialatlascivil/htlm/index_en.htm) (see Chap. 11 for a more detailed account).

The European regulations have attempted in various ways to simplify procedures in order to make things easy for the users. In theory, superimposing a unique pan-European procedure on the pre-existing multitude of heterogeneous national procedures offers EU citizens and businesses a unique standardised procedure working in each MS. Formal requirements have been kept as simple as possible: the simple handwritten signature, with no requirement of being certified by a local authority or being supported by any additional document, is accepted as valid; pro se litigation is accepted; and cases can be filed using normal postal services. Finally, the data to be entered into the various forms to be exchanged in the judicial transaction are relatively simple and standardised. Only in a few cases do the parties have to provide relatively complex written statements (such as the description of the claim). Even if the language barrier and the need to provide such statements in the language of the seized court may be problematic, efforts have been made to design a procedure accessible to citizens and businesses without the involvement of professional lawyers and without going to court. Therefore, in terms of accessibility and user-friendliness, the procedure appears to represent a remarkable improvement compared to several national judiciaries in which the certified authenticity of the defendant's signature is required, legal patronage is needed and plaintiffs and defendants must go in person to the court counter to file cases.

In spite of such efforts at procedural simplification, the experiment highlighted a number of problems affecting the circulation of agency that make it difficult for a generic user to handle the procedure in practice. The first problem the UK-based user encountered was how to identify the jurisdiction and the seized court. If the claimant most likely is not familiar with the country-specific jurisdictional rules and structure, she might seize the inappropriate court, and if the seized court is not the one having the jurisdiction, the court could dismiss the case. Secondly, before filing a case, the claim has to be described by using the language of the seized court, in this specific case, Italian, with which a British citizen may not be familiar. A translator must then be called in to solve the problem. Thirdly, court fees have to be paid, and in order to proceed to payment the exact amount must be calculated and a suitable means of payment identified. Here, another problem emerged, since the e-justice portal (the official site where information for this kind of procedure can be found) did not mention the possibility of online payments. Consequently, the claimant had to find a way to pay the court fee without going to Italy: anything but easy. Even more telling was the late discovery that, despite what is stated in the e-justice portal, in Italy it is possible to pay EPO and ESCP court fees with a normal bank order to a specific account, raising the problem of how to keep the portal information updated in real time in the face of continuous local changes. Finally, once the case was filed and the EPO issued, the Italian registry did not serve the document to the plaintiff and the defendant, as it was supposed to do according to the European regulations. The court decided that, in this case, instead of following what was stated by the European rules, it was better to stick to the national rules. The plaintiff therefore had to find a way to get the EPO from the court counter, if possible without travelling to Italy.

Even these simple illustrations suffice to show how difficult it is to meet the goals established by the Commission. The circulation of agency from one jurisdiction to another is hampered not only by language barriers or procedural complexity but also by a number of administrative and procedural micro-issues and by the questionable (or wrong, contingent or simply whimsical) interpretation of European regulations by national courts. Minimal as these procedural slippages may be, they still produce the effect of interrupting the procedure and forcing users to do extra work or to hire a lawyer, thus burdening them with transaction costs. A further likely consequence will be the user's frustration. It is therefore critical that the development of an effective e-justice system supporting the circulation of agency in transborder procedures take care of these problems, otherwise people will not be motivated to use the new tools.

From the data collected, we know that in the early development phase national courts handle a very small number of EPOs and ESCPs, resulting in a low frequency of transactions throughout the system. A critical issue, then, is how to create conditions and a mechanism that will attract a high number of users in the early phases. In order to do this, it is necessary to deliver some value to the users right at the outset, and at the same time to make the digital procedure as accessible and friendly as possible for the naïve user. Systems and procedures must be simple enough in the early stages so that users will find them more convenient to use, for example, because they are faster and less expensive than the conventional ones. The requirement of low complexity and high accessibility for the design of the digital procedures are even more critical if we consider that such European remedies are in competition with national payment orders and small claim procedures. A potential claimant, before filing an EPO or an ESCP, may still consider the option of requesting a local payment order. Geographic and linguistic barriers can reduce access to justice for some users, but not for others. For a normal citizen to hire a lawyer in a different country may be a serious problem, but not for many companies doing their business in the EU. Therefore, EPO, ESCP and the ICT systems that must enable and support them have to be designed with a focus on the potential users who may have problems in accessing cross-border proceedings through the conventional national remedies.

The practical test of the EPO and ESCP shows that the circulation of legal agency throughout the EU, that is, the possibility for a user to obtain justice and for a system to deliver it in practice, depends on system interoperability across national borders, media and functional domains. Poorly interoperable systems create problems and bottlenecks in the circulation of agency, generating unwanted local sources of complexity and a rough, impervious territory through which legal agency will encounter obstacles and will be slowed down by frictions. As a consequence, desired effects will not be produced. Moreover, the test also shows that the scope of interoperability reaches well beyond the simple exchange or transport of electronic data and legal documents across systems and borders. It should actually encompass the whole legal procedure, from facilitating users' access and operations to supporting the judges and the judicial offices that receive the claim and issue a decision. Electronic data exchange and e-filing are therefore important aspects of the procedure but do not by themselves grant the circulation of legal agency. In light of the above considerations, in the following section we take our next step by discussing the concept of interoperability, its limits and its relations to the broader notion of infrastructure.

1.5 Beyond Interoperability: The Critical Role of Infrastructure

1.5.1 Interoperability and Adaptability

The idea of interoperability originates from the technical field of computer-based communication and standardisation. It usually denotes what kind of communication and integration one wants to achieve between computer systems by enforcing a set of shared standards in order to support electronic data exchange. Interoperability stands as a key concept in the EU strategy for developing pan-European e-government solutions but is given a much broader and essentially non-technical definition. In the European Interoperability Framework, it is defined as

> the ability of disparate and diverse organisations to interact toward mutually beneficial and agreed common goals, involving the sharing of information and knowledge between organisations via the business processes they support, by means of the exchange of data between their respective information and communication technology (ICT) systems (EIFv.2.0: 2).

In other official documents, interoperability is generically defined as 'the ability of organisations to work together to common goals', a phrasing that emphasises the outcome of interoperability rather than the conditions that make it possible.

In several documents of the European Commission, the idea of interoperability is illustrated through the analogical image of a chain (EIFv.1.0), or else a train of gears (www.e-codex.eu). Both these analogies are at the same time suggestive and misleading, inasmuch as they convey an image of interoperability as a static property, giving it the quality of a tight mechanical coupling, whereas the means by which interoperability is provided must necessarily evolve as technological, legal and institutional conditions change. Whilst such images point to 'connectedness' and 'transmission', they keep out all conceptions of flexibility and adaptability.

One might question, then, whether this concept, in its current formulation, can help us to understand fully the aspects and issues that matter when we try to develop and implement pan-European e-government solutions (Hanseth 2011). For instance, one might reasonably doubt whether the original meaning and scope of the concept can be maintained when it is transposed to non-technical domains, such as the different national legal codes, the organisational settings and the semantic domains, that must also be made 'interoperable' to enhance the circulation of agency. In addition, one might wonder whether interoperability captures everything that needs to be taken into account when developing pan-European transborder procedures (in the judiciary or other domains). What's more, one might question whether high or full system interoperability is an absolute value or whether the interoperability requirement should be balanced with the equally critical requirements of flexibility and adaptability. It could be the case that too much interoperability at a specific level and at a specific time yields undesired consequences at a different level or at a later time. In the end, one might legitimately ask how much interoperability is desirable or necessary to enable the circulation of agency, and how interoperability, once built into the European e-government framework, can be maintained and adapted over time. Elements of a processual and evolutionary approach are curiously absent in the current version of the EIF, but in our opinion they are critical and should not be left out of any design endeavour.

Indeed, if we delve more deeply into the meaning and scope of interoperability, we are led to reframe our ways of looking at interoperability as the major focus of design. We should look beyond interoperability. To begin with, all designs must maintain a balance between interoperability and adaptability, and this puts limits on the amount of interoperability that can or should be achieved. Building interoperability cannot be framed only as the design of interfaces and linkages between different systems through the implementation of technical standards or the alignment of administrative and legal systems, or by enforcing a semantic reduction of linguistic variety. More critically, interoperability is not an intrinsic property of interacting computer systems, never mind of the systems that are in place and operating here and now. It cannot be designed simply as a result of a convergence and homogenisation among systems, procedures and applications, whereby NIFs must adapt to and comply with the EIF guidelines in resetting their procedures, applications and organisational equipment. This, we surmise, will most likely feed variety and inflate an unmanageable complexity.

We should also look at the conditions that make interoperability possible rather than at its outcomes. The conditions of interoperability do not reside in the systems that happen to be in place and run at a specific point in time at a specific location, but in the underlying infrastructure that supports system operations and communication along with a whole set of various and changing functionalities. The concrete possibility of attaining interoperability depends on the existence and the quality of the infrastructure—technical, legal, institutional and semantic—and on the features of the agency to be supported. A consideration of infrastructure will allow us to develop a broader view of the complexity involved in the making of e-justice and construct a richer conceptualisation of interoperability.

1.5.2 *Infrastructure*

Around the idea of infrastructure, a number of scholars have done substantive research in recent years with a specific focus on ICT infrastructures (Bowker and Star 1999; Broadbent and Weill 1999; Hanseth 1996; Hanseth and Lyytinen 2010; Monteiro and Hanseth 1999; Ciborra et al. 2000; Contini and Lanzara 2009; Star 1999). An infrastructure has been defined as 'a shared, open (and unbounded), heterogeneous and evolving installed base' (Hanseth and Lyytinen 2010, 4). In turn, the installed base is 'a set of ICT capabilities and their users, operations and design communities' (Hanseth and Lyytinen 2010, 4). ICT infrastructures result from the convergence of information technologies and systems and telecommunication technologies. Due to its elusive and ever-shifting features, it is definitely not easy to grasp what an infrastructure is as a stable empirical object. An infrastructure is made of standards, protocols, gateways, converters, linkages, channels and other components that allow for certain functionalities to be implemented, connected and operated in a network. In our own reformulation, an infrastructure is the underlying base and support for the circulation of agency. Infrastructures retain relational and ecological qualities. They are not 'things' or fixed entities that can be designed ex ante, developed by sticking to a blueprint and eventually built into a finished state. In addition, they evolve over time: they are built from pre-existing components, grow in reach and range, and adapt to changes in user requirements and enabling technologies. With infrastructures, the scope of design is conspicuously narrowed. The only thing that can be reasonably done is to cultivate and nurture them along the way in a piecemeal fashion as they evolve and reconfigure (Ciborra 2000; Dahlbom and Janlert 1996, Hanseth, Chap. 2 in this book; Hanseth and Lyytinen 2010; Lanzara 2009b).

In order to provide European interoperability in the domain of civil justice, as in any other e-government domain, an infrastructure must be assembled that is shared by all MSs and by the potential users (citizens, enterprises, etc.) as a sort of common good. The European infrastructure can be here provisionally defined as a shared platform that allows some forms and levels of interoperability and communication among diverse domains, sectors and territories. As one can distinguish different types of interoperability (see EIFv2.0 2010), so one can distinguish different types of infrastructure in different domains. Thus, an information infrastructure consists of a set of standards, protocols and gateways that link the running applications, programs and systems. It connects, supports and enables the exchanges of bits, data and information between different technological and human agents. A legal infrastructure is made by shared legal principles, rules and procedures that link the several national jurisdictions and help them communicate and inter-operate. In legal terms, this is mainly based on the EU principles of legal cooperation and mutual recognition. A more practical aspect is that legal objects (files, sentences, utterances) must keep their legal validity when they cross the borders of a jurisdiction. A semantic infrastructure provides mechanisms for inter-language communication, including human and automatic translators between different languages, in order to retain meaning. An institutional infrastructure consists of bureaucratic procedures and organisational routines that can carry out the relevant administrative and business processes across national borders.

More to the point, infrastructures make interoperability possible as a particular kind of agency. When the components of an infrastructure are well functioning and not obtrusive to human action, they tend to be taken for granted by the user. Indeed, the user perceives herself to be handling an application or a tool, or interacting with a simple interface, rather than using the underlying infrastructure that makes the application run and the use of the tool possible. Agency can then be carried smoothly across systems, media and territories. When this happens, it means that the infrastructure has absorbed and hidden away from the user most of the complexity involved in the transactions. However, the infrastructure itself can reach high levels of complexity that might run against the maintenance and the smooth functioning of the infrastructure or make it impossible for the infrastructure to evolve over time. This is why it is so important to design infrastructures in modular components that 'unpack' and 'unbundle' complexity (Hanseth and Lyytinen 2010).

1.5.3 Problems with Building European Infrastructure: The Schengen Information System

The European Union's Schengen Information System (SIS) represents a good example of the complexities involved in the development of infrastructures. SIS is the set of databases, applications and the underlying infrastructure used by the MSs to collect and exchange data relevant for border control and law enforcement purposes (such as the European Arrest Warrant). Since the nineties, SIS has evolved, providing new services and progressively including new MSs. The original system was improved with the deployment of SIS 1+, allowing Denmark, Sweden, Finland, Norway and Iceland to exchange and share data within the Schengen Information Systems and thus join the Schengen area in 2001. The original design of SIS had a number of limitations that made the extension to a larger number of countries and the inclusion of new categories of data and information difficult, however. At the same time, the efforts to replace SIS and SIS+ with a new SIS II were not successful. Therefore, pending the roll-out of SIS II, some new functions for SIS 1+ were developed, and in 2007, due to further delays in SIS II development, a temporary solution called SISone4all was introduced. This solution enabled the new EU MSs (the Slovak Republic, Slovenia, Estonia, Hungary, Latvia, Lithuania, Malta, Poland and the Czech Republic) to join Schengen by October of the same year.

If the SIS infrastructure has proved to be able to evolve up to a certain stage in order to generate new services and include new users, it now seems to be reaching a dead end. Its high complexity makes it impossible (or at least quite difficult and expensive) to add new modules to provide additional functions and features that are included in SIS II. However, the decision to set up SIS II dates back to 1996. After 15 years and more than 130 million euro spent, the new platform is still under development. The difficulties faced by SIS II—analysed in detail in one of our project case studies (see Chap. 8)—highlight a mix of technological failures at the development level, the difficult and risky migration from the old to the new databases and entanglements between the legal framework (i.e., the regulations enacted to legalise and regulate the use of SIS II) and the technological developments. Building a large information infrastructure from scratch while assuring at the same time the required compatibility with pre-existing infrastructural components soon reaches unmanageable levels of complexity.

Strangely enough, in spite of the central role of infrastructures in supporting interoperability, in most of the documents of the European Commission there is only an occasional mention of infrastructure. The infrastructural dimension is not analytically distinguished from the system dimension, that is, from the systems and applications that run upon and by means of the infrastructure. Thus, for example, in the technological domain, interoperability is often conceptualised as a property of a stand-alone system connected to other stand-alone systems by means of technological devices placed in-between (gateways, interfaces, standard protocols, guidelines, etc.), yet interoperability is not just that, being a consequence of the features and the dynamics of the infrastructure.

Accordingly, standards, protocols, formats and guidelines are indeed mentioned as critical elements to ensure interoperability, but their infrastructural significance is insufficiently stressed. They are not regarded as critical infrastructural elements that have a dynamics of their own. This is not at all surprising, because an infrastructure is not a 'thing' defined by boundaries and is often deeply entangled with the mundane artefacts and systems of everyday use. Similarly, there is an insufficient consideration of the infrastructural dimension in the legal and organisational domains. Here, the concern for interoperability is essentially associated with the issue of how to enforce alignment of MSs' legal systems and organisational structures and processes in order to do joint business. Pressures to or efforts at aligning systems without consideration for the underlying, and at present rather thin, European institutional infrastructure may become a further source of complexity, however.

We submit that many of the phenomena and issues we encounter in the development of the European Payment Order and the European Small Claims Proceedings Online fall outside the scope of the concept of interoperability; that is, they cannot be reduced to the problem of obtaining straight 'linkability' and communication between systems. Rather, they involve the design and evolutionary change of complex infrastructures that are necessary for supporting interoperability-over-time. The concept of interoperability must therefore be assessed within the broader field of infrastructure development, which is precisely what we should investigate if we want to provide sound indications for building interoperability in EU Civil Proceedings Online.

1.5.4 Institutional Infrastructure

Up to this point, we have mainly discussed the role of infrastructures in enabling the exchanges of bits and data. We have mainly looked, therefore, at specific features of information and communication technologies. When technologies enter the public sector to support e-government and e-justice systems, however, the exchange of bits and data enabled by the infrastructure is useless if it is not made legal. Technologies and technology-enabled activities must be made legal to produce the expected results within legal or administrative proceedings. This is the only way by which agency can circulate and yield effects with legal validity. Unfortunately, the present state of affairs in the EU is that, while an email can be adequate enough to stipulate a complex contract between private companies, in the judicial domain only one European judiciary (Finland) accepts simple emails as a legal means to file a lawsuit. Not only legal issues but also the bureaucracy can hinder the circulation of agency.

As we have discovered with the simple simulation of EPO and ESCP, and as confirmed by studies carried out by consumers' associations, local administrative oddities, ambiguous regulation and unnecessary procedural complexity can create bottlenecks and frictions, slowing down and even blocking the smooth execution of the procedure. Legal and institutional infrastructure thus consists of all the legal and organisational gear necessary to support legal and institutional interoperability and the circulation of legal agency.

The requirement of institutional interoperability originates from the peculiar nature of the emerging institutional configurations that unfold from the encounter of existing institutional frameworks with ICT infrastructures. Even a cursory look at the development of ICT infrastructures leads us to appreciate that achieving technical and institutional interoperability requires radical changes in the ways organisations work. In other words, as the existing organisations and administrative bodies increasingly come to share a technical infrastructure, they must change their procedures and routines and must develop new ones if they want to interoperate for the purpose of managing data, being accountable to one another, jointly assessing problematic situations and delivering public service. In this respect, new technology brings about new organisation. Rules, routines and capabilities must be increasingly shared across organisations; that is, they become part of a shared institutional infrastructure. Public sector organisations tend to lose their character of self-contained systems, owning their own inhouse operations and technology, and become components 'hooked up' or 'plugged in' to larger assemblages connected by interfaces, linkages and gateways of various kinds. As Dunleavy et al. (2006) remark, such organisations do not run their own operations, at least not entirely, nor are they fully in control of their own information resources. The classical Weberian model of formal bureaucratic organisation no longer seems adequate to account for their characteristics and behaviour in the newly emerging institutional landscape. While organisations struggle to keep their stability and performance, infrastructural changes unsettle and reshape them from underneath or from within. New organisational morphologies and inter-organisational linkages emerge.

This process of restructuring is visible with exemplary clarity in some of the cases we have studied (see Chap. 4). Even the relatively simple administrative procedures contemplated by the delivery of e-services, such as Money Claims OnLine in England and Wales (MCOL), are never exclusively owned by a single organisation but require the coordinated and synchronised contributions of multiple agents, which must be able to map and acknowledge one another's procedures, so that issues of legitimacy, mutual recognition, accountability and validity are not raised all the time and are swiftly resolved (Kallinikos 2009; Lupo, Chap. 4). In the specific case of MCOL, we notice that the overall functionality of the service is jointly operated by a number of functionally dedicated organisations, both public and private, which share large bodies of data and help legal agency circulate across the assemblage:

1. The accounting company must be able to connect to software companies and to the Country Court Bulk Centre in Northampton;

2. The banks and the credit card companies must be made compatible with the legal requirements for access and identification by the software applications, and vice versa;
3. Backup systems, dedicated interfaces and offline/online switch points must be designed in order to assure system redundancy and resilience in the case of intervening problems and interruptions; and
4. Connections to other services and functions of the public sector must be devised, for example demographics, bio-medical data, real estate, etc.

These emerging functional linkages require higher levels of understanding and coordination among the several public and private agents involved in the project. The effective execution of new functions and operations calls for the development of a sound institutional infrastructure, assembled from available components, without which a seamless functioning of the system will not obtain. We have reason to think that the same requirements will emerge, at a higher level of complexity, in the development of European transborder services.

In practice, the development of full institutional interoperability at the European level is a long and difficult endeavour, and the roadmap available to date is just a rough sketch so far. It definitely involves integrating and enriching the various Government Interoperability Frameworks existing in the EU, but the grounds and the strategies by which that can be accomplished are still a matter of discussion. Interoperability wants 'shared' resources rather than 'owned' resources; it wants open technologies, systems and software applications, as opposed to a proprietary approach; it also wants a common ground of reliable organisational routines and legal regulations so that the European public agencies can generate results capable of being interconnected, re-used and shared to the purpose of the circulation of legal agency. The dominant organising logic of most national bureaucracies is still proprietary, however, based on owning and controlling resources. This logic hinders the development of effective institutional infrastructures and the diffusion and sharing of platforms, frameworks, solutions, tools and components. As a consequence, the novel institutional capabilities associated with 'sharing' an infrastructure do not consolidate and transborder collaboration among agencies is difficult to achieve.

1.6 Sources of Complexity

As we have argued in the previous sections, building transborder interoperability for European e-government, and specifically for European judicial e-services, involves the development of an infrastructure, and depending on what kind of infrastructure is developed, a dramatic increase in interactive complexity may ensue. The sources of complexity are multiple. Firstly, the making of e-government enacts new interdependencies between heterogeneous functional domains, namely, the law, the technology, politics, the economy and the bureaucracy. Secondly, bringing together the European MSs to cooperate in the production of e-services increases the number and heterogeneity of interactions among the national jurisdictions. Thirdly, the migration from conventional to digital services entails the emergence of new practices and procedures, and the integration between multiple media calls for the mobilisation of a complex mix of stakeholders, technologies, regulations, public agencies and private providers that must be coordinated. Fourthly, all processes of interaction happen in time, thus adding an inter-temporal dimension to the problem of complexity. Complexity is both interactive and dynamic, and it affects the infrastructure. Research has shown that one of the reasons why carefully designed and engineered systems do not meet expectations after implementation is a complexity that often grows beyond the handling capabilities of the single individual or overarching management authority (Hanseth and Lyytinen 2010). Complexity is the most serious hindrance to the circulation of legal agency and the design of pan-European judicial e-services. Therefore, critical challenges to building interoperability and fostering the circulation of legal agency are the reduction and control of complexity and then the balanced allocation of complexity to the different (human and nonhuman) components of the infrastructure. Let's articulate the sources of complexity in more detail.

(a). First of all, complexity is produced by the systemic interactions between different functional domains. We shall focus specifically on technology, law and organisation. Each domain works according to its internal rules, its own code, and enjoys a certain degree of autonomy. The interactions between domains produce both intended and unintended consequences, especially when multiple domains claim rights of control or priority over specific issues simultaneously. In other words, the different codes tend to generate competitive regulatory regimes, with tensions and frictions that must be resolved and streamlined. In this respect, technology is a regulatory regime in its own right, which may enter into a rival relationship with law (Kallinikos 2009). Some illustrations are laid out below:

   - The law may feed technological complexity, for instance, when it requires or dictates some solutions or constraints in the design of digital technologies (procedures, devices, systems) in order to meet legal requirements, such as those concerning privacy, security, publicity or fair judgement. For the law, technical objects must first be turned into legal objects if they are to be adopted and have legal effects. Therefore, legal regulation may induce unnecessary technological complexities and intricacies that may cause technical suboptimisation and create problems for users.
   - Conversely, technology can inscribe and absorb organisational and legal complexity and can take care of control tasks previously carried out by humans. That is facilitated by means of functional simplification of legal procedures and organisational routines (Kallinikos 2009; Lanzara 2009b). For instance, simplified procedures for the identification of users, the transmission of documents and the registration of case-related data can be partially or totally inscribed into and delegated to technological machinery.

However, the amount of delegation allowed depends on the different legal rules of each national jurisdiction; it is likely, for example, to be more extended in the UK and Finland and more limited in Italy and Portugal. This will generate asymmetries and differences in the service to the public that will need to be bridged by means of additional applications, which will increase complexity.

- The delegation of legal and administrative procedures to technology may lead, in turn, to increased bureaucratic and legal complexity. An increased number of regulations (and thus higher legal complexity) may be required to specify how technology must work or how users should operate it. Moreover, a higher number of public and private organisations may be involved in the electronic delivery of the services, thereby increasing the overall organisational complexity. More often than not, complex technologies and systems need to be supported by additional organisational machinery and regulated by additional legal procedures, particularly in the case of exceptions and unexpected events.
- The adoption of simple shared solutions, such as email (in Finland), debit/credit card (MCOL in the UK) or open standards and open source software applications may speed up the growth of the infrastructure in terms of the number of integrated components and number of users. Such solutions enlarge the potential number of users who can have easy and low-cost access to the system, and consequently facilitate the adoption of the procedure and the circulation of agency. These simple solutions are not (or not yet) considered legal in other national jurisdictions, however (for example, Italy).
- The process of choice among competitive technical solutions may lead software development firms and vendors to heavy lobbying and to business strategies that turn e-government development into a political and market battleground (De Nardis 2011). As a result, a high level of political complexity may render the adoption of simple, cost-effective solutions unfeasible or make the law-making process overly time- and energy-consuming.

The interdependencies and the frictions between the different functional domains must be dealt with through smart mediations that make communication and inter-operation possible without paying far too high a price in terms of complexity. A whole set of interoperability problems arise from the fact that each one of these functional domains strives to work as an autonomous regulatory regime in its own right, but at the same time should communicate and coordinate with the other domains. As we will see in the chapters reporting the case studies, the efforts at making smart mediations have produced unequal results in the different countries and in the European applications. In many instances, the mediations themselves may become a further source of complexity.

(b). A second source of complexity arises as a result of the cultural heterogeneity of the EU MSs. European peoples speak different languages and rely on multiple legal frameworks and organisational routines that make transborder communication and coordination problematic. For example, coming to the transborder scope of EPO and ESCP, multiple language translation services may generate high semantic ambiguity and/or high bureaucratic costs, whereas the simplified solution of using one common language for all transactions puts the burden on the users, who must pay the costs of learning the language, and is politically unfeasible or unacceptable (see Chap. 12).

In addition, the different institutional and technological installed bases of the judiciaries of the MS may contribute to the increase in complexity. As large components of the national installed base are made up of national legislation and country-specific bureaucratic and technological equipment, it is likely that pressures to adapt to the EIF guidelines will require changes that will make them become bigger and more complex. Each national judiciary will try to align with the EIF according to its own specific characteristics, by introducing changes compatible with its own specific installed base and with its own path-dependent history. In the end, that might result in the development of an increasingly fragmented European infrastructure—indeed, an unintended consequence with respect to the goal of developing common European systems in the judiciary. This will make the search for common standards solutions for user identification and secure transmission of data and documents more difficult.

The solutions currently adopted for user identification and signature in the four national case studies illustrate this point. Money Claim OnLine/UK uses a combination of registration (providing user name and password) and use of credit or debit cards (see Chap. 4). In COVL/Slovenia, identification is based on the registration on an ad hoc web portal and on the payment of court fees (see Chap. 5), whereas CITIUS/Portugal (Chap. 6) and Trial OnLine/Italy (Chap. 7) adopt digital signature and external certification authorities. The last two systems work just for professional lawyers, while in MCOL and COVL, identification is also possible for normal citizens. Each country has the legitimate interest to promote and push for a European solution compatible with its own system. It is unreasonable to ask the English or Slovenian judiciary to develop a PKI infrastructure for digital signature, and very difficult to convince the Italian Ministry of Justice to get rid of the current bulky but reliable infrastructure.

In line with the findings of earlier European projects, (iDABC 2009a, b; Cimander et al. 2009) our national case studies confirm that even the technological standards for user identification and signature adopted in the different member countries (as well as in eCuria) show a high degree of heterogeneity that adds to the difficulty of designing interoperable systems.

To find an acceptable technological mediation between these heterogeneous installed bases may be extremely difficult. In addition, the problem is also legal because each national technological solution is consistent with a national legal framework. The search for viable mediations between the legal and technological infrastructures of the 27 MSs is the task currently faced by e-Codex (see Chap. 13), and at the present stage of development it is apparent that it will be rather difficult to identify a simple and viable solution.

(c). A third source of complexity is multimediality. In online procedures, the digital medium remediates legal agency, its instruments and the channels through which it flows. When legal and administrative procedures migrate to the digital medium, on the one hand they tend to assume emergent features brought in by the new medium, and on the other hand they carry over to the digital medium the legacy of the conventional medium (meanings, practices, uses, mindsets) (Lanzara 2009a). All mediations are ambivalent and ambivalence generates a design dilemma: whether to freely exploit the features of the digital medium to 'think differently' and design entirely new procedures and objects that may add to the legal capacity of the users, or to maintain the stability of familiar legal objects and procedures as much as possible, that is, transpose them into the new medium and try to make them work (Lanzara 2010). Our research findings show that the import of legal requirements into the digital environment tends to generate complexity and that in the design of e-services an appropriate balance must be struck between the necessary functional simplification and legal requirements.

While the circulation of agency in the conventional configuration is relatively straightforward, it may not be so in the digital environment, due to the rising complexity generated by the interdependencies among systems and components that were not originally connected but can now be connected in the digital medium. If complexity is not reduced or absorbed through appropriate strategies, several impediments may slow down, restrict or block the circulation of agency.

(d). A fourth source of complexity stems from the time dimension. As we said above, interoperability is not just a matter of 'here and now', it cannot be built once and for all by fixing a final, 'closed' solution, but must be maintained and adjusted over time. Conditions for interoperability change over time: new users and user needs emerge, the underlying infrastructure shifts and drifts, standards and requirements vary, legislation is modified and new technical solutions and ICT innovations pop up in the market. All the components (legal, institutional, technological, etc.) evolve over time and the inter-temporal interactions among them generate dynamic complexity. The problem of inter-temporal harmonisation affects both the different types of infrastructure at the national level and the transborder interactions between the different national jurisdictions. What must be achieved, then, is system coordination and communication over time.

The discussion above shows how the growth of complexity can affect the development of European transborder judicial systems and lead to a range of interconnected consequences, some of which are unintended and not necessarily predictable. We want to stress here the highly interactive and dynamic character of the complexity effects we have described. In particular, one may notice how an excessively high legal-procedural density, which may be called for by the adoption of leading-edge ICT applications in legal proceedings, might itself call for more organisational and administrative complexity. This might lead to the paradoxical consequence that ICT-based innovations, originally designed with the purpose of procedural and bureaucratic simplification, bring instead more bureaucratisation (as it has been the case of Trial OnLine in Italy) (Fabri 2009).

1.7 Procedural and Infrastructural Complexity: The Search for a Dynamic Balance

All sources of complexity described above have an influence on building interoperability and on the agents' capacity to undertake effective action to issue a claim or obtain a service online. In other words, ineffective reduction of complexity may create conditions that seriously impair the circulation of agency across different national jurisdictions, functional domains and media.

The growth of complexity may generate problems both at the level of the procedure and at the level of the infrastructure, and the two levels are closely interrelated. Firstly, complexity may affect the interfaces, procedures and tools available to the users of e-services. For example, non-ambiguous personal identification may be difficult, access to service may be problematic, procedures may be awkward and time-consuming, critical information may not be readily available. Unfriendly interfaces and procedures, as well as highly demanding and not widely diffused technological components, make the use of e-justice applications difficult and keep down the number of users. In turn, the small number of users may hinder or slow down the growth of the infrastructure, thus negatively affecting the development and deployment of the application (see Chap. 2). This was the case with the adoption of digital signature in Italy's Trial OnLine a decade ago, and it could well be the case with the European Small Claims Procedure Online, as our simulated experiment of ESCP and EPO indicated. Ideally, in order to develop the system effectively, access to the new EU judicial procedures should be made possible through technological components that are already available to potential users—citizens, lawyers, court staff and judges. It is the approach followed by e-Curia (Chap. 9), MCOL (Chap. 4) and COVL (Chap. 5), all easily accessible by users.

Secondly, complexity may affect the multiple infrastructures underpinning the e-service system. The development of the system requires the assemblage of a large number of technological, organisational and normative components, often leading to a growing number of private companies and public bodies upon whom service delivery is increasingly dependent and which must be held accountable. These actors, individuals or companies, public or private, are usually connected through a network of contractual and functional relations. In addition, they often use different technical standards and normative codes in their operations, which must be aligned in order to obtain coordination, thus further increasing the complexity of the overall architecture. An infrastructure comprising heterogeneous standards, multiple normative codes and nonaligned organisational routines will make the circulation of agency difficult. As a result, emerging frictions between market requirements and public values, conflicts of interests, technical incompatibilities and contractual ambiguities may slow down the development of the system.

For sure, there is an ambiguous relationship between procedural and infrastructural complexity, which requires further scrutiny. If we wish to design simple and easy-to-use interfaces and procedures so that the EU civil justice system becomes largely accessible to the mass of European citizens (this is a basic requirement of EU policy and a critical element for success), then the infrastructure must be able to absorb and hide complexity away from the hands and sight of the users (an operation called 'black-boxing'). This can lead to thickly entangled configurations that are hard to maintain and adapt when needed, however, unless specific design strategies are adopted to prevent the rise of infrastructural complexity (Contini and Lanzara 2009; Hanseth and Lyytinen 2010; Hanseth, Chap. 2 in this volume). On the other hand, a thin and fragmented infrastructure may overburden the users with operations that they cannot handle in practice, thus hampering system adoption and the further expansion of the infrastructure. The design problem can then be formulated as one of dynamic balance in the allocation and containment of complexity: at each stage of the system development process, the question is how much complexity should go into the procedure without hindering user agency, and how much complexity should go into the infrastructure without undermining its manageability, evolvability and financial sustainability. As the balance shifts over time, it is reasonable to start with simple procedural solutions delivering some consistent value that will attract the users, who can then learn to use the system, which can subsequently be further developed with richer functionalities, which in turn will attract more users, and so on and so forth in a positive, self-amplifying feedback.

This positive feedback is precisely what characterised the development of MCOL in the United Kingdom. The early web forms were made progressively more complex to allow for a better description of the cases, and the identification engine was moved from an initial ad hoc solution to a general purpose one, taking advantage of concurrent infrastructural developments. Similarly, Italy's TOL, after a long and painful development process, finally went online with a simple payment order procedure and is currently extending its functionalities to include the digital handling of more complex cases, such as civil executions and bankruptcy. A concurrent dynamic could be the development of the infrastructure to make system access and use easier. MCOL switched from the ad hoc identification described above to the multipurpose identification provided by the DirectGov portal. Slovenia's COVL has been designed for easy user access and use, too. It also provides additional functionalities, such as a search for attackable assets, that make debt recovery easier and thereby render it more attractive to users. Even e-Curia, which enables digital procedures at the European Court of Justice, has been designed to be easily accessible and support the complex litigation handled by the court. Here, one of the design principles was to have a system open to the lawyers working in most peripheral areas of the Union, not just to big law firms specialising in EU law (see Chap. 9 for details).

1.8 A Dual Design Strategy: Maximum Feasible Simplicity Versus Maximum Manageable Complexity

In this last section, some design strategies are presented that respond to the critical requirement of handling complexity. Here we shall only discuss strategies affecting the design of procedures, applications and systems and only hint at the complexity of the infrastructure (installed base). As we said in the previous section, the two are stuck in an ambiguous relationship, in the sense that a fragmented or complexly entangled infrastructure, as well as a lack of it, will not support interoperability and will make the adoption of simple procedures and applications difficult, thus hampering the circulation of agency. Inversely, a high complexity of user interfaces and judicial procedures will hinder access to the system and the extended use of it. As a consequence, the system will never take off, the underlying infrastructure will never develop and increasing returns will not be generated. A positive, self-reinforcing learning process will not begin. Thus, both procedural and infrastructural complexity affect the circulation of agency.

By taking inspiration from John Maeda's work (2006) we propose here a 'dual strategy' for designing viable e-government systems and procedures and helping complexity absorption: systems should take shape in a dynamic design space between Maximum Feasible Simplicity (MFS) and Maximum Manageable Complexity (MMC). Maeda has synthetically condensed the critical design space we are confronting by asking the dual questions: How simple can you make it? versus How complex does it have to be? (Fig. 1.2).

Duality means here that the design problem can be expressed through two distinct and related formulations, where in each formulation the design objective becomes a constraint in the other one. This amounts to saying that the pursuit of simplicity is subject to the requirement of variety, and the pursuit of variety is subject to the requirement of simplicity. These dual questions mark off a dynamic space of design solutions crossed by a tension between opposite and simultaneous design requirements. The design artefact—application, procedure, system—should take shape at the critical point or in the critical area where pressures for functional

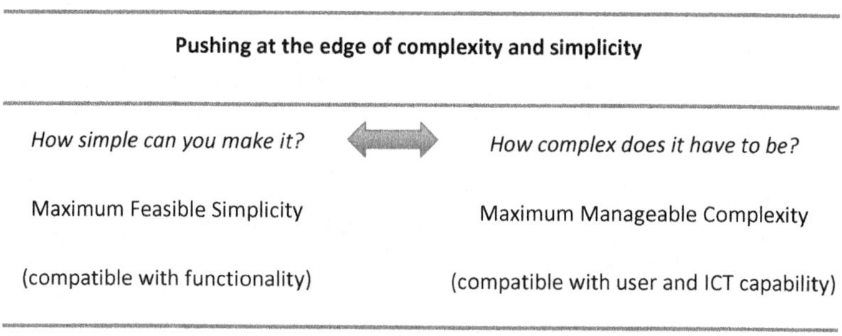

Fig. 1.2 Pushing at the edge of complexity and simplicity

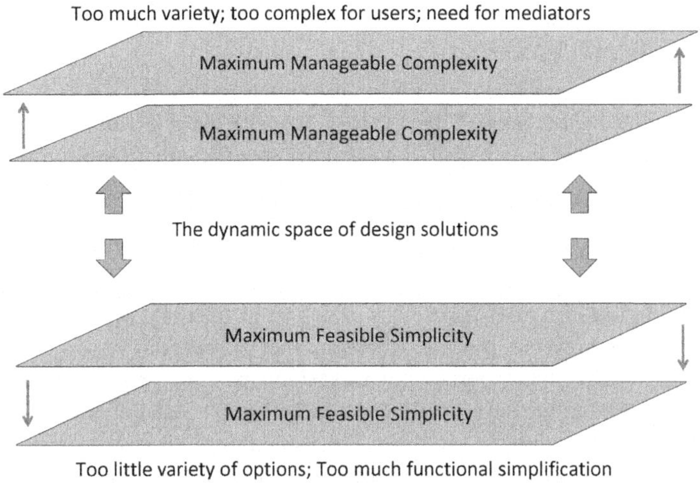

Fig. 1.3 The dynamic space of design solutions

simplification balance pressures for requisite variety, that is, in the bounded space between the floor of maximum feasible simplicity and the roof of maximum manageable complexity (Fig. 1.3).

1.8.1 Maximum Feasible Simplicity

Whoever sets out to design judicial procedures online should start with the following question:

- What is the Maximum Feasible Simplicity for an online procedure compatible with functionality and with fair legal and administrative procedure?

In other words, how far can functional simplification of legal and administrative procedure go without jeopardising or nullifying the legal validity and fairness of that procedure? How much functionality (legal specificity, detail, controls, safeguards) can be 'safely' removed from the procedure without detracting too much value and usefulness from it? These questions point to a dilemma:

> On the one hand, assuming the user-centricity principle espoused by the EIF policy, if we want to attract a critical mass of users fast enough, we must design simple online procedures that deliver some value and are perceived by the users as attractive and convenient to use. In other words, we must create systems that act as 'attractors' to users (Hanseth and Lyytinen 2010). On the other hand, however, simplicity cannot go below a minimal threshold, where the range of functionalities provided to users become too narrow and the agency enabled is too limited. As a case in point, the European Small Claim Procedure at the present stage of development does not provide users with an engine to calculate and pay court fees. This is a case in which the procedure does not meet a critical user requirement and therefore fails to

generate substantial user value. As a result, the system cannot take off and will not be able to attract a critical mass of users.

The threshold for maximum simplicity is ultimately decided or discovered by the users themselves on the basis of their experience with the procedure. If users do not feel at ease with a procedure and do not use it because they find it too complex, it will require further simplification, as was the case with Italy's Trial OnLine. Conversely, users may be dissatisfied with far too simple a procedure, which delivers poor value and does not meet basic agency requirements; in this case, they will push the threshold of simplicity upwards so as to incorporate more complex functionalities, as happened in the case of e-Curia. This endogenous design process can only begin and be carried on, however, if a reasonable number of users can experiment with the simplified early versions of a procedure or system and can learn from them. In turn, the latter will be further developed, updated and improved, for instance, through debugging and fine tuning, as long as more users are motivated to adopt it, that is, system and user will learn from each other in a mutual learning process.

1.8.2 Maximum Manageable Complexity

The dual question cited above also points to the opposite problem of excessive variety, that is, Maximum Manageable Complexity. The upper threshold for 'manageability' depends both upon the user's competence and upon the technology's or the organisation's capabilities to handle the complexity:

- What is the maximum manageable complexity of a system or procedure that users can handle, compatible with the limits of their capabilities, attention and time?
- What is the maximum manageable complexity that available technology and organisation can accommodate?

In other words, how much real-life variety should be kept and embodied in the online procedure before it risks overwhelming the user's competence or the ICT's functional capabilities, and consequently jeopardising the system's overall ability to support the circulation of agency? How much legal and organisational complexity can be 'safely' retained and embodied in the procedure without it turning into a hindrance for the circulation of agency?

In principle, the requirement of embodying a certain degree of complexity in the online procedure to better serve a wider range of potential demands (present or future) is sound. One could, for example, imagine that online procedures and services should be able to respond to litigations that involve reasonably high values and are complex enough, but still within a maximum threshold of complexity above which procedures, interfaces and transactions become too complex to be handled effectively. Too much complexity becomes incompatible with the smooth and timely circulation of agency. If the maximum threshold of complexity is passed, agency does not flow smoothly or is blocked.

What can be done, then, to deflate complexity and restore the circulation of agency when the roof is reached and agency cannot flow through? One strategy is to delegate specific agency components to agents that come into play to handle problems and situations the technology or the users cannot take care of, such as expert mediators (lawyers, consultants, interpreters, etc.) or organisations that support the service and the users by processing specialised data and performing relay functions. However, expert inter-mediation will also increase the number of transactions needed to manage the procedure and the system, which will produce higher transaction costs. The more agency components are delegated, the more principal-agent chains of delegation are set up, the larger the complexity of the system. A further strategy is to build some redundancy into the system by providing it with online/offline switch points, where one can disconnect from the 'mainstream' online procedure and proceed along a conventional offline channel in case of low-frequency transactions or when unexpected problems (contingencies, blockages, bottlenecks) arise in the system and must be dealt with as exceptions (Kallinikos 2009).

An alternative to delegation/inter-mediation and to the online/offline switch could be user learning as an effort to bridge the gap between user competence and system complexity. This option is problematic, though, because it involves learning costs that most users are unwilling to pay. This is particularly true for EPO and ESCP, since for many users it will be a once-in-a-lifetime experience and the expected benefits will not pay off for the learning effort sustained.

All the above-mentioned strategies play with the dynamic tension within the design space and produce the effect of moving both the floor and the roof upwards and downwards. Learning and, in general, the accumulation of experience with the system tends to raise both the floor and the roof of the design space: the floor, because it will deflate pressures to functional simplification; the roof, because it will expand or better allocate the maximum complexity that can be handled by the technology and the user. The online/offline switch and the delegation of agency to intermediating agents will lower the maximum complexity that can be dealt with by the user or the technology by shifting the complexity to human agents, organisations and infrastructures. Complexity will not be cancelled out, just absorbed differently. When the roof goes down and the floor goes up, the design space for viable solutions becomes narrower. At the extreme, if the design of online procedures and systems does not proceed according to the functional simplification requirement, the floor will rise up to reach the roof, meaning that the system incorporates, by design, maximum manageable complexity.

As a case in point, the results of the simulated experiment of the European Payment Order and the European Small Claim procedures (see Chap. 11 of this volume) give us further indications as to the levels of feasible simplicity and manageable complexity involved in the present design of the European judicial e-services. One of the points highlighted by the experiment is that the procedural and semantic complexity that a pro se litigant must face is too high in relation to the very low value of the case. This calls for the support of other actors, such as lawyers, translators and other officers, to take charge of the complexity faced by the litigant, thus relieving her from a number of tasks, but in turn increases the complexity of the transactions, thus raising the cost of the procedure—a solution that would be viable (and cost-effective for the user) where the value of the case is substantial or the frequency of the transactions is high, but this does not seem to be the case for EPO and ESCP.

At the present stage of development, the dual design imperatives of maximum feasible simplicity and maximum manageable complexity are met by the national and European case studies to different degrees. In general, while the UK's MCOL and Slovenia's COVL strike a good balance between system simplicity and functional richness both at the procedural and infrastructural level, Italy's TOL and Portugal's CITIUS still present a number of problems. In particular, the design of TOL has for a long time ignored the imperative of maximum feasible simplicity and in the beginning chose to position itself above the upper threshold, well beyond user, technological and organisational capabilities for handling complexity. In recent years, however, intractable problems arising during development have produced a re-positioning of TOL design goals and aims within a design space in which simpler and more manageable solutions can be searched.

Both the national case studies and the simulated experiment of EPO and ESCP have been carried out within the existing architectures and the legal frameworks of the Civil Proceedings (national and European). The case findings and the previous discussion of sources of complexity and design criteria now put us in a better position to spell out and assess alternative institutional architectures for European Small Claims Online and, at large, for European e-government (see Chap. 14).

The dual requirements of maximum feasible simplicity and maximum manageable complexity also apply to infrastructures, whether ICT-based, legal or institutional, although the strategies for keeping infrastructural complexity in check are different from the strategies addressing procedural complexity, as will be shown in the next chapter. Infrastructures, too, live within a dynamic design space: on the one hand, they must meet basic simplicity requirements, compatible with the ability to support basic functionalities that create user value; on the other hand, they must not reach levels of complexity beyond which governance, sustainability and evolvability become problematic and costly.

1.9 Concluding Remarks

In this chapter we have argued that, in order to enable and support the circulation of legal agency across Europe, systems for transborder civil proceedings online must be designed to meet basic requirements of simplicity and ease of use while simultaneously delivering perceivable value to users from the early development stages. Circulation of agency and system interoperability must be supported by European-wide technical, legal and institutional infrastructure that should be at the same time robust and adaptable to future demands. We discussed the idea of circulation of agency and stressed the critical importance of infrastructures for building and sustaining European interoperability; then, we unpacked and analysed sources of procedural and architectural complexity arising in the development of even simple judicial procedures, such as those described in the case studies; finally, we proposed a set of design strategies to keep complexity in check and enhance the circulation of agency.

The ideas and remarks presented here have been laid out as a conceptual introduction to the topic of the book and to the case studies. They are also intended to be an invitation to reframe and reconsider several critical aspects in the design of European transborder e-services in the judiciary and more broadly in the development of European e-government. Our findings suggest that a sound EU strategy for developing pan-European e-government services should shift its current focus in three major respects: from building straight system interoperability to assembling open and shared infrastructures that can host multiple and ever-changing applications; from the provision of complex functionalities to systems and facilities that are attractive to users; and from an outcome-oriented to a more process-oriented design methodology, allowing for adaptation and change.

References

Arthur, B. 1994. *Increasing returns and path dependence in the economy*. Ann Arbor: University of Michigan Press.

Bowker, G., and S.L. Star. 1999. *Sorting things out: Classification and its consequences*. Cambridge, MA: MIT Press.

Broadbent, M., and P. Weill. 1999. The implications of information technology infrastructure from business process redesign. *MIS Quarterly* 23(3): 159–182.

Callon, M. 1992. The dynamics of techno-economic networks. In *Technological change and company strategies: Economic and sociological perspectives*, ed. R. Coombs, P. Saviotti, and V. Walsh, 72–102. London: Harcourt Brace Jovanovich.

Ciborra, C.U. (ed.). 2000. *From control to drift: The dynamics of corporate information infrastructures*. Oxford: Oxford University Press.

Cimander, R., M. Hansen, and H. Kubicek. 2009. Electronic signature as obstacle fo cross-border E-Procurement in Europe, Institut für Informationsmanagement. Bremen. http://www.ifib.de/publikationsdateien/2009-06-15_eSig_article_final_ePractice.pdf. Accessed 26 June 2013.

Contini, F., and G.F. Lanzara (eds.). 2009. *ICT and innovation in the public sector: European studies in the making of e-government*. Basingstoke: Palgrave Macmillan.

Dahlbom, B., and L.E. Janlert. 1996. *Computer future*. Unpublished manuscript.

David, P.A. 1985. Clio and the economics of QWERTY. *American Economic Review* 75: 332–337.

Deleuze, G., and F. Guattari. 1980. *Mille plateaux*. Paris: Editions de Minuit.

De Nardis, L. 2011. *Opening standards: The global politics of interoperability*. Cambridge, MA: MIT Press.

Dunleavy, P., H. Margetts, S. Bastow, and J. Tinkler. 2006. *Digital era governance: IT corporations, the state, and e-government*. Oxford: Oxford University Press.

Fabri, M. 2009. E-justice in Finland and in Italy: Enabling versus constraining models. In *ICT and innovation in the public sector: European studies in the making of e-government*, ed. F. Contini and G.F. Lanzara, 115–146. Basingstoke: Palgrave Macmillan.

Fabri, M., and F. Contini, eds. 2001. *Justice and technology in EU: How ICT is changing the judicial business*. The Hague: Kluwer Law International.

Hanseth, O. 1996. Information technology as infrastructure. PhD diss., Goteborg University.
Hanseth, O. 2011. *From interoperability to installed base cultivation. Report to the EU project building interoperability for European civil proceedings online*. Bologna: IRSiG-CNR.
Hanseth, O., and K. Lyytinen. 2010. Design theory for dynamic complexity in information infrastructures: The case of building internet. *Journal of Information Technology* 25: 1–19.
Henman, P. 2010. *Governing electronically: E-government and the reconfiguration of public administration, policy and power*. Basingstoke: Palgrave Macmillan.
iDABC. 2009a. *Study on mutual recognition of esignatures: Update of country profiles: Analysis and assessment report*. Bruxelles: European Communities. http://ec.europa.eu/idabc/en/document/6485.html.
Kallinikos, J. 2009. Institutional complexity and functional simplification: The case of money claim OnLine service in England and Wales. In *ICT and innovation in the public sector: European studies in the making of e-government*, ed. F. Contini and G.F. Lanzara. Basingstoke: Palgrave Macmillan.
Lanzara, G.F. 2009a. Reshaping practice across media: Material mediation, medium specificity and practical knowledge in judicial work. *Organization Studies* 30(12): 1369–1390.
Lanzara, G.F. 2009b. Building digital institutions: ICT and the rise of assemblages in government. In *ICT and innovation in the public sector: European studies in the making of e-government*, ed. F. Contini and G.F. Lanzara. Basingstoke: Palgrave Macmillan.
Lanzara, G.F. 2010. Remediation of practices: How new media change the ways we see and do things in practical domains. *First Monday* 15(6–7). http://firstmonday.org/ojs/index.php/fm/article/view/3034/2565
Latour, B. 1992. Where are the missing masses? The sociology of a few mundane artifacts. In *Shaping technology/building society: Studies in socio-technical change*, ed. W. Bijker and J. Law, 225–259. Cambridge, MA: MIT Press.
Latour, B. 2000. Technology is society made durable. In *Work and society: A reader*, ed. K. Grint. Malden: Blackwell.
Maeda, J. 2006. *The laws of simplicity. Design, technology, business, life*. Cambridge, MA: MIT Press.
Mohr, R., and F. Contini. 2011. Reassembling the legal: The wonders of modern science in court-related proceedings. *Griffith Law Review* 4: 994–1019.
Monteiro, E., and O. Hanseth. 1999. Developing corporate infrastructure: Implications for international standardization. In *Proceedings from standardization and innovation in information technology (SIIT'99)*, ed. K. Jacobs and R. Williams, 75–79. New York: IEEE.
OECD. 2009. Annual report 2009. Paris.
Star, S.L. 1999. The ethnography of infrastructure. *American Behavioral Scientist* 43(3): 377–391.

European Commission Websites

EIFv2.0. 2010. Tracking the loss of interoperability, FSFE. Accesses 16 Dec 2010.
IDABC. 2004. European interoperability framework for pan-European e-Government services: Version 1.0. http://ec.europa.eu/idabc/servlets/Docd552.pdf?id=19529. Accessed 11 Jan 2011.
IDABC. 2009. EIF—European interoperability framework for pan-European egovernment services. http://ec.europa.eu/idabc/en/document/2319/5938.html. Accessed 17 Dec 2010.
IDABC. 2010. Documentation on the European interoperability framework. http://ec.europa.eu/idabc/en/document/3473.html#finalEIF. Accessed 17 Dec 2010.
ISA Strategy—Commission's Communication on Interoperability. http://ec.europa.eu/isa/strategy/index_en.htm. Accessed 16 Dec 2010.

Chapter 2
Developing Pan-European e-Government Solutions: From Interoperability to Installed Base Cultivation

Ole Hanseth

Abstract In this chapter I address some of the complexities of ICT systems like Pan-European e-Government solutions, the challenges we are regularly confronted with when developing such solutions, the kinds of strategies that can help us cope with these challenges, and the extent to which an EU strategy with a strong focus on interoperability is an appropriate approach to dealing with them. I conclude that complex solutions like those discussed here can appropriately be seen as IIs. These IIs are not designed from scratch: they just evolve. A strategy for developing such solutions must therefore concentrate on how to make an II evolve in the desired direction. Standards are indeed crucial to infrastructures but the way standards are developed and their various properties have to address the need for an infrastructure to be flexible in order to grow and adapt to changing user requirements. The way the concept of interoperability is understood and used implies a static view of infrastructures that does not take into account the need for flexibility.

2.1 Introduction

The European Union's e-Justice programme aims at developing a large number of ICT solutions that should contribute to the establishment of harmonised and integrated judicial services, i.e., the circulation of legal agency across all EU member states (Lanzara, Chap. 1). This is a very ambitious task. The development of well-working ICT solutions within the judicial area has proved to be a complex and demanding undertaking at the national level (Contini and Lanzara 2009). There are good reasons to believe that the development of integrated and harmonised services and ICT solutions at the EU level will be considerably more challenging due to the

O. Hanseth (✉)
Department of Informatics, University of Oslo, Oslo, Norway
e-mail: ole.hanseth@ifi.uio.no

F. Contini and G.F. Lanzara (eds.), *The Circulation of Agency in E-Justice*, Law, Governance and Technology Series 13, DOI 10.1007/978-94-007-7525-1_2,

increase in complexity, in terms of the number of ICT solutions, actors, languages, legislations, judiciary systems and traditions, etc. This chapter will discuss some issues related to what kind of strategy and approach is required for coping with this complexity.

The EU's e-Justice programme covers one area within an ambitious program aimed at developing what the EU calls pan-European e-Government solutions. These are solutions aiming at establishing what are referred to as pan-European e-Government Services, which the EU trusts '... will enable citizens and businesses from all member states to access e-Government services in all member states. In future these services will eliminate or reduce the current limitations on the free flow of people, goods, capital and services across all member states of the European Union.'

Activities continue to aim at establishing such pan-European e-Government solutions in many sectors, like health care and customs, in addition to the justice sector. The EU has developed a set of documents outlining its strategy for developing these solutions in general and for e-Justice in particular. A major question, then, is if this strategy is appropriate or how it could/should be improved.

The key concept in the EU's strategy and approach is interoperability. This is a concept that emerged and became popular in the computer communications standardisation field during the 1980s. It usually denotes what kind of communication and integration one wants to achieve between computer systems. The way to achieve interoperability is usually considered to be by reaching agreement on a set of shared standards. The term is particularly popular among communities involved in formal standardisation activities where standards are supposed to be established by means of bureaucratic committees and based on a top-down specification-driven approach. A typical example is the failed ISO/OSI effort, which was heavily sponsored by the EU and the governments of the OECD countries.

The pan-European e-Government solutions that are being developed include a number of new solutions at the same time as they are linking together numbers of existing (and modified) solutions in each member state. This means that the overall pan-European solutions will be very complex, and so, it follows, will the organisational arrangements of the development activities. Accordingly, a successful strategy for developing these solutions needs to address this complexity in a proper way.

2.2 Pan-European e-Government Solutions and Information Infrastructures

2.2.1 From Interoperability to Complexity

Increased processing power and higher transmission and storage capacity have made it possible to build increasingly integrated and versatile Information Technology

(IT) solutions, which have dramatically increased complexity (BCS/RAE 2004; Kallinikos 2007; Hanseth and Ciborra 2007). In addition, the complexity of IT solutions has been growing continuously as existing systems, new and old, have been increasingly integrated with each other. Complexity can be defined here as the dramatic increase in the number and heterogeneity of included components, relations and their dynamic and unexpected interactions in IT solutions (Hanseth and Lyytinen 2010).

The Software Engineering Institute (SEI) at Carnegie-Mellon University describes this trend as the emergence of Ultra-Large-Scale (ULS) systems (Northrop et al. 2006). The report argues that these systems will push far beyond the size of today's systems and systems of systems by every measure:

- Number of technological components of various kinds
- Number of people and organisations employing the system for different purposes
- Number of people and organisations involved in the development, maintenance and operations of the systems
- Amount of data stored, accessed, manipulated and refined
- Number of connections and interdependencies among the elements involved

The report argues further that the sheer scale of ULS systems will change everything: ULS systems will necessarily be decentralised in a variety of ways; developed and used by a wide variety of stakeholders with conflicting needs, so that they will be evolving continuously; and constructed from heterogeneous parts. Furthermore, people will not just be users of a ULS system; rather, they will be elements of the system. The acquisition of a ULS system will be simultaneous with its operation and will require new methods for control. These characteristics are, according to the report, emerging in today's systems of systems; in the near future, they will dominate.

The SEI report notes that the scale of ULS systems presents challenges that are unlikely to be addressed adequately by incremental research within the established paradigm. Instead, they require a broad new conception of both the nature of such systems and new ideas on how to develop them. We will need to look at them differently, not just as systems or systems of systems but also as socio-technical ecosystems.

The growth in complexity has brought to researchers' attention novel mechanisms to cope with complexity, such as architectures, modularity and standards (Baldwin and Clark 2000; Parnas 1972; Schmidt and Werle 1998). Another, more recent, line of research has adopted a more holistic, socio-technical and evolutionary approach, putting the growth in the combined social and technical complexity at the centre of empirical scrutiny (see, e.g., Edwards et al. 2007). These scholars view these complex systems as new types of IT artefacts and identify them by the generic label of Information Infrastructures (IIs) (e.g., Hanseth and Lyytinen 2010; Star and Ruhleder 1996; Tilson et al. 2010).

Hanseth and Lyytinen (2010) define an II, consistent with the characterisation of ULS systems above, as a shared, open (and unbounded), heterogeneous and evolving socio-technical system (called an installed base) consisting of a set of IT capabilities and their user, operations and design communities. Typical examples of IIs are the Internet, solutions supporting the interaction among manufacturers along a supply chain and portfolios of integrated applications in organisations (often several thousand in number).

Pan-European e-Government solutions obviously fit this definition of ULS systems and the emerging paradigm around the concept of IIs seems an appropriate one to cope with the challenges that the development of such solutions raises.

2.2.2 The Key Characteristics of Information Infrastructures

The most distinctive feature of IIs and ULS systems is their overall complexity. Developing and managing IIs, then, is about understanding and managing complexity. More specifically, IIs, like all complex systems, are evolving and not designed from scratch. Thus, managing IIs means managing their evolution.

In reality, IIs are radically different from the way information and software systems are presented in the literature. Infrastructures have no life cycle—they are 'always already present'. This is strictly true of some infrastructures, such as our road infrastructure, which has evolved through modifications and extensions ever since animals created the first paths. IT infrastructures certainly have a much shorter history, but an II like the Internet has now been around and constantly evolving for roughly 40 years since its inception in the late 1960s. The same is true for IIs like portfolios of integrated ISs in larger organisations. Developing IIs, then, requires approaches that are different from the traditional 'design from scratch' ones (Hanseth and Lyytinen 2010; Edwards et al. 2007; Tilson et al. 2010). It rather requires an approach, which is the opposite of this, i.e. an approach which sees designing a new II as modifying (changing and extending) the installed base, the existing IIs, so that the installed base evolves as far as possible towards what is desired (user requirements).

The evolution of IIs regularly involves a large number of actors. All these actors cannot be strictly controlled from one single point (like, for instance, a manager at the top of a hierarchically structured project organisation). They will often act independently. In the case of the Internet, there are thousands, if not millions, of actors developing new services on top of the existing Internet or adding new features to lower-level services, such as quality-of-service mechanisms. This means that even though there are many institutions (ICANN, IETF, etc.) that are involved in the governance of the Internet, the Internet is not evolving in a strictly planned or controlled way. Its evolution is mostly the aggregated result of the various autonomous actors' actions. Institutions having responsibility for the governance of the Internet can have an impact and shape its evolution in a way similar to how we might influence the growth of an organism or a piece of land. The same is the case for large application portfolios. The individual applications and their relations (degree of integration) will change continuously and no single actor will have a total overview of these changes. Accordingly, we call our approach to how we can shape the evolution of an II 'installed base cultivation' (Hanseth and Lyytinen 2010).

If infrastructures are 'always already present', are new infrastructures never emerging? Wasn't the Internet a new infrastructure at some point in time? Yes, of course it was. New IIs are indeed emerging. This happens primarily in two ways. One, a system may be growing in terms of the number of users and along that path gradually changing from being a system (or application) of limited reach and range into a large-scale II. Email, for instance, was introduced into the Internet (or rather the Arpanet) at a time when the Net consisted of only four computers. Those computers (and the email service) did not constitute an II, but a distributed system of limited complexity. As the Net grew in terms of connected computers, services, developers and users, however, it increasingly took on the character of an infrastructure. The other way an II may emerge has been seen in most large organisations. Over time, the number of applications has continuously been growing at the same time as old and new applications have been increasingly integrated. During this process, the application portfolio has grown from being an initial, stand-alone item to a few loosely integrated ones and towards an increasingly more complex II.

The next section will present a brief outline of the key challenges related to the management of the evolution of IIs and the kind of 'tools' available for this task.

2.3 Design Challenges and Management Tools

Successful development of IIs requires appropriate management of the tension between standardisation and flexibility. Key to the management of this tension is the management of two main, and related, challenges: the bootstrapping and adaptability challenges (Hanseth and Lyytinen 2010). I will briefly describe these challenges and then discuss how a strategy focusing on interoperability is able to cope with them.

2.3.1 Design Dilemmas

2.3.1.1 The Tension Between Standards and Flexibility

Infrastructures are made up of a huge number of components. Accordingly, standards defining the interfaces between components are essential features of IIs and the specification and implementation of standards are important activities in the establishment of IIs. Standards are closely associated with stability. This is the case partly because keeping a standard stable is required so that it is possible, for example, to store data today and read them at a later time. Standards are also stable, however, because widely diffused standards are so hard to change when necessary (because of the lock-in problem). Nonetheless, standards need to change over time. Just like information systems, IIs need to change and adapt to changing user requirements, and some of these changes mean that implemented standards need to change, too. At the same time, the scaling and growth of an II can generate the need for changes in standards even though user requirements stay unchanged (Hanseth et al. 1996; Tilson et al. 2010). Accordingly, IIs will evolve as a dynamic driven by a tension between standards (stability, uniformity) and flexibility (change, heterogeneity). Managing this tension is a key to the management of IIs (Hanseth et al. 1996).

2.3.1.2 Bootstrapping: Adaptability

The dynamic complexity of IIs poses a chicken-egg problem for the II designer that has been largely ignored in the traditional approaches. On the one hand, IT capabilities embedded in IIs gain their value by being used by a large number of users demanding rapid growth of the user base. Consequently, II designers have to come up early on with solutions that persuade users to adopt while the user community is non-existent or small. This requires II designers to address head on the needs of the very first users before addressing the completeness of their design or scalability. This can be difficult, however, because II designers must also anticipate the completeness of their designs. This defines the bootstrap problem of II design. On the other hand, when the II starts expanding by benefitting from the network effects, it will switch to a period of rapid growth. During this growth, designers need to heed unforeseen and diverse demands and produce designs that cope technically and socially with these increasingly varying needs. This demands infrastructural flexibility so that the II adapts technically and socially. This defines the adaptability problem of II design (Edwards et al. 2007; Hanseth and Lyytinen 2010). Clearly, these two demands can contradict and generate tensions at any point of time in II design (Edwards et al. 2007).

2.3.1.3 Interoperability and Design Dilemmas

Among those who use it, the concept of interoperability has mostly positive connotations: according to the received wisdom, interoperability is the only thing one needs to focus on in order to successfully develop large-scale distributed solutions, and the more interoperability the better. Unfortunately, things are more complicated than that. If we relate the concept of interoperability to the design dilemmas mentioned above, a different picture emerges. In actuality, the concept of interoperability and the EU's Interoperability strategy and framework do not help us much in understanding or coping with any of them. The EU's strategy for developing pan-European e-Government solutions focuses on standards. Nothing is said about the need for flexibility, the tensions between standardisation and flexibility, the deeper issues related to the complexity of the solutions and the complexities of their user and development communities. This means that a strategy for coping with the bootstrapping or adaptability challenges is totally absent.

Research on the development of pan-European e-Government solutions in the customs area, the EU's eCustoms programme, has revealed conflicting issues and demands related to interoperability (Henningsson and Hanseth 2011). The aim of the eCustoms programme has been to develop ICT solutions for electronic customs declaration in all member states, harmonise customs declaration procedures among the member states and integrate these solutions in order to reduce the costs of traders related to customs declarations (Henningsson and Hanseth 2011). In this initiative, it emerged that there was a conflict between interoperability at the national level (i.e., interoperability between the solutions involved in the overall customs declaration processes) and interoperability between the solutions at the EU level. The more interoperability at the national level, the less interoperability could be achieved at the EU level. It also turned out to be the case that the actors involved at the national level were working more closely together at the national level than at the EU level, meaning that interoperability at the national level was given the highest priority. The overall result of this was a more fragmented system for customs declaration at the EU level and increased costs for traders (Henningsson and Hanseth 2011)!

2.3.2 Management Tools

So what kinds of 'tools' are available for managing the evolution of IIs—or for installed base cultivation? The answer given here is process strategy, architecture and governance regime. The rationale behind the focus on these three aspects is, first of all, the fact that these three 'tools' are what development efforts are all about: the steps to be taken to develop some new technology (bottom-up or top-down, incremental/iterative or 'big bang', evolutionary and learning driven or specification driven, etc.); the architecture and overall design of the technology (the modularisation of a system determines how and how easy it may be maintained and modified); and how to govern, manage and organise the effort. Secondly, these 'tools' have been at the centre of extensive discussions and research on the evolution of the Internet, and they have been key factors behind its success: an experimental bottom-up development strategy (which includes a strategy and rules for bottom-up development and settlement of standards), the end-to-end architecture and distributed control and governance structures combined with Open Source software licenses (Lemley and Lessig 2000; Hanseth et al. 1996; Benkler 2006; Zittrain 2006).

Traditionally, the management of ICT has focused on the management of projects developing ICT solutions. Such projects are typically organised as a hierarchy of sub-projects, each with a sub-project manager. Each manager has the right to make decisions within the domain of the sub-projects and give instructions to the managers at the level below. The management of such a project organisation is normally supported by various management tools, such as detailed plans and establishment of milestones. In addition, the production of detailed plans and the monitoring of the progress made in the project—if it is progressing according to plan or not—are supported by various computer-based project management tools. Together, this package of project organisation, decision rights and management tools is an example of what I call a governance regime. Governing the complexity of IIs requires new and different governance regimes. In the case of the Internet, for example, its successful evolution has been shaped by a governance regime consisting of a few central institutions, like IETF and ICANN. Another important part of this regime has been the fact that most of its technology has been distributed using Open Source licenses (like the GNU Public License). Maybe the most important feature of the governance regime, however, has been the organising of the development activities as a loosely connected network of individuals who coordinate their work through extensive use of email and by making all software and relevant information publicly available on ftp and Web servers.

Software and IS development often takes place by following specific methodologies. The central element of such methodologies is a specification of the steps to be taken, and in which sequence, to develop a specific IS solution. This is what I call a process strategy. The complexity of IIs requires process strategies different to those prescribed for traditional IS development efforts. In particular, we need process strategies that address the role of network externalities and path-dependence; that is, we need strategies that address the bootstrap and adaptability problems.

The architecture of an IS is traditionally considered important for its maintenance. In general, modularisation is an important strategy for coping with complexity and, in the case of IIs, the architecture plays a crucial role. This is illustrated by the role attributed to the Internet's architecture in explaining its successful evolution. The Internet's so-called end-to-end architecture (in which the functionality is located in the ends of the network, that is, in the computers connected to the Internet, and not in the network itself, which has been the case within traditional telecommunication networks) has made the Internet extremely flexible in the sense that anybody having a computer connected to the Internet can develop and provide new services.

The management of IIs, then, requires process strategies, architectures and governance regimes that in combination make an II evolve along the desired path. Exactly which combinations are appropriate for specific IIs is still a major research issue.

The concept of interoperability relates particularly to architecture. Accordingly, in the next section, a richer picture is offered of how architectural features shape the evolution of infrastructures and of the roles architectural features play in the cultivation of an installed base.

2.4 Architectural Shaping of Infrastructure Evolution

Traditionally, research on technological architectures in general and ICT architectures in particular has focused on how to decompose a system into modules so that system flexibility is maximised. This is assumed to be best achieved through loose coupling among components and strong internal cohesion (Henfridsson et al. 2009; Parnas 1972). Loose coupling, as opposed to tight coupling, between components means that the inner working of a component is largely irrelevant and can be hidden from other components (Baldwin and Clark 1997; Sanchez and Mahoney 1996). This is what Parnas (1972) called encapsulation. Loosely coupled components are consequently easier to modify and more available for new relationships in the reconfiguration of a modular system. Research on technological architectures has traditionally concentrated on one single software system. More recently, however, as the number of systems has been growing and their integration has increased, more attention has been directed towards architectures specifying the relations between individual solutions. This research has directed much of its focus towards Service Oriented Architectures (SOA) (Vassiliadis et al. 2006), in which the modular structure consists of services. The implementation of SOA may vary, from simple ASP solutions to Web services, to more complex SOAs based on Enterprise Software Bus middleware (Rosen et al. 2008).

The literature on ICT architectures focuses mainly on projects and solutions located within one single organisation. Pan-European e-Government solutions are different in the sense that they will be shared by a large number of independent organisations. Such large-scale solutions raise a lot of new challenges. These challenges are addressed within a growing body of research—to which the research presented here belongs—conceptualising these large-scale solutions' IIs (see for instance Ciborra et al. 2000; Edwards et al. 2007; Hanseth et al. 1996; Star and Ruhleder 1996; Tilson et al. 2010). To some extent, this literature also addresses architectural issues. It does not relate risks to specific architectures, i.e., specific ways of modularising (or decomposing) an II, but to the degree of modularisation, i.e., to what extent the modules are loosely or tightly coupled. The literature is, for instance, demonstrating how larger IIs emerge as responses to the felt need of tighter integration of applications to enable more smooth information flow and sharing in order to enable more smooth co-ordination of work tasks and more efficient ways of organising them (Hanseth and Ciborra 2007). Tighter integration leads to more complexity and new challenges for managing the IIs.

Here, I will try to move beyond this research by focusing on how specific architectures, i.e., specific ways of modularising, have an impact on challenges related to the management of IIs. I will do so by drawing upon three emerging streams (Table 2.1) of research on technological architectures that focus on, and demonstrate, how architectures relate to a broad range of issues beyond the flexibility of the technological artefact.

Table 2.1 Three emerging streams of research on ICT architectures

Stream	Key issue	References
Strategic architecting	ICT architecture and platforms win technology wars	Morris and Ferguson (1993), Tiwana et al. (2010), Woodard (2008), Rodon et al. (2012)
Mirroring and structural alignment	Technological architectures and organisational structures are mirroring each other	Henderson and Clark (1990), Baldwin and Clark (2000), Garud et al. (2002), Colfer and Baldwin (2010)
Innovations and generativity	Generativity denotes a technology's capacity to create innovation driven by large and uncoordinated networks of actors	Saltzer et al. (1984), Abbate (1994, 1999), Benkler (2006), Zittrain (2006)

2.4.1 Strategic Architecting

Morris and Ferguson (1993) argued that 'architecture wins technology wars' in complex high-tech markets. Companies being successful over time in such markets achieve this not primarily because of the superior qualities of their products or their production processes but because they control architectures that have become de facto standards in a product domain. Important examples supporting this hypothesis are IBM in the mainframe area and Intel and Microsoft in the PC (desktop) area. Morris and Ferguson argue that Borland and Lotus were losers in the competition with Microsoft for exactly this reason (lack of control of architecture), although they at a certain point in time had superior product families in terms of functionality. They conclude that technological architectures are crucial for the long-term competitiveness and commercial success of high-tech firms.

Research on architectural strategies is limited, but growing. In particular, there is a rapidly growing number of what Tiwana et al. (2010) call platform-centric ecosystems and a correspondingly growing research interest related to such platforms covering the importance of platform-centric architectures, how specific platforms emerge as dominant within an ecology and strategies that platform owners can pursue in order to control the evolution of the platform as well as the whole ecology (Cusumano and Gawer 2002; Gawer 2009). Tiwana et al. (2010) mention a number of areas where such platforms are emerging: browsers (e.g., Firefox, Chrome and Opera), smartphone operating systems (iPhone, Android), Web services (Google Payments, Amazon Elastic Cloud), social media (Facebook, Apple's Ping), marketplaces (SABRE, eBay) and gaming consoles (Xbox, Apple's iPod Touch, Sony PlayStation). Platform-centric architectures are examples of what Jason Woodward (2008) calls architectural control points, i.e., architectures that contain certain components of strategic importance in the sense that if an actor is controlling the evolution of this component (i.e., the platform), she can control the evolution of the whole ecology.

Rodon et al. (2012) report on a case in which the issue of strategic architecting and architectural control points were central. In mid-2004, the Catalan Health

Service (CHS) set the foundations for the development of an electronic prescription system in Catalonia. The CHS started the project in a spirit of cooperation and invited all the stakeholders, among them the Catalan College of Pharmacists (CCP), the natural spokespersons of pharmacists, to participate in the project. The CCP described its role in the project, and particularly in the IT architecting phase, as a way to protect the interests of community pharmacies and minimise any potential negative impact on the collective of pharmacists. Early in the project's history, CHS designed an architecture for the II with a central database where all prescriptions were stored. This architecture did not assign any role to the CCP in the operations of the II. The CCP strongly objected to this, and through series of strategic and political manoeuvres the college was able to make modifications to the architecture which meant that the pharmacies were accessing prescriptions in a database operated by the CCP that was mirroring the database operated by CHS and which General Practitioners accessed. Through this strategy, the CCP was able to modify the architecture so that it included one component that the CCP controlled, and through the control of this component the CCP also obtained substantial control over the whole infrastructure.

2.4.2 Mirroring and Structural Alignment

Recently, the scope of research related to technological architectures has expanded. This includes research related to the relations between a product's architecture and the structure of the organisation developing or producing it, and how these relations shape each other's evolutionary dynamics. Within the field of Organisation Studies, substantial empirical material has been collected supporting the hypothesis that technological architectures and organisational structures are mirroring each other. In a critical test of this hypothesis, Colfer and Baldwin (2010) found that it was strongly supported by empirical evidence, both at the firm and at the industry level. Henderson and Clark (1990) found that as a consequence of this mirroring, established firms are systematically unable to come up with architectural innovations—only component innovations. This mirroring is also an important part of Clayton Christensen's (1997) explanation for established firms' inability to come up with disruptive innovations.

At the industry level, the mirroring of technological architecture and organisational structure also has important implications. For instance, Utterback (1994) argues that virtually all industries are evolving according to a life-cycle process. In the early phases, the diversity of products and producers proliferates until the industry reaches a certain level of maturity and a de facto standard architecture (often called the 'dominant design') emerges. At this stage, the degree of product variety and number of producers decrease dramatically at the same time as the products are assembled out of standardised components produced by a growing number of component suppliers. This transformation occurred in the car industry in the 1920s and in the computer industry in the 1980s. Baldwin and Clark (1997) argue that the evolution of the concept of modularity has had a significant impact on the evolution of high-tech industries in general and the computer and software industry in particular. For this reason, increasingly complex but modular architectures have emerged and, because of their high degree of modularity, computer and software architectures have changed considerably over time at the same time as the individual modules have evolved. Overall, they argue, the computer and software industries have changed over time in terms of a co-evolution of modular technological architectures and what they call modular clusters (of companies). Further, 'managing in the modular age' (Baldwin and Clark 1997) requires new strategies: managers need to focus on, and understand, how the overall ecology (the technological architecture and the structure of the modular cluster) is evolving and how their companies' products and overall strategy can continuously adapt to this.

The research presented above focuses on the relations between a product and its producer (both at the company and industry level). This relationship is also found to be important within the II domain. For example, significant investments have been made by the powerful actors in the European mobile communications industry to implement the very successful Japanese mobile Internet service i-mode in many European countries. According to Tee and Gawer (2009), however, they all failed because of the differences in organisational structures in the mobile communications industry in Japan on the one hand and in Western European countries on the other; i-mode's architecture was congruent with the former but not the latter. Sæbøe et al. (2011) have been doing research on the implementation of a national health II in Malawi. The actors involved in this effort tried to build the II based on a set of standards initially developed in South Africa. They found that in order to succeed, they had to redesign the II's overall architecture and the individual standards so that they reflected relations between the vendors of the various Health Information Systems being integrated through the national II. In the case of IIs, however, it is not only the mirroring of the structures of the producer and the product that matters. Forster and King (1995) have, for instance, found the mirroring of the structure of an II and the structure of the user community to be a critical success factor—or the cause of failure. They found that efforts aiming at adapting the very successful booking systems for air passenger transport to air cargo transport failed even though the functionality required to support both processes is more or less exactly the same. Forster and King argue that these efforts failed because of the differences in organisational structures in the air cargo and passenger transport industries.

Some research is also emerging on interactions between an II's architecture and the unfolding of an II's development and implementation processes. In a comparative study of two Danish projects aimed at developing nationwide Electronic Patient Records infrastructures, Aanestad and Jensen (2011) found that the one project that developed an II based on a modular architecture that allowed for incremental implementation emerged as the national II. The architecture of this solution was mirroring the structure of the collaborative arrangements with health care. The other project failed in spite of extensive funding and political support, according to Aanestad and Jensen, because it was based on an architecture that required all modules to be implemented before the solutions could be used for meaningful purposes.

Table 2.2 Comparing the two approaches

	INA approach	SPA approach
ICT architecture	Many applications, sending messages to each other	Single application, distributed to clients
Project organisation	Co-ordinated teams in many organisations	Single team, within one organisation
Overall risk	High	Medium to low

2.4.3 Architecture, Organisational Complexity and Project Risks

Hanseth and Bygstad (2012) have studied the evolution of 10 IIs within the health care sector of Norway for a period of more than 20 years. They found that the chosen architectures had strong implications for the organisation of the development activities and that different architectures generated development organisations of hugely different complexities, which again had a huge impact on development costs and outcomes. Hanseth and Bygstad also found that the infrastructures examined were developed by basing them on two different architectures. The first architecture was an integrated part of a broader paradigm, which they call the EDI paradigm, a paradigm which says that an II should be built by extending existing applications so that they can send and receive (standardised) messages. They call this architecture 'Institutional Interface/Application Centric Architecture', or INA, to reflect the fact that the overall infrastructure is built by focusing on existing applications and that the main interfaces between the main modules of the infrastructure reflects the 'interfaces' between the organisations. The second architecture they call 'Service Provider/Communication System Centric Architecture', or SPA, to point out that the infrastructures based on it are focused on service providers offering service consumers electronic access to their services and that the infrastructure is built by developing a separate module taking care of as much as possible of the communication (and leaving the applications untouched).

The architectures and the roles they play in shaping the respective infrastructures will be described in more detail below. The main findings are summarised in Table 2.2.

2.4.3.1 The INA Approach

All the INA projects were problematic. They all suffered from various problems associated with complexity: the large number of involved actors, the heterogeneity of technical solutions and the many dependencies that created postponements and frictions when schedules were not kept. The key to these problems are illustrated in Fig. 2.1. The chosen ICT architecture was (as usual in EDI solutions) based on the data flow between the involved organisations. This led to a relatively complex ICT architecture, with a large number of messages flowing between a large number

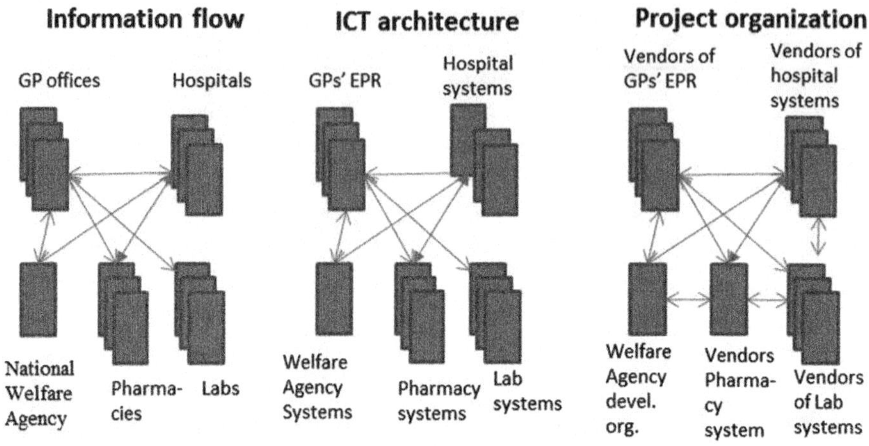

Fig. 2.1 The INA approach

of systems, meaning that many local applications had to be modified in order to produce and receive messages. In practice, each vendor had to develop their own client modules of the solution. For example, in the ePrescription project, of the six vendors of EPR systems present in the Norwegian market (three GP and three hospital systems), each had to make their own version of a quite complex piece of software with exactly the same functionality.

Further, the INA solution implies a project organisation with participants from all involved actors, usually organised as a number of sub-projects, with a central co-ordinating actor. As observed by van der Aalst (1999), this increases the challenge of co-ordination. The co-ordinating actor cannot usually instruct the other participants (since they represent independent organisations), but will have to manoeuvre by means of compromises and politics. This combination of technical and organisational complexity increases significantly the risk of postponements and even failure, as revealed by the cases presented.

2.4.3.2 The SPA Approach

The SPA projects, although different in type and scope, were all successful. The analysis shows that the overall reason was the chosen ICT architecture. This architecture did not reflect the information flow between the numerous organisations but was based on a solution from one application service provider. As illustrated in Fig. 2.2, this greatly simplified the design solution.

In the SPA-based solutions, the important interfaces within the overall solution are the interfaces between the communication solution and the applications, not the interfaces between the different modules of the communication system that are running within different organisations. In the SPA architecture, there is a tight coupling between the different components of the communication system and weak

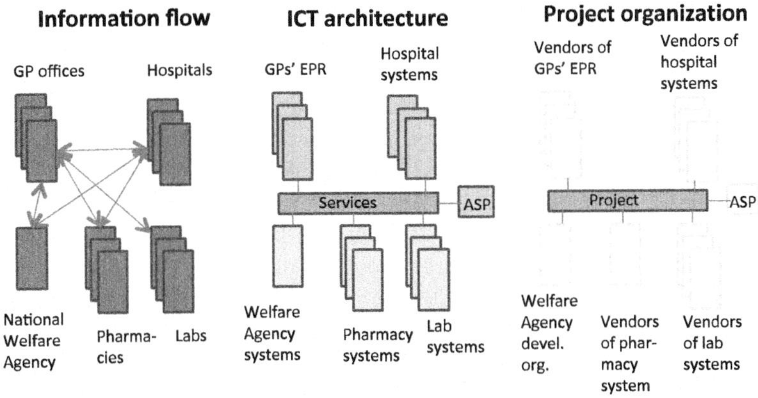

Fig. 2.2 The SPA approach

coupling between the communication system and the applications, whereas the INA-based solutions are based on tight coupling between the applications and the communication system (i.e., the module running within the same institution) and loose coupling between the modules within the communication system.

The most crucial aspect of the SPA-based solutions, in the context of this chapter, is the fact that the architecture of the communication solution allows the complete solution to be developed by one single project team within one single formal organisation. Only minor development work needs to be done by other organisations, such as application vendors. In more general terms, the important aspect of the SPA architecture is the fact that the complexity of the development organisation becomes dramatically reduced compared to that of the INA-based solutions.

To sum up, the increased risks of the INA approach compared to the SPA approach are:

- A more complex technical solution, with a higher technical risk;
- A more complex project organisation, with very challenging co-ordination;
- Higher costs, because the vendors will all have to develop their own client solutions; and
- Higher implementation risk, because the INA solution requires that all actors start at the same time. Such a 'big bang' strategy is more risky than an incremental approach (Bygstad et al. 2010) that the SPA allows for.

2.4.4 *Innovations and Generativity*

The role of technological architecture on the evolution of an II has been extensively discussed in relation to the Internet. Its end-to-end architecture is widely held to be a prime and distinguishing feature of the Internet compared to traditional telecommunication (Saltzer et al. 1984; Abbate 1994, 1999). This means that the functionality ('intelligence') of the overall network is located in the ends—its terminals (i.e., computers in the Internet case)—rather than in the network, as in the case of traditional telecom architecture. This end-to-end architecture made the Internet extremely flexible: anybody who had a computer could develop and provide a new service. Abbate (1999) also illustrates how the successful development of Internet services has been based on an approach in which each layer of services acted as a platform for experimental development of the next layer. The importance of the end-to-end architecture has also been forcefully argued by Lawrence Lessig (2001) in debates about issues like network neutrality.

Yochai Benkler (2006) developed this 'end-to-end' argument one step further by underscoring the mutual dependence of the end-to-end architecture of the network and (easily) programmable terminals, in the form of general purpose computers. Benkler makes a conceptual contrast between programmable computers and appliances. An appliance is a device with a limited and well-defined set of functions that (normally) cannot be modified after the users have bought it. Typical examples include washing machines, radios and phones (traditional ones, at least). Most such devices have computers inside but their software cannot usually be modified by their users. Benkler also makes a strong link between the Internet's architecture and its model for organising and governing development activities. Central here is the Open Source model, which implies a loosely organised system with distributed control, and the Open Source software license.

Jonathan Zittrain takes this argument one step further by means of the concept of generative technology. Generativity 'denotes a technology's overall capacity to produce unprompted change driven by large, varied, and uncoordinated audiences' (Zittrain 2006). Zittrain argues that the grid of PCs connected by the Internet has developed in such a way that it is consummately generative. Zittrain defines generativity in more detail as a function of a technology's capacity for leverage across a range of tasks, adaptability to a range of different tasks, ease of mastery and accessibility. Leverage describes the extent to which these objects enable valuable accomplishments that would otherwise be either impossible or not worth the effort to achieve. Adaptability refers to the breadth of a technology's use without change and the readiness with which it may be modified to broaden its range of uses. A technology's ease of mastery reflects how easy it is for broad audiences to adopt and adapt it: how much skill is necessary to make use of its leverage for tasks they care about, regardless of whether the technology was designed with those tasks in mind. Accessibility refers to the ease with which people can come to use and control a technology (along with what information might be required to master it).

Even though the Internet's end-to-end architecture has contributed significantly to the Net's successful evolution, its future is uncertain. The Internet's growth has generated new demands. For instance, issues such as security and the illegal distribution of spam, music and child pornography have become major concerns. Many actors are arguing that these issues demand technological mechanisms (filters and security technologies, such as trusted computing) to be put into the Net. Network providers also argue that they have to implement quality of service mechanisms to guarantee better services for those willing to pay for them, in order to afford further expansion of their bandwidth capacities. Scholars such as Benkler (2006), David (2005), Lemley and Lessig (2000), Wu (2003) and Zittrain (2006) are worried that the proposals for addressing these issues will destroy the end-to-end architecture and turn the Internet into an appliance, as well as dramatically reducing the rate of innovations related to the Internet in the future. Other researchers argue that the Internet's architecture has to change to allow further growth (Clark et al. 2005). This relates to 'tussles in cyberspace' emerging out of the growth in number and variety of Internet Service Providers. This makes their relationships complex and the conditions for sustainable and co-ordinated growth of the Internet are eroding. A new architecture is also considered necessary to maintain, or preferably enhance, the Internet's resilience (Trimintzios 2011).

2.5 Conclusion

In this chapter, I have addressed some of the complexities of ICT systems like pan-European e-Government solutions, the challenges we are regularly confronted with when developing such solutions, the kinds of strategies that can help us cope with these challenges, and the extent to which an EU strategy with a strong focus on interoperability is an appropriate approach to dealing with them.

I have concluded that complex solutions like those discussed here can appropriately be seen as IIs. These IIs are not designed from scratch: they just evolve. A strategy for developing such solutions must therefore concentrate on how to make an II evolve in the desired direction. Standards are indeed crucial to infrastructures but the way standards are developed and their various properties have to address the need for an infrastructure to be flexible in order to grow and adapt to changing user requirements. The way the concept of interoperability is understood and used implies a static view of infrastructures that does not take into account the need for flexibility.

I have argued that there are three 'tools' that are of particular importance when discussing how to control the evolution of infrastructures: process strategies, architectures and governance regimes. Of these three 'tools', the concept of interoperability is most directly linked to architecture. For this reason, I have presented existing research on how an infrastructure's architecture is linked up to a broad range of organisational and strategic issues. This research demonstrates the breadth of ways in which an architecture shapes the evolution of an infrastructure by linking up and interacting with a huge range of organisational features. This implies that an appropriate strategy for developing pan-European e-Government solutions need to be based on a much more nuanced and richer understanding of architectural issues.

References

Aanestad, M., and T. Jensen. 2011. Building nation-wide information infrastructures in health care through modular implementation strategies. *The Journal of Strategic Information Systems* 20(2): 161–176.

Abbate, J. 1994. The Internet challenge: Conflict and compromise in computer networking. In *Changing large technical systems*, ed. J. Summerton, 193–210. Boulder: Westview Press.

Abbate, J. 1999. *Inventing the Internet*. Cambridge, MA: MIT Press.

Baldwin, C.Y., and K.B. Clark. 1997. Managing in an age of modularity. *Harvard Business Review* 75(5): 84–94.

Baldwin, C., and K. Clark. 2000. *Design rules*. Cambridge, MA: MIT Press.

BCS/RAE. 2004. The challenges of complex IT projects. The report of a working group from the Royal Academy and the British Computer Society. http://www.bcs.org/upload/pdf/complexity.pdf. Accessed Aug 2009.

Benkler, Y. 2006. *The wealth of networks: How social production transforms markets and freedom*. New Haven: Yale University Press.

Bygstad, B., P.A. Nielsen, and B.E. Munkvold. 2010. Four integration patterns: A socio-technical approach to integration in IS development. *Information Systems Journal* 20(1): 53–80.

Christensen, C.M. 1997. *The innovator's dilemma: When new technologies cause great firms to fail*. Boston: Harvard Business School Press.

Ciborra, C.U., K. Braa, A. Cordella, B. Dahlbom, A. Failla, O. Hanseth, V. Hepsø, J. Ljungberg, E. Monteiro, and K.A. Simon. 2000. *From control to drift: The dynamics of corporate information infrastructures*. Oxford: Oxford University Press.

Clark, D.D., J. Wroclawski, K.R. Sollins, and R. Braden. 2005. Tussle in cyberspace: Defining tomorrow's Internet. *IEEE/ACM Transactions on Networking* 13(3): 464–475.

Colfer, L., and C. Baldwin. 2010. The mirroring hypothesis: Theory, evidence and exceptions. Harvard Business School working papers no. 10-058.

Contini, F., and G.F. Lanzara (eds.). 2009. *ICT and innovation in the public sector: European studies in the making of e-Government*. Basingstoke: Palgrave Macmillan.

Cusumano, M.A., and A. Gawer. 2002. The elements of platform leadership. *MIT Sloan Management Review* 43: 51–58.

David, P.A. 2005. The beginnings and prospective ending of "end-to-end": An evolutionary perspective on the Internet's architecture. SIEPR Discussion Paper No. 01-04. http://www.stanford.edu/group/siepr/cgi-bin/siepr/?q=system/files/shared/pubs/papers/pdf/01-04.pdf. Accessed 18 Jan 2013.

Edwards, P., S. Jackson, G. Bowker, and C. Knobel. 2007. Report of a workshop on 'History and theory of infrastructures: Lessons for new scientific infrastructures'. University of Michigan, School of Information. http://www.si.umich.edu/InfrastructureWorkshop/documents/UnderstandingInfrastructure2007.pdf. Retrieved 15 March 2007.

Forster, P.W., and J.L. King. 1995. Information infrastructure standards in heterogeneous sectors: Lessons from the worldwide air cargo community. In *Standards policy for information infrastructure*, ed. B. Kahin and J. Abbate, 148–177. Cambridge, MA: MIT Press.

Garud, R., S. Jain, and A. Kumaraswamy. 2002. Institutional entrepreneurship in the sponsorship of common technological standards: The case of Sun Microsystems and Java. *Academy of Management Journal* 45(1): 196–214.

Gawer, A. 2009. Platforms, markets and innovation: An introduction. In *Platforms, markets and innovation*, ed. A. Gawer, 1–16. Cheltenham: Edward Elgar Publishing.

Hanseth, O., and B. Bygstad. 2012. ICT architecture and project risk in inter-organizational settings. ECIS 2012 Proceedings. Paper 130. http://aisel.aisnet.org/ecis2012/130mt1312. Accessed 18 Jan 2013.

Hanseth, O., and C. Ciborra (eds.). 2007. *Risk, complexity and ICT*. Cheltenham: Edward Elgar Publishing.

Hanseth, O., and K. Lyytinen. 2010. Design theory for dynamic complexity in information infrastructures: The case of building Internet. *Journal of Information Technology* 25(1): 1–19.
Hanseth, O., E. Monteiro, and M. Hatling. 1996. Developing information infrastructure: The tension between standardization and flexibility. *Science, Technology and Human Values* 21(4): 407–426.
Henderson, R.M., and K.B. Clark. 1990. Architectural innovation: The reconfiguration of existing product technologies and the failure of established firms. *Administrative Science Quarterly* 35: 9–30.
Henfridsson, O., L. Mathiassen, and F. Svahn. 2009. Reconfiguring modularity: Closing capability gaps in digital innovation. Sprouts: Working papers on information systems. http://sprouts.aisnet.org/9-22. Accessed 18 Jan 2013.
Henningsson, S., and O. Hanseth. 2011. The essential dynamics of information infrastructures. ICIS 2011 Proceedings. Paper 14. http://aisel.aisnet.org/icis2011/proceedings/projmanagement/14. Accessed 18 Jan 2013.
Kallinikos, J. 2007. Technology, contingency and risk: The vagaries of large-scale information systems. In *Risk, complexity and ICT*, ed. O. Hanseth and C. Ciborra, 46–74. Cheltenham: Edward Elgar Publishing.
Lemley, M.A., and L. Lessig. 2000. The end of end-to-end: Preserving the architecture of the Internet in the broadband era. UC Berkeley Law research paper no. 37, http://papers.ssrn.com/sol3/papers.cfm?abstract_id=247737. Accessed 18 Jan 2013.
Lessig, L. 2001. *The future of ideas*. New York: Random House.
Morris, C.R., and C.H. Ferguson. 1993. How technology wins technology wars. *Harvard Business Review* 71(2): 86–95.
Northrop, L., P. Feiler, R.P. Gabriel, J. Goodenough, R. Linger, T. Longstaff, R. Kazman, M. Klein, D. Schmidt, K. Sullivanand, and K. Wallnau. 2006. *Ultra-large-scale systems: The software challenge of the future*. Carnegie Mellon Software Engineering Institute.
Parnas, D.L. 1972. A technique for software module specification with examples. *Communications of the ACM* 15(5): 330–336.
Rodon, J., J. Trullen, L. Silva, and F. Sese. 2012. Counter-designing power in healthcare interorganizational information systems: The design of an electronic prescription system. Unpublished manuscript.
Rosen, M., B. Lublinsky, K.T. Smith, and M.J. Balcer. 2008. *Applied SOA: Service-oriented architecture and design strategies*. Indianapolis: Wiley.
Sæbø, J.I., E.K. Kossia, O.H. Titlestada, R.R. Tohouria, and J. Braaa. 2011. Comparing strategies to integrate health information systems following a data warehouse approach in four countries. *Information Technology for Development* 17(1): 42–60. doi:10.1080/02681102.2010.511702.
Saltzer, J.H., D.P. Reed, and D.D. Clark. 1984. End-to-end arguments in system design. *ACM Transactions on Computer Systems* 2(4): 277–288.
Sanchez, R., and J.T. Mahoney. 1996. Modularity, flexibility, and knowledge management in product and organization design. *Strategic Management Journal* 17: 63–76.
Schmidt, S.K., and R. Werle. 1998. *Coordinating technology: Studies in the international standardization of telecommunications*. Cambridge, MA: MIT Press.
Star, S.L., and K. Ruhleder. 1996. Steps toward an ecology of infrastructure: Design and access for large information spaces. *Information Systems Research* 7(1): 111–134.
Tee, R., and A. Gawer. 2009. Industry architecture as a determinant of successful platform strategies: A case study of the I-mode mobile Internet service. *European Management Review* 6: 217–232.
Tilson, D., K. Lyytinen, and C. Sørensen. 2010. Research commentary—digital infrastructures: The missing IS research agenda. *Information Systems Research* 21(4): 748–759.
Tiwana, A., B. Konsynski, and A.A. Bush. 2010. Platform evolution: Coevolution of platform architecture, governance, and environmental dynamics. *Information Systems Research* 21(4): 675–687.

Trimintizos, P., ed. 2011. Inter-X: Resilience of the Internet interconnection ecosystem. Summary Report Enisa. http://www.enisa.europa.eu/activities/Resilience-and-CIIP/critical-infrastructure-and-services/inter-x/interx/report/interx-report. Accessed 18 Jan 2013.

Utterback, J. 1994. *Mastering the dynamics of innovation: How companies can seize opportunities in the face of technological change*. Boston: Harvard Business School Press.

Van der Aalst, W.M.P. 1999. Process-oriented architectures for electronic commerce and interorganizational workflow. *Information Systems* 24(9): 639–671.

Vassiliadis, B., A. Stefani, J. Tsaknakis, and A. Tsakalidis. 2006. From application service provision to service-oriented computing: A study of the IT outsourcing evolution. *Telematics and Informatics* 23(4): 271–293.

Woodard, C.J. 2008. Architectural control points. Research Collection School of information systems. http://works.bepress.com/cjwoodard/14. Accessed 18 Jan 2013.

Wu, T. 2003. Network neutrality, broadband discrimination. *Journal of Telecommunications and High Technology Law* 2: 141. doi:10.2139/ssrn.388863. http://ssrn.com/abstract=388863. Last access 18 January 2013.

Zittrain, J. 2006. The generative Internet. *Harvard Law Review* 119: 1974–2040.

Chapter 3
How the Law Can Make It Simple: Easing the Circulation of Agency in e-Justice

Francesco Contini and Richard Mohr

Abstract The chapter analyses the ways in which technology and law disperse, channel and reassemble agency in ICT enabled legal proceedings. It works from five of the case studies of e-justice discussed in the book, assessing how different approaches magnify or reduce complexity and affect systems development and use. The law can legitimate ensembles of technological and performative procedures, but it cannot construct them by regulation through a legal blueprint. Attempts at excessive legal regulation quickly raise complexity to unmanageable levels. Technology is assessed as a distinct regulative regime that opens new channels of communication, potentially duplicating existing legal and traditional channels. The regulation of technology could take advantage of this state of affairs. Machines and software codes identify and admit participants and direct human activity. Some of the difficulties in reproducing legal processes in technologically enabled environments are explained by the demands of the performative, where meanings exceed the demands of simple information flow. The chapter explores the requirements of meaning making, by which participants recognise the context and the legal consequences of ICT enabled procedures. The interfaces of law and technology rely on the interpretive context in which messages are understood as well as the legal forms in which they are transmitted. Each of these elements is essential to assure the circulation of agency in ICT enabled legal proceedings, while ensuring the legality of the entire ensemble.

F. Contini (✉) • R. Mohr
Social Research, Policy and Planning, Sydney, Australia
e-mail: francesco.contini@irsig.cnr.it

F. Contini and G.F. Lanzara (eds.), *The Circulation of Agency in E-Justice*, Law, Governance and Technology Series 13, DOI 10.1007/978-94-007-7525-1_3,

3.1 Introduction

Information and communication technologies (ICTs) have been one of the main drivers of change in courts and judiciaries. Initially considered as tools to increase productivity or make judicial operations more transparent and streamlined, now ICTs are deeply seated in the judicial machinery and organization, affecting also the ways in which justice is administered through trials and judicial proceedings.[1] This has affected the ways in which relevant information (including documents) and the agency of judges and parties to proceedings circulate in civil proceedings, thus changing the institutional landscape. The case studies discussed in the book, namely Money Claims OnLine (MCOL), COVL, CITIUS, Trial OnLine (TOL), and e-Curia, show how the regulation of technology and the effects of e-justice deployment in the regulation of proceedings are becoming key issues. The new goal is to bring e-justice from the national to the European level, thus enabling transborder civil proceedings such as the European Small Claims Procedure (ESCP) (Regulation (EC) No. 861/2007) and the European Payment Order (EPO) (Regulation (EC) No. 1896/2006). From a technological and legal perspective this leads e-justice into unexplored terrain, in which legal agency has to be projected by from one member state to another without human facilitators or intermediate bodies. Complexity may become unmanageable due to the difficulties of interoperability between technological, institutional and legal frameworks of the 26 member states adopting the procedures. The dynamics between the rule of law and the "rule of technology" have to be investigated. This chapter, considering the findings emerging from five case studies, identifies ways in which the regulation of technology can contribute to lowering complexity, and conversely how it might inject complexity into the systems. Such findings are then used to suggest a different approach to regulating EPOs and ESCPs in order to ease the circulation of agency in transborder proceedings.

[1]This chapter is a revised and expanded version of Mohr, R. and Contini, F. 2011. "Reassembling the Legal: 'The wonders of modern science' in court-related proceedings". Griffith Law Review 20: 994–1019. The authors are grateful to the editors of the Griffith Law Review for permission to use a considerable part of that article. While the work is the result of a joint effort of the two authors, the evaluation exercise of the Italian research systems requires the attribution of specific sections to individual authors. In response to this evaluation requirement individual sections may be attributed as follows. Contini: Law, technology and courts; Regulation of technology and technology as regulative regime; Regulative approaches to e-Justice, Lowering complexity in ICT enabled legal processes, Identity and agency; Technology regulation in EPO and ESCP; Mohr: Introduction, Identity and the performance of legal agency; Legalise, Reassemble, Signify; Making technology legal; Contexts of the performative; Performing the legal; Pathways and the reassembling of agency.

3.2 Technology and the Performance of Law

3.2.1 Law, Technology and Courts

Law has always worked with technology, even if it was not called by that name. If we think of technology as those things that people use to achieve a desired effect (Latour 2005),[2] then the technology of law has encompassed documents, signatures and files (Vismann 2008). The courtroom is a technology of the law, providing a place for the parties and the judge to come together and communicate, for witnesses to be sworn and to give evidence, and for judges to pronounce binding decisions. The bench with its raised position facilitates the judge's surveillance and control of the court, as well as framing (with a motto, flag or other symbol of authority) the legal pronouncement of a sentence or interlocutory orders (Mohr 2000). This well-known ensemble of people in specific roles, and things that set the scene of their roles and record the statements they make, has accompanied and developed with the law over many centuries (Garapon 1995; Jacob 1995–96). Some of the interactions between the law, people and things have been written into procedural law and court rules while others, gradually established by convention and habitus, remain unwritten.

Over the past 20 years information and communication technology (ICT) has burst into this peaceful scene. Even if a promised 'paperless' future is yet to come, a growing number of tasks previously accomplished in courts by humans working with paper have been delegated to or inscribed onto machines. One of the outcomes is that 'judicial and legal procedures, together with the agencies that come with them, are inscribed, although not entirely, into technical procedures and objects' (Lanzara 2009, 13). The effort has not been just technological but also legal and regulatory, since the placement of technologies into highly regulated court environments has required new sets of formal rules. As stated by Lanzara and Hanseth in the two previous chapters, e-justice development is affected and hindered by many sources of complexity. The interaction between functional domains, in particular law and technology, may at the same time inject complexity into the system, making it difficult to develop and use, or contribute to reduce it. This is magnified in transborder proceedings, due to the interactions between multiple legal and institutional frameworks, and between the different e-justice platforms developed at national level.

This chapter expands this argument, assessing how the approaches to the regulation of technology identified in the case studies affect the complexity to be faced in developing and using the system. From a theoretical perspective the goal is to better grasp the dynamics between the two functional domains. By doing this we aim to identifying approaches for regulating technology in a way that keeps

[2]Latour considers this and other relations between people and technology in his Reassembling the Social: an introduction to actor-network-theory (Latour 2005).

digitally enabled judicial proceedings accessible and simple for the users, while properly signalling the consequences of the actions undertaken in the digital media. At the same time, we single out some general principles to regulate technologies in a way that doesn't clash with the technology itself, lowering complexity at design and development stage. In doing this, we aim to identifying criteria to support the dual design strategy identified by Lanzara in Sect. 1.8: pursuing the 'maximum feasible simplicity' in system design, development and use, as well as avoiding to reach the threshold of 'maximum manageable complexity'.

The rapid introduction of ICT, the degree of formality of its software codes, and its relative distance from the courts (through out-sourcing and other forms of public-private partnerships) have all highlighted the degree of competition and potential conflict between the laws of technology and the technology of law. We consider the interactions between the legal frameworks that regulate the technologies that the courts use, and the codes that specify how the technology is to be operated. As will be seen, this interaction is unstable and liable to lead to unanticipated consequences.

We begin, in the following two subsections, by introducing the key concepts of our inquiry: regulation and agency. First we consider the different ways law and technology regulate and circulate human agency. Then we identify certain essential functions that must be performed in constituting and implementing a legal order. Having established the conceptual tools of our analysis, we introduce the case studies, discussing how the law has regulated technology. We focus specifically on the digital means for the circulation of legal agency. Our particular focus is on the ways in which parties to a case can be identified. The agency of the parties to simple civil proceedings is first of all expressed in their statement of claim or filing of an action. In traditional proceedings this was achieved in place and in person: a document was signed or an oath was sworn. The challenge for the interaction of law and technology is to enable such a declaration of agency to circulate from remote to central (and back to remote) locations, or across national boundaries. A legal declaration is distinguished from a simple message by its performativity (see Sect. 3.2.3). That is to say, it must effect legal or social change: initiating a legal action, responding to a claim, or allocating responsibility for a debt or other binding legal commitment. How can technology convey legal agency, and not just information? The transfer of information and agency across national borders and between jurisdictions adds complexity to the difficulties of distance.

In the fourth and final part of the article (Sects. 3.4. and 3.5) we draw a number of conclusions about how the law can simplify the development of e-justice and the circulation of agency in judicial proceedings and, conversely, how it can hinder or even paralyse it. Law, technology and the people who use them do not work in isolation. Instead we understand them as shifting assemblages which bring together rules, objects and actors to carry out particular functions associated with exchanging procedural documents in civil trials. This perspective clarifies the roles of law as a legitimating device, of technology as enabling functions and of people as actors who need to know the implications and consequences of their performances.

3.2.2 Regulation of Technology and Technology as Regulative Regime

e-Justice entered into the courts and into the public sector at least in part with the aim of reducing bureaucratisation (Cordella and Willcocks 2009; Velicogna 2008). The effect, however, has been quite different. Technology brings into play a new, thick layer of regulations (Lessig 2007), which may be clearly seen in the fields we are considering. Norms proliferate in order to specify how technological artefacts must (or are supposed to) operate. They are particularly visible from a system development perspective, since at this level rules (and behaviours) have to be inscribed into the machine. This is 'a particular mode of institutionalization' through which norms are inscribed 'onto tangible technical installations and apparatus' and conventional procedures are absorbed into machines (Czarniawska and Joerges 1998, 372). In this way, action is directly delegated to the machines that do (or that automate) what humans were doing.

In the case studies, we can observe rules prescribing which technology can be used to perform specific functions (such as proof of identity); norms indicating the technical features of the technology (such as the protocols to be used to secure data interchanges), norms indicating machine behaviour ('data are exchanged through an HTTPS protocol'[3]), and also norms indicating how one must behave vis-à-vis a machine (such as to log in before being enabled to do a particular operation). Just as procedural norms are part of the institutional structure of any judicial system, 'technical norms are the institutional structure of machinery' (Czarniawska and Joerges 1998, 378). The first obvious consequence is that instead of reducing bureaucracy and regulation, the massive deployment of ICT often requires a massive deployment of regulation.

In the case of e-justice, it is important to make a distinction between the regulations established within the technological domain, such as the features of technological standards, and regulations established within other domains: the parliaments, the government or the courts. The former respond to the need to regulate the functioning of the machine, the second to the requirement that a given technology must act effectively as a performative. (This requirement is clarified in the following part of the chapter.)

From another angle, the (technically regulated) machine guides or even dictates human behaviour, whether as with speed bumps regulating traffic, (Latour 1999, 186) home banking moving money securely or e-justice transmitting legal performatives remotely. Technology therefore has its own 'normativity', i.e. the capacity to 'actually constrain human actions, inviting or enforcing, inhibiting or prohibiting types of behaviour' (Hildebrandt 2008, 5). It can direct human behaviour by means

---

[3]Each of these regulations is linked to other regulations and standards developed in various technological sectors, such as the A4 page (International Standard ISO 216) or the https protocol (combining http and ssl technical standards).

of an 'invisible hand', often made of software codes, in a much more compelling manner than can traditional regulation (Lessig 2007). Lastly, technology, law and social systems tend to tie each other up in composite assemblages (Lanzara 2009) or sociotechnical regimes shaping day to day actions as well as the evolution of the entire system (Cordella and Iannacci 2010).

The power of technology to regulate such a range of activities has led Kallinikos to argue that technology may be seen as 'a major regulative regime', which he defines as 'a technical, social and institutional system of forces that shape human agency both in the direct way of embodying functionalities that engrave particular courses of action and in the rather unobtrusive fashion of shaping perceptions and preferences, forming skills and professional rules' (Kallinikos 2009b, 70).

From this perspective, formal laws (including procedural codes) and technology (together with its own codes and regulating impulses) constitute different regulative regimes. Both engage 'normativity' but they constitute distinct modes of regulation, and operate in different ways (Hildebrandt 2008).

Technology is outcome oriented: it either works, which is to say that it produces the expected outcomes, or it does not work (Weick 1990, 3–5). It is judged teleologically. A given e-filing application is good from a technological point of view if it allows users to send online files to the court; that is to transfer bits and data. But the effective electronic delivery of such files may not be sufficient to constitute a valid filing of the case from a legal perspective.

Formal regulations, on the other hand, are judged deontologically: they separate the legal from the illegal. What works from a technological perspective is not necessarily legal. A case may be filed via an online system approved by the court and not by other means; identity may be ascertained online by using a given technology (e.g. a security protocol), but not using any other, and so on. In the case studies analysed in this book, as well as in transborder proceedings (EPO and ESCP), it is not possible to file a case using regular email. Legal changes can outlaw technology even though it may have been used effectively for some time (Velicogna and Ng 2006). At the same time there are many technologies that are legal, since some authority endorsed their use, but are failures from a technological point of view, since they do not produce the expected outcomes or, simply speaking, do not work (Fabri 2008). Any legal process, whatever technologies it uses, must be judged both teleologically, for its effect, and deontologically, for its legitimacy. Kelsen said as much (Kelsen 1967, 211–212). Finally, the interactions between these two regulative regimes have major effects on complexity. They may increase complexity, pushing the system development or its use up to the threshold of maximum manageable complexity, as when the law prescribes the use of technological components that may become difficult to develop or use. In this case, system development may become slow, difficult or even impossible. Even once it is developed it may fail to be diffused because users find its protocols or its technical requirements too onerous. However, legal–technological interactions can also reduce complexity, pursuing the goal of maximum feasible simplicity without hampering effective performativity, as illustrated by the case studies. This chapter investigates these dynamics, focusing on how the regulation of technology and of technological procedures can help to maintain legal and performative efficacy without exceeding manageable complexity.

3.2.3 Identity and the Performance of Legal Agency

The following case studies cast some light on the interaction of intersecting regulative regimes: how they increase or reduce the complexity of the system and how they affect the circulation of agency.

We analyse the entanglements between technology and formal rules in the operations of online civil claims, and of the trans-national proceedings handled by the Court of Justice of the European Union. Even if the proceedings of the Court of Justice are not properly 'civil', their structure and the functions they have to perform are similar to those of civil claims. Indeed, our focus is on the functions of courts and related legal processes that can go online. Courts resolve disputes, provide a forum for testing legal issues of public interest, pronounce decisions favouring one party or another, and determine penalties, all of which must be verified and recorded. In these myriad functions the law and the technology interact in carrying out numerous operations: inputting data, generating process, communicating with respondents, identifying parties, recording and communicating judgment or outcomes, acknowledging receipt, and so on.

Law iterates and re-iterates a legal order (Butler 1997, 33–40). The legal order may be seen as a key guarantee of the social order, and indeed unless law is to be a formalistic end in itself, it must serve such broader social ends. A key element of law's iteration of the legal order is to manage and record the status of subjects, including the legal obligations between them and their relationships to certain material assets.[4] Law does not only record, but also confers changes of status. One cannot make a transition from single to married, from free to detained, from debtor to bankrupt, unless the proper legal forms are followed (Austin 1980; Benveniste 1966, 269).

Legal processes and the utterances that constitute them are made up of performatives, intended to institute specific changes to the social order, and to re-establish relations between citizens within a legal order. All courts and other binding legal procedures must have the capacity to pronounce these decisions in a legitimate and effective way. Even before arriving at the final decision, law and the courts deal with performative utterances in numerous ways. These include undertakings made by the

---

[4] As seen in more detail below, legal pronouncements underpin 'The "the force of law" that supports human societies, [through] linguistic enunciations that stably obligate living beings' (Agamben 2011, 70).

parties, either in court proceedings or in antecedent contractual or administrative arrangements, statements made under oath, and the oath itself.[5]

These performative utterances are essential to the operation of law, and for e-justice to be possible they must be carried out in new, electronic forms as well as in traditional legal settings. So the focus of our analysis is on the forms and conditions of successful performatives found in our case studies, for comparison with the baseline conditions found in the conventional (face-to-face and paper-based) forms of traditional courts. Performatives enact agency; ICT must be utilised in order for their efficacy to circulate beyond the immediate contact points of the face-to-face and the material.

Successful performatives underlie each of the many functions of courts and their electronic counterparts. For the purposes of this study we limit our focus to specific crucial moments, or functions, which are fundamental to any proceedings: identifying the parties and recording their statements and legally relevant acts, including outcomes leading to changes of legal status. We consider these functions before returning to a more detailed discussion of our approach to the performative mechanisms by which they are achieved.

The first task of legal agency is to identify the party making a performative utterance. The proper identification of parties and any related actors is crucial to the effective work of the law. Latour found the identification of the énonciateur, the author of the statement, to be central to the operations of the senior French administrative court, the Conseil d'état. 'The whole of law can be grasped as an obsessional effort to make the enunciation assignable (rendre l'énonciation assignable).' The parties must be known, the author of the statement acknowledged. Latour identified 'the signature, the archive, the text, the file' as 'the perilous tracks' by which the law seeks to reattach the statements to their speakers ('les énoncés à leurs énonciateurs') (Latour 2002, 295, 297).

Also in our cases, whether an uncontested money claim or a high profile case before the European Court of Justice the same 'obsessional efforts' must be made: the parties must be identified; their statements must be assignable; their oath must be binding. They must be recognised for who they are, what they have said, and what their obligations are. Pleadings have to be properly exchanged and the tracks must be preserved so there is a record for future reference and for publicity.

Identification in legal proceedings is usually achieved by performative, not descriptive, means. A descriptive statement is judged by its veracity, i.e. its correspondence with some independent state of affairs, so that it is an accurate representation. Courts and other legal processes normally spend little effort in empirically discovering the identity of a party. The signature has been the traditional legal means to signify identity and agency in a single gesture. By signing a declaration, one is initiating a legal action and asserting one's identity. In some

[5]The expression 'oath' here covers both the religious form of swearing by God, and the secular form, distinguished by the term 'affirmation' in some English-speaking jurisdictions. The legal effect is equivalent.

proceedings, as in the European Payment Order, it is enough to sign one's name on a paper form. In others, a signature must be validated or witnessed by third parties, or it may be necessary to swear one's name and address under oath. By declaring their identity, parties are recognised for who they are and for their claim to recognition as a legal agent.[6]

The traditional signature or oath can only project agency into their immediate surroundings: the space of the courtroom where the oath is uttered or, thanks to the efficacy of postal and document delivery systems, the place where the signed document is received. ICT enables a wider circulation of agency, and this is the promise and the attraction of e-justice. Yet for e-justice to successfully replicate the immediate effect of the oath or signature, it must fulfill equivalent conditions of identification, security and non-repudiation. If this has led to difficulties at the national level, in transborder cases it seems to be almost impossible.

As will be discussed below, adequate conditions of identification and security are generally met in important realms of online banking or commerce by simple means such as user name, password and perhaps some additional security code. Yet as will also be seen, courts are sometimes reluctant to resort to such simple solutions. What does e-justice require that is lacking in e-commerce?

Legal agency is usually enacted through some solemn ceremony. In addition to confirmation of identity and the security of the transaction, the non-repudiation and serious consequences of legal acts are signified in performative terms. Austin's theory of the performative showed that language did not simply communicate information, but effected transitions in social relations (Austin 1980). Its effect relies upon a public record (Vismann 2008) and other elements of social context (Foucault 2002, 31; Derrida 1988, 18). The context includes the material setting of the utterance as well as the institutional context within which it is performed. The material setting may include certain actions that must accompany the words, or particular architectures within which it is set (Austin 1980, 8). The broader institutional context involves the legal and cultural actions which authorise the setting and the various actors within it. The introduction of ICT into courts changes both the material and institutional settings of judicial proceedings.

Once the entire context–social, spatial and temporal–is admitted to the proactive landscape of the affirmation of the social (and not just legal) order, then new actors are recognised: not just the judge, but all the interlocutors; not just the bench, but all the furniture, equipment and architecture that frame and authorise the enunciation; not just the signature, but the bodily gesture that enacts it, and the context in which the commitment is made.

In summary, our study examines the role of performative utterances in identification and status change to bind the telos of technology to the deon of law.

[6]Recognising the parties for who they are is not simply a formal legal requirement, but goes to the heart of political and moral life. Honneth (1995) and Ricoeur (2004) have placed the relationship of recognition at the very foundation of the polity and of social life, respectively. Here we focus on its role in legal proceedings as a driver of legal agency.

Legal discourse has consequences. To make admissions, to accept responsibility, to blame or to deny culpability are all means by which we and our actions are recognised. There must be records of those transactions (now rarely oral, usually written, increasingly digital) if their effects are to be lasting and not ephemeral. The law courts have long managed those processes of performance, enunciation and recording. As we come to recognise the fuller social context of the courts and related procedures, it is no longer possible to isolate their discourse within the exclusive 'system' of law and legal formalism. The collective assemblages[7] that confer authority and recognition include the various files, databases, and communication channels through which the parties interact and in which their statements, including oaths, commitments, admissions and denials, is recorded.

A number of questions flow from this focus. How is performative efficacy of legal agency projected beyond the courtroom and the signed document? ICT enables virtually instant communications across vast distances, but information is not equivalent to agency. Here we have tried to analyse some of the elements required to circulate legal agency through e-justice's radically different physical and informational architecture. In the following section we analyse some alternative approaches to the digital reassemblage of gestures, words, signatures and evidence beyond the traditional settings of the courtroom and the original signed document.

3.3 Regulative Approaches to e-Justice

3.3.1 Five Case Studies

The e-justice initiatives discussed in this book, Money Claim Online, COVL, CITIUS, TOL and e-Curia, as well as the e-justice platform currently developed by e-Codex to enable EPO and ESCP have in common the needs of effectively performing the identification of citizens and lawyers, granting access to judicial procedures, and enabling the exchange of utterances (documents and data) in judicial proceedings. Each of these requirements is built in at the design and development stage as well as at the day by day use of the e-justice application. They faced such functional and legal need with different approaches, which we summarise below in order to assess how the different approaches impact on complexity.

Money Claim Online (MCOL) is a web-based service for issuing money claims and resolving fixed money disputes introduced by the Department of Constitutional

[7]Giovan Francesco Lanzara helpfully pointed out, in commenting on earlier versions of this work, that 'assemblage' in this context is more closely related to the French 'agencement', a richer and more precise term that refers to the social circulation of agency, in space and time, through persons and objects, than the French 'assemblage'. We have now been able to address the question of agency in greater depth, thanks to Lanzara's previous comments and his elaboration in Chap. 1 of the present book.

Affairs (DCA) of England and Wales to improve access to justice by opening a digital channel for dispute resolution (see Chap. 4) (Timms et al. 2003). One of the reasons for its great success is the way in which it has been regulated. MCOL development took place without having to come to terms with regulations establishing the features of the technological components. The legal ground for system development was provided by the pre-existing back-end systems delivering a similar service for bulk users through the County Court Bulk Center and for the entire country (Kallinikos 2009a, 183). Building on the top of this installed base, the mandate of the DCA was to develop the system in a short time to facilitate access to justice in accordance with the recommendations of the Woolf Report (1996). Once the system had been developed and tested, the DCA mandated the legality of filing and handling a well-defined set of civil suits. This was done through Practice Direction 7E which regulates the terms of use and the procedure to be followed when using the system, but not its technical features. Art 1.1 states that 'This practice direction provides for a scheme in which ... a request for a claim form to be issued and other specified documents may be filed electronically ('Money Claim Online')'.

Article 1.2 simply enables claimants 'to start certain types of county court claims by requesting the issue of a claim form electronically via Her Majesty's Courts Service website' without even specifying the basic features of that site.

The approach of the DCA has been designed to increase users' access to justice by taking advantage of technologies already deployed by the courts (like the Bulk Centre systems) and those familiar to potential users (like debit and credit card payment). This functional simplification allowed the use of the same standard components already adopted for e-commerce to permit identification, and hence access to MCOL, to all English and Welsh 'consumers' owning a credit or debit card.

COVL, the Central Department for Enforcement in Slovenia, further expands the MCOL approach toward law-driven functional simplification (Chap. 5). The Supreme Court, leading the project, promoted changes at the code of civil proceedings so as to create a legal framework conducive to ICT developments. These included a unique national jurisdiction in charge of handling electronic procedures, and simplified procedural requirements to better accommodate technological developments. For example, while based on pre-existing regulations requiring digital identification to be based on digital signature, a new regulation states that the Ministry of Justice is entitled to prescribe other 'less secure means for specific procedures'. Taking advantage of this amendment, the Supreme Court designed COVL to accept claims based on valid email, statement of truth declaration, and payment of court fees (see Sect. 5.2.3). These and other legal changes gave to the project team a legal ground to develop the system. Other amendments to the code of procedure eased the payment of court fees and the submission of copies of the documents supporting the claim in the new digital environment. Finally, a practice order has provided that the Supreme Court may validate a digitally enabled procedure as a legal performative once it has been successfully tested. These legal changes have been effected mainly at the procedural level. They do not establish the technological features of the application. Rather, technological features are the result of the analysis of other e-justice applications (such as MCOL and the Finnish e-filing system), of the assessment of the installed base, and of determinations taken within the project team and endorsed by the Supreme Court.

CITIUS, the e-filing application developed in Portugal, casts further light on the dialogue between law and technology. In 1996 the code of procedure was amended to allow the use of electronic means to handle and complete pleadings. Further amendments of 1999 prescribed the simultaneous and compulsory use of digital and conventional means to exchange procedural documents. But legal changes cannot impose the use of a given technology, especially when that technology is not available (see Sect. 6.1.2.). Later on, in 2006 when case management technologies had been implemented, and the technological and organisational installed bases of courts were technologically ready, legal changes allowed civil procedures to take place electronically in the terms to be defined by the competent government agency. As in the two case studies previously discussed, this general framework gave the green light to the more ambitious project known as CITIUS. In 2008, while a group of technicians and clerks of the Ministry of Justice had developed the system, the Ministry passed the regulation that specifies the functioning of the electronic procedure in terms of presentation of the pleadings, electronic writs of notice, payment of court fees and other procedures. This was integrated into a new legislative framework which provided the data protection system (see Sect. 6.1.3). In this case, too, the legal framework is general, and does not enter into the technical features of the systems. Technical specifications are rather the result of the step-by-step development carried out by a team of the Ministry of Justice over the years, and redesigned after an audit carried out by a specialised company in 2009. After initial difficulties in 1999, the Portuguese experience tells of a dialogue between law and technology. The law provides a broad framework for e-justice development. Technologies are developed and tested. Then their use in judicial proceedings is made legal.

The same evidence emerges in the case of e-Curia, the e-justice platform of the European Court of Justice. In contrast to the other case studies, in which e-justice applications affect simple money orders procedure, e-Curia has been developed to support the entire set of high profile judicial proceedings handled by the Court. Even in this case, however, the development has been carried out within a very general legal framework. In 2005 a first legal change to the rules of procedure set up the legal ground for technological development, establishing that the Court may decide the criteria for the electronic exchange of procedural documents which would 'be deemed the original of that document'. This provided the legal ground for system development, and after years spent in inscribing the complex procedures of the court into the digital media, and after successful testing of the application, in 2011 the Court legalised the 'lodging and service of procedural documents by the means of e-Curia'. The use of the system is not mandatory, and applicants must first accept the conditions of use, as with any e-service provided by private companies. If they don't accept such conditions, they can always use traditional paper-based procedures.

The dynamics between law and technology in Trial OnLine (TOL) is quite different. TOL is an ambitious project launched in 2000 by the Italian Ministry of

Justice to fully digitise all civil proceedings and achieve a paperless court (Carnevali 2010, 124). The development of TOL was driven first of all by formal rules, approved several years before the first running applications.[8] Instead of providing a general framework legitimising ICT development Italian rules pre-established the features of the technologies to be adopted. In particular they established that the digital signature, based on EU regulation, was the only technology capable of properly identifying users and verifying documents, and ensuring security and non-repudiation of communications. The Ministry of Justice, acting as rule maker and system developer, mandated a public key infrastructure (PKI) and digital signature for all procedures requiring identification and signature. Less demanding technological solutions, such as those adopted in each of the other e-justice applications except CITIUS, were not considered to be sufficient to meet the legal requirements of security, confidentiality and non-repudiation (Fabri 2009). This led to the need to develop a large number of infrastructural components from scratch for both courts and lawyers. As a consequence the development phase was long and expensive. It was only after 6 years, at the end of 2006, that the court of Milan became the first in Italy to begin using the system, and then only for money claims and not for any other procedures.

3.3.2 Legal Blueprint or Iterative Development?

MCOL, COVL, CITIUS and e-Curia show a similar dynamics between law and technology. First the establishment of a legal ground for e-justice development based on a general framework stated that 'e-justice can be developed in a given area'. This was followed by technological development carried out in house.[9] The systems were then checked for technical issues and also for the legal requirement that the system supported the exchange of performative utterances with effects on legal proceedings and status management. This entails also to check if the system is properly signifying the consequences of the actions undertaken in the digital environment. Once these checks were satisfied, the system was authorised by another legal act of the competent authority.

This iterative approach was not adopted in TOL, which was instead developed starting from a blueprint established by formal rules. The Italian authorities attempted to regulate the technical features of the software and hardware application with 'technical rules'. After the publication of the first framework regulation,[10] the

[8] Law no. 59 of 1997 established the legal value of digital documents and digital signature based on PKI standard (L. n. 59/1997), and the Presidential Decree no. 123 of 2001 endorsed Trial Online based on that law (D.P.R. n. 123/2001).

[9] In MCOL technological development was carried out by the private company that was managing the pre-existing systems at the Bulk Centre, and therefore without a specific tender.

[10] D.P.R. n. 123/2001.

Ministry of Justice had to approve an incredible number of technical regulations defining, from a legal perspective, every single detail of the technological components. The system development had to follow the specification of the formal regulation enacted to clarify the features of the applications, how the technology was to operate, and how users were to act vis-à-vis the technological applications (Fabri 2009, 130) It took almost 3 years just to draft the regulations required to develop the systems of the Ministry of Justice and of the courts.[11] Then it was necessary to draft technical regulations for the applications to be developed by the lawyers' associations, since nothing had yet been developed in this second area (also due to the lack of technical specification).

This can be understood if we consider that the Italian Ministry of justice had to develop the system with a private company selected after an open tender, and technical rules and specifications were required to draft the tender itself. This was not necessary in the other case studies since they were developed in house, or by companies having long-term service contracts with the courts (as in MCOL). In such cases technical specification can be identified in a step-by-step approach during the design and development stage. The effects of this dynamic in increasing or reducing complexity are self-evident: iterative approaches help to keep complexity at a manageable level, while legal blueprints inject complexity in design and development stages. At the design stage, it requires pre-established technical specifications that could be identified more easily and effectively at a more advanced stage. Legal blueprints established before the development stage restrict options and solutions, regardless the complexity to be faced. As will be discussed below, the European legislator, even without a legal blueprint, has pre-established technical solutions that are complicating the development of a European e-justice platform supporting EPO and ESCP.

This analysis also illustrates the effects of functional simplification in lowering the level of complexity to be faced in the development and application of e-justice systems. Indeed, functional simplification is a powerful design tool in e-justice development (MCOL). Even if it can be pursued without legal changes, the possibility of enacting legal changes magnifies its effects. All the case studies, even if in different ways and with different timing, experienced the benefits of law-based functional simplification. It affects areas like payment of court fees, simplified requirements for exchanging procedural documents, reduction of the data to be entered into the forms, just to mention a few. However the most revealing area of functional simplification entails the identification of the parties and signature protocols.

EPO and ESCP have been functionally simplified in various ways, but problems remain in the common implementation of the rules at national level.

---

[11] Decree of the Ministry of Justice n. 264 of 2000, Ministerial decree of 27 March 2000 (D.M. n. 264/2000), followed by other regulations.

3.4 Lowering Complexity in ICT Enabled Legal Processes

3.4.1 Identification and Access

There are strict limitations on who may be admitted to judicial or other legal proceedings. One must have standing, a recognised role in the process. In injunctive orders as in high profile cases at the European Court of Justice the proceeding must begin with the identification of the parties. This must be ascertained in a formally appropriate manner, using the ceremonial and contextual elements of the performative discussed above. Established legal conventions allow identity to be ascertained by a set of traditional practices endorsed by formal regulations, such as a signature on a procedural document, the exhibition of an identity document, or certain statements under oath. The question of online legal identity, on the other hand, is still problematic.

Indeed, while many technologies can provide more or less robust technical solutions, such solutions are not necessarily acceptable from a legal point of view. Electronic identity cards are not widely used in Europe. Simple systems based on user names and passwords, accepted in so many areas of online transactions, grant access to e-justice platforms, but are not generally accepted as a legal substitute for a signature. Here we encounter two intertwined issues: access to e-services and the signature. The question of digital identity remains a quintessential case of the difficult mediations between technology and the law, but also an effective test bed to assess the effects of the legal framework on the complexity (or simplicity) of architectures and procedures.

The case studies face the question of digital identity in different ways. During the development of MCOL, the first idea was to identify users through the 'Government Gateway', a common point of entry to e-government services. But since the Gateway was not fully functional yet,[12] the Department of Constitutional Affairs preferred to use a ready-made component provided by a private company, integrated with a payment system engine based on credit and debit cards (Kallinikos 2009a). Some years later, when the Gateway was ready, they moved to the new identification engine. In both cases, however, the plaintiff has to register on a web site to receive a customer ID and a password. Once logged in to MCOL, the 'customer' can file a new case entering data into web forms. At the end of this procedure, plaintiffs first write their name to sign the 'statement of truth', and then pay the court fees with their own debit or credit card. No signature is needed. Article 10 of the practice direction states that 'Any provision of the Civil procedure rules which requires a document to be signed by any person is satisfied by that person entering their name on an online form.' This reduces to a minimum the functional and technical requirements of the signature. The name provided during the customer enrolment and typed under the statement of truth must correspond to the name of the owner of

[12]MCOL switched to the Government Gateway in 2010, 8 years after the launch of the system.

the card used to pay the court fee. The analogy between this procedure and those commonly used in e-commerce is apparent. The citizen's identity is established digitally as their 'customer ID', and the typing of one's name substitutes for the hand-written signature. The defendant, having received the claim pack from the Court, may choose from several possible responses, such as to ignore it or pay the amount claimed, using the online channel or the conventional one.[13]

As noticed above, an identical approach has been used in COVL thanks to the legal amendment, authorizing the Ministry of justice to use identification systems less secure than digital signature for specific procedures. At the Court of Justice of the European Union the procedure is similar, even if the enrolment is more complex, with checks carried out by the Court's staff. Indeed, once the enrolment request is received (on a duly signed paper form) the registries of the courts verify the identity of the applicant and his/her practising certificate is attached to the request. Only if all the conditions are fulfilled do the registries provide the credentials to the applicant.

3.4.2 Simplicity Versus Complexity

In the e-justice platforms of MCOL and COVL, the user (whether plaintiff, defendant or court staff), once identified and logged into the system, can submit or serve procedural documents or data without having to sign them. Indeed, the legal and functional features of the signature (identity and agency) are fulfilled by the identification process (enrolment, credentials, and correct log in), by the decision to submit the document (i.e. ordering to the computer interface to submit the document, often with a click of the mouse), and by an associated statement of truth (stating for instance, that the facts described in the procedural document and its annex are true). In MCOL and COVL this is further enforced by the payment of the court fee by the same subject who is submitting the application. If all the conditions are fulfilled, the document submitted through the e-justice application is legally valid and becomes a performative utterance with legal consequences. In all these systems, therefore, access and signature, with the joined needs of identification and the projection of agency, are merged together. Access and signature initiate the process by which legal agency is circulated. This approach, which is largely self-contained, has contributed to minimizing the architectural and procedural complexity without hampering the performativity of the judicial proceedings. In all these examples the legal framework has set up a context that has supported the simplification at functional and architectural level, as better clarified by comparison with the other two case studies.

---

[13]If the defendant ignores the claim a judgment by default will be issued by the Court of Northampton.

In CITIUS and TOL the legal framework requires digital signatures based on public key infrastructure. For Italian lawyers to file a case electronically they must first buy a smart card with digital signature issued by a certification authority contracted by their local lawyers' association. Only then may they connect to the systems of the Ministry of Justice and the courts through access points provided by each bar association, of which there are 165 throughout Italy.[14] To file a money claim the lawyer must draft the petition using a specific software application developed by private companies. Everything is signed with the lawyer's digital signature, and attached together inside a digital envelope. Only at this stage can the lawyer, using the smart card, connect to the access point provided by the lawyers association, and send the application and attachments to the court system via the central system of the Ministry of Justice.[15] The architecture was too complex and expensive to be fully deployed at national level, and after a recent legal change procedural documents can be delivered to the court with certified mail. Clerks and judges, using ad hoc software, analyses the case, prepares and digitally signs the order, and sends it to the registry of the court. A similar procedure has to be followed by Portuguese lawyers, clerks and judges. The main difference is that the digital signature and access points are provided at centralised level.

Digital signature was the EU legal standard, and represented the best possible option from a legal point of view. But what was simple and rational from a purely legal perspective has been almost impossible to develop from a technological perspective. Here the conflict between the requirements of the law, and the requirements of technology (in particular information infrastructure growth) are clearly visible. Complexity increases to levels that have been difficult to manage.

At the time these development took place digital signatures were not widely used by lawyers, and the decision to assign to each local bar association the authority to provide digital signatures to their members made their diffusion even slower. As Hanseth and Lyytinen (2010) have clearly pointed out, the bootstrapping of any information infrastructure requires a fast growing number of users. Since the use of digital signatures was not diffused at all, and bar associations were not well equipped to provide the infrastructural components required for access and identification (digital signature and point of access), the development has been almost impossible. The problem is twofold. On the one hand digital signatures were not available to many potential users. At the same time, the architecture envisaged was too complex to develop, maintain and evolve. Here the technology regulation lost a great chance to pursue simplification until it legalised the use of certified mail, a method that was more accessible and diffused among potential users.

[14]This has recently been substituted by the use of certified email.

[15]Ministero della Giustizia, 'Processo Civile Telematico', http://www.processotelematico.giustizia.it. Accessed 8 August 2011.

3.5 Legalise, Reassemble, Signify

In this section we draw on the findings of the case studies to identify some dynamics of law and technology in judicial proceedings and suggest some modest means to keep them well matched. First, we consider the ways law and technology may work together in valid and effective identification of parties. Then we move the analysis to a more general level, identifying an approach to the regulation of e-justice in which law and technology are developed together. Third, we point out that processes rarely stay on one technological track: instead they switch between electronic, paper and oral modes of communication. Rather than considering this as a drawback, we propose taking advantage of it, and regulating the system accordingly. After having explored how specific approaches to the regulation of technology can contribute to reducing complexity we consider the issue of maximum feasible simplicity. Indeed, simplicity cannot be pursued too far, and it is necessary to identify minimum criteria to assure the performativity of the proceedings.

3.5.1 Identity and Agency

The question of digital identity is central to each of the case studies. Looking behind the different flow of actions and procedures, and the specific technology involved in establishing identity, we see several similarities. All the systems of digital identification are based on common elements: digital records are linked to a piece of hardware. This is achieved with smart cards in TOL and CITIUS, debit or credit cards in MCOL and COVL, and attachment of an ID document in e-Curia. To allow digital identification, some paper-based procedure must be followed. A contract must be signed to buy a smart card; application forms are lodged with a bank to issue a credit card or open a bank account; a duly signed request attaching the required documentation has to be provided at the Court of Justice of the European Union.

The procedure becomes streamlined once a user is registered to access the platform. Access is granted once a computerised system has automatically cross checked and verified that the credentials (embedded in the hardware or provided by the users) are those required to access the system. Even though the process of identification is at this stage handled in the digital domain, it can be supported by other media (e.g. paper) and alternative procedures. Different tracks are available to reassemble the components required for identification. Agency is circulated through different domains, and the regulation of e-justice should be aware of and take advantage of this (see also Sect. 14.4.3).

In regulating the use of technologies in judicial proceedings, it must be considered that technology has its own dynamics of development, change and evolution. The technological domain is largely decoupled from the legal one: attempt to couple them too tightly may lead to a number of unexpected consequences. The law can capture technology, but so too can technology capture the law. Judicial procedures cannot take advantage of new technological developments without legal changes inaccessible to project developers. Conversely, the costs of redesigning and redeploying technological infrastructures may inhibit legal changes if they are too tightly coupled with existing regulations. Law and technology remain distinct regulative regimes, and regulating technology requires an understanding of technology's relative autonomy. Technology, and particularly large information infrastructures such as e-justice are not as malleable as some legislators may believe.

In the cases of MCOL, COVL and e-Curia, this autonomy was respected so that ICT was used effectively to increase access to justice. MCOL was developed very quickly (it was online in 6 months) taking advantage of technological components–online use of bank cards–that were already in place. The fact that key components of the information infrastructure were shared by a large number of potential users is one of the reasons for the fast development and rapid deployment of MCOL to many users and its success in terms of the number of cases processed (Kallinikos 2009a). We can see, therefore, that apparently small differences in the technologies used may have profound consequences in terms of complexity, cost and access to technology and to justice alike. To pursue simplicity at the design stage as well as in executing digitally enabled judicial proceedings, the law must authorise the use of technological components already available to the majority of expected users. As discussed below, this is limited by the needs of performativity and signalling.

3.5.2 *Making Technology Legal*

It is clear now that ICT cannot be used to manage and record status changes (whether in simple money disputes or high profile litigation) without appropriate regulation. We have, however, identified two distinct approaches. In the first one, the legal blueprint, with formal (i.e. legal) regulations, drafted by lawyers and enacted by the parliament, aims to design the architecture and the internal features of the technology. This is clear in the Italian case of TOL, in which the legal codes first tried to establish the configuration of the software codes and system architecture. This approach begins from the formal rules, stating what is legal and what it is not (i.e. which kind of technology can and cannot be used), as well as how technology should operate. In this development model, first the technology appears in the official gazette, then formal prescriptions have to be transformed into running applications. As has been seen, the consequence in the case of TOL was a system architecture which was extremely complex, difficult to develop, inaccessible and very expensive.

By contrast, in the MCOL case, the first step was the development of the technology by the Department and by contracted private companies. This allowed the developers to assemble a system taking advantage of the technologies already available and to postpone the use of systems (like the electronic Government Gateway) that were not yet ready. The law authorising the use of MCOL for handling specific types of claims was only passed once the system was successfully tested.

As noted, the law did not prescribe the technological details of each component of the applications (as in TOL) but simply legalised the ensemble of ICT enabled procedures. E-Curia took a similar approach, first with legislation that cleared the legal ground for e-justice development, followed by a long and meticulous process of system development, testing and finally a further change in the procedural law that authorised the use of the system. CITIUS adopted a mixed approach, in which the regulation and development of technology proceeded piecemeal over many years. Also in this case, however, when the law anticipated what technology-enabled procedures had to do, as in the 1999 regulation, the result was a fiasco (6.1.2). In the following years the development and regulation of technology went hand in hand and the achievements have been positive. In all these examples, the existing regulation does not prescribe in detail (or in advance) the technical features of the system, but rather specifies the main features of the overall system and legalises its use.

Divergent rules can also originate in those external organisations to which the courts outsource particular functions. This creates difficulties for the conceit of law-makers and lawyers that law is the sovereign source of all regulation. The technology of law cannot simply overturn the rule of technology. The development of large ICT-based communication systems has its own autonomous rules (Hanseth and Lyytinen 2010). As long as the courts and legislators fail to recognise that they are operating in a hybrid environment of cross-cutting regulative regimes, they will continue to be surprised and frustrated by unintended consequences, public misconceptions and failure to integrate law and technology.

There is a converse to this argument that law does not make all the rules: law does not only make rules. Following a rule always requires communication between people and their actions which encompass corporeality and the world of objects (Taylor 1993). Filing a case in a registry, giving evidence from a witness box, cross examining from the bar table, and recording judgment in a file are the taken-for-granted practices of law that have grown with it over centuries. They are well inscribed in habitus and communication protocols even where the formal rules are silent.

To resolve the difficulties that arise from legal misconceptions that rules can create technological solutions, one must understand the different levels of operation of legal and technological regulation. Law creates the conditions for new social facts: changes of status that are institutionally constituted. Technology manipulates information and things, 'brute facts', that enable or block actions and produce physical effects (Hildebrandt 2008). Law's role in designing technological solutions is necessarily very limited. Its more appropriate role is to legitimate already existing solutions. Where law has been used to specify the technological conditions of particular interactions ex ante, it creates unworkable monsters. Not only does the technology proliferate to the point that it is almost impossible to use; the law proliferates to the point that it is almost impossible to understand. There is a rule for every tool, every packet of data, almost every keystroke (Fabri 2009).[16] The threshold of maximum management complexity is rapidly reached,

---

[16]Since 1997 the implementation of TOL has required 'a never-ending string of regulations' that Fabri describes as a 'legal soap opera' (Fabri 2009, 130).

technological development is almost impossible, and circulation of agency almost comes to a halt.

The alternative solution to using law to design technology would be to create the technology and then legitimate it. This too can create difficulties if the technology was not designed with legal requirements in mind. Law requires permanent and (to an extent) public records, unambiguous identification, and solemn declarations. Ticking the box, 'I have read and understand the terms and conditions', while it is adequate to authorise an online sale, would be insufficiently secure and too performatively weak for legal processes that change our social or civil status. The lawyers need to communicate the security and performative needs to the technologists, but the solution can only be a joint effort. Once the solution is technologically workable and legally robust, then the law can authorise it.

3.5.3 Contexts of the Performative

Up to this point of our conclusions we have been dealing mainly with the dynamics between law and technology focusing on how they may increase complexity up to the threshold of maximum management complexity, and identifying how technology can be regulated to avoid this risk. But on the other side, the performativity of the system may fail if is too simple, or if it is not signalling the legal consequences of the actions undertaken in the digital domain. We have therefore to consider the lower level of maximum feasible simplicity. To do this, we now shift focus to the consequences for social reality outside the legal realm.

Projecting legal agency impacts on the very being of the legal and social person in ways that go beyond the simple acts of online shopping or exchanging information. Swearing an oath, entering a contract or making a legal declaration have far-reaching implications. To lose ones case, become obligated to pay a debt or lose a credit rating or drivers licence have more serious consequences that buying a concert ticket or posting to Facebook.

We have seen that it matters whether one swears an oath rather than signs a form or enters a password. If the law legitimises these procedures, architectures and outcomes, then they may be considered to have the required legal effect. However, swearing and entering into an agreed change of status go beyond the letter of the law. Their implications extend into a wider range of social relations: whether I lose my case or become obligated to pay a debt.

We have noted that e-justice development is eased by the use of technological components and already developed in other domains, such as e-commerce or e-banking. However, this design approach must be balanced by another principle. We cannot design e-justice adopting digital identities provided by Facebook, or summoning parties using Twitter. If processes are adopted that are familiar from other social interactions–e.g. invitations to pay online, entering user names and passwords–then the source of authority and legal consequences may not be accurately signalled to the participants. If the context of a legal commitment appears to be one of online shopping or tweeting, then this can equally lead to performative failure. The agency to be circulated must be just that which is intended by the agent: neither amplified nor diminished. An architecture which mimics Twitter or online shopping to project legal agency is misleading, and may not be recognised as legally binding. In such a case the performative is expressed within a structure of rules, but in a new context.[17] The rules have been inscribed into a divergent technology, institutional architecture or social context. Old rules inscribed into new tools can change their effect. Technology is not a neutral medium which conducts whatever is introduced at one end, spitting it out, unchanged, at the other.

The question is not just how to secure the identification, or the exchange of procedural documents, but also, whether an online procedure fulfils the performative requirements of context. Limiting the focus on technology to its formal legality or its technical efficacy fails to appreciate the important semiotic weight that is carried by the context (including the technology itself). The traditional rituals of the oath, the legal declaration and the signature carry an excess of signification beyond that which is required to convey information or meaning. Agamben proposes that it is this very excess that carries with it the power to make changes to the social world (Agamben 2011, 68). In order to be legally identified we are bound to our words; our good faith is guaranteed on pain of perjury. The oath or the signature, as performative, binds the speaker to their statement, the person to the deed. Only then can legal agency be put into circulation.

Social power and legal agency always go beyond the note in the file or the entry to the database. Those are necessary but not sufficient conditions to register a change of status, whether to debtor or offender. The change of status must be recognised, not just by the law but by the parties to an action and by the society at large. Any interaction between law, technology and society can only be understood as an assemblage of regulation, legitimation and the way in which people use and understand the things placed a their disposal. To the familiar categories of law's deontology and technology's teleology must be added the social efficacy of the performative. The interfaces of law and technology rely on the interpretive context in which messages are understood as well as the legal forms in which they are transmitted. Each of these elements is essential to the circulation of agency between people and things that constitutes and reassembles legal and social relationships.

[17] We identified a problem of this sort in Australian speed infringement notices, where paying a fine is as easy as paying a bill, but with legal consequences (including possible loss of a driving licence) that are not apparent from the familiar, bill-paying environment (Mohr and Contini 2011, 1008).

3.5.4 Pathways and the Reassembling of Agency

When law works with technology it entangles numerous actors, techniques and regulations. Judges and court staff, lawyers, software and hardware providers all interact with the technology and the regulations (both legal and technical) to reassemble new composites of actors and techniques. As Lanzara has pointed out, these composites or assemblages 'are based as much upon communications and functional relations as upon authority and norms': they work through the social circulation of agency in space and time (Lanzara 2009, 12).[18] They determine who is empowered to do what, which objects authorise, record and transmit agency. If law is to legitimate effective new techniques it must authorise the composite of people, regulations, tools and organisations (public and private) that make it work. Instead of legislating a tool for every rule, legislation must encompass the functional composite of actors, technologies and practices that make it work.

We now turn to look at how this entanglement of technology and law affects the agency required to effect changes of status. As we have seen even digital identification is also based on paper and conventional procedures. This observation can be extended to the entire process. All the case studies use records kept in electronic format as well as in traditional paper files. Notifications to defendants can be made through conventional means (post or bailiff) or through the e-justice platform, at the election of either party. The final certifications of the change of status (such as injunctions, orders to pay or judicial decisions) are recorded on paper as well as in digital systems. Far from being paperless, all these procedures continuously jump between different media: paper, digital, and face-to-face. The effective management of changes of status requires different things, sometimes material (computers, cards, identity documents etc.) and sometimes immaterial (software codes and data). Further, it requires a web of relations between the material and the immaterial (such as the link between ownership of a bank account and a credit card). Law regulates or legitimises the overall system, and requires the proper distribution of agency through different domains: law, technology, bureaucracy and even the market, where technological components are developed or purchased. Each of these domains tends to regulate agency and judicial procedures in different ways, introducing different requirements, incentives and constraints to action. Keeping the domains assembled in a way that allows identification and changes of status requires difficult mediations and courageous legal approaches (Contini 2009, 266).

Clearly the twin risks of excessive complexity or deceptive simplicity can never be completely eliminated. More complexity inevitably proliferates risk (Ciborra 2007). Excessive simplicity may compromise security or the performative

[18] See also footnote 6.

projection of agency. We may, however, propose that the ICT enabled system be considered as just one of the channels that guarantee performative efficacy. Digital proceedings cannot eliminate conventional ones, and it may be better if the 'paperless court' were to stay in the realm of science fiction. Paper will coexist with the digital, using the strategy of 'smart redundancy'. We have already seen that all the systems analysed in this research retain a two-track system, both to accommodate the preferences of the parties and to ensure the availability of the systems. We also suggest that new ways of understanding the operations of law and technology can ameliorate the problem. Again, the answer lies in the level of interactions that are encompassed by the legal system, which should not focus on authorising and maintaining a specific tool or rule. Laws and legal and managerial practices need to define the spheres of responsibility and agency appropriate to the functional ensemble of actors, rules and things. The unit of analysis, of legitimation and of accountability must be the reassembled functional composite, rather than any particular code, actor (e.g. a company or a judge) or machine.

3.6 Technological Regulation in EPO and ESCP

We can now use the findings of our analysis to assess the way in which the rules establishing EPO and ESCP regulate the use of technology in legal proceedings. The European Small Claims Procedure (ESCP) (Regulation (EC) No. 861/2007) and the European Payment Order (EPO) (Regulation (EC) No. 1896/2006) are transborder civil proceedings recently introduced by the EU to facilitate access to transborder proceedings by European citizens and companies. They require strong mechanisms of legal cooperation among member states since, typically, a case filed by an applicant located in one country will be handled by a court of another member state. They are therefore good examples to assess the condition of circulation of agency across the legal and judicial systems of member states and the dynamics between law and technology in transborder e-justice platforms.

A quick assessment of the regulations illustrate that the procedures have been designed pursuing a degree of functional simplification. The most visible effort is the mandatory use of pre-established forms to exchange procedural data. Plaintiffs, defendants and also the courts handling the case in each member state must use the forms. There are many other areas, however, in which the procedure is not simple at all, such as the identification of the jurisdiction, or the payment of court fees. The legal analysis conducted by Marco Mellone (Chap. 10) and the simulation conducted by Gar Yein Ng (Chap. 11) demonstrate how further simplifications may facilitate access to the procedure and its execution by parties and courts. Accordingly, we propose that further simplification would ease the development of technological applications supporting their use (for more details see Sect. 14.4.1).

As previously discussed, identification and signature are also key issues to be considered in EPO and ESCP. If the procedures are carried out through conventional means (printed forms delivered to the courts or to the case parties through the postal service), a hand-written signature is sufficient to ascertain the subject's identity and volition: that this person intends to circulate legal agency in accordance with the content of the document. The signature continues to have unchallenged performative effect, as indicated by the court's unquestioned acceptance of the filing of the case (see Sect. 11.3). Having been approved in the digital era, the regulations establishing EPO and ESCP provide legal grounds for their electronic implementation. But the requirements for identification in the digital domain are much more demanding than those prescribed in the conventional one. Indeed, as in Portugal or in Italy, the regulations require the use of digital signatures carried out according to the pre-existing European Directive 1999/93/EC. This is the rock that will wreck the digitalization of the procedures: a tiny piece of legal code that triggers an unbelievable amount of software codes and technological problems. Here we can only expect a situation similar to the one faced in Italy, magnified by the fact that digital signature is neither diffused nor easily available to a large proportion of European citizens, that in some member states it is not available at all, and that ensuring interoperability of digital signatures issued in the various member states would be very demanding. Here again, the law comes first and technology has to follow. But when the law enters into the domain of the technology, prescribing ex ante the use of a given system, problems are bound to arise when the rule of law tries to impose itself on the rules of technology.

The law could reduce the complexity of establishing identification mechanisms, to make them less demanding from a technological and organisational point of view. It could take advantage of technological components already available to the prospective users: European citizens and businesses. The case studies provide various examples of identification mechanisms based on web enrolment and payment of court fees. Other approaches could be explored. If a hand-written signature on the paper form is sufficient, then surely a scanned copy of the same signed form, possibly supported by a scanned copy of an ID document, would satisfy the legal and security requirements of digitally enabled EPO and ESCP.

The e-Codex project and the e-justice portal are attempting to digitize EPO and ESCP procedures. Marco Velicogna, in Chap. 13, discusses the problems currently faced in this effort, and the costs to European citizens. We surmise that e-Codex will demonstrate, also from a practical perspective, that the identification requirements established by the current regulation are neither in line with the possibilities offered by ICT nor sustainable in the mid–term; that the rule of law is not matching the rule of technology.

A way out, explored in detail in the concluding chapter (see Sect. 14.4), is to take advantage of the circulation of agency between the two channels, avoiding the perils of the digital signature by leaving this procedural component in paper proceedings. But we have also learned that a dialogue between law and technology is needed as in CITIUS and in TOL. If e-Codex identifies that the complexity of the technological architecture is too high, too expensive, too difficult to develop, and still inaccessible to prospective users, then changes to the regulations will be needed to establish a legal framework more attuned to technological development. Technologies are not as malleable as the European legislator may believe. Having a technological solution up and running, ready to be formally legalised, is much better that having a sophisticated regulation that cannot be translated into a performative legal practice.

More specifically we propose development of a running pilot that may not respect the prescription of digital signature and other technological requirements currently established by the law. It could, however, support an effective and meaningful exchange of procedural information across Europe and facilitate prospective users' access to transborder legal remedies. Then the law could play its proper role. It would check that the performative conditions required by transborder judicial proceedings are fulfilled. Once the judges and legislators were satisfied with these conditions, they would then legalise these assemblages of technologies, procedures and actors that had been shown to effectively circulate legal agency across Europe.

References

Agamben, G. 2011. *The sacrament of language: An archeology of the oath* (trans: Kotsko, A). Stanford: Stanford University Press.

Austin, J.L. 1980. *How To Do Things With Words*. Oxford: Oxford University Press.

Benveniste, E. 1966. *Problèmes de linguistique générale*, vol. 1. Paris: Gallimard.

Butler, J. 1997. *Excitable speech: A politics of the performative*. New York: Routledge.

Carnevali, D. 2010. Vent'anni di informatica negli uffici giudiziari: un percorso in (chiaro)scuro. In *Soggetti Smarriti. Perchè innovazione e giustizia non si incontrano quasi mai*, ed. D. Carnevali, 101–167. Milano: FrancoAngeli.

Ciborra, C. 2007. Digital technologies and risk: A critical review. In *Risk, complexity and ICT*, ed. O. Hanseth and C. Ciborra, 23–44. Bodmin: Edward Elgar.

Contini, F. 2009. ICT, assemblages and institutional contexts: Understanding multiple development paths. In *ICT and innovation in the public sector. European studies in the making of e-government*, ed. F. Contini and G.F. Lanzara, 244–271. Basingstoke: Palgrave.

Cordella, A., and F. Iannacci. 2010. Information systems in the public sector: The e-Government enactment framework. *Journal of Strategic Information Systems* 19(1): 52–66.

Cordella, A., and L. Willcocks. 2009. ICT, marketisation and bureaucracy in the UK public sectors. In *ICT and Innovation in the Public Sector. European studies in the making of e-government*, ed. F. Contini and G.F. Lanzara, 88–111. Basingstoke: Palgrave.

Czarniawska, B., and B. Joerges. 1998. The Question of Technology, or How Organizations Inscribe the World. *Organisation Studies* 19(3): 363–385.

Derrida, J. 1988. *Limited Inc*. Evanston: Northwestern University Press.

Fabri, M. (ed.). 2008. *ICT for the Public Prosecutor's Offices*. Bologna: Clueb.

Fabri, M. 2009. E-justice in Finland and in Italy: Enabling versus constraining models. In *ICT and innovation in the public sector European perspectives in the making of e-government*, ed. F. Contini and G.F. Lanzara, 115–145. Basingstoke: Palgrave.

Foucault, M. 2002. *Archaeology of knowledge* (trans: Smith, A.M.S). Abingdon, Oxon: Routledge.

Garapon, A. 1995. Il Rituale Giudiziario. In *I Diritti Nascosti: Approccio Antropologico e Prospettiva Sociologica*, ed. A. Giasanti and G. Maggioni, 289–305. Milano: Raffaello Cortina Editore.

Hanseth, O., and K. Lyytinen. 2010. Design theory for dynamic complexity in information infrastructures: the case of building internet. *Journal of Information Technology* 25: 1–19. doi:10.1057/jit.2009.19.

Hildebrandt, M. 2008. Legal and technological normativity: More (and less) than twin sisters. *Techné: Research in Philosophy and Technology* 12(3): 169.

Honneth, A. 1995. *The struggle for recognition: The moral grammar of social conflicts* (trans: Anderson, J.). Cambridge, UK: Polity Press.

Jacob, R. 1995–96. The historical development of courthouse architecture/La formazione storica dell'architettura giudiziaria. *Zodiac* 14:30–43.

Kallinikos, J. 2009a. Institutional complexities and functional simplification. The case of Money Claims Online. In *ICT and innovation in the public sector. European studies in the making of e-government*, ed. F. Contini and G.F. Lanzara, 174–210. Basingstoke: Palgrave Macmillan.

Kallinikos, J. 2009b. The regulative regime of technology. In *ICT and innovation in the public sector: European studies in the making of e-government*, ed. C. Francesco and L. Giovan Francesco, 66–87. Basingstoke: Palgrave.

Kelsen, H. 1967. *Pure theory of law (Reine Rechtslehre)* (trans: Knight, M.). First published 1934 edn. Berkeley, CA: University of California Press.

Lanzara, G.F. 2009. Building digital institutions: ICT and the rise of assemblages in government. In *ICT and innovation in the public sector*, eds. F. Contini and G.F. Lanzara, 9–48. Basingstoke: Palgrave.

Latour, B. 1999. *Pandora's hope: Essays on the reality of science studies*. Cambridge, MA: Harvard University Press.

Latour, B. 2002. *La fabrique du droit. Une ethnographie du Conseil d'État*. Paris: La Découverte.

Latour, B. 2005. *Reassembling the social: An introduction to actor-network-theory*. Oxford: Oxford University Press.

Lessig, L. 2007. *Code and other laws of cyberspace*. New York: Basic Books. Version 2.0.

Mohr, R. 2000. Authorised performances: The procedural sources of Judicial authority. *Flinders Journal of Law Reform* 4(1): 63–79.

Mohr, R., and F. Contini. 2011. Reassembling the legal. 'The wonders of modern science' in court-related proceedings. *Griffith Law Review—Special Symposium: The Laws of Technology and the Technology of Law* 20(3): 994–1019.

Ricoeur, P. 2004. *Parcours de la reconnaissance: Trois études*. Paris: Gallimard.

Taylor, C. 1993. To follow a rule. In *Bourdieu: Critical perspectives*, ed. C. Calhoun, E. LiPuma, and M. Postone, 45–60. Cambridge, UK: Polity Press.

Timms, P., J. Plotnikoff, and R. Woolfson. 2003. Judicial electronic data interchange in England and Wales. In *Judicial electronic data interchange in European civil proceedings and criminal matters*, ed. M. Fabri and F. Contini, 171–201. Bologna: Lo Scarabeo.

Velicogna, M. 2008. *Use of information and communication technologies (ICT) in European Judicial Systems. CEPEJ Studies N.. 7. European Commission for the Efficiency of Justice (CEPEJ)*. Strasbourg: Council of Europe.

Velicogna, M., and G.Y. Ng. 2006. Legitimacy and Internet in the Judiciary: A lesson from the Italian Courts' websites experience. *International Journal of Law and Information Technology* 14(3): 370–389.

Vismann, C. 2008. *Files: Law and media technology* (trans: Winthrop-Young, G.). Stanford: Stanford University Press.

Weick, K.E. 1990. Technology as equivoque: Sensemaking in new technologies. In *Technology and organisations*, ed. P.S. Goodman and L.S. Sproull, 1–44. San Francisco: Josey Bass.

Woolf (Lord). 1996. *Final report to the Lord Chancellor on the civil justice system in England and Wales*. HMCS, London.

Part II
Building e-Justice: National and European Experiences

Chapter 4
Law, Technology and System Architectures: Critical Design Factors for Money Claim and Possession Claim Online in England and Wales

Giampiero Lupo

Abstract The study of two e-justice services developed in England and Wales helped to shed some light on the designing principles of ICT systems in the justice sector. The literature on ICT and on e-justice has stressed the importance of a set of design principles for the implementation of complex systems based on information and communication technology, such as modularity, bootstrapping, and the smart exploitation of the pre-existing installed base. The study consists of a comparative analysis of MCOL and PCOL from multiple perspectives. The analysis addresses firstly the historical development of the two systems, secondly the implications of their installed base for design, and thirdly the daily use of MCOL and PCOL. Some theoretical conclusions based on the comparison of the two systems are drawn. Based on my findings, I argue that the design principles espoused by the existing literature on information infrastructures and e-justice may not be enough to assure effective system implementation performance, because other intervening factors like the system's architecture and the interactions between law and technology may also have a considerable influence.

4.1 Introduction

The literature on information infrastructure has stressed the critical relevance of a set of design principles for the implementation of complex systems based on information and communication technology. Hanseth and Lyytinen (2010) have explored the influence of strategies such as the modularisation of systems and bootstrapping on the success of information infrastructure development by focusing

G. Lupo (✉)
Department of Political Sciences, University of Bologna and Research Institute on Judicial Systems, National Research Council of Italy (IRSIG-CNR), Bologna, Italy
e-mail: gampiero.lupo@irsig.cnr.it

F. Contini and G.F. Lanzara (eds.), *The Circulation of Agency in E-Justice*, Law, Governance and Technology Series 13, DOI 10.1007/978-94-007-7525-1_4,

Table 4.1 Civil work initiated online (MCOL and PCOL). Table gathered from Her Majesty's Court Service Annual Report and Account, 2009–2010

Increase of the amount of civil work initiated online			
65 % of eligible possession claims to be made through Possession Claim Online (PCOL)			
75 % of specified money claims to be made online through Money Claim Online (MCOL) or through the Claim Production Centre (CPC)			
2007–2008 performance	*2008–2009 performance (%)*	*2009–2010 target (%)*	*2009–2010 performance (%)*
This measure was reconfigured in 2008 so comparable data are not available	PCOL 73 MCOL/CPC 67	PCOL 65 MCOL/CPC 75	PCOL 79 MCOL/CPC 67

on the history of Internet. In the e-justice literature, Kallinikos (2009), in his study of Money Claim Online (MCOL), acknowledged the importance of building on an established installed base.

In this chapter, the comparative analysis of two e-justice services developed in England and Wales allows us to explore the validity of the aforementioned design notions. Our leading research question is whether these principles can be applied to every context and information system and whether it is plausible that other factors may influence the performance of e-justice services. The study focuses on MCOL and Possession Claim Online (PCOL), two web-based facilities for issuing money and possession claims in England and Wales available to individuals and private organisations. The website allows English or Welsh citizens to issue and defend a claim or ask for a warrant of execution online.

The two web services are a successful online translation of paper-based procedures. In addition, statistics confirm the widespread use of the two systems in place of the traditional procedures that involve county courts.[1] According to the annual report of Her Majesty's Court Service for 2009–2010, 79 % of possession claims were issued online in the year of analysis, while 75 % of money claims were issued online or electronically through the Claim Production Centre (CPC) based in Northampton (Sects. 4.2, 4.4 and 4.5.1 of this chapter will deal with these agencies of the United Kingdom justice system; see Table. 4.1).

Despite the widespread use of the services, our empirical analysis and, in particular, the interviews with court staff identified differences in the performance of MCOL and PCOL, specifically regarding the day-to-day application of procedure in the institutions involved. MCOL is generally considered a successful service (Timms et al. 2003; Timms and Woolfson 2006; Kallinikos 2009; Velicogna 2008; Falletti 2009; Fabri and Contini 2003), being rapid, easy to use and appreciated by the public: the online survey[2] administered by Her Majesty's Court and Tribunal

[1]See HM Court Service 2008 and HM Courts and Tribunals Service (2011).

[2]Her Majesty's Court, Magistrates and Tribunals Service (HCMTS) by utilising the online service 'Survey Monkey', which offers survey facilities for free or at low prices (government cuts linked

Service (HMCTS) in 2011 to MCOL users has shown user satisfaction with the overall service: Of respondents, 46.5 % are very satisfied and 28.6 % are fairly satisfied (see Table. 4.1). Moreover, 92.7 % of users who utilised MCOL facilities declared that they would use them again.

In contrast, PCOL is facing many problems, principally due to the heterogeneous application of procedure in each county court. The service is characterised by a decentralised structure with a web server directly linked to several county courts that manage possession claims issued online. This aspect will be investigated in the empirical analysis with the goal of shedding light on the factors that have contributed to the different performances of the two services.

The empirical investigation is based on a comparative analysis of the two systems using multiple methods: I combined study of the main official documents (such as Ministry of Justice reports and legislation) and of previous scholars' contributions to the topic, the analysis of official statistical data and qualitative analysis of semi-structured interviews with court staff and ICT team managers. The comparative analysis is methodologically feasible thanks to the many similarities of the two systems (indeed, PCOL can be considered a spinoff of MCOL) and it allows the highlighting of factors that may have had a role in the success or failure of the two services.

In the following pages, I will analyse the two services from several points of view: first, I will investigate the history of their development; second, I will analyse the implications of their installed base; third, I will deal with MCOL and PCOL's day-to-day use. In the final part of the chapter, I will draw some theoretical conclusions that refer to the old and new design principles that the empirical analysis of MCOL and PCOL make evident.

4.2 The Implementation of Money Claim Online

MCOL is the result of a modernisation effort by the United Kingdom justice system that started with Lord Woolf's report in the 1990s. The report[3] (and the related White Paper, 'Modernising Justice') had the objectives of improving access to justice, reducing the costs of litigation, limiting the complexity of the rules and in general enhancing the performance of the justice system. A large part of the reform concerned the employment of information technology (IT). In this regard, Lord Woolf proposed the introduction of a case management system and the

to the international crises affected the Ministry of Justice as well). A link to the survey has been included in the final steps, both for claimants or defendants on the MCOL website.

[3]In 1994, because of the growing criticism regarding the inefficiencies of the judiciary, Lord Woolf was asked to conduct an inquiry into the civil justice system and to formulate proposals for its innovation (Timms and Woolfson 2006). Lord Woolf's final report, titled 'Access to Justice' (Woolf 1996) made clear the most critical issues that affected the civil justice at that time, namely, delay in and heterogeneity of outcomes, costs, complexity and the domination of trials by lawyers who

establishment of the Civil Justice IT Strategy Development Group with the aim of making recommendations for the role of IT in the civil justice system (Civil Justice IT Strategy Development Group 1998; Susskind 2000). Following Lord Woolf's reform and recommendations, several IT services in the justice system have been developed, aside from MCOL and PCOL. In 2000, the British and Irish Legal Information System (BAILII) was launched to provide access to Irish and British legislation and case law at no cost. In 2002, 'Just Ask', the website of the Community Legal Service, which provides legal information and help on the Internet, was launched.

Lord Woolf's reform also fostered important innovations in civil procedure, particularly the constitution of the Civil Procedure Rules[4] (CPR), a new code of procedural regulations that substituted the Rules of the Supreme Court and the County Court Rules. The reform's objective was to improve access to justice by making legal proceedings faster, cheaper and easier to understand for non-lawyers (Dwyer 2009). This affected the two e-justice services' development in terms of legal interoperability. The CPR are supplemented by detailed practice directions[5] that are supplemental protocols to the rules of civil and criminal procedure in the courts. The procedure for drafting and amending practice directions is simpler and faster compared to the CPR[6] (Dwyer 2009). As the norms ruling the use of MCOL and PCOL are included in two practice directions[7] (PD 7E for MCOL and PD 55A for PCOL), the processes with which the technologies have been made legal

habitually drew out processes in order to increase costs (Susskind 2000). Reform was approved in 1999 by the Labour Party in the White Paper 'Modernising Justice' (Lord Chancellor's Office 1998), which accepted the suggestions advanced in the 'Access to Justice' report. In particular, reform aimed at associating the complexity of cases' procedures with the amount of money involved, at imposing stricter timetables for processes and the reduction of adversarial techniques, at diffusing the use of information technology and at avoiding the abuses of the right of appeal. The White Paper 'Modernising Justice' provided for the identification of 'pre-action protocols that set standards and timetables for the conduct of cases before court proceedings are started' ('Modernising Justice', December 1998). See also Ng 2010.

[4]Civil Procedure Rules 1998 (SI 1998/3132) were approved on 10 December 1998 and came into force on 26 April 1999.

[5]The practice directions for the Civil Procedure Rules apply to civil litigation in the Queen's Bench Division and the Chancery Division of the High Court and to litigation in the county courts other than family proceedings.

[6]While amending or drafting CPR, secondary legislation was required that involved both branches of parliament. With the coming into force of the Constitutional Reform Act (CRA) of 2005, the power to approve the practice directions fell to the Lord Chief Justice (with the approval of the Lord Chancellor in most instances; Woodhouse 2007).

[7]At the time of MCOL practice direction approval, the Lord Chancellor authorised Lord Justice May to draft practice directions. For county courts, the section 74A of the County Courts Act (1984) authorises the Lord Chancellor or a person authorised to act on his behalf to make practice direction. At the time of PCOL practice direction approval, the Lord Chancellor authorised Lord Justice Dyson to make practice directions for the county courts; the CRA (2005) approval provided for the Lord Chief Justice to have the power to nominate a judicial office holder to perform his functions with regard to making designated directions (Malleson 2005).

have been rapid and, in the case of MCOL, simultaneous to the development of the service.

Following the wave of modernisation of the justice system, in 1999 the Department of Constitutional Affairs (DCA, nowadays HMCTS) initiated the project for an online service for handling small money claims. The system would remove the paper-based administrative work related to money claims from county courts. DCA believed that money claims could be managed through an online procedure accessible to lay users, given that a many money claims act as a reminder in order to stimulate payment or a debt reduction. Usually, money claims are settled without a court hearing and convert into administrative work for court staff (Reeves 2004).

The development of the project has seen the collective effort of public and private actors. Two offices of the Department of Constitutional Affairs, the business area and the ICT team, and the private company that at the time had an overarching contract with the DCA, that is, EDS, cooperated in the implementation of the project.

Initially, the DCA and EDS formulated a business case, a feasibility analysis and, through the use of user-interface prototypes[8] (screen mock-ups), established MCOL requirements. The architecture of the system reflected the joint team's decision to exploit the organisational, institutional and technological components already in use for claims issued electronically. MCOL has been developed as a user-friendly interface (Kallinikos 2009) of two DCA agencies that were already dealing with money claims issued in electronic form, that is, the CPC and the County Court Bulk Centre (CCBC). Both agencies are based in Northampton and operate under Northampton County Court.

The CPC deals with money claims issued electronically by magnetic tapes or floppy disks.[9] The Centre manages the court fees, produces the claim creating the court's record and then despatches the claim to the defendant. MCOL designers made use of the CPC data files' validation function: before the MCOL claim enters a successive processing stage, an electronic identifier verifies if the claim's data file fits the specification for the CPC. The CPC has a set of scripts that validate the data; for instance, it determines whether the specified amount of data allowed for the claim's details is respected.

The CCBC[10] deals with bulk money claims, that is, massive claims issued by different types of organisations, such as banks, insurance companies or any public utility company.[11] MCOL developers exploited the Centre's Exchange Data system

[8]Prototypes have been demonstrated in several judicial conferences in order to spread information about the project.

[9]The claims are issued in the name of the county court at the request of the claimant (based on area of residence). Claims can be issued by magnetic tape, floppy disk, electronic transfer (FTP - File Transfer Protocol) and, in future, by a secure email address. For more information, see http://www.justice.gov.uk/about/hmcts/.

[10]Please see http://www.justice.gov.uk/courts/northampton-bulk-centre.

[11]The Centre manages 'straightforward debt collection' (HMCTS website), that is, principally that not defended in county courts. In contrast to the CPC system, in order to utilise the CCBC

(EDI), called CaseMan,[12] which manages bulk claims: once a claim is submitted, and after CPC validation, the claim enters automatically as a data file in CaseMan. Here, CCBC staff can handle the claim under the name of Northampton County Court.

In parallel with the implementation of the technological/organisational components of the service, the DCA policy unit worked on the draft of PD 7E,[13] which controls MCOL and allows citizens to file money claims through the online website.

In order to accelerate the implementation of the project, EDS subcontracted to EzGov the development of the website. EzGov was the owner of the Flex Foundation Library, which includes software libraries for implementing several types of website. The company provided a website form-creation facility with the option of setting validation, verification criteria and rules; the ability to include a multi-step process; a registration-based environment; and a payment engine (Kallinikos 2009). EzGov supplied the use cases and the user-interface prototypes and coded the project after the DCA's approval. EDS worked on the integration of the system with the CCBC; consistent modifications to the Bulk Centre working practices were not needed.

During development, designers considered the option of integrating the system with the Government Gateway website, which would provide the accounting system and a payment engine. At the present time, Government Gateway is the portal where UK citizens can register in order to have access to government services (Government Gateway[14] website 2011). It provides the accounting engine for MCOL. At the time, however, the Government Gateway project was not ready, so the DCA opted for utilising the already implemented Flex Foundation user-registration, login system and payment engine in order to respect the tight schedule.

---

system, companies need to become members and respect a set of parameters. CCBC users submit a single data file containing the particulars of a claim, such as claim number, claimant, defendant name, etc., along with an individual payment of the correct fee for each case to the CCBC, which then processes the data files. Data files can be transmitted to the CPC system by magnetic tape, floppy disk and electronic transfer (FTP - File Transfer Protocol). Claims are issued in the name of Northampton County Court, but the CCBC's role is limited to the issuing of electronic claims once they are verified by the CPC; to the entry of judgment by acceptance, default or determination; and to the entry of a warrant of execution or transfer to any other court for types of enforcement different from a warrant.

[12]CaseMan is the 'core' of the CCBC system, a multi-user relational database management system (Plotnikoff et al. 2001) that replaced manual record cards and allows court staff from any court in England and Wales to log in and deal with claims.

[13]Practice Direction 7E 'provides for a scheme in which, in the circumstances set out in the practice direction, a request for a claim form to be issued and other specified documents may be filed electronically (Money Claim Online)' (Ministry of Justice 2011). The MCOL practice direction supplements Civil Procedure Rule Part 7, which refers to the rules for starting and managing a civil proceeding for money claims. As soon as PCOL is involved, PR 55B allows for the issuing of a possession claim online and supplements CPR Part 55, which controls claims for the recovery of possession of land (including buildings or parts of buildings).

[14]For more information, see http://www.direct.gov.uk/en/index.htm.

The service was tested by the project managers, involving the court service's staff, who tried the claim submission facility. Developers at first opted for a soft launch by making the service available to users but without advertising it (Kallinikos 2009). Successively, the project managers promoted MCOL with posters in the courts, with press releases and advertisements aimed at civil services' users associations (Civil Courts Users Associations). Nowadays, MCOL is advertised on the most important government websites, such as Government Gateway, Direct Gov and Business Link.

Since the 2001 launch, many amendments and updates have been introduced. In 2002, in order to allow for more equality between claimant and defendant, DCA provided significant functionalities for the latter so that they can defend against claims online.[15]

When the contract with EDS came to an end, HMCTS, which had replaced the DCA, signed a new contract with Logica. This ICT service provider for the public sector won the competitive tender for the management of MCOL technological components. Due to this change, claim packs are no longer printed and posted by EDS in Mitcheldean but by Logica in its office in Bridgend. Logica added two other functionalities to MCOL: the postal code lookup[16] and the synchronisation of events, allowing a rapid update of claim status on the website when the Bulk Centre's staff move claims through the case management system.

A fundamental change to MCOL concerned its accounting and payment engine. Initially, the Flex Foundation software dealt with accounting, using debit card details. The recent MCOL update finally integrated the system with Government Gateway (May 2010), an online process that checks users' identity when they sign up to government services and provides a user ID.

4.3 The Implementation of Possession Claim Online

The Civil Operational Business initiated the PCOL project in 2006 in order to increase automation and provide a more efficient way for processing possession claims. As for MCOL, different offices of HMCTS and the private companies that supplied the main technology cooperated in order to implement the project. The principal actors involved were the Civil Operational Business, which attends to the civil courts' administrative operations; the ICT team of HMCTS; the Policy department of the Ministry of Justice, which looks after the overarching policy

[15]Given the consistent interoperability between MCOL and its back office system, that is, the CCBC, the Bulk Centre also needed to be updated, to include a defence option for the CCBC's bulk users.

[16]The postal code lookup enables users to control and look for the exact address of claimants or defendants. This is also allowed by the UK's peculiar system of postal coding, which codes not only the postcode area and the district but also the street, part of a street or a single address.

and changes in legislation; and EDS, the private company that provided the main technology for the online facility.[17]

The development strategy followed HMCTS's standard project methodology. This foresaw the requirements as, first, high-level requirements signed off by the Civil Policy Business and second, low-level requirements signed off by the ICT team and the supplier. When requirements were gathered, HMCTS and suppliers signed off the commercial contracts and proceeded to development, testing and deployment.

An important difference with MCOL's strategy of development concerns the legislation that allows users to issue a possession claim online, that is, PD 55B. In contrast to PD 7E, which controls MCOL, PD 55B had been approved before the requirement gathering and presented ICT developers with Hobson's choice. In the case of possession claims, the legislation guided the technological change. The most considerable Hobson's choice regarded the architecture design. Instead of centralising the service in one county court, Possession Claim Online involves several county courts in England and Wales in which the service is available. This choice was dictated by the PD rule that designated the claimant's home court as the competent county court for issuing the claim. Possibly, the explanation for the missed adaptation of the law to a functional technological solution resides in the procedure for possession claims. In contrast to the money claim procedure, as soon as a possession claim is issued, the competent county court fixes a date for the hearing. The administrative work and the different stages of the procedure that precede a potential hearing in money claims are not present in possession claims, where the hearing follows directly upon the issuing of the claim. Consequently, the design of PCOL foresees that electronic data are transferred from the web server to the competent county court. The website utilises a postcode look-up facility in order to retrieve the competent court.

Possession Claim Online designers utilised several technological components developed in MCOL; screen mock-ups are the same and the accounting and payment engine is the one provided by Government Gateway for Money Claim Online.

PCOL has been tested live in an environment as close as possible to real life, and including all interfaces and printing. Court staff tried the system by making possession claims on one another. As the system involves local authorities, the online system has been advertised in all county courts involved in the project through court leaflets and court guidance updates.

After the implementation of the e-justice service, Logica substituted EDS in dealing with the technological components (web server and database) of the system. An important amendment that this change brought about was the integration with Direct Debit's system of payment. Direct Debit is an automated system of payment that allows citizens to pay bills with a direct deduction from a bank account. The

[17] All of this section concerning PCOL derives from the analysis of website guidelines, precedent contributors to the topic (Falletti 2009; Cortes 2011) and interviews with court staff and the ICT team of the CCBC and HMCTS. For more information, see http://www.pcol.org.

integration with PCOL allowed possession claim bulk users to pay fees by having them collected on a monthly basis from the nominated account in Direct Debit.

4.4 Advantages and Disadvantages of the Exploitation of the Installed Base

A number of contributions on information infrastructure (Ciborra and Hanseth 1998; Hanseth and Lundberg 2001; Hanseth and Lyytinen 2010) and several other studies specifically concerned with e-justice (Lanzara 2009; Kallinikos 2009) have highlighted the advantages of exploiting an established installed base for ICT development. Hanseth and Lyytinen (2010) supported the use of the installed base in the implementation stage of an ICT system in order to reduce adoption barriers and safeguard capabilities already in place. The contribution of the two authors mainly deals with the technological components of the installed base and specifically analyse the story of Internet development. Other studies (Contini and Lanzara 2009) explored other components of the installed base, such as the organisational and institutional arrangements and the legal framework. In this study, too, the installed base is considered to be made of technological, organisational, institutional and legal components; these will be discussed through the MCOL and PCOL cases.

In addition, the e-justice literature and more specifically Kallinikos's (2009) analysis of MCOL considered the use of a 'pre-existing technological set-up' (Kallinikos 2009) as a strong point of the English and Welsh service.

The analysis of MCOL and PCOL development, conducted in Sects. 4.2 and 4.3, shows that developers relied on institutions, agencies and technological solutions already available at the time of implementation. As previous studies have acknowledged (Kallinikos 2009), this may represent an advantage, but my empirical analysis also highlights possible negative outcomes of the use of an installed base. These refer to technological components of the two services that are stable and resilient to change and consequently that hinder the evolution of the e-justice services. Lanzara (2009) stressed the dual character of the installed base: on the one hand, the installed base 'constitutes a pool of available resources that can be turned into convertible and usable materials'; on the other hand, it can foster inertia and hinder 'the development of new configurations' (Lanzara 1998, 19).

Moreover, the comparative analysis of the two systems will show that the installed base design principle is not enough to assure quality performances of the ICT system. Other factors, such as the design of the system architecture, may have an impact on the outcomes.

The organisational and technological installed base of Money Claim Online is constituted by the agencies of the civil court services that were already dealing with money claims issued electronically, that is, the Claim Production Centre (CPC) and the Country Court Bulk Centre (CCBC). While the CPC provides the data file validation facility, the Country Court Bulk Centre manages money claims issued online through its case management system. As happens with all other claims that arrive in electronic forms in the CPC and the CCBC, the staff of the two agencies based in Northampton manage the claims issued online using CaseMan and under the name of Northampton County Court. In the case of a hearing, data are transmitted through the case management system to Northampton County Court, which deals with MCOL claims and all the claims electronically admitted through the CPC or CCBC service. Therefore, a fundamental institutional and organisational installed base's component of Money Claim Online is the Northampton County Court.

Even though the wise exploitation of functional components of the installed base may bring about many advantages, such as in terms of reduction of adoption barriers (Attewell 1992; Hanseth and Lyytinen 2010), some components, such as the aforementioned Claim Production Centre may be too rigid and hinder change. The interviews with the ICT staff of HMCTS confirmed that the stable parameters of data interchange through CPC become a substantial obstacle for MCOL evolution. Any modification of the claims' submitting functions in Money and Possession Claim Online would need a change in CPC parameters, which are considerably stable and are the same as those used by claimants who issue claims through magnetic tape or floppy disks.

The MCOL installed base is not constituted only by its technological components but also by standards and legal frameworks. Developers relied on the United Kingdom's e-Government Interoperability Framework (UK e-Gif) as a set of guidelines for choosing between multiple standards and technologies (UK Government, 2005). The UK's e-Gif provides policies and standards for accomplishing interoperability and facilitates data exchange across the public sector. The frameworks are based on the government's commitment to making possible exchange of data between the LCD/Court Service intranet, the Government Secure Intranet (GSI) and the Internet. UK e-Gif specifies the XML language as required for rapid exchange of data in the public sector. Moreover, it recommends the use of Internet browsers as the principle user interface and TCP/IP (internet protocol) network connectivity (UK Government 2005). The e-Gif also provides for the compliance to the United Kingdom Government Category List (GCL), a taxonomy that facilitates the automatic categorisation. The UK e-Gif guidelines foresee the adherence to the Government Metadata Standards (e-GMS) that specify how public sector bodies should label documents and content as web-pages in order to facilitate access and management to public documents.

Given the mandatory nature of e-Gif for public bodies, developers followed strictly the UK e-Gif specifications, utilising the XML language, allowing the use of Internet browsers and opting for TCP/IP connectivity. The choice of a more open and accessible system that can exploit the evolutionary potential of the Internet and a simple design of the website fostered the rapid generation of a critical mass of users (Lanzara 2009). The other side of the coin is that opting for openness and easier access in order to foster the evolvability of a technology also means becoming exposed to security problems (Hanseth and Lyytinen 2010). As HMCTS's chief of the ICT team stated in an interview, most of the costs of MCOL implementation are due to compliance with security requirements. For instance, data exchanged through MCOL need to comply with IL3 data classification standards. IL3 stands for Impact Level 3, which refers to data considered 'restricted'. More recently, the payment engine needed to be revised in order to comply with the Payment Card Industry Security Standards (PCI). The PCI are set by the Payment Card Industry Security Standards Council and include rules and parameters to be respected in order to reduce credit card frauds. Given that an external Qualified Security Assessor (QSA) does the validation annually and that standards may be amended from time to time, compliance with PCI standards translates into a permanent cost for HMCTS.

At the time of the implementation of MCOL, the legal installed base (the civil justice system and its procedures) had been affected by a considerable modification, due to the approval of the government's White Paper 'Modernising Justice' of 1998, which introduced a new code of procedural regulations, the Civil Procedure Rules (CPR). This was integrated with ad hoc practice directions that can be drafted and amended through a fast procedure by the Ministry of Justice alone. The simplified and rapid procedure for practice directions' drafting introduced by the reform has been an advantage for MCOL implementation: the adaptation of the legal system to the new online service has been rapid and concurrent with MCOL's development. In addition, the Civil Procedure Rules that control money claims contributed to make the procedure faster, cheaper and easier to understand for citizens even without the assistance of a lawyer, thanks also to the use of plain English (Dwyer 2009). It is possible to say that most of the 'procedural' complexity of MCOL (and in part of PCOL) is absorbed by its legal infrastructure, which guarantees a simple procedure available to common citizens in its offline version.

Similarly, the design of Possession Claim Online is based on the exploitation of technological and institutional components already in use, such as the screen mock-ups, and many functionalities of the website shared with MCOL. Possession Claim uses the same payment and accounting engine developed for other public services in England and Wales and integrated with Money Claim Online (provided by Government Gateway). The several county courts in which the online service is available and that manage possession claims issued online can be considered the basic institutional installed base of Possession Claim Online.

Even in the case of the online service for possession claims, old technological and institutional components, such as CaseMan, the case management system developed in the 90s and still in use in the English and Welsh county courts, may hinder the evolution of the system (Plotnikoff et al. 2001).

PCOL designers relied on the UK e-Gif standards, the same utilised for Money Claim Online, which foster the creation of accessible systems and interoperability between public administration services (the main e-Gif guidelines are resumed above in this section). In addition, the legal instrument that disciplines the online procedure for possession claims is based on antecedent changes in the civil law that facilitated the amendments to civil procedure by the introduction of the Civil Procedure Rules and the practice directions. In this case, the possession claim practice direction may represent a further example of an installed base component—in this case a legal component—that influences its design and evolution. This happens because the PD 55E was approved before the implementation of the service and consistently affected the implementation of the decentralised architecture of the e-justice service.

4.5 The Functioning of the Systems: Two Architectures, Two Different Ways of Performing Legal Tasks

In this section, I will show how the two e-justice services work by describing the procedures for money and possession claims. The possibility of judgement and enforcement that the two services provide for claimants will also be explored. The description will show the 'architectural' differences between the two systems and the consequences that they have for the procedure and its performance.

4.5.1 The Centralised Configuration of Money Claim Online

Citizens who want to issue a claim or to defend a claim online can access the Money Claim Online website (www.moneyclaim.gov.uk). The online procedure for both issuing and defending a claim is a replication of the paper-based procedure based on specific paper forms. Some limitations to the use of the online service apply to claims against more than two people, if the case falls under the Mental Capacity Act 2005 and if the address of the defendant is not in England or Wales; MCOL is a service for fixed amounts of money claims (up to £100,000), so it is not available for cases in which claimants do not know exactly the value of the claim, as for example in claims for damages or compensation for loss or injury.

When a claimant enters MCOL in order to issue a claim, he needs to register to a Government Gateway account (see Fig. 4.1).

He will provide his details, then choose an ID (identifier) and password. Government Gateway checks the user identity looking at the National Insurance number and provides a user ID that can be utilised only for a government service, in this case MCOL.[18] After the user logs in, MCOL provides a claim code that he can use during the entire process of claim submission (and to be identified by the help desk office in Northampton, in case of problems).

MCOL fees[19] stimulate the use of the online service instead of the traditional procedure, which directly involves county courts. Higher amounts of money claimed are associated with a further reduction in fees compared to the paper-based

[18] As anticipated, this procedure is an amendment to the original website, where accounting was managed directly in MCOL (see Sect. 4.3.1).

[19] http://www.justice.gov.uk/courts/northampton-bulk-centre/money-claim-online.

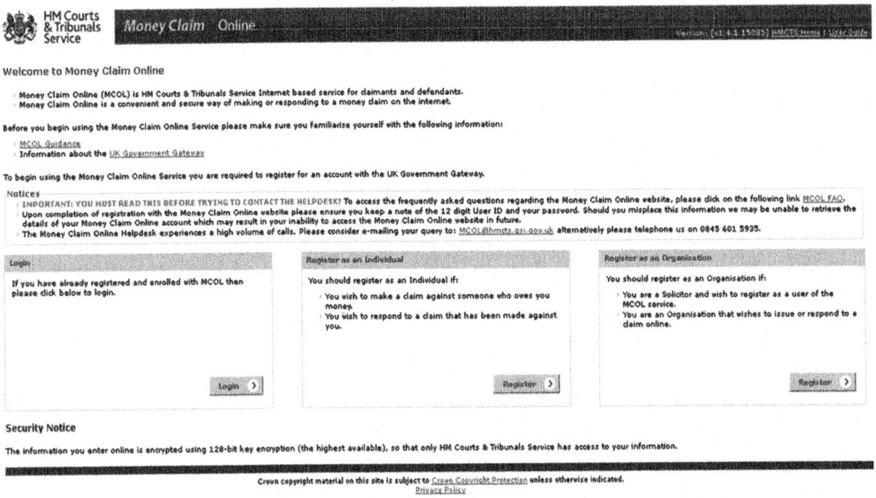

Fig. 4.1 Screenshot of money claim online registration

procedure. On average, MCOL court fees are 14.64 % lower than county court fees.

The claimant issues the claim through an eight-step procedure that corresponds to eight screens on the website (for an account of the procedure see Table 4.1). The first one provides a guidance screen with information on the MCOL claim submission system, the details needed and a fee table. In four successive steps, the claimant will provide his personal data, a correspondence address, the defendant's data (with the possibility of distinguishing between an individual or organisation and the possibility of adding another defendant), the details of the claim and the amount claimed, with or without interest applied. For the Claim Particulars screen (fifth screen), users need to describe the claim details in no more than 1,080 characters (including spaces); if the claims' details cannot be included within this allowance, the user can state in the Particulars section that detailed particulars will follow: this document needs to be sent by post within 14 days to the defendant. The following three screens provide a summary with the statement of truth (Summary step), a screen where credit/debit card details need to be submitted (Payment Details step) and a confirmation screen were the user can download the claim as a pdf or plain text (Confirmation step).[20]

Once the claim pack is served, defendant has 14 days to respond.[21] In the claim pack, defendants will find a user ID, a password and a claim code; the ID

[20] The Claim form that the claimant can download from the MCOL website reproduces the N1 form that claimant needs to fill out in order to submit a claim directly in a county court.

[21] As the CCBC has no capacity to check if a claim pack has been correctly received, the 14-day period begins from the date of service, that is, 5 days from the date the claim was issued.

and password allow the defendant to log in to MCOL and respond to the claim. Defendants can act by utilising the Money Claim Online facilities or by post/paper, utilising the forms included in the claim pack. Not all actions available in the small claim procedure can be pursued using MCOL, however. The defendant has several options at his disposal, from admitting the claim in full (by paper), to asking for more time to pay (online or by paper form), to admitting only part of the claim (online or by paper form), to filling an acknowledgement of service (online or by paper form) in order to extend the time to respond to the claim.[22] The defendant may dispute the claim by filing a defence in MCOL or completing N9B form and sending it by post to the competent court. If the defendant issues a defence online, MCOL will transfer the claim to the competent court (see Table 4.3). If the defendant has a counterclaim against the claimant, he can submit it through MCOL or by completing the paper forms included in the claim pack.

In MCOL, the claimant may ask for a judgement in the absence of the defendant's response (default judgement) or where claim is admitted (judgement by admission) without paying any additional fee (see Table. 4.2.). If a claimant fails to request a judgement within a 6 month period, the claim will automatically be stayed and no further action may be taken. Claimants may use their MCOL ID and password to log in and ask for a judgement. A judgement by default can be issued only if defendant failed to respond to the claim within the 14 days allowed (or 28 if an acknowledgement of service has been issued). The option of judgement by default will appear in MCOL only after the 14–28 day period has passed. The judgement by admission can be issued only if the claimant has received from the defendant a signed admission (the court can ask the claimant to submit proof of this admission at any stage).

If a defendant fails to comply with a court judgement, the claimant has different enforcement options at his disposal. The enforcement is a decision of the court regarding the outcome of a claim. Warrant of execution is the only method of enforcement available on MCOL (see Table. 4.2).

The claimant needs to be sure that the defendant has enough attackable assets, which could be sold at auction to raise money for the judgement, or the money that the claimant is asking for on the warrant. A warrant can be issued only after the claimant has asked and obtained a judgement. Whenever a judgement in default with immediate payment has been entered, MCOL allows the claimant to apply for a warrant. This also happens when a judgement has ordered the defendant to pay by a particular date or by instalments and the defendant has failed to pay.

The study of MCOL architecture reveals the simplicity of the system, which is composed of a few (only seven) stable sub-systems organised hierarchically and in a centralised structure. MCOL's 'simple' system facilitates a smooth circulation of

[22]The acknowledgement of service refers to the opportunity given to defendants to extend the 14-day period at his disposal to respond to a claim (to a maximum of 28 days). The acknowledgement of service can be issued in MCOL or using the form included in the claim pack.

Table 4.2 Options available to defendant in MCOL

1. Admit a claim in full	Utilising the paper forms received with the claim pack and sending it directly to the claimant within 14 days after service of the claim. In this case, the use of MCOL is not allowed. Defendants need to pay court fees, costs and any interest directly to the claimant at the address for service provided in the claim pack
2. Admit the claim in full but wish to ask for time to pay	In this case, the defendant needs to complete admission form N9A and send it to the claimant. If the claimant accepts the proposal, MCOL may be used to issue a judgement by admission. If the claimant wants to reject the proposal, he must notify the CCBC in Northampton by post and provide a copy of the N9A form. In this case, the CCBC will settle how the defendant should pay
3. Part admission	Defendants may issue a part admission either using MCOL or by filling the N9A and N9B forms and sending them directly to Northampton County Court. With a part admission, defendants may defend the disputed amount and either (a) pay the admitted amount (payments must be sent directly to the claimant), (b) ask for time to pay the admitted amount (option present in the part admission form both offline and online) or (c) make a counterclaim against the claimant
4. Acknowledgement of service	The defendant may want to extend the 14 day period. In this case, he may issue an acknowledgement of service in MCOL or by using the form included in the claim pack. Total time to file a response can be extended for more than 14 days, to a maximum of 28 days
5. Defence	The defendant may want to dispute the claim by filing a defence in MCOL or completing N9B form and sending it by post to the competent court. If the defendant issues the defence online, MCOL will transfer the claim to the competent court. If the defendant is an individual, usually the case will be transferred to the defendant's home court. If the defendant is an organisation, the case will be transferred to the claimant's home court
6. Counterclaim	If a defendant has a claim against the claimant, he can issue a counterclaim. This action is allowed only if the defendant is making a defence against part of the claim or the claim in full. The counterclaim procedure foresees the payment of fees; the amount to be paid depends on the money claimed and counterclaim fees are the same as fees for submitting a claim offline or online

agency (see Chap. 1, by Lanzara) through its main components. This is also due to the simplicity of its 'legal installed base', that is, the civil procedure for money claims in England and Wales, which involve only a few stages and a small amount of bureaucratic and administrative work (Table 4.2).

Table 4.3 Options of judgement and enforcement available to claimant in MCOL

1. Judgement by Admission: can be issued only if the claimant has received from the defendant a signed admission (the court can ask the claimant to submit proof of the admission at any stage). If the claimant receives a part admission from the defendant asking for time to pay, he should decide whether to accept the proposal or not. If the claimant accepts the payment proposal, he can issue a judgement by admission in MCOL. If the claimant does not accept it, he must complete a paper form (the N225) and send it to Northampton County Court with a copy of the defendant's admission form. The court will settle the rate of payment and send the order to both parties 2. Judgement by Default: can be issued only if the defendant fails to respond to the claim within the 14 days allowed (or 28 if an acknowledgement of service has been issued). The option of judgement by default will appear in MCOL only after the 14-28 day period has passed	Judgement is a decision of the court regarding the outcome of a claim. If the decision of the court imposes payment on the defendant, judgement will be entered on the public Register of Judgements, Orders and Fines. If the judgement has been paid in full within one calendar month of the date of the judgement, the entry in the public register can be cancelled and removed completely
Enforcement. Warrant of execution is the only method of enforcement available in MCOL. The warrant can be issued only after the claimant has asked and obtained a judgement. Whenever a judgement in default with immediate payment has been entered, MCOL allows the claimant to apply for a warrant. This also happens when a judgement has ordered the defendant to pay by a particular date or by instalments and the defendant has failed to pay. The minimum amount a claimant can issue a warrant for is £50, or one monthly instalment, whichever is the greater amount; the maximum amount that a warrant can be issued for is £5,000 (including costs, as happens in any other county court). If a judgement totals more than £5,000, the claimant can issue additional warrants in order to recover the balance at a later stage, but the case will be transferred to the competent court. When a warrant is issued, it is sent electronically to the bailiffs at the defendant's local county court, because only the bailiffs at that court have jurisdiction to enforce the warrant	

4.5.2 *The Decentralised Configuration of Possession Claim Online*

In order to issue a possession claim online, citizens need to register on the website (see Fig. 4.2). Users can register as an individual or as a solicitor acting on behalf of a firm or a private organisation (see screen 6 in the Appendix). Government Gateway provides the accounting and identification facility, as happens at Money Claim Online. After registration, the claimant receives an identification number and a claim number. In Possession Claim too, the claim number will identify the claim during the entire process of claim submission (and in order for the claim to be identified by the help desk office in Northampton, in the case of problems).

The website enables the claimant to issue a possession claim, to check the status of the claim or to issue a judgement and/or a warrant. Any individual or organisation that has an address in England or Wales and wants to issue a claim against a defendant can utilise the system (the defendant must also have an address for service

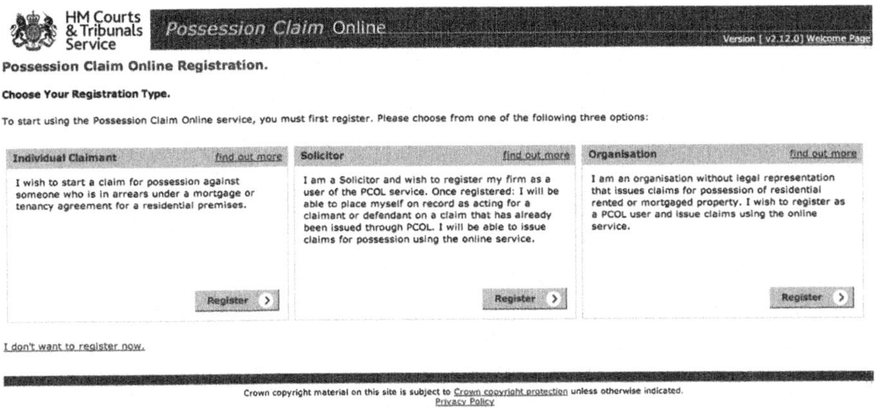

Fig. 4.2 Screenshot of possession claim online registration

Table 4.4 Steps and procedures in possession claim online

Screens and Steps	
Step 1	Submit claimant's details
Step 2	Provide a correspondence address and a postcode to which the system associates the competent county court
Step 3	Submit claim details and specify the types of arrears
Step 4	Add defendant's details and address
Step 5	Add claim particulars
Step 6	Submit the history of payment and the payments due
Step 7	See a résumé of the claim and sign a statement of truth
Step 8	Fees payment screen

in England or Wales). In contrast to the offline procedure, the value of the property and the amount of any financial claim issued should not be higher than £100,000. The online service has some restrictions that resemble MCOL restrictions.[23]

Claims are issued through an eight-step procedure (see Table 4.4) that allows the claimant to find the competent court, submit claim details and pay any fees. The possession claim is then electronically transferred from the web server to the competent county court, which will fix a date for a hearing and print and post the details of the claim to the defendant.

[23]Individuals under the age of 18, patients under the Mental Health Act of 1983 or anyone forbidden by a High Court judge to issue proceedings without permission (vexatious litigants) cannot utilise the system.

The date of the hearing will be not before 28 days from the date of issue of the claim form (CPR Part 55).[24] During this period, the defendant may issue a defence both online on PCOL or offline by issuing it to the competent county court. If the defendant does not file a defence within 28 days, he may take part in the hearing but the court may take his failure to file a defence into account when deciding about the case.

Claimants can utilise Possession Claim Online to issue a warrant of possession. Warrant of possession is an official termination order to end a residential tenancy. Defendants can go to PCOL to request a suspension of eviction. This applies when the defendant is able to make payments again and wants to ask the judge to 'suspend the warrant for possession'.[25] Claimants and defendants can pursue these legal actions both online through PCOL or by presenting the appropriate forms to the court.

Possession Claim Online provides several other facilities that help claimants and defendants during the possession claim procedure, such as a tool for hearing adjournment, the option of 'terminating party representation' (that is, to remove a party's solicitor acting as his representative) or the messaging service for communications with the courts.[26]

The Possession Claim Online architecture described here is clearly decentralised. The web server and the PCOL database are connected to the local county courts that individually manage the claims and print and post the claim documents and forms to the claimants and to the defendants. Despite the massive use of the system by English and Welsh citizens (see Table. 4.1), interviews with HMCTS staff revealed that PCOL is facing many problems due to an uneven application of the procedure. Possession Claim experience reveals that a decentralised architecture constituted by several de-localised components may foster heterogeneous performance and different applications of the same institutional innovations (Lanzara 1998). This may signify, aside from the factors described by the information infrastructure and e-justice literature, the influence of other variables on e-justice services' performance. This aspect will be discussed in the following section.

---

[24] Civil Procedure Rule Part 55, 'Possession Claims'.

[25] In a case where a previous warrant has been suspended by the court and the defendant has breached the terms of the suspension, the claimant can 're-issue a Possession Warrant' through PCOL.

[26] Practice Direction 55B clarifies that 'if the PCOL website specifies that a court accepts electronic communications relating to claims brought using Possession Claims Online the parties may communicate with the court using the messaging service facility, available on the PCOL website ("the messaging service")'. The messaging service is only for 'brief and straightforward' communications with the court staff and does not accept attachments. The PCOL website contains a list of examples of when it will not be appropriate to use the messaging service. The court normally replies via messaging service or by email if the sender has provided an email address.

4.6 Theoretical Discussion: Old and New Design Principles for e-Justice

The implementation of the two e-justice systems is an example of compliance to several principles identified by the e-justice (Carnevali 2010; Cortes 2011; Contini and Fabri 2001; Contini and Fabri 2003; Contini and Lanzara 2009; Fabri 2007; Kallinikos 2009) and information infrastructure (Lessig 1999; Hanseth 2004; Ciborra and Lanzara 1994; Ciborra and Hanseth 1998; Hanseth and Lundberg 2001; Hanseth and Lyytinen 2010; Fountain 2001) literatures. However, the empirical analysis confirmed that respecting the design principles of e-justice systems is not always a guarantee of success. The comparative analysis highlighted the architectural differences between the two systems that may be the cause for their different performances. Let's analyse first the points in common between the two systems. These refer to the e-justice systems' design principles that developers appeared to follow in implementing the two services.

Both systems exploited an installed base, that is, antecedent technological solutions, institutions and organisational structures. Money Claim has been built as the front end of an already developed back office system, that is, the CCBC exchange data system and the county courts' case management system (CaseMan). The organisational installed base is constituted by different agencies and offices that were already dealing with money claims filed electronically, namely, the Claim Production Centre, the County Court Bulk Centre and Northampton County Court.

For Possession Claim, the several courts that enable the issuing of possession claims online and that manage them can be considered the organisational and institutional installed base of PCOL.

By exploiting the existing infrastructure, a stable organisational structure, existing institutions and their functions, costs are lowered and the barriers to adoption for the user could be reduced. The argument for '*cultivation*' of an installed base is not peculiar to the information infrastructure literature (Aanestad and Jensen 2011). In 1962, Simon acknowledged the importance of building on hierarchically structured systems constituted by stable sub-systems. Only stable sub-systems (an already established installed base) can provide the basis for the evolution of a system. This happens by proceeding from patterns of behaviour, routines and components that are already stable, through small changes and trial and error (Simon 1962; see also Lane 2006).

MCOL and PCOL developers dealt with the boot-strap problem, that is to say, they made an effort to attract initial users by directly targeting their needs, thus fostering the creation of a critical mass of users (Hanseth and Lyytinen 2010). Often, the evolution of a system is facilitated by the contribution of its large and diverse user base: users may 'start to deploy the IT capability in unexpected ways through learning by doing and trying or re-organising the connections between the user communities and the IT capability' (Hanseth and Lyytinen 2010, 13), thus fostering the evolution of the system. Hanseth and Lyytinen also suggested that the system initially should target users' problems and needs, but in a way that does not assume a complete solution or a large base of users; in this way, the new system's requirements will be added to with the expansion of the user base. In the beginning, the technological solution must be simple, in order to attract users, and only later should new functionalities be added, thus attracting more users and fostering a sort of snowball effect (see also Lanzara, Chap. 1). For MCOL and Possession Claim the use of the Internet, the openness of the service to lay users, the simplicity of the procedure and the advertisement of the system through Court Users associations and in county courts all facilitated the creation of a critical mass of users. In MCOL in particular, system requirements were also in some way limited and represented a simplified technological innovation capable of attracting early users: for instance, the system was only dedicated to claimants, and only when a critical mass of users was reached was the option for defendants to use MCOL added (see Sect. 4.2 in this chapter).

MCOL and PCOL designers developed a modularised system constituted by different 'layers of infrastructure' (Hanseth and Lyytinen 2010) with different functions. For Hanseth and Lyytinen (2010), it is essential to decompose the system in different layers connected by gateways and to maintain loose couplings (Contini and Lanzara 2009) between different components. Simon (1962) previously acknowledged this principle by focusing on the stability and evolvability of an architecture constituted by several sub-systems. Through the watchmaker story, Simon (1962) showed that relatively independent sub-systems facilitate problem-solving and the overall evolution of the system (if one of the several pieces of the watch is broken, it is easier to substitute it if the parts of the watch are built independently [Simon 1962, 473]). Above all, the MCOL story confirms these arguments. The Money Claim Online architecture is constituted by several loosely coupled components; moreover, as most of its components can be combined and recombined in different combinations, its architecture is also modularised. This structure facilitated the evolution of the system and problem-solving. For instance, over the years, some system components changed but this did not hinder the performance of the system nor modify its main characteristics and functions. One of MCOL's components that has changed considerably is the private company that runs and manages the ICT technological elements of the system: in the beginning, it was EDS but more recently it has been Logica (this change also affected PCOL, see above). Moreover, the accounting engine has changed as well. Previously, it was the FlexFoundation accounting system based on credit card, whereas now it is the Government Gateway accounting system, based on citizens' fiscal code. These events did not require an overarching change of the all architecture and did not hinder the system's performance.

Can these features of the e-justice systems under study (reflecting the principles of information infrastructure design) be considered adequate for implementing performative systems? Like Money Claim, also Possession Claim Online is built on an established installed base and can be considered a modularised e-justice system, but the uneven application of the possession claim procedure in the county courts seems to disconfirm this hypothesis. The differences in performance between the two systems may be due to factors that characterise and differentiate the history of

MCOL and PCOL's implementation. The factors pertain to the relationship between law and technological change and to the different outcomes of decentralised and centralised architectures. Let's discuss these two points and the influence of these factors on the performances of the two systems.

A remarkable difference between Money Claim Online and PCOL implementation concerns the drafting and approval of the norms that discipline the offline and online procedure for claims. In a recent work, Mohr and Contini (2011) acknowledged the strict entanglement between law and technology and the 'unstable, unreliable relationship between norms and ICT' (Mohr and Contini 2011, 995). Thus, an important factor that may affect the performance of e-justice services relates to the different types of relationship that may interest law and technology: is it the law that legitimates a given technological solution or do ICT developers simply inscribe the law into the technology? The case of MCOL and PCOL confirms what Mohr and Contini recognised in their study of Australian e-justice technologies: a parallel change of legislation and technological regulation or norms that legalise technological artefacts contribute to reduce complexity; by contrast, a strategy that inscribes legal procedures into ICT systems is inefficient and contributes to the creation of more complexity, thus affecting an e-justice service's performance negatively. While in the case of MCOL, technological change went hand in hand with policy change (the draft of a practice direction that disciplines the online service), in the case of PCOL, an already established norm constrained the developers' work so that they had to opt for a particular type of decentralised architecture (see Sects. 4.3 and 4.5.2 in this chapter).

Another factor that differentiates the two systems is the system architecture. MCOL structure is centralised; even though different modules (HMCTS, CPC, CCBC, Northampton County Court, Logica offices) constitute the layers of the system, the governance and the functions of the e-justice services are centralised and unique for all users in England and Wales. By contrast, the PCOL architecture is decentralised. Several courts in England and Wales manage the possession claims inputted through the online service. It is plausible that this architecture is the main cause for the different implementation of ICT innovation and of the different performances of the service provided, on the basis of the county court involved (HMCTS interviews). This result confirms that a decentralised architecture may foster a different implementation of the same institutional innovation (Lanzara 1998) and, therefore, differences in performance and in the quality of service provided by its several components. In the justice sector, this issue is of great importance because quality of justice also involves equal treatment of cases before the law.

The theoretical discussion adds new aspects to Lanzara's analysis in Chap. 1. In particular, the argument suggests that even if the conditions for a quality e-justice service are respected, such as the use of an installed base, modularisation of the infrastructure and keeping complexity below a certain threshold (see the argument on maximum manageable complexity in Chap. 1), the configuration of the infrastructure may still negatively or positively affect the performance of an e-justice service. This is indeed a factor that designers should take into account.

The MCOL and PCOL case demonstrates that a centralised infrastructure ensures a homogeneous product and service, even though it will absorb all the complexity in a centralised manner so that backups cannot easily be provided (for instance, in the unlikely event that MCOL's main component, the CCBC, experiences a malfunction, the entire service is interrupted). A decentralised service, by contrast, even if constituted by several modules, as in the case of PCOL, may foster a heterogeneous application of the new routines and practices and, as a consequence, may produce a heterogeneous service. This happens because its modules and components are not connected in a hierarchical fashion (thus unpacking the procedure in different stages and sharing 'large bodies of data and helping legal agency circulate across the assemblage' [Lanzara, Chap. 1, 20]), but independent, and each component independently interprets the new procedure.

4.7 Concluding Remarks

The study of the MCOL and PCOL cases sheds some light on the strategy of development and on the evolution of e-justice services. The lessons learned concern the utilisation of an already functioning installed base, the parallel development of the law that controls civil procedures and the technology, and the modularisation of the infrastructure. The most important argument advanced here concerns the 'shape' of the architecture and the differences between the application of the same innovation in centralised and decentralised architectures. I am aware that this last point, even if confirmed in the case of Money and Possession Claim Online, cannot be generalised and considered a general design principle for civil justice services; instead, it is very context laden. It is not clear that an application of the same principle (centralised architecture) in other areas or contexts will bring about a reduction of complexity, an equal application of the same institutional innovation and a performing service.

A final remark worth making. The option given PCOL and MCOL users to use both the online and offline procedures at every stage of possession and money claim cases confirms the commitment of the justice system of England and Wales to optimising the accessibility of justice services. From a different perspective, however, this point presents a remarkable paradox. On the one hand, if the purpose of policy in the judiciary is to make procedures faster, easier and less costly by utilising ICT facilities, on the other hand the incomplete diffusion of ICT literacy and the commitment to the accessibility of court services limit and will limit in the future a complete translation of conventional legal procedures into digital media.

References

Aanestad, M., and T.B. Jensen. 2011. Building nation-wide information infrastructures in healthcare through modular implementation strategies. *Journal of Strategic Information Systems* 20: 161–176.

Attewell, P. 1992. Technology diffusion and organizational learning: The case of business computing. *Organization Science* 3: 1–19.

Carnevali, D. (ed.). 2010. *Soggetti smarriti: Perché innovazione e giustizia non si incontrano (quasi) mai*. Milano: Giuffrè Editore.

Ciborra, C.U., and O. Hanseth. 1998. From tool to gestell: Agendas for managing the information infrastructure. *Information Technology and People* 11(4): 305–327.

Ciborra, C.U., and G.F. Lanzara. 1994. Formative contexts and information technology. *Accounting, Management and Information Technologies* 4: 611–626.

Civil Justice IT Strategy Development Group. 1998. Civil Justice: Resolving and avoiding disputes in the information age.

Contini, F., and M. Fabri (eds.). 2001. *Justice and technology in Europe: How ICT is changing the judicial business*. Dordrecht: Kluwer Law International.

Contini, F., and M. Fabri. 2003. Judicial electronic data interchange in Europe. In *Judicial electronic data interchange in Europe: Applications, policies and trends*, ed. M. Fabri and F. Contini, 1–23. Bologna: Scarabeo.

Contini, F., and G.F. Lanzara (eds.). 2009. *ICT and innovation in the public sector: European studies in the making of e-government*. Basingstoke: Palgrave Macmillan.

Cortes, P. 2011. *Online dispute resolution for consumers in the European Union*. London: Routledge.

Dwyer, D. 2009. *The civil procedure rules ten years on*. Oxford: Oxford University Press.

Fabri, M. (ed.). 2007. *Information and communication technology for the public prosecutor's office*. Bologna: Clueb.

Fabri, M., and F. Contini (eds.). 2003. *Judicial electronic data interchange in Europe: Applications, policies and trends*. Bologna: Scarabeo.

Falletti, E. 2009. *E-justice: Esperienze di diritto comparato*. Milano: Giuffrè.

Fountain, J.E. 2001. *Building the virtual state: Information technology and institutional change*. Washington, DC: Brookings Institution Press.

Hanseth, O. 2004. Knowledge as infrastructure. In *The social study of information and communication technology*, ed. C. Avgerou, C.U. Ciborra, and F. Land, 103–118. Oxford: Oxford University Press.

Hanseth, O., and K. Lyytinen. 2010. Design theory for dynamic complexity in information infrastructures: The case of building internet. *Journal of Information Technology* 25: 1–19.

Hanseth, O., and N. Lundberg. 2001. Designing work oriented infrastructure. *Computer Supported Cooperative Work* 10: 347–372.

HM Court Service. 2008. *HM court service framework document*. London: Her Majesty Stationary Office.

HM Courts and Tribunals Service. 2011. Corporate reports. Ministry of justice.

Kallinikos, J. 2009. Institutional complexity and functional simplification: The case of money claim online service in England and Wales. In *ICT and innovation in the public sector: European studies in the making of e-government*, ed. F. Contini and G.F. Lanzara, 66–86. Basingstoke: Palgrave Macmillan.

Lane, D. 2006. Hierarchy, complexity, society. In *Hierarchy in natural and social sciences*, ed. D. Pumain, 81–120. New York: Springer.

Lanzara, G.F. 1998. Self-destructive processes in institution building and some modest countervailing mechanisms. *European Journal for Political Research* 33: 1–39.

Lanzara, G.F. 2009. Building digital institutions: ICT and the rise of assemblages in government. In *ICT and innovation in the public sector: European studies in the making of e-government*, ed. F. Contini and G.F. Lanzara, 9–48. Basingstoke: Palgrave Macmillan.

Lessig, L. 1999. *Code and other laws of cyberspace*. New York: Basic Books.
Lord Chancellor's Office. 1998. *Modernising justice. White paper Cm 4155*. London: Her Majesty Stationary Office.
Malleson, K. 2005. *The legal system*. Oxford: Oxford University Press.
Ministry of Justice UK. 2011. Solving disputes in the county courts: Creating a simpler, quicker and more proportionate system. A consultation on reforming civil justice in England and Wales. Consultation paper CP6/2011.
Mohr, R., and F. Contini. 2011. Reassembling the legal: 'The wonders of modern science' in court-related proceedings. *Griffith Law Review* 20(4): 944–1019.
Ng, Y.G. 2010. Quality management in the justice system in England and Wales. In *Quality management in courts and in the judicial organisations in 8 Council of Europe member states*, CEPEJ Studies, 18. Strasbourg: Council of Europe Publishing.
Plotnikoff, J., R. Woolfson, and S. Lyons. 2001. The technological challenge of a fragmented justice system: ICT in England and Wales. In *Justice and technology in Europe: How ICT is changing the judicial business*, ed. F. Contini and M. Fabri, 233–256. Dordrecht: Kluwer Law International.
Reeves, A. 2004. *The path to justice: A review of the county court system in England and Wales*. Brighton: Emerald Publishing.
Simon, H.A. 1962. The architecture of complexity. *Proceedings of the American philosophical society* 106(6): 467–482.
Susskind, R. 2000. *Transforming the law: Essays on technology, justice and the legal marketplace*. New York: Oxford University Press.
Timms, P., J. Plotnikoff, and R. Woolfson. 2003. Judicial electronic data interchange in England and Wales. In *Judicial electronic data interchange in Europe: Applications, policies and trends*, ed. M. Fabri and F. Contini, 171–184. Bologna: Scarabeo.
Timms, P., and R. Woolfson. 2006. Un successo tra molti fallimenti. In *Tecnologie per la giustizia*, ed. D. Carnevali, F. Contini, and M. Fabri, 177–196. Milano: Giuffrè Editore.
UK Government. 2005. *UK e-Government interoperability frameworks*. Technical Standards Catalogue.
Velicogna, M. 2008. Use of information and communication technologies (ICT) in European Judicial Systems. CEPEJ Studies No. 7, Council of Europe. www.coe.int/t/dghl/cooperation/cepej/series/Etudes7TIC_en.pdf.
Woolf (Lord). 1996. *Access to justice: Final report to the Lord Chancellor on the civil justice system in England and Wales*. London: HMSO.
Woodhouse, D. 2007. The constitutional reform act 2005: Defending judicial independence the English way. *The International Journal of Constitutional Law* 5: 153–165.

Website

http://www.possessionclaim.gov.uk
http://www.justice.gov.uk
http://www.justice.gov.uk/about/hmcts
http://www.supremecourt.gov.uk
http://www.dca.gov.uk
http://www.justice.gov.uk/about/moj
http://www.justice.gov.uk/about/hmcts/
http://www.direct.gov.uk/en/index.htm
http://www.gateway.gov.uk
http://www.justice.gov.uk/courts/northampton-bulk-centre/money-claim-online

Legislation

Civil Procedure Rule 7, 'How to start proceedings - the Claim form'.
Constitutional Reform Act 2005 (Commencement No. 11), Order 2009, Statutory Instrument 2009 No. 1604.
County Court Act 1984.
Civil Procedure Rule Part 22, 'Statement of Truth'.
Civil Procedure Rule Part 55, 'Possession Claims'.
Electronic Communication Act, 2000. HMSO.
Electronic Signature Regulation, 2002. HMSO.
Mental Capacity Act, 2005. HMSO.
Practice Direction 7E, 'Money Claim Online'.
Practice Direction 55B, 'Possession Claim Online'.
Public Contracts Regulations 2006 as amended by the Public Contracts and Utilities Contracts (Amendment) Regulations, 2007. HMSO.

Chapter 5
Functional Simplification Through Holistic Design: The COVL Case in Slovenia

Gregor Strojin

Abstract COVL case study examines the design, development and functioning of an automated judicial enforcement system for monetary claims in Slovenia. The development of the system, initiated by the Registry Department of the Supreme Court, was divided into four concurrent components: legislative, technological, organisational and promotional. Decisions made in all components show that maximum simplicity and operational efficiency of the system were strived for since the very beginning. Complexity was intentionally avoided with the establishment of a single national jurisdiction and reduction of traditional legal formalisms. The new system introduced e-filing, avoided free text, simplified identification of debtor's assets and claim processing. The system started its operations in 2008. Prior to this, backlogs in enforcement procedures inhibited debt recovery and negatively affected the economy. The transformation of a traditionally paper-based and decentralised system into a centralised and automated procedure significantly reduced the number of court staff and operational costs, but also increased the access to justice, and shortened average decision times from 6 months to 2 days. Modular development and the use of open standards allowed the system to expand and be reused by other judicial procedures.

5.1 Introduction

In 2004, the Supreme Court of Slovenia (SC) proposed a solution to the problem of judicial backlog and inefficiency in the field of enforcement procedures. By 2008, the project had developed into an efficient system for enforcement of monetary claims.

G. Strojin (✉)
Public Affairs Office, Supreme Court of Slovenia, Ljubljana, Slovenia
e-mail: gregor.strojin@sodisce.si

F. Contini and G.F. Lanzara (eds.), *The Circulation of Agency in E-Justice*, Law, Governance and Technology Series 13, DOI 10.1007/978-94-007-7525-1_5,

Court backlogs, especially those related to the enforcement of monetary claims, were one of the acute problems of the Slovenian judicial system. Prior to 2008, 44 different local courts were responsible for enforcement on the basis of their territorial jurisdiction, and work involved approximately 350 employees. The procedure was paper-based and computer systems were used only for basic case management but did not allow any connectivity. Average time to issue a decision on the requested enforcement often exceeded 6 months, and practices among different courts varied greatly. Long procedures, inefficiency and unpredictability in this field caused a significant burden for the economy and contributed to low confidence in the judiciary.

Previous attempts to reduce the backlog were done through normative (legislative) reforms in 1998 and 2002, but the courts remained overburdened with work. Steps that would lead to major improvements were yet to be implemented.

It was well understood that any major process-optimisation reform required the use of a modernised ICT infrastructure; otherwise, it would be neither economic nor rational. At the same time, however, technological renewal would most likely be insufficient because enforcement faced wider legislative and organisational issues. The solution was based on a systemic reform through a combined implementation of custom-made ICT solutions, business process modifications and changes of legislation.

The main objective was to systematically reorganise the management of the enforcement procedure up to the phase of finality of the decision on an enforcement claim, in a one-stop manner and with the assistance of effective information support. Creditors should get a decision on their claim in as short time as possible and should have the capacity to track the procedure by direct web access.

The strategic goal was to provide users with a user-friendly information and organisation environment that would enable efficient management of judicial procedure without unnecessary delays. Through this, it was believed, the project would increase the transparency and efficiency of the courts, make their resources available for other activities and types of procedures and improve the payment discipline in the economy.

COVL, an acronym for the Central Department for Enforcement on the Basis of Authentic Documents, began its operations on January 1, 2008, as part of the Local Court in Ljubljana. In 2011, 65.04 % decisions were issued within 2 days of receipt of the claim, and 84.26 % within 5 days. Only 2.6 % of claims were submitted on paper in 2011, the remaining 97.4 % being submitted in electronic form (Registry Department of the Supreme Court of Slovenia 2008).

The project strived to achieve maximum simplicity and by doing this dispensed with many traditional formalities and legal requirements. Among other specifics, the user-friendly approach to case filing enabled direct access to courts without any need for representation by attorneys. Previous formal requests for enforcement were replaced by form filling and completely avoided free text and the attachment of related documents. At the organisational level, court activities were centralised in one unit, and many activities that were previously performed by judges were systematically delegated to court personnel at lower levels of decision-making. Similarly, technological solutions were designed in line with the SC's strategic technological development guidelines, which promoted uniformity, modularity, reusability, scalability, compatibility, interoperability and open standards (Supreme Court of the Republic of Slovenia 2008).

In this way, the project increased the potential for circulation of legal agency. This chapter will attempt to identify the building blocks that were required for the implementation of the initial concept, retrace the paths and solutions used by the project team and describe the functioning of the new system with particular regard to its potential for transborder submission, recognition of data validity and the constancy of the meaning of data.

While the author of this case study has also been involved in the creation of the draft project in 2004, interviews were held with a number of individuals directly involved with the design, implementation and the production phases of the project in order to create a comprehensive case study, and project documentation as well as the final product were thoroughly studied and analysed.[1]

5.2 History

5.2.1 Starting Point

Prior to 2008, the Law on Enforcement and Securing of Claims (ZIZ)[2] allowed for a large number of different legal instruments in different phases of the enforcement procedure and required the court to perform a number of activities that in comparative systems are usually left to creditors (e.g., acquisition of data from external registries). Claims were filed in traditional, paper form and e-filing was not possible. Case parties had to submit attached documents as proof, submissions were not uniform and consequently many were incomplete or difficult to interpret.

While legislation on electronic signatures existed, its implementation into judicial procedures was inefficient. Civil Procedure Law (ZPP),[3] which is used as a subsidiary of ZIZ, had a number of mandatory requirements that limited its introduction, even though it had nominally allowed for submission of claims by means of information technology (105 ZPP) if they conformed with conditions

[1]Since the project documentation is just partially available to the public and is written mostly in Slovenian, the chapter does not refer specifically to individual documents that were used for the analysis, such as Twinning Interim Quarterly Reports and Reports of the Working Parties specified in the References.

[2]Zakon o izvršbi in zavarovanju (ZIZ), Official Gazette of the Republic of Slovenia, 51/1998 (17 July 1998) and its subsequent changes.

[3]Zakon o pravdnem postopku (ZPP), Official Gazette of the Republic of Slovenia, 26/1999 (15 April 1999) and its subsequent changes.

set by the Law on E-Commerce and E-signature (ZEPEP).[4] Analysis showed that such change alone did not offer real possibilities for e-filing because other articles relevant for the filing of claims in civil procedures remained unchanged. Examples of this were a rule that multiple copies of documents had to be submitted by the case parties, otherwise the submission was to be declared incomplete and consequently dismissed, or the requirement to include a personal signature on submissions.

Enforcement procedures use a number of external information sources, and many of these were available but could not be accessed easily by judicial information systems because personal data protection law required a specific legal ground for access to data from various registries. Moreover, many judicial procedures that were written prior to data protection legislation did not include explicit formulations, including both civil procedure and enforcement legislation.

Organisationally, enforcement was greatly fragmented. Claims for enforcement were filed by creditors (i.e., citizens and companies) at 44 local courts based on the residence of the debtor (general rule of geographic jurisdiction). Information on debtors' debtors (e.g., banks, employers, etc.) and from external base registries (e.g., bank accounts, real estate, stocks, etc.) was collected individually and mostly by paper-based inquiries to managing institutions. Identification of debtors alone was done in a similar manner, which often caused mistakes, necessitated corrections, delayed processing time by months and consequently resulted in relatively high levels of objections and appeals, thus additionally increasing the workload at appellate levels.

Because most courts did not even have specialised enforcement departments, a disproportionately high number of court employees were responsible for the procedure. The whole system was operated by 350 full-time court employees, and while the average time to get a decision on the claim was 6 months, the entire procedure could take years to complete. The situation made it impossible to ensure the upkeep of trial in reasonable time and a lengthy procedure represented a significant inhibitor for the economic environment and investments.

The practice of mid-sized and smaller courts was that judges, and consequently other employees (e.g., judicial assistants, typists, ledger managers) covered different material areas. In addition, many courts did not employ clerks to handle enforcement cases, so these remained a responsibility of the judges themselves. At smaller courts, only one judge was usually responsible for all enforcement cases, which not only caused disproportionate workloads but also created significant differences in the application of law where legislation was ambiguous. Similar discrepancies and inharmonious case law were observed at appellate courts, and this further exacerbated timely judicial resolution of claims and was often exploited by larger or more frequent debtors to prolong the proceedings.

---

[4]Zakon o elektronskem poslovanju in elektronskem podpisu (ZEPEP), Official Gazette of the Republic of Slovenia, 57/2000 (23 June 2000) and its subsequent changes.

The management practice of enforcement departments at local courts was neither unified nor transparent. Slovenia's courts did not collect statistical data on individual events and procedural steps regarding the enforcement of authentic documents, despite their importance for the setting up of an efficient organisational scheme. It was therefore necessary to rely on relatively subjective analyses and assessments by individual clerks or typists who were doing the work at the time.

Consequently, the inefficient activities of some enforcement officers were also a big problem because there was no clear overview of cases that were concluded by the court and submitted to the enforcement officers for physical finalisation. These tended to work on the cases according to their own priority lists, often leaving indefinitely open many cases that were formally final, without the courts being aware of that.

Technologically, a decentralised information system from the 1990s was written in Clipper and allowed only basic case management. Although it was updated a number of times, it did not allow network connectivity and, consequently, no interoperability. The old IT solution also did not allow centralised maintenance or upgrades, thus increasing the costs and dependence on the original external developers. Hardware was also outdated, because it did not support work with the newer technological solutions. All printing was done by individual clerks at a departmental level, and printers were mostly matrix based. The appearance of printouts differed greatly and costs were high. The solution was used only for internal and partial case management of enforcement procedures because it was basically built around a paper-based procedure, defined by legislation for decades. Although the technological base did, to a certain extent, support the basic case management, it did not facilitate preparation of statistical and analytical reports, even though these are essential for efficient court management and prevention of unnecessary delays at the organisational level. As a consequence, organisational solutions at local courts varied (e.g., number and quality of personnel allocated to the procedure) and resulted in different approaches to solving similar legal or substantive issues, as well as in different resolution times. Obviously, the old system did not allow e-filing.

5.2.2 Project Development

A project was initiated by the Registry Department of the SC (RDSC). While originally responsible for the uniformity of judicial practice, RDSC has heavily relied on informatisation of judicial procedures since the 1980s, and in 1996 it formed its own Centre for Informatics (CIF). Since its inception, CIF has been in charge of computerisation and informatisation of the national judicial system, providing all 66 courts with technological, pedagogical and procurement support, as well as application development and optimisation of procedures. CIF has developed strategic guidelines[5] both for providing information support to courts' management, as well as for the development of IT solutions (Supreme Court of the Republic of Slovenia 2008). Among information support to court management, uniformity of information solutions, use of open standards, security, economy, scalability and compatibility are the most important. CIF is especially encouraging the use of information solutions based on open standards, which are publicly published, generally adopted and completely documented, and which give the users the free option of further development of their products in line with these standards. The result is greater transparency and better comparison of particular solutions in the market, which thus allows a choice between more providers and prevents vendor lock-in. Technological guidelines include uniform, three-tier architecture of information systems' development, the modular basis of information solutions, reusability, interoperability, standard formats for data interchange (XML) and creation and saving of documents (Open Document Format ISO/IEC 26300 and PDF/A ISO 19005-1), Java for codings, ownership of the code, vendor neutrality and independence from the vendor. All projects led by RDSC and CIF are based on a combination of technical and substantive groups, consisting of judges and other lawyers from the judiciary and CIF's engineers (Supreme Court of the Republic of Slovenia 2008).

On the basis of such an approach and prior experience with large-scale reorganisation of judicial procedures (mainly digitisation of Land Registry), the COVL project was initiated as an extension of the Enforcement Procedures project group. It soon received financial support in the form of EU Phare funding, and Germany (Deutsche Stifftung für Internationale Rechtliche Zusammenarbeit E.V.) was chosen as the twinning project partner.

The project made it clear from the start that its goal was to achieve a transition from a decentralised, bottom-up system to a centralised, top-down system. As noted, some of the major problems with the installed base, both technologically and organisationally, related precisely to its decentralised nature.

The new solution, however, aimed to utilise the developments and possibilities of the technological advances of the last decade and build a new system by their integration with the core principles of the procedure and the necessities of efficient court management.

Research was thus a significant part of the design phase. Project specifications were initially limited to the way the project should be conducted and what its general results should be, and have not focused on any chosen solution but rather on the general principles of ICT project management. It is worth noting that project partners firstly signed a project covenant, which defined some of

[5]Similarly, technological solutions were designed in line with the SC's strategic technological development guidelines, which promoted uniformity, modularity, reusability, scalability, compatibility, interoperability and open standards.

these principles, along with benchmarks and mandatory results for various phases (Supreme Court of the Republic of Slovenia, German Foundation for International Legal Cooperation 2006).

Initial design of the project identified the need to divide work into four distinct components: legislative, technological, organisational and promotion. All project components worked concurrently under the supervision of the steering committee and adapted their tasks to each other's findings and to the committee's decisions. Specifications for the final solutions in all components were drafted and completed only at the later stages of the project and contained some significant solutions that were not included or even mentioned during the inception phase. The centralised organisational component, for example, was included only at a later stage.

Decisions made in all components show that simplification of the system was on the minds of the project leaders from the very beginning and that complexity was intentionally avoided. The project team tried to look at the widest possible picture from the very start and included a wide variety of stakeholders in the process of designing the solution. Extensive input from internal and external users, as well as other stakeholders, was collected, and a detailed analysis of the existing installed base (in all of the components) was made, identifying obstacles, bottlenecks and drawbacks and looking to a number of comparative models for possible solutions to avoid or overcome them.

A part of the research involved study visits to Germany, the UK and Finland. A training course in the organisation and functioning of a centralised court was conducted at the Local Court in Mayen, Germany. The UK system of Money Claims Online at Northampton Bulk Centre (see Chap. 4) was interesting primarily due to its web interface, which allowed authentication simply on the basis of an email address: if the user is prepared to pay a court fee and carry the legal consequences, then this is his choice. It also gave some insight into their mass filing system. While they noticed that the system was developed as a proprietary solution, which caused problems to the users when additional requirements emerged, such a pragmatic project management approach provided long-term stability and usage of the systems. The Finnish system of process management turned out to be organised in a similar manner to the methodology that was adopted by Slovenia, and this realisation strengthened project management's confidence regarding the correctness of their strategic directions and decisions. Most important in terms of the project at hand were the data connections of the Finnish judiciary to various external registries and a pragmatic approach regarding e-filing procedure. Such an approach was, for example, not possible in Germany due to stronger data protection legislation, but it allowed for the faster and simpler processing of claims. Study visits helped clarify dilemmas and enabled project management to combine the best practices and solutions of all three systems into a new working solution.

Legal, technological and organisational frameworks of the existing system were significantly adapted to serve the functional objectives of the project and were aimed at increasing the efficiency of enforcement procedures, both from the customers' as well as the courts' perspective.

5.2.3 Normative Components

Despite a detailed analysis of the legislative environment, which identified a number of structural faults and suggested solutions for them, project leadership experienced difficulties in getting relevant input and feedback from the executive branch and certain stakeholders from the business sector, which caused delays. The executive also showed reluctance in implementing certain suggestions, especially regarding some organisational and legislative aspects (e.g., exclusive jurisdiction of only one appellate court, minimum debt limit for attachment of real estate, creation of a frequent debtors database, etc.), which could have increased the efficiency of the procedure even more.

Nevertheless, suggestions relating to technological modernisation of the procedures were accepted and implemented in the legislation almost fully. Legislative changes aimed at creating an environment that avoided traditionally obvious elements of formality in favour of functionality and effectiveness. Some requirements were the result of paper-based procedures but were not necessary in an e-context, or even presented a burden. Cooperation of the judiciary and the executive was thus critical for the general success of the project.

During 2007, a number of normative changes were implemented. Changes to the Civil Procedure Law (ZPP)[6] aimed at fully enabling the informatisation of civil procedures by the introduction of electronic communication, including e-filing, e-decision and e-inspection. E-filing changed the rules related to identification of case parties and introduced a qualified certificate as a basic identifier but also allowed the minister to prescribe other, less secure means for specific procedures. This allowed the submission of claims on the basis of a valid email address only but required payment of the court fee. It also allowed all e-filing through information systems designed by the SC and on e-forms confirmed by the SC. This has, in a way, formalised the convention that all changes to legislation that relate to e-justice become fully operational only after the SC validates the technological conditions. Courts were allowed to issue and sign decisions in e-form (meaning that judges do not have to physically sign decisions when they are generated automatically), and e-serving was made equivalent to paper-based serving. Other changes stipulated that courts can work on electronic case files and exchange them, and that no paper receipts need to be submitted as proof of fee payment if the fee was paid by electronic means. In addition, the general requirement that multiple submissions need to be made (in as many copies as there are case parties plus one for the court) was relativised, allowing for a more specific definition of the necessary forms in a by-law.

[6]Zakon o spremembah in dopolnitvah Zakona o pravdnem postopku (ZPP-C), Official Gazette of the Republic of Slovenia, 52/2007 (12 June 2007).

A by-law to ZPP (rules about the envelope for mail serving in civil procedure)[7] specified the format and quality of the envelope required for the automated postal dispatch system.

Changes to the Courts' Law (ZS)[8] gave exclusive competence over cases related to enforcement of authentic documents, and over objections regarding these, to one Local Court in Ljubljana, which enabled formation of COVL (99a ZS) as a centralised unit. Even more importantly, it created a general obligation for operators of collections of personal and other protected data to provide these to the courts free of charge and as quickly as possible, if they were required for determination or evaluation of facts related to judicial procedures. It also stated that the information system of the courts can establish connections with official registries and public ledgers, which possess data required by the court for its procedures (13 ZS). This gave the project a legal ground to start working on technological interoperability with other data registries.

Changes to ZIZ[9] described the exclusive competence in more details and declared COVL responsible for the identification of the means of enforcement from electronic registries for the purpose of serving decisions (40c ZIZ). It prescribed a mandatory filing on a standardised form (41 ZIZ). It changed the rule that requested submission of related documents (e.g., copies of the claimed authentic document) and required only their specification and date of maturity (41 ZIZ). It specified conditions for e-filing in enforcement procedure, defined that e-claims are filed when the information system confirms its receipt and allowed for automated processing of claims and preparation of decisions (29 ZIZ). It also introduced a unique identifier as a basis for payment of court fees in e-filing and made an exception to the rule that a claim is made when the fee is paid, stating that in e-filing these can be paid within 8 days of the claim being submitted to the information system (29b ZIZ).

A by-law to ZIZ (rules about forms, types of enforcement and practice of the automated enforcement procedure)[10] specified the standardised structure of forms and the permitted methods for filing of claims.

The Courts' Fee Law[11] allowed for the differentiation of fees filed in e-form and specified fees for various stages of COVL procedure.

---

[7]Pravilnik o ovojnici za vročanje po pošti v pravdnem postopku, Official Gazette of the Republic of Slovenia, 93/2008 (30 September 2008) and its subsequent changes.

[8]Zakon o sodiščih (ZS), Official Gazette of the Republic of Slovenia, 19/1994 (13 April 1994) and its subsequent changes; Zakon o spremembah in dopolnitvah Zakona o sodiščih (ZS-F), 127/2006 (7 December 2006).

[9]Zakon o spremembah in dopolnitvah Zakona o izvršbi in zavarovanju (ZIZ-E), Official Gazette of the Republic of Slovenia, 115/2006 (10 November 2006).

[10]Pravilnik o obrazcih, vrstah izvršb in poteku avtomatiziranega izvršilnega postopka, Official Gazette of the Republic of Slovenia, 121/2007 (27 December 2007).

[11]Zakon o sodnih taksah (ZST-1), Official Gazette of the Republic of Slovenia, 37/2008 (15 April 2008).

Because of the relative ease of access to court proceedings, the Penal Code (KZ-1)[12] was also more clearly formulated, in particular, defining abuse of enforcement procedures as a crime, punishable by a fine or prison for up to 2 years (216 KZ-1).

The adopted solutions consequently not only enabled the basic scope of the project but also provided the ground for subsequent projects and the development of other legal procedures. Some solutions, especially those related to e-serving, were not used directly in the COVL project but for other projects that were developed simultaneously or subsequently (e.g., Insolvency, Land Registry, etc.).

5.2.4 *Organisational Components*

At the organisational level (which also had to be defined in the legislation) business process was significantly modified and automated with the intention of bridging bottlenecks in determining the validity of claims and issuing decisions.

Decision-making was to be transferred from judges to clerks in a number of procedural activities. Preparedness of the first-level judges and presidents of the courts to accept and adopt the suggested organisational changes was an important factor. This allowed the establishment of a new, centralised department with newly employed personnel, as opposed to using the installed organisational and institutional scheme with the existing employees.

COVL, as a special organisational unit of the Local Court of Ljubljana, took over the competence of all other 44 local courts in the field of enforcement of authentic documents.

Involvement of judges was limited only to the legally most demanding tasks, such as decisions on received objections and verification of legal merits for appeals, while other activities were either to be automated or delegated to clerks.

Judicial clerks manage the majority of cases and issue decisions allowing the claims for enforcement of authentic documents according to the change in Courts' Law (53a ZS). ZIZ also allowed the judges to delegate the decision-making regarding objections to clerks (6 ZIZ).

Typists and administrators are a very important segment of the business process at COVL, especially in the phase of scanning control, data verification, verification of conditions for fee exemption, etc.

Other local courts' enforcement departments gain competence over COVL's cases only after the finality of the decision, and the COVL project did not deal with their reorganisation (this was, however, the role of the Enforcement Special Programs Working Group).

[12] Kazenski zakonik (KZ-1), Official Gazette of the Republic of Slovenia, 55/2008 (4 June 2008).

5.2.5 Technological Components

Time- and resource-consuming activities, such as the preparation of outgoing mail and the scanning of incoming mail, were delegated to outsourced companies. Nevertheless, software solutions that were to be used by outsourced contractors for these tasks were developed by the project itself.

The pre-existing technological base was completely replaced by the new solution, along with hardware. The new solution was based on CIF's strategic technological guidelines, such as three-tier architecture, modularity, reusability, interoperability, vendor neutrality and independence and, most importantly, open standards.

The technological component was based on automation of the procedures by introducing new centralised information modules, which replaced the old case management system (CMS). The new CMS, which is written in Java, incorporated the new organisational methods and decision-making process.

CIF's strategic guidelines and principles were applied at all levels of the project, and were significant for the choice of the system's technical standards. Uniform architecture of information systems' development, which is used for all centralised information systems that are intended for simultaneous use at all courts, was employed at COVL. It utilizes a three-tier architecture with a user interface level (front applications, in charge of communication between the user and the system), application level (where all business logic for a specific solution is found in form of a service, usually reusable in other information systems) and database level (tool or permanent storage and access of data in the information system). All functionalities and services that can be used by more information systems are consistently joined into service modules, thus shortening the development and simplifying maintenance. Both three-tier architecture and modularity are closely related to reusability of developed information solutions for new tasks and procedures. Special attention is given to interoperability of the planned systems with other systems, especially regarding data formats (these must allow interoperability with as many systems) and suitable conception of services (must allow simple access). In order to achieve this, the development of solutions is always carried out by CIF. When external contractors are used, development code is constantly verified by CIF, and copyrights are owned by CIF for unlimited use in its own (SC) information systems (Supreme Court of the Republic of Slovenia 2008).

The system uses XML based service calls (SOAP, web services) to connect different information systems in a service-oriented architecture. While XML is the standard format for data exchange, Open Document Format (ISO/IEC 26300) and PDF/A (ISO 19005-1) are used for creation and saving of documents. Significantly, CIF is strategically oriented in the use of open standards (e.g., servers operating on LAMP, system written in Java (Java Enterprise Edition), Open Office used for document creation, PDF-A for document exchange, XML for communication, etc.), and the development of COVL was an example of their use. While the use of open standards gives room for the use of alternative technological standards, it also and even more importantly allows the system to adapt quickly to new or changed requirements. Strategic prevention of vendor neutrality and independence is closely related to the principle of using open standards. In order to prevent vendor lock-in each solution must consider the possibility of potential replacement of the chosen contractor and the effects of such a change (incl. economic effects) on the information system.

An example of this is the automated postal dispatch system, which was (as planned) outsourced to a contractor who possesses the required industrial-scale hardware. The contractor accepts documents from the court in e-form (pdf); prints, collects and folds them; prints data on envelopes; mechanically envelops documents in the matching envelopes (using bar codes for pairing); controls the quality of outgoing mail; creates a post ledger for all mail that is submitted to the Post Office; and delivers the post to the Post Office. Such an approach makes COVL an almost paperless environment, save for the small amount of paper-based claims received directly at COVL. The envelope, which is crucial to the effective functioning of such a system, was initially developed by CIF in connection with the first contractor. Although the contractor was changed in 2010, the process did not experience any setbacks due to the change, which shows the correctness of the open standard approach.

The only exception to the open standards involved the development of the scanning and OCR module, where a proprietary platform (KOFAX) was adapted to the requirements of the process. However, because the platform is a widely adopted platform in the commercial sector, scanning of return-of-service slips was also eventually outsourced to private contractors.

Servers are physically located at COVL (scanning and OCR), the Ministry of Public Administration (MJU) holds servers with CMS and a third location is used for security copies.

A module for payment of court fees, E-Payments, which is used by the Public Payments Administration at the Ministry of Finance, was developed by MJU and their contractor, Banka Koper d.d. (Bank of Koper). CIF established interoperability with their system to allow payments by credit card according to the requirements of the procedure. Users can employ any other means of e-payment through their e-banking systems, however, as long as they use the claim ID number as a reference. The judicial information system EOBVEZ (E-Obligations) is dedicated to control of payments and regularly controls the status of payments at the E-Payments server, pairing the results of e-payment data with data received from the COVL system. As the payment is done directly to the MF, not to the courts themselves, in the past this process could take quite some time.

Connections were also established with operators of a number of external and internal base registries, both for identification of case parties, as well as their means and assets (e.g., Tax Authority, Central Registry of Citizens at Ministry of Internal Affairs, Registry of Bank Accounts at Bank of Slovenia, Central Securities Clearing Corporation Registry, Employment Office, Land Registry, Registry of Land Units at Surveying Authority, Company Registry, etc.).

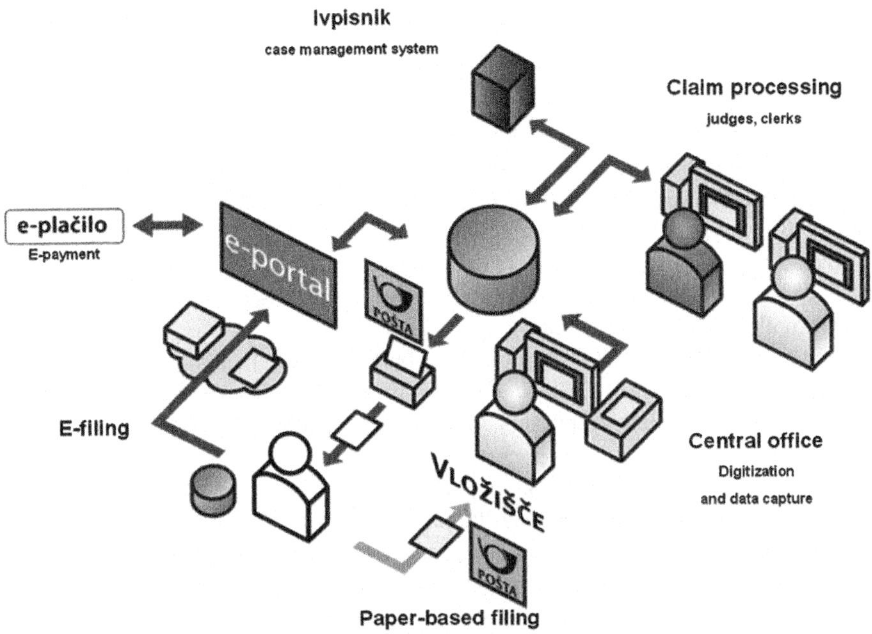

Fig. 5.1 A simplified presentation of the COVL business process (Source: Supreme Court of the Republic of Slovenia.2008. mag. Pavel Reberc, Centre for Informatics. Presentation: "Legal Enforcement Procedure for Money Claims as E-Service" (2. 6. 2008); translated and adapted by Gregor Strojin)

Data exchange protocols, which are based on XML structured requests and use web service calls between servers over a minimum 128-bit encryption, are established with each operator individually by contract and adapted to specific technological requirements. All connections also include a request log, which allows control of all requests and their pairing with actual cases, thus satisfying the requirements of data protection legislation.

Experiences from the previous projects led by the RDSC and CIF have shown the importance of a strategic commitment to open standards and of the sustainability of the final solution, which has significantly influenced project development. It was well understood that other approaches (e.g., proprietary solutions) would create the risk of vendor lock-in and prevent modularity, as well as the customisation and adaptation of features according to changes and requirements of the courts' business environment. This also led to the creation of a principle of not committing to a certain solution at a legislative level in advance, but rather creating a technological solution according to the requirements of the new legislation and in line with the SC's strategic technological guidelines, within a time slot prescribed by the legislation. Only after such a solution is developed and tested can a ministerial decree be issued, officially confirming that the solution had been verified by the SC and that the conditions for the implementation of the new legislation have been met (Fig. 5.1).

5.3 Current Functioning of the System: Getting Ready to File a Case (Identification and Access)

Claims for enforcement can be submitted in two ways: via a smart electronic form or on the strictly defined paper forms, which are available at the local courts.

A web portal was developed for registration of individual users, filing of claims and status tracking.[13]

Individual users (mostly creditors or their attorneys) can register online to receive a password to their email account. No additional authentication but a name and a valid email address are required.

A B2G interface was also developed for bulk filing of claims by large creditors, and the description of the XML scheme was published online, which allowed them to implement it in their proprietary systems (e.g., accounting software) or buy it from other developers.

Bulk (also referred to as mass or package) filing is suitable for creditors who require filing of many simultaneous claims.

All forms have data fields that are connected to the XML scheme. Each form has a unique identifying number (paper forms use a pre-printed ID, e-form IDs are generated), which enables users to pay the required court fees by using the ID as a reference number.

Only claims for enforcements can be submitted in electronic form. All other submissions (e.g., withdrawals, requests for court fee refund, objections, complaints, etc.) must be sent in paper form.

Claims can be submitted online only during working days (Mon–Fri) from 8.00 to 20.00.

Registration and submission of claims are available to non-national users from other countries. Claims can also be submitted against debtors from other countries if the means of enforcement are located in Slovenia. Existence of such means is verified by COVL immediately after the receipt of a claim during the first data control, because COVL would otherwise have no jurisdiction over the subject matter, and represents an exception to the general rule where this is checked only after the finality of the decision.

5.3.1 Preparation of the Claim (Filling Out the Claim Form)

User guidelines for submission of a claim, either in paper or electronic form, as well as an explanation of court fee structure, are published online in separate

[13]On 1 March 2012, a web portal for enforcement was added to a wider platform, which also allows e-filing in land registry and insolvency cases. As many functionalities were changed or added to the system, this chapter describes the functioning of the web interface prior to this date: https://evlozisce.sodisce.si/esodstvo/index.html.

pdf documents, which can be found in the menu of the web portal used for filing claims. FAQs are regularly updated and the help desk is available via email (covl@sodisce.si).

A smart web form guides the users during the process of claim preparation and notifies them where errors or omissions occur in the input data.

Paper form COVL-1 allows the input of data for only one creditor, one debtor or one authentic document, but these can all be expanded by annexes. If a claim is filed by many creditors, the appropriate field must be ticked on COVL-1, and as many COVL-2 forms filled out and annexed to the claim as necessary. The same can be done when there are many debtors (COVL-3). If there are multiple authentic documents, each separate COVL-4 annex form makes possible the addition of data for up to five additional documents.

The web form allows for the additional expansion of fields regarding multiple creditors, debtors or authentic documents by a simple click ('Add additional ...'). The user can also claim enforcement for an unlimited number of claimed documents related to a specific debtor.

No documents need be submitted together with the claim. The user need only identify the type of original document (on the basis of a catalogue) and its reference to allow its identification by the debtor. Dates of issuance and maturity must be stated, as well as the amount and currency (on the basis of a catalogue of abbreviations used by the Bank of Slovenia). Users only need to state the interest rate, the calculation period for contractual interests and their initial date; they do not need to state the claimed amount of interest because it is calculated by the court.[14] Users can also claim their expenses related to the specific enforcement, including postage, court fee and other expenses, such as attorney's fee, according to the Court Fees Law (ZST) rate.

Users are responsible for the veracity of the claims relating to the existence of an original document. In practice, control of this is also in the hands of the debtor, who can object to the decision and claim that no such document exists or that it had already been paid, etc.

The user can specify the means for enforcement or leave the identification of available means to the court. At least one of the means must be specified, but users often choose two or more, depending on their assessment of the debtor's assets.

Types of information that need to be submitted regarding each specific means of enforcement are defined by ZIP and its by-law.

If the creditor chooses movable assets, real estate that is not registered with Land Registry, other property or material rights or securities that are not traded at the Stock Exchange, they must also designate an enforcement officer.

The user must submit his personal information (an individual must submit his name, surname, address and country of residence and one of the following

[14]Users can calculate interests by using a web application developed by SC (http://izo.sodisce.si).

options: either tax number, personal ID number or date of birth), information on his legal representative or agent (in some cases the user is an attorney but the system is largely used by citizens and companies without the support of a legal advisor) and information about the account to where the enforced means are to be transferred.

The user must provide the debtor's basic identification data: name, surname, address and country of residence and either date of birth, tax number or any other suitable identifier, or company name and address and registry or tax number.

Claim forms must be completed fully and a smart web form prevents incomplete claims from being filed. It also automatically verifies most of the data fields, including the accuracy of data inputs regarding the most important identifiers. Automatic control is performed by requests to external connections regarding accuracy or existence of numerical data (e.g., citizen's ID number, bank account number), existence of street and house number, of name and surname, of currency and country, of company name and registry number, of a registered security and of date.

If the system detects an error in the claim form data, it informs the user via a two-colour warning scheme. Absolutely erroneous fields have a red text with the description of the error and potentially erroneous fields have a yellow text (e.g., names are verified in the citizens' or companies' register but there can be exceptions or variations in spelling). If the users believe that yellow warnings are immaterial to their claim, they can submit the form regardless.

5.3.2 *Submitting the Claim and Paying the Fee*

Although forms can be pre-filled and printed out from the web portal and then mailed to the court by post, their multiplication is not allowed because it would create a multiplicity of claim IDs. Users are cautioned to make sure that printed forms are equivalent in appearance to the outlook of the web form (e.g., field borders must be visible), otherwise COVL will consider such a claim to be submitted on an improper form and call upon the creditor to correct it by sending a prescribed form. Printed forms are available free of charge at all local courts.

No signature is required on electronic forms but they are required on paper forms.

Court fees are approximately 20 % lower for the users of the electronic form and depend on the number of specified means of enforcement.

Fees for claims specifying only one means of enforcement, which are sent by paper, are 45 euro, and those sent by electronic form cost 36 euro. Any additional means of enforcement (e.g., enforcement on movable AND immovable property) cost 5 euro for each additional means.

If a claim is withdrawn or dismissed, one third of the fee must still be paid. After a claim is submitted online, users receive a reference number and details of the amount required for payment of the court fee.

If conditions are met, users can also request exemption from court fee payment, submitting such a request on paper.

Users can choose to pay the court fee either through their own (or their bank's) payment system or by using the system's credit card payment application. Fees must be paid within 8 days of submitting the claim, otherwise it is considered withdrawn. If the fee is not paid or if an insufficient amount is paid, the system notifies the user by email; users can also track the status of their claims in their account. If the system does not detect receipt of payment (or detects insufficient payment) within 10 days of submission, the claim is returned.

5.3.3 Court Activity (Claim Processing, Preparation and Sending of Decisions)

Claims are processed and validated through an automated information system. Some of the information is verified during input (Fig. 5.2).

Paper form claims are digitised (scanning + OCR) and additionally validated by eye if errors are reported by the system. Verification of paper-based claims' content is done during the scanning phase by typists. Currently, approximately 30 % of paper-based claims still need human verification in some respect.

CMS uses all the collected information and creates a complete electronic case file, which enables an automated creation of the final decision.

On average, decisions are generated within two working days after submission.

All decisions are equipped with a digital facsimile of the court's stamp; a signature is not required.

All outgoing mail is printed, packed, labelled and sent from one central automated postal dispatch system, which makes the 'inner' COVL working environment mostly paperless.

The decision is sent to the creditor and the debtor, who have 8 days to respond after being served.

An external contractor receives return-of-service information from the Post Office.[15] All returns of service slips are scanned and information on date of service is added to the case file.

5.3.4 Receiving the Decision and Replying

After receiving the decision, the debtor can decide either to pay the debt, default (wait for enforcement) or file an objection. Objections (by debtors, approximately

[15] Previously this was done by COVL, but the work was creating bottlenecks and an industrial-scale facility was required.

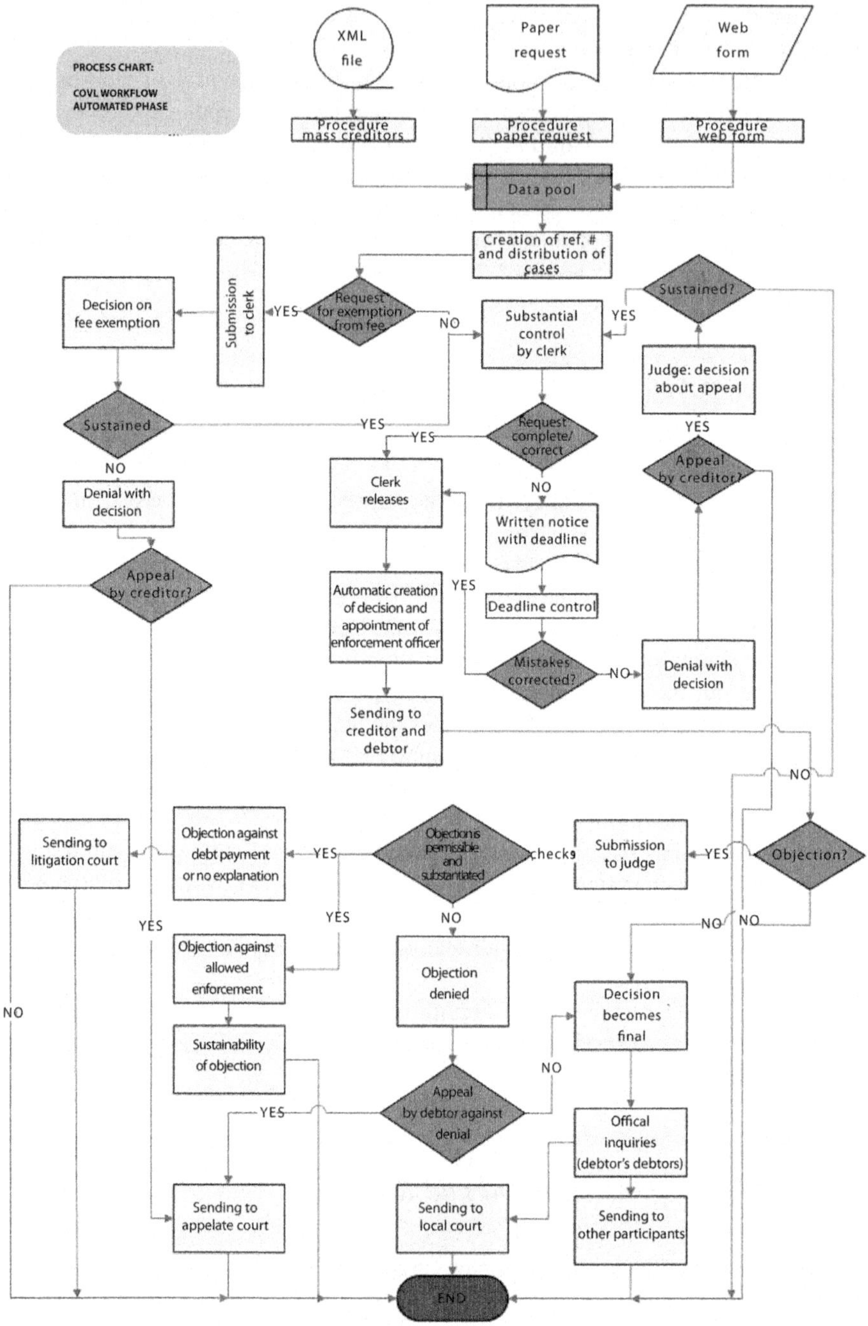

Fig. 5.2 Detailed workflow of the automated phase at COVL (Source: Supreme Court of the Republic of Slovenia, German Foundation for International Legal Cooperation. 2006. Twinning Interim Quarterly Report, Number 3, Annex XV (14 November 2006): Workflow Phase 2-automated work–Stand: 21.09.2006, Peter Werle; Ljubljana: Supreme Court of the Republic of Slovenia. translated and adapted by Gregor Strojin)

11 % of all claims) are decided on by a judge at COVL and the procedure is completely paper-based. If the objection is successful, the case is transferred to a competent litigation court (local or district, depending on the amount). Fee for an objection is 40 euro and an appeal against a decision regarding an objection is 100 euro.

A creditor can at that stage also appeal the decision (e.g., if the claim was denied), withdraw or partially withdraw the claim. If the creditor withdraws the claim before its finality, he must still pay one third of the fee. Creditors' appeals (approximately 1.5 % of all claims) are forwarded to the appellate court. The fee for an appeal against a decision is 80 euro.

Appeals are sent to the appellate or higher court, which decides in a senate of three judges (6 ZIZ). Initially, all four higher courts served as appellate courts. Since 2011, only one appellate court (the appellate court in Ljubljana) has competence over the appealed cases.

Appeals, objections, withdrawals, etc., can be filed only in paper.

In all cases, the complete electronic case file is available to the competent judge handling the objection, appeal or litigation and is usually printed out for the trial/appeal phase. Because the type of procedure changes from enforcement to litigation, the file is also transferred from enforcement CMS to litigation CMS.

5.3.5 Sentence and Enforcement (Determination of Finality)

Date of finality is determined on the basis of returns of service. These are scanned and archived and the date of the receipt by case parties is automatically added to the electronic case file.

Until the finality of a decision, COVL has competence regarding all additional means of enforcement, deferments, withdrawals or partial withdrawals and other submissions, and they have to be sent in paper. Correction of an electronic claim by electronic means is not possible, except if the court fee has not yet been paid (i.e., by simply resending the claim).

Additional means of enforcement cost 12 euro if only one was requested initially, or 6 euro for each additional one if two or more were requested initially.

After the finality of the decision, all available information on the debtor's financial means (e.g., bank accounts, securities, land property, company shares, employer data, other assets, etc.) is automatically collected from official databases and registries by COVL, if the user so chooses, by not entering specific details regarding the requested means.

COVL then sends the decision to the debtor's debtor (e.g., bank, employer, etc.), enforcement officer, Land Registry, Company Registry and/or CSCC, depending on the requested means of enforcement. In this way, COVL participates in the enforcement of the decision itself, because it is important that a decision is executed immediately.

Competence is then also transferred from COVL to one of 44 local courts, which is specified in the decision and is primarily based on debtor's residence, which is responsible for realisation of the decision on real estate or movable assets. The electronic case file also allows other courts to access its contents.

If it is established (after finality) that no means for enforcement exist, the competent local court calls upon the creditor to request a new means of enforcement or the creation of a list of debtor's assets within 15 days. If the creditor fails to do so, the case is closed.

5.4 Functioning in Numbers

The main goal of the project was to increase the efficiency of enforcement procedures, which were a major contributor to judicial backlogs due to exponential increases in new claims. The objectives were to decrease the number of pending enforcement claims and to shorten the decision-making time.

The work, which was previously done by approximately 350 court employees and judges at 44 different courts, is now concentrated at a specialised court with only six judges and 62 support personnel (two judges were added to the initial four in 2011 to help COVL deal with increasing numbers of claims). This has enabled other local courts to reassign their resources to other types of claims, thus additionally contributing to their backlog reduction. Introduction of the automated postal dispatch system alone (which processed more than a million postal parcels in 2009) saved approximately 60–70 people/year.

In 2008, COVL received 131,167 claims; in 2009, the number was 208,302 (an increase of 60 % in 1 year) and rose slightly in 2010 (213,886) and 2011 (218,779).[16]

New cases at COVL represented 81 % of all new enforcement cases in 2010 (other local courts received 20,340 claims in other types of enforcement).

The first objective, a decrease in pending cases, was achieved, as COVL relieved local courts and allowed them to focus on other types of enforcement with greater intensity. Until 2007, the number of pending cases was increasing each year. At the end of 2007, there were 305,321 pending enforcement cases at local courts. Introduction of COVL (on 1 January 2008) helped to lower the number of pending enforcement cases by 6.6 % in 2008 (to 285,043 by 31 December), by an additional 5.6 % in 2009 (to 269,072) and by 7.3 % in 2010 (249,465). While there will always be unresolved cases due to a daily inflow of new ones, it is important to recognise

[16]Ministry of Justice and Public Administration. 2007-2012. Sodna statistika (Judicial Statistics). Republic of Slovenia, Ljubljana.

Quantitative data on cases is based on annual Judicial Statistics (Sodna statistika) reports of the Ministry of Justice, available on://www.mpju.gov.si/si/storitve_in_mnenja_mpju/uporabni_seznami_imeniki_in_evidence/sodna_statistika/. Last accessed 30 January 2013.

Other data is based on various reports of the Enforcement Working Group and RDSC.

the reduction in numbers because they represent faster resolution times, especially in light of a general increase in quantity of new cases.

The second objective, of shortening the decision-making time, was achieved despite a significant and unexpected increase in claims, which shows that the system can efficiently cope even with an overload. The optimum business goal was set at 2 days per decision. Decision-making time has been lowered from an average of 6 months to less than five working days for over 90 % of the claims. In 2009, a decision was sent within two working days of the receipt of a claim in 66 % of all cases, but the rate fell a bit in 2010 to 54.9 %. It reached 65 % again in 2011, most likely as a consequence of organisational measures aimed at decreasing the workload of the employees by outsourcing part of the work and by adding two judges for the task of working on objections (Registry Department of the Supreme Court 2008-2012).

Although one contributory factor to the significant increase in new claims in 2009 may have been the general financial crisis, the shortening of the time period between the due date for payment and the date of claim-filing (the average in 2010 was 69 days)[17] suggests that another reason may have been greater awareness on the part of creditors of the available court procedure. Rather than wait and spend resources on notices to debtors, creditors seemed to decide earlier on submitting a claim for enforcement.

Enforcement claims at COVL were used for 876,012 original documents (2010),[18] which shows that creditors usually claimed on average four due original documents on each claim. This suggests that creditors preferred to wait in order to have more original documents against a specific debtor, and only then decided on submitting a claim. One of the reasons for this is, naturally, the court fee, which is paid only once, regardless of the number of claimed documents.

The amount of all enforced claims (not including statutory default interests or contractual interests) in 2010 was 1,215,870,990.49 euro or, on average, 1,387.96 euro per original document and 5,693.64 euro per claim.[19]

In the majority of cases, garnishment of funds available at the organisations for payment transactions is proposed as the primary means of enforcement. Data for 2011 show that garnishment is used in 47.99 % of the cases, followed by attachment of salary (27.23 %) and movable assets (18.84 %).[20] The absolute numbers are higher than the number of claims because many different means may be requested for each claim.

---

[17] Information provided to the author by Mr. Andrej Gogala from the Center for Informatics of the Supreme Court upon request to analyse the data in the enforcement information system.

[18] ibid.

[19] ibid.; The data, however, also includes claims which were later rejected on material grounds. As some of these might have been in the values exceeding 6-figure numbers, the average of validated enforced claims is lower.

[20] Ministry of Justice and Public Administration, 2007-2012. Sodna statistika 2011 (Judicial Statistics 2011), p. 63.

Approximately 10 % of claims are withdrawn by creditors before the conclusion of the decision at COVL, and an additional 20 % before enforcement takes place through the competent local court,[21] which often signifies the debtors' immediate voluntary fulfilment of the obligation after receipt of the decision. An increased awareness of potential additional costs incurred by the debtors (e.g., fees, interests, etc.) seems to play a part of the incentive.

Although the percentage of objections and appeals was expected to be at 20–30 % during the design phase of the project, it has remained consistently low, at an average of 11 % of objections and 1.5 % of appeals (2009) (Registry Department of the Supreme Court 2008–2012).

Objections were submitted in 23,058 cases in 2010 (more objections are possible in a single case) and 13,376 cases (58.01 %) were forwarded to litigation courts, while the others (41.99 %) were dismissed (Registry Department of the Supreme Court 2008–2012).

There were 6,055 appeals in 2010, and appellate court data (for 2010) shows that initial decisions are upheld in 64.1 %, annulled in 19.8 %, and changed in 16.1 % of appeals.[22]

Of all claims in 2009, 94 % were in e-form (62 % individual, 32 % bulk) and only 6 % in paper form. That year, 98 % of e-claims and 72 % of paper-based claims were completed fully and correctly (i.e., all fields required for processing were fully and correctly completed). By 2011, the percentage of paper submissions had fallen to 2.6 %, while the rate of fully correct claims rose. In 2011, creditors were asked to correct their claims in 16.27 % of paper-based claims and only in 1.54 % of e-claims (Registry Department of the Supreme Court 2008–2012).

The automated dispatch system processed 1,109,649 exit mailings in 2010, which consisted of 9,444,600 pages (or 4.26 sheets per mailing). COVL sent 223 packages of mailings to the subcontractor in 2010, with an average of 4,976 mailings and 42,352 pages per package.[23]

In 2010, around 10 million euro of court fees were collected by COVL, and almost 11 million euro in 2011. Development costs before 2008 were around 3.2 million euro, and annual operation costs are around 5.5 million to 6 million euro: 3.5 million euro for mail, 0.5 million euro for external contractors (printing, scanning), 1.2 million euro for salaries and only 0.2 million euro for material expenses and overhead.[24] The amount received through court fees thus surpasses the budget required for its functioning almost double. The investment had been fully returned already in the second year of COVL's operation. Court fees go directly into the

[21] Info provided by Ms. Nataša Kosec, the Head of COVL during the interview with the author.

[22] Information provided to the author by CIF upon request to analyse the data in the enforcement information system.

[23] Information provided to the author by CIF upon request to analyse the data in the enforcement information system.

[24] Information provided to the author by Mr. Bojan Muršec, director of CIF during the interview with the author.

national budget, however, and not to COVL or the judiciary, which may pose issues in regard to maintenance of the project in the future.

The cumulative amount of the enforced claims, however, is over 1.2 billion euro, which makes it highly cost-efficient, and through this, it seems, also an economical and highly attractive option for the economy.

The speed and efficiency of the procedure suggest that the new approach could even have a positive effect on voluntary and regular payments of monetary obligations in society. This will only be evident in the long run, however, through a significant decrease in new claims.

5.5 Discussion: Achieving Interoperability

It could actually be said that both legislative and organisational developments were initiated by the technological developers and ICT specialised lawyers from within the judiciary, and that this probably represents the most important factor affecting the design and development of the project. The results of the COVL project stand in direct relation to the centrally led and goal-oriented approach of the RDSC and its CIF.

The simplicity of the final result required highly complex and meticulous work during the design and development phases. Most of the internal business process is hidden away from the user's eyes, although its complexity can be glimpsed, for example, when the user receives error notices for entering a non-existing surname, street, company name, registration number, date or any other data that is simultaneously verified through external connections.

For this purpose, but more importantly for the internal gathering of all necessary data required for the identification of case parties and means of possible attachment or garnishment, connections with external information systems had to be established anew, because they were previously paper-based. One of the major issues affecting the interoperability was related precisely to the formal right of the judiciary to automatically access personal data from other registries and databases. While it was relatively easy to establish technological interoperability between COVL and external operators, a new methodology in line with the strict requirements of the personal data protection legislation had to be developed by the project. Legislation relating to general organisational aspects of the courts (Courts' Law) was amended by a general provision creating an obligation for operators of collections of personal and other protected data to provide data to the courts free of charge, as well as by allowing the creation of automated connections between the courts and these institutions.

Such connections are based on web service calls and message passing of clearly defined XML requests, thus resulting in relatively low coupling. This allows significant changes in the assembled modules with little cost of maintaining or re-establishing interoperability, as long as agreed standards are maintained.

Claim submission was simplified by preparation of the XML structured forms and minimisation of the required data. Documents, which were traditionally attached to the paper-based claims as proof of transaction on which the claim is based, are no longer required. Simple email access is sufficient for user identification because it is the subsequent payment of the fee that implies users' legitimacy. Similarly, no signature is required on e-claims. Free text was avoided almost completely and most inputs are verified for accuracy while the user is entering the data into the form, through the above-mentioned connections with external databases.

The e-form has significantly contributed to the simplification and speed of claim processing. Only 1.54 % of e-claims need to be corrected or amended, as opposed to 16.27 % of paper-based claims.

An alternative, slightly more complex solution has been developed for larger users, who may implement bulk filing in their own systems. Its open code also allows users to modify it for further adaptation to their internal requirements. For such users a digital certificate is required.

As a consequence, users can file claims without any legal training. Numbers show that the new approach significantly simplified the complexity of filing a claim for non-professional users, because they had previously relied on specialist assistance, either from a lawyer or some other professional. This raised their initial costs, as well as the costs of the debtor, and led to frequent hesitation or delays in requesting a judicial decision.

Significantly more complex solutions could be imagined, though, and potential elements of those were contemplated during the design phase, such as electronic serving to debtors, e-filing of appeals and objections, creation of an e-file for second and third instances, an extension of the CMS to the external enforcement officers, etc. It could be envisaged that such attempts would have increased technological complexity, with more costs at the development stage, longer development timeframe and more risks, as well as requiring additional normative changes. Nevertheless, the modular assemblage allows further developments in the future.

Further simplicity of the system could always be achieved at the user-interface level, because different functional and e-literacy levels of users require different means of presentation, but the proof of the pudding is in the eating. The project had to draw the line somewhere, and that was at the finality of the decision allowing enforcement. This covers the majority of work, however.

The system has since proven to be able to evolve and adapt to new functional needs. The technological solution was assembled with largely independent modular components, which permit modification in light of legislative or organisational changes and with relatively low costs. Many modular solutions from the project (e.g., centralised filing, unique case ID, electronic case file, modules, automated postal dispatch system, etc.) are now being reused and implemented at a national level for modifications or development of other judicial information systems, according to their procedural and logistical specifics and requirements (e.g., Criminal Law Information System, Land Registry, Company Register, etc.) and in line with the SC's information strategies. The project became a model for successful transformation of a judicial procedure from a paper-based to an electronic format, and such an approach also seems to provide a comfortable adaptation of users to the new environment. Compatibilities of a number of similarly constructed applications eventually led to the creation of a new judicial portal for e-filing of different claims (Land Registry, Insolvency, Enforcement), which utilises many of the same modules. COVL was added to the new portal on 1 March 2012, and the above-mentioned user interface was changed.

5.6 Lessons

The COVL project shows the importance of a holistic approach during the phases of design and development and the need for avoiding complexity in the final product. The latter can be achieved by focusing on the crucial functional elements of the system and by designing its building blocks on the principle of modularity, thus allowing subsequent modifications and additions in the future. The former, however, depends on the willingness of all major stakeholders to commit to finding a working, efficient and sustainable solution.

Efficient governance of any judicial procedure depends on the statistical and analytical capabilities of the system. These allow monitoring of the system's performance and enable its potential adaptations based on empirical data, and not merely on assumptions. At the same time, however, such monitoring needs to be performed by a dedicated management that has the responsibility, as well as the tools, for ensuring that the system remains stable and sustainable.

Some organisational and technological elements could be applied generally. Enforcement of monetary claims, or any similar judicial procedure, should be viewed as a service for citizens and the economy, and its optimisation as a business process. Tasks should be standardised and the routine administrative work should be outsourced wherever possible. Among other effects, this relieves the judges of non-judicial work, accelerates processing and lowers costs.

A centralised department model, such as COVL, which is also used to a certain extent by the UK and Germany, could offer a possible EU solution, but its effect also depends on the automation of data gathering for the purpose of claim processing. This might be possible in Slovenia or Finland but was not legal in Germany (at least at the time when comparative research was conducted). It is therefore questionable whether similar controls and data exchange with external registries could be established at a pan-European level with the same methodology and within the same timeframe.

Modularity, use of open standards and independence from vendors and external contractors seem to stand out most from the technological elements. Independence, however, implies an independent development unit that is dedicated primarily to a sustainable implementation of such solutions (and not necessarily making a profit), or at least a highly professional and stable IT management team directly connected to the judicial system and capable of effectively managing the external contractors through all the phases of the project.

While it is necessary to have professionals to organise the judicial management of such a procedure as a business process, it is at the same time equally important to have them cooperate closely with the judges and other legal professionals in the creation of efficient and stable solutions. Legal, especially judicial, knowledge of procedural and operational aspects is crucial and seems to be indispensable for effective optimisation or reform of any judicial procedure. It should not be attempted without their inclusion; otherwise, it is reasonable to expect practical problems to emerge at later stages.

References

Ministry of Justice and Public Administration of the Republic. 2007–12. *Sodna statistika* (English translation: Judicial Statistics). Republic of Slovenia, Ljubljana: Ministry of Justice and Public Administration. http://www.mpju.gov.si/si/storitve_in_mnenja_mpju/uporabni_seznami_imeniki_in_evidence/sodna_statistika/. Accessed 30 Jan 2013.

Ministry of Justice and Public Administration. 2007–2012a. *Sodna statistika (Judicial statistics)*. Ljubljana: Republic of Slovenia.

Ministry of Justice and Public Administration. 2007–2012b. *Sodna statistika 2011 (Judicial statistics 2011)*, 63.

Quantitative data on cases is based on annual Judicial Statistics (Sodna statistika) reports of the Ministry of Justice. Available on http://www.mpju.gov.si/si/storitve_in_mnenja_mpju/uporabni_seznami_imeniki_in_evidence/sodna_statistika/. Accessed 30 Jan 2013.

Registry Department of the Supreme Court of the Republic of Slovenia. 2008. Zapisniki delovnih skupin (English translation: Reports of the Working Parties). vol 1/2008, vol 2/2008 (7 March 2008), vol 3/2008 (18 April 2008), vol 4/2008 (23 May 2008), vol 5/2008 (20 June 2008), vol 6/2008 (26 September 2008),vol 7/2008 (24 October 2008), vol 8/2008 (28 November 2008), vol 1/2009 (23 January 2009), vol 2/2009 (16 March 2009), vol 3/2009 (8 April 2009), vol 4/2009(8 May 2009), vol 5/2009 (19 June 2009), vol 6/2009 (18 September 2009),vol 7/2009 (23 October 2009), vol 8/2009 (20 November 2009), vol 1/2010 (22 January 2010), vol 2/2010 (5 March 2010), vol 4/2010 (14 May 2010), vol 5a/2010 (24 June 2010), vol 6/2010(24 September 2010), vol 7/2010 (29 October 2010), vol 8/2010 (3 December 2010), vol 1/2011(28 January 2011), vol 2/2011 (18 February 2011), vol 3/2011 (1 April 2011), vol 4/2011 (6 May 2011), vol 5/2011 (17 June 2011), vol 6/2011 (15 July 2011), vol 7/2011 (30 September 2011), vol 8/2011 (28 October 2011), vol 9/2011 (2 December 2011), vol 10/2011 (15 December 2011), vol 1/2012 (27 January 2012), vol 2/2012 (2 February 2012), vol 3/2012 (5 April 2012). Ljubljana: Supreme Court of the Republic of Slovenia.

Registry Department of the Supreme Court of Slovenia. 2008. Zapisnik delovnih skupin vol 1/2012 (27 Jan 2012). Ljubljana: Supreme Court of Slovenia.

Registry Department of the Supreme Court. 2008–2012a. Zapisniki delovnih skupin (Reports of the working parties) vol. 1/2010 (22 Jan 2010).

Registry Department of the Supreme Court. 2008–2012b. Zapisniki delovnih skupin (Reports of the working parties) vol. 1/2011 (28 Jan 2011).

Registry Department of the Supreme Court. 2008–2012c. Zapisniki delovnih skupin (Reports of the working parties) vols. 1/2010 (22 Jan 2010), 1/2011 (28 Jan 2011), 1/2012 (27 Jan 2012). Ljubljana: Supreme Court of the Republic of Slovenia.

Supreme Court of the Republic of Slovenia. 2008. *Strateška izhodišča za delo Centra za informatiko pri Vrhovnem sodišču RS* (English translation: Strategic Guidelines for the Work of Centre for Informatics at the Supreme Court of Slovenia), in *Zapisnik sestanka Sveta*

uporabnikov (English translation: Report of the Meeting by the Council of Users). Ljubljana: Supreme Court of the Republic of Slovenia.
Supreme Court of the Republic of Slovenia. 2008. mag. Pavel Reberc, Centre for Informatics. Presentation: "Legal Enforcement Procedure for Money Claims as E-Service" (2. 6. 2008). Ljubljana: Supreme Court of the Republic of Slovenia.
Supreme Court of the Republic of Slovenia, German Foundation for International Legal Cooperation. 2006. European commission, Transition facility 2004 for Republic of Slovenia, EU-Twinning project: SI2004/IB/JH-06, Reduction of judicial backlog. Twinning interim quarterly reports; vol 1 with annexes (12 April 2006); vol 2 with annexes (6 July 2006), vol 3 with annexes (14 November 2006), vol 4 with annexes (6 February 2007), vol 5 with annexes (17 May 2007), vol 6 with annexes (12 July 2007). Ljubljana: Supreme Court of the Republic of Slovenia.
Supreme Court of the Republic of Slovenia, German Foundation for International Legal Cooperation. 2006a. European commission, Transition facility 2004 for Republic of Slovenia, EU-Twinning project: SI2004/IB/JH-06, Reduction of judicial backlog. Ljubljana: Supreme Court of the Republic of Slovenia.
Supreme Court of the Republic of Slovenia, German Foundation for International Legal Cooperation. 2006b. Twinning interim quarterly report, Number 3, annex XV (14 November 2006): workflow phase 2—automated work—stand: 21 Sept 2006, Peter Werle. Ljubljana: Supreme Court of the Republic of Slovenia. Translated and adapted by Gregor Strojin.
Supreme Court of the Republic of Slovenia. 2008a. Strateška izhodišča za delo Centra za informatiko pri Vrhovnem sodišču RS (Strategic guidelines for the work of centre for informatics at the Supreme Court of Slovenia). Ljubljana: Supreme Court of Slovenia.
Supreme Court of the Republic of Slovenia. 2008b. Zapisnik sestanka Sveta uporabnikov (Report of the meeting by the council of users). Ljubljana: Supreme Court of Slovenia.
Supreme Court of the Republic of Slovenia. 2008c. mag. Pavel Reberc, Centre for Informatics. Presentation: "Legal Enforcement Procedure for Money Claims as E-Service" (2 June 2008). Translated and adapted by Gregor Strojin.
Supreme Court of the Republic of Slovenia. 2008d. mag. Pavel Reberc, Centre for Informatics. Presentation: "Legal Enforcement Procedure for Money Claims as E-Service" (2 June 2008). Ljubljana: Supreme Court of the Republic of Slovenia.

Legislation

Kazenski zakonik (KZ-1) (English translation: Penal Code). 2008. Official Gazette of the Republic of Slovenia, 55/2008. Adopted on 4 June 2008.
Pravilnik o obrazcih, vrstah izvršb in poteku avtomatiziranega izvršilnega postopka (English translation: Rules on forms, types of enforcement and steps of the automated enforcement procedure). 2007. Official Gazette of the Republic of Slovenia, 121/2007. Adopted on 27 Dec 2007.
Pravilnik o ovojnici za vročanje po pošti v pravdnem postopku (English translation: Rules about the envelope for mail serving in civil procedure). 2008. Official Gazette of the Republic of Slovenia, 93/2008 and its subsequent changes. Adopted on 30 Sept 2008.
Zakon o elektronskem poslovanju in elektronskem podpisu (ZEPEP) (English meaning: Law on E-Commerce and E-signature). 2000. Official Gazette of the Republic of Slovenia, 57/2000 and its subsequent changes. Adopted on 23 June 2000.
Zakon o izvršbi in zavarovanju (ZIZ) (English meaning: Law on enforcement and securing of claims). 1998. Official Gazette of the Republic of Slovenia, 51/1998 and its subsequent changes. Adopted on 17 July 1998.
Zakon o pravdnem postopku (ZPP) (English meaning: Civil procedure law). 1999. Official Gazette of the Republic of Slovenia, 26/1999 and its subsequent changes. Adopted on 15 April 1999.

Zakon o sodiščih (ZS) (English meaning: Courts' law). 2006. Official Gazette of the Republic of Slovenia, 19/1994 (13 April 1994) and its subsequent changes; Zakon o spremembah in dopolnitvah Zakona o sodiščih (ZS-F), 127/2006. Adopted on 7 Dec 2006.
Zakon o sodnih taksah (ZST-1) (English meaning: Courts' fee law). 2008. Official Gazette of the Republic of Slovenia, 37/2008. Adopted on 15 Apr 2008.
Zakon o spremembah in dopolnitvah Zakona o izvršbi in zavarovanju (ZIZ-E) (English meaning: Law on changes and amendments to law on enforcement and securing of claims). 2006. Official Gazette of the Republic of Slovenia, 115/2006. Adopted on 10 Nov 2006.
Zakon o spremembah in dopolnitvah Zakona o pravdnem postopku (ZPP-C) (English meaning: Law on changes and amendments to civil procedure law). 2007. Official Gazette of the Republic of Slovenia, 52/2007. Adopted on 12 June 2007.

Chapter 6
The Piecemeal Development of an e-Justice Platform: The CITIUS Case in Portugal

Paula Fernando, Conceição Gomes, and Diana Fernandes

Abstract Citius is the system developed by the Portuguese Ministry of Justice to dematerialise proceedings by treating electronically all information belonging to the proceedings, thus reducing their physical form to a minimum. The Citius-Payment Order Procedure is one of the Citius applications. We show that the development of Citius in the Portuguese Justice system constitutes an example of piecemeal development and cultivation of the installed base. It therefore benefits and suffers from the limitations of being a further development of H@bilus, a former application used by court clerks and registrars in courts to manage the acts of registries. We unpack the ICT design infrastructure of the Portuguese Justice system at the legal, organisational and technological level, with a special focus on small civil claims and the payment order procedure. We offer a description of the system's characterisation, concentrating on its various applications and latest developments, and illustrate the daily functioning of Citius, with its virtues and drawbacks as experienced and perceived by the users. We bring forth the most noteworthy aspects of the experience and discuss its future prospects.

6.1 Introduction

The present chapter is based on research carried out on the Portuguese experience of Citius, the system developed by the Ministry of Justice to dematerialise proceedings.[1] In order to assess the level of circulation of agency in the Portuguese judicial

[1] The dematerialisation of proceedings aims at providing all judicial documents by electronic means of communication but, as will be seen in this chapter, this goal cannot be fully achieved.

P. Fernando (✉) • C. Gomes • D. Fernandes
Centre for Social Studies, University of Coimbra, Coimbra, Portugal
e-mail: pfernando@ces.uc.pt

F. Contini and G.F. Lanzara (eds.), *The Circulation of Agency in E-Justice*, Law, Governance and Technology Series 13, DOI 10.1007/978-94-007-7525-1_6,

system, this case study aims at unpacking the ICT design infrastructure at a legal, organisational and technological level.

The starting point of the research was the collection and study of literature, comprising relevant doctrine and studies (national and international) and legislation (national and European). The technical overview of Citius's components, strengths, weaknesses and future possibilities was enriched by the results of an audit to the Citius system by a private national company, Critical Software. The audit took place using three analytical vectors: security, architecture and technology, and performance. Its results were presented in a very comprehensive report (Critical Software 2009, 2010). This documentary analysis was deepened by means of collection and statistical treatment of data concerning the use of the payment order procedure, several interviews with key actors (including ministerial officers, court clerks, registrars, judges and public prosecutors), registry observation and a focus group with experts (gathering practitioners, academics and researchers).

The Portuguese case is an example of a process led and controlled by the executive branch, with ministerial bodies holding the monopoly of ICT implementation in justice. The Ministry of Justice (*rectius*, some of its agencies) has taken the lead in terms of the use of ICT in justice. The Directorate-General of Justice Administration of the Ministry of Justice (DGAJ) developed the computer application in close connection with the Institute of Information Technologies in Justice (ITIJ) and provided technical support to court staff users. ITIJ is generally responsible for the management and monitoring of the justice network, for issuing the electronic signature cards for all court officers and for supporting the users of Citius with a special telephone line; the Directorate-General of Justice Policies (DGPJ) has been monitoring the Citius project, as well as ensuring training sessions for judges and public prosecutors.

The Higher Judicial Council and Public Prosecution General maintain either an advisory and/or an instrumental role in what concerns judicial data. The Bar Association takes on a greater role, but only with regard to providing lawyers with the necessary tools to access Citius, such as the digital signature. A strengthening of the Higher Judicial Council and Public Prosecution General's intervention is still a controversial topic. Intervention of external entities, especially private, is rare and carefully watched.

In the next pages, the system's background, with its various stages and applications, including those that deal specifically with small civil claims, will be dissected. Section 6.1 presents the legal, technological and institutional background of the use of ICT in civil jurisdiction, specifically addressing the regime of small civil claims and payment order procedure. The system's characterisation, concentrating on its various applications and latest developments of Citius, and the daily functioning of Citius, with its virtues and drawbacks as experienced and perceived by actors, is the subject of Sect. 6.2. In Sect. 6.3, we offer a critical overview, bringing forth the most noteworthy aspects of the experience, discussing its panorama and future prospects.

6.2 The Introduction of ICT in Civil Jurisdiction

6.2.1 Civil Jurisdiction: The Courts Affected by the Innovation

In compliance with the 1976 Constitution of the Portuguese Republic,[2] the national justice system is divided in two different jurisdictions: the civil (which also encompasses the criminal justice system) and the administrative. To this edifice must be added the Constitutional Court (competent in matters of a legal-constitutional nature), the highest authority concerning the fundamental text and principles, and the Court of Auditors (competent for the verification of the legality of public expenditure). Administrative and Fiscal courts benefit from a different electronic system (SITAF) adapted to administrative proceedings and therefore are outside the scope of the present case study. Civil jurisdiction is mainly ruled by the Act on the organisation and functioning of judicial courts (LOFTJ), as well as the Code of Civil Procedure.

On the top of the pyramid within civil jurisdiction, there is the Supreme Court of Justice, the highest authority in all regards. It is followed by five Courts of Appeal. Finally, the first instance of recourse is composed by judicial circles, and within them the district jurisdictions, where the District Courts are based.

District Courts belong to one of three categories, depending on the subject and value at stake: (1) courts of general jurisdiction (general courts of law); (2) courts of specialised competence (criminal instruction, family, minors/juvenile, labour, commercial, maritime and execution of sentences); (3) courts of specific competence (civil, criminal and mixed jurisdictions; civil courts and criminal; civil small instance courts and criminal small instance courts).[3]

This structure is on the verge of change, however, with the implementation of reforms of the judicial map.[4]

---

[2] Articles 209 and following.

[3] With specific reference to dealing with payment order procedures, see 1.4.

[4] Back in 2008, after a long debate and the publication of scientific studies (Santos and Gomes 2006), from August 28, Law no. 52/2008 brought forth significant changes to LOFTJ with the introduction of a new judicial map. This not-so-silent revolution entered into force on 14 April 2009, in three jurisdictions: Alentejo Litoral, Grande Lisboa Noroeste and Baixo Vouga. A deep reform places the emphasis on specialisation of all sorts, introducing a brand new territorial matrix, a new model of competences (specialised courts and divisions in all territory, not only in urban centres) and a new model of court management (administrative tasks traditionally belonging to the judge president of each court are now distributed by court administrator and registrar, thus leaving judges free to exercise their technical legal competences). The new model is still being tested in the three jurisdictions, since the foreseen trial period of 2 years was extended. In 2010, it was determined that from 1 September 2010, the new model would be applied gradually until it filled the whole territory on 1 September 2014. The process entered on permanent hiatus until early 2012, however, when the new Ministry of Justice announced that reform of the judicial map would use a different matrix. On 22 November 2012, the Cabinet Council approved the draft law

6.2.2 *The First Steps: A Light Legal Background Intertwined with the Development of the First Applications (GPCível and H@bilus)*

The use of new technologies in judicial acts was first addressed back in 1995, with an amendment brought to the Code of Civil Procedure[5]:

> [t]he chapter on pleadings—one of the most marked by the erosion of time and the application of new technologies to forensic activity—deserved significant amendments, reformulating numerous solutions of the current Code, in order to prevent the maintenance of unnecessary or disproportionate formalisms, thus operating a real progress in simplifying and streamlining the causes.[6]

In the following year, a new amendment was introduced to 'allow the use of electronics for the treatment and completion of any act or pleading, as long as rules concerning protection of personal data are respected and their use is mentioned'.[7]

Nonetheless, it was only in 1999 that the Act on the organisation and functioning of judicial courts (LOFTJ)[8] was amended with an article on the use of information technology, stating that, 'Information technology will be used to treat data related to judicial courts management and procedure, in accordance to constitutional and legal provisions in force'.[9]

After this, the legal provision of the use of information technologies in judicial courts came step by step. The following year, the possibility of lawyers presenting pleadings in digital form and using certified email addresses for their delivery was added. Presentation of pleadings by email[10] and the compulsory presentation of pleadings, appeal allegations and counter-allegations in digital format, in addition to paper copy,[11] were specifically foreseen.[12]

This legal framework[13] was revoked soon after and replaced (in 2003)[14] by one that foresaw, 'in a more realistic fashion' (Lameiras 2008, 119) that

---

that comprised the reform of the judicial map. The new judicial map has been approved by Law n.° 62/2013, August 26. However, it is waiting for its regulamentation to come into force. The major purposes of specialisation are maintained, but with a strong focus on concentration and centralisation of services and courts.

[5]Decree-Law no. 329-A/95, from December 12.

[6]Preamble.

[7]Article 138, no. 5, from the Decree-Law no. 180/96, from September 25.

[8]Law no. 3/99, from January 13.

[9]Article 132.

[10]Amended Article 143, no. 4, from the Code of Civil Procedure.

[11]Amended Article 150, no. 1, from the Code of Civil Procedure.

[12]More detailed regulation was introduced by Ordinance no. 1178-E/2000, from 15 December, and afterwards Ordinance no. 8-A/2001, from January 3.

[13]Decree-Law no. 183/2000, from August 10.

[14]Decree-Law no. 324/2003, from December 27. Came to amend the code of civil procedure. It ruled on the presentation of pleadings by email (amended Articles 260–A, 254, and 229-A, from the Code of Civil Procedure), and the form of pleadings presented to the court (amended Articles 150 and 152, from the Code of Civil Procedure).

dematerialisation could not be compulsory at such a stage; its rules (concerning presentation of pleadings by email and the form of these pleadings presented to the court) took a step back and were accepted as 'possibilities', rather than 'realities' (Lameiras 2008, 119), as the legislator had too hastily advanced 3 years before. The use of email for the presentation of pleadings and for writs of notice was introduced the following year.[15]

Practice had been running ahead underneath these somewhat slow legal developments, however. In fact, the implementation of ICT owes more to common practice than to written law, and specifically to the action of court clerks and registrars, within the authority of the Ministry of Justice. In the meantime, it was the administrative and fiscal jurisdiction that took decisive steps towards the accomplished use of information techniques, aiming at implementing a fully electronic procedure.[16]

Back in 1999, when no relevant legal developments on this matter were to be expected any time soon, a group of court clerks and registrars started a project called GPCível (from *Gestão Processual Cível*, or Civil Procedural Management). This was the first attempt to use information technology for case management and the direct ancestor of electronic procedure and dematerialisation processes in Portugal. The GPCível Project was sponsored and flourished within DGAJ, resulting in the birth of the application named H@bilus. This new case management tool was used in registries of both civil and criminal competence courts. Using the technology available at the time, each court worked on its own, much like an island, because the application was client–server, supported by modems and telephone lines.

Working ahead of legal developments, H@bilus was applied to a growing number of courts, under the aegis of DGAJ, until it covered all civil and criminal courts in 2005. By then, technology had evolved immensely and modems had been replaced by local servers. Nonetheless, each court was isolated because there was no network.

6.2.3 *Major Step Forward: The Arrival of Citius*

The ancestor of the dematerialisation of proceedings was H@bilus, when court clerks became able to make writs of notice directly in the platform, but a concrete procedural dematerialisation only became real with Citius, which finally allowed the actual electronic lodging of a proceeding.

A larger legislative step was finally taken in the year 2006. Mirroring the outline drafted in the law on the organisation and functioning of judicial courts, a norm

---

[15]By Ordinance no. 337-A/2004, from March 31, followed and revoked by Ordinance no. 642/2004, from June 16.

[16]Decree-Law no. 325/2003, from December 29, introduced electronic procedure in administrative and fiscal courts (see Article 4). It was later regulated by Ordinance no. 1417/2003, from December 30, concerning the brand new Sitaf, an electronic system adapted to administrative proceedings. It was this Article 4, from Decree-Law no. 325/2003 (more precisely, its no. 1), that inspired said Article 138-A, as we will see below.

specifically concerning electronic procedure was finally added to the Code of Civil Procedure in 2006[17]: 'Procedure takes place electronically in the terms defined by ordinance from the member of the government responsible for the area of justice; procedural rules concerning acts from judges, public prosecutors and judicial offices shall be adapted when necessary.'[18]

Citius was announced the following year by means of a brand new law,[19] with the legislator now offering a platform that could host electronic pleadings of judges and public prosecutors. The project, named Citius—meaning 'faster' in Latin—was specifically developed by the Ministry of Justice (DGAJ) with the same team of registrars and court clerks (currently inserted in ITIJ) that created and developed H@bilus. As said before, this new system is a further development of H@bilus, aiming at procedural dematerialisation by treating electronically all information belonging to proceedings, thus reducing their physical form to a minimum.

A year later, the Code of Civil Procedure was amended,[20] [21] dictating that 'electronic procedure guarantees its own integrity, authenticity and inviolability'. In the meantime, the formulation of the law on the organisation and functioning of judicial courts (LOFTJ) was maintained throughout various amendments, to be completed nearly 10 years later[22]: it was only after these specifications within the Code of Civil Procedure that the law on the organisation and functioning of judicial courts was adapted with regard to electronic procedure.[23]

In fact, the legal implementation of the *desiderata* present in Law no. 14/2006 came only 2 years later: in order to fill the legislative gap, the Ministry of Justice[24]

---

[17]Law no. 14/2006, from April 26.

[18]Article no. 138-A.

[19]Complementing the regime of Law no. 14/2006, ground-breaking Ordinance no. 593/2007, from May 14, introduced the Citius platform.

[20]Decree-Law no. 303/2007, from August 24, added Section no. 2 to Article 138-A, from the Code of Civil Procedure.

[21]This norm's entry into force was then subjected to the publication of the foreseen Ordinance from the Ministry of Justice, as specifically ruled in Section no. 2 from Article 11, of Decree-Law no. 303/2007. The Decree-Law was subjected to Rectification no. 99/2007, from October 23, which did not bring any alteration to these specific norms. Therefore its transitory norms (Article 8, especially no. 1) kept alive, when needed, the dispositions altered or revoked until the publication of that ordinance.

[22]Law no. 52/2008, from August 28.

[23]A brand new Article 159 came to replace former Article 132, thus complementing its broad formulation. It reads as follows: '1—Information technology is used for the treatment of data related to judicial courts management, procedure and archive. 2—Procedure takes place electronically in the terms defined by ordinance from the member of the government responsible for the area of justice; procedural rules concerning acts from judges, public prosecutors and judicial offices shall be adapted when necessary. 3—Said ordinance shall regulate, among other issues: (a) presentation of pleadings and documents; (b) file assignment; (c) electronic pleading by judges, public prosecutors and court officials; (d) acts, pleadings, minutes and procedural terms that may not exist in paper.'

[24]Ministerial Ordinance no. 114/2008, from February 6, from the Ministry of Justice.

introduced the regulation of several aspects of electronic procedure in first instance courts, by means of the new system, Citius.[25] This Ordinance no. 114/2008 came to regulate several matters[26]: the presentation of pleadings, compulsory copies, publicity of the procedure, electronic case assignment, publication of said electronic case assignment, electronic writs of notice and proof of court fees payment.

As such, the regulation of the Citius system in terms of technology and operability is extremely light, as these norms focus on the work of the registry, i.e., mostly procedural terms. Still, further legal production came to conform to the regime, such as amendments to the legal regime of court fees,[27] which became another decisive step. Indeed, at first, the legal regime of court fees foresaw important incentives to lawyers who chose to use only electronic means of communication with courts. Afterwards, the dematerialised lodging of pleadings became compulsory for lawyers and solicitors.[28] Finally, new legislation concerning the transmission and protection of judicial data[29] was introduced in 2009 and came to offer the needed data protection framework; it also presented new key entities and re-defined the competences of others.

In 2009, an audit to the Citius system was commissioned by the ITIJ, carried out by a private national company, Critical Software. After this audit, Citius was subjected to a redesign, conducted by the team of Critical Software together with the DGAJ-ITIJ team. The project's name was Citius Plus. Its main objectives were to correct security issues pointed out in the audit and to evolve the technology, from VB6 to VisualBasic.NET. This process also enabled the documentation of the application and, indirectly, also made knowledge less restricted because there were, finally, written documents that could be passed on to new members of the team. Some problems could not be solved, though, as they were of a structural nature, depending on the very architecture of H@bilus.

Ministerial Order no. 11388/2010, from the Minister of Justice, legally introduced Citius Plus and stated its objectives: (1) reformulation of the technological infrastructure of the Citius platform, ensuring an efficient response to requests from various types of users, both in its ability to evolve and in supporting legal changes; (2) adequate levels of quality, control and security in access to procedural information and the guarantee of audits to ensure their access and actions; (3) homogenisation of environments and technological solutions, in order to pursue synergies in the use of the platform; (4) introduction of practices, tools and procedures that will allow the support of development activities and to increase service levels and quality management in a subsequent evolution of the platform;

[25] It has subsequently been altered by Ordinances no. 457/2008, from June 20; no. 1538/2008, from December 30; no. 195-A/2010, from April 8; and no. 471/2010, from July 8.

[26] In the sequence of what had been earlier stipulated in Article 11, no. 2, of Decree-Law no. 303/2007.

[27] Such as Decree-Law no. 34/2008, from February 26.

[28] Decree-Law no. 34/2008, from February 26, which entered into force on 5 January 2009.

[29] Law no. 34/2009, from July 14.

(5) raising the level of knowledge about the system, through the description of its core functionalities and its behaviour, and the specification of tests that should serve to support the validation and acceptance of any evolutionary solutions.

Citius Plus is currently in use in two courts after a period of pre-tests conducted with a limited number of judges in simulated proceedings. The two courts are the Court of Appeal of Coimbra—providing a second-instance experience—and the District Court of Figueira da Foz, a coastal town near Coimbra that has a workload considered to be average and therefore appropriate for a first-instance try-out. The migration of the code, from VB6 to Visual Basic.NET, was in the charge of Critical Software. The changes are solely related to software; the functionalities remain the same, with virtually no visible changes to the user accustomed to Citius.

As for future evolutions of Citius beyond Citius Plus, some constraints were highlighted during fieldwork. In short: a limited team working at ITIJ; a still working obsolete technology (VB6); and stumbling blocks in terms of decision-making capacity to alter and improve the system. The e-Justice program, like other judicial reforms, is highly dependent on political choices. In this context, the development of the program tends to run in contradictory directions whenever there is a change in political strategy.

6.2.4 Use of ICT in the Payment Order Procedure

Traditionally, dealing with small claims has been interwoven with the use of information technology in courts. Thus, the payment order procedure is undoubtedly a landmark both for the use of ICT in courts and for dealing with small civil claims in a simplified way. This ground-breaking law[30] specifically deals with small claims and payment order procedures for debts originated by contracts. The main target upon its publication was to speed up small claims litigation, where proof is simple and document based and statements of objection rare. To this end, its regime gathered up previous legislative initiatives concerning both small civil claims procedures and payment order procedures, now further developed with the use of ICT, especially for the latter.

The payment order procedure was introduced back in 1993[31] as a quick and swift way of recovering debts, most of them unchallenged. It consists of a

[30] It has subsequently been amended/republished by a series of regulations: Rectification no. 16-A/98, from September 30; Decree-Law no. 383/99, from September 23; Decree-Law no. 183/2000, from August 10; Decree-Law no. 323/2001, from December 17; Decree-Law no. 32/2003, from February 17; Decree-Law no. 38/2003, from March 8; Decree-Law no. 324/2003, from December 27; Rectification no. 26/2004, from February 24; Decree-Law no. 107/2005, from July 1; Rectification no. 63/2005, from August 19; Law no. 14/2006, from April 26; Decree-Law no. 303/2007, from August 24; Law no. 67-A/2007, from December 31; Decree-Law no. 34/2008, from February 26; and Decree-Law no. 226/2008, from November 20.

[31] By means of Decree-Law no. 404/93, from December 10.

simplified pre-judicial procedure that allows for a swift enforceable title without the intervention of a jurisdictional organ (in the case of unchallenged claims). It is a specific mechanism for the collection of debts arising from unpaid bills. Its *iter processualis* is extremely simplified: (1) by filling in a form and paying a court fee (initially, a court fee stamp), the creditor requires the notification of the debtor to pay, under penalty of said payment order becoming an enforceable title; (2) the debtor may present a defence, by means of a statement of objection. In the case of unchallenged claims, there is no intervention of jurisdictional organs; otherwise (or when it is impossible to notify the debtor), the proceeding is presented to a judge; (3) after the writ of notice takes place, if the debtor does not pay the debt or does not present a statement of objection in due time, the payment order procedure form becomes enforceable, acquiring the nature of an enforceable title with the intervention of the court registrar; (4) if the debtor presents a statement of objection, a trial takes place in 30 days, and the final ruling from the judge becomes enforceable.

In terms of jurisdiction value, this procedure started off with a maximum of €1,870.49, raised to €3,740.98 in 1998[32] and to €14,963.94 in 2005.[33] In 2007, the jurisdiction limit value was rounded up to €15,000. A big breakthrough came in 2003, with the Decree-Law[34] that transposed Directive 2000/35/Ec of the European Parliament and of the Council on combating late payment in commercial transactions. According to this Directive, debts from commercial transactions[35] could be claimed by means of a payment order procedure regardless of its value.

Common civil procedure did not experience relevant changes with the arrival and implementation of ICT. The use of ICT in payment order procedures walked side by side with the development of the legal framework, as well as with organisational reforms. The latest legal (*rectius*, procedural) amendments to the payments order procedure regime are tightly interwoven with the development of electronic tools and the creation of a sole forum (BNI) with a specific Citius application to deal with the procedure. In fact, the application's development team was deeply involved in the procedural novelties, thus truly adapting one to the other. The evolution of the competent fora to present the payment order procedure's forms and of the ways of presenting them are intertwined (Fig. 6.1).

Until 1999, the payment order procedure's form was to be presented, in paper format, at the district courts or, more accurately, at their registries, according to the rules on territorial competence. The creditor could choose to present the payment order procedure in the registry of the court from (1) the place of performance of the

---

[32] Decree-Law no. 269/98.

[33] Decree-Law no. 197/2005.

[34] Decree-Law no. 32/2003, from February 17.

[35] Defined as "transactions between undertakings or between undertakings and public authorities which lead to the delivery of goods or the provision of services for remuneration"—article 2, of the Directive.

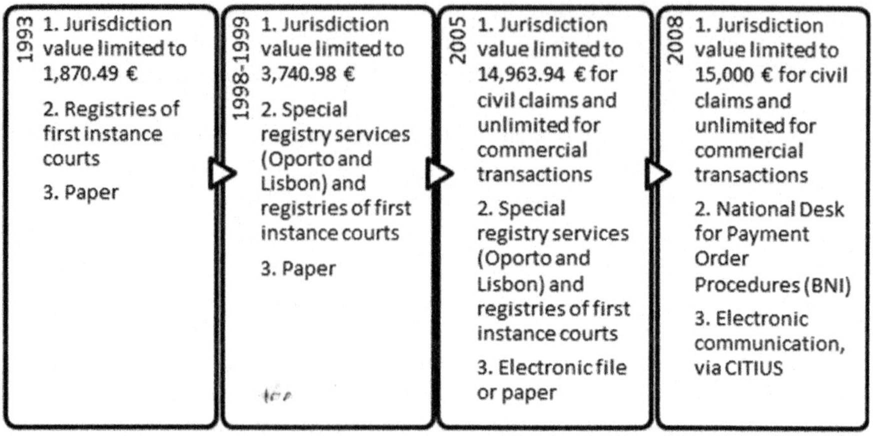

Fig. 6.1 Overlapping reforms in the payment order procedure: legal framework, organisational framework and use of ICT

underlying obligation or (2) the place of the debtor's address. That is, all district courts received the payment order procedure's form.

In 1999, the Ministry of Justice created special registry services with exclusive jurisdiction for payment order procedures in Lisbon and Oporto, for their respective territorial jurisdiction.[36] At first, the form could only be personally presented in paper or sent by fax or regular mail in that format at the competent registries referred above.[37] Later on,[38] it also became presentable in electronic form (CD, CD-ROM, floppy disk, pen-drive) at the same registries.

Almost a decade later, a general registry was installed,[39] with national jurisdiction over payment order procedures,[40] called the National Desk for Payment Order Procedures (the *Balcão Nacional de Injunções*, or BNI), located in Oporto. Oporto and Lisbon registries worked until the 31 May 2008.[41] BNI is today the general registry with exclusive national jurisdiction for this electronic procedure. In 2008,[42] electronic delivery via Citius became compulsory for lawyers and solicitors. However, the form can be delivered in person or by regular mail in paper from when

[36] Ordinance no. 433/99, from June 16.

[37] The registry of the court from the place where the underlying obligation should have taken place, or the place of the debtor's address, in accordance with Decree-Law no. 269/98 (Article 8 of the Annex).

[38] By means of Article 1, of Ordinance no. 809/2005, from September 9.

[39] Ordinance no. 433/99was later amended (overruled, rather) by Ordinance no. 220-A/2008, from March 4 (in compliance with Article 8, no. 4, of the Annex of Decree-Law no. 169/98).

[40] See Article 3.

[41] See Article 4.

[42] By means of Decree-Law no. 34/2008, from February 26, which amended Article 19, no. 1, of the Annex of Decree-Law no. 269/98.

the creditor is not represented by a lawyer or solicitor. Thus, BNI only receives forms electronically—it receives directly those that are sent over the Internet, by lawyers or solicitors, and indirectly those that are delivered in paper from, since the information on those forms is introduced into the computer application when it is received.

The BNI is always the competent forum for the procedure. Thus, all information on the *iter processualis* became accessible online, through the Citius platform, in a way such that the enforceable title within may also be created and used electronically if needed. Still, whenever the creditor presents a statement of objection, the proceeding is presented to a judge and acquires judicial status, following the rules of the small civil claims procedure[43]; in such cases, the court territorially competent may be one of the two previously addressed.

As mentioned before, Citius comprises several applications, databases and services that communicate with one another: computer applications for public prosecutors, judges and court staff, as well as for lawyers and solicitors, complement each other in order to achieve full electronic pleading. For the payment order procedure, a special application has been created that has allowed the lodging of a small claim procedure request, payment of court fees and electronic procedure for that specific registry (BNI) since 2008: the BNI platform or the Citius-Payment Order Procedure.

Specifically, the application was developed by a team made of court clerks and registrars within the DGPJ-ITIJ in order to (1) lodge the request electronically through the Internet, at the website http://citius.tribunaisnet.mj.pt, by form or computer file; (2) pay court fees electronically by ATM or home banking; (3) provide full electronic procedure of the payment order by BNI; (4) remit the payment order to the competent court electronically if a statement of objection is lodged by the debtor; (5) send warnings by email to the creditor in order to fully accompany the procedure; and (6) create an enforceable title that makes it possible to start an enforcement procedure.

The electronic application working at this registry is in VBNet format. The development team, formed by court clerks, was also different from the H@bilus one, though under the wing of DGAJ and afterwards ITIJ. It is different from Citius-H@bilus, even though both interact. It has a centralised server, a specific application for writs of notice and deals exclusively with the electronic procedure. Citius-Payment Order Procedure connects to Citius-Web to allow lawyers to lodge payment order procedures and to give them access to virtual proceedings. It also connects with Citius-H@bilus when a statement of objection is lodged and when it transits to an enforcement procedure. Connection also takes place with other entities and services, as seen in the following section.

---

[43] Also ruled by Decree-Law no. 269/98.

6.3 Current Functioning of the System

6.3.1 The Configuration of the System: A Broad Picture

The project named Citius aims at a dematerialisation of proceedings by treating electronically all information belonging to the proceedings, thus reducing their physical form to a minimum. It is therefore composed of several applications, databases and services that communicate with each other[44] The Citius-Payment Order Procedure is one of the Citius applications, that is to say, it is just a piece of the puzzle (Fig. 6.2).

H@bilus is a component of the Citius system used by court clerks and registrars in courts to manage the acts of registries, such as reception and distribution of pleadings, file management, registration and archiving. It has a two-level architecture and is therefore composed of two essential parts: (1) a client application, which implements the functional requirements and all the functionalities required to the presentation of contents and functionalities; and (2) a management system database (SGBD)[45] that implements the support for the functionalities of creation, reading, updating and data removal in a relational and structured way. In this architecture, the H@bilus applications (one for each workspace) connect to an SGBD at the

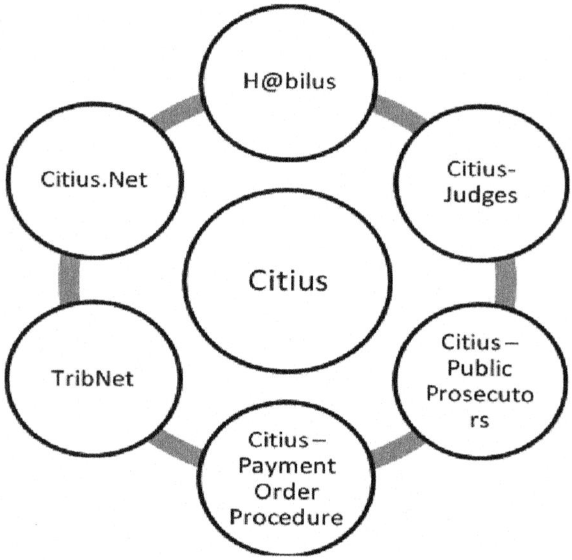

Fig. 6.2 Citius–payment order procedure: a piece of the puzzle

[44]This section is based on data collected and provided by Critical Software during the commissioned audit of the Citius system (Critical Software 2009, 2010). We therefore follow their final report closely. For further technical detail, see Critical Software (2009: Sect. 5).

[45]From the Portuguese: *sistema de gestão de base de dados*.

court (implemented in MS SQL Server 2005) to perform SQL queries in a database. The connection of H@bilus to the SGBD occurs by remote web authentication. In this kind of architecture, the business application is installed at the specific user's workplace, although there may be administrator restrictions. Sensitive information circulates in the network connecting the workplace and the respective database servers (Critical Software 2009, 2010).

Citius-Judges and Citius-Public Prosecution, as their names suggest, are the two versions of H@bilus used by judges and by public prosecutors, respectively. More specifically, Citius-Judges is a work tool intended to reduce bureaucracy and provide better management tools for judicial courts. With said purposes in mind, this application was specifically created to enable judges to (1) make sentences, court orders and other judicial decisions directly in the application; (2) sign sentences, court orders and other judicial decisions with electronic signatures, by means of a card (smartcard) associated with a PIN code, with no need to sign said decisions in the paper proceedings; (3) receive and send proceedings electronically to the registry, with no circulation of the paper proceedings; and (4) immediately know all procedures assigned to them and their stage in the process (Ministry of Justice 2009a). Similarly, Citius-Public Prosecution is adapted to the activities of their officers, thus allowing them to (1) make and sign court orders, with no need to print them; (2) receive and send proceedings electronically to the registry, with no circulation of the paper proceedings; (3) organise and manage the titular officer's own proceedings; (4) connect electronically between the public prosecution, police forces and courts; and (5) conduct national inquiries concerning defendants electronically (Ministry of Justice 2009b).

Citius-Judges and Citius-Public Prosecution became operational in July 2007, but their use only became compulsory from 5 January 2009. To prepare for these ground-breaking changes in the judicial actors' activity, laptops and digital certificates were assigned to judges and public prosecutors throughout 2008, and DGPJ gave intensive training courses to them all. These courses were decentralised (i.e., across the territory, rather than just in Lisbon) and a team of 112 instructors was assembled, with DGPJ hiring 80 extra staff members to fulfill the task.

Citius.Net (lodging of pleadings and documents) is a web application that allows legal representatives such as lawyers and solicitors to lodge their pleadings and to keep track of the progress of the procedures they are related to. This system makes the use of pleadings in paper obsolete, 'which is seen as a great breakthrough in reducing bureaucracy in the connection between legal representative and court' (Critical Software 2009, 25). Furthermore, common citizens may use the application to access public information concerning the justice system, namely, publicity of sales and bankruptcies. This work tool specifically allows its users (lawyers and solicitors) to use the Internet to (1) lodge pleadings and other documents; (2) know the results of the distribution; (3) consult proceedings and related court hearings; and (4) follow the status of their due payments within legal aid action.

TribNet, also called Citius-Public Access, is an application that provides information about compulsory publication to the general public by means of direct access to the central databases of the Citius system or to local court databases.

The information at stake specifically concerns issues such as public lists of case assignment, publicity concerning sales and publicity concerning insolvency, public court sessions, edictal writ of summons or addresses and contacts of courts.

As well as these applications allowing direct interaction between different types of user, the Citius system also enables communication with other information systems from external entities. For instance, links with entities such as the Central Department of Investigation and Criminal Action (DCIAP), the BNI, the Directorate-General for Social Reinsertion (DGRS) or police forces enables Citius to both request and receive information in a quick and integrated way from other information systems (Critical Software 2009, 26). The communication with external users is effected through the following functionalities: (1) direct connection to Web Services made available by other agencies (such as the Chamber of Solicitors); (2) connection to Web Services made available by other agencies through a central gateway of Web Services (such as the Bar Association); (3) connection to central Web Services (such as civil registries data bases); (4) direct connection to the central server (by SQL).

On the other hand, external users have three main options to access Citius (1): through a internet based web service dealing with bankruptcy cases; (2) through a database (GatewayCS) lodged in the central SGBD accessible by the Chamber of solicitors; (3) through a Web Service to which the criminal police can have access in order to lodge official reports. When the access is through a Web Service, the aforementioned service access the central SGBD to read and write the needed information (Critical Software 2009).

H@bilus, Citius-Judges and Citius-Public Prosecution use VB6, an outdated technology (since discontinued by Microsoft), whereas Citius.Net and TribNet are developed in .NET. H@bilus, Citius-Judges and Citius-Public Prosecution function at a local level, with a local server, in all courts of the civil jurisdiction. These servers are then connected via the web. Unlike the others, Citius.Net is not local in structure, having a central database. Thanks to the law on the protection of data,[46] a legal background to create a central database was available, to accompany the headline for each proceeding. This headline contains the basic data of the proceeding, such as court, serial number and name of the pleading parties. The complete proceeding is lodged at the local server of each court, which the lawyer accesses through Citius-Web, which then connects the user to the local court server. The central database is currently lodged—physically—at ITIJ. As for the local databases of each court, they are usually physically lodged at the building of the respective court. However, since some were not in the best environmental conditions, a few are currently physically lodged at ITIJ but retaining their autonomy and work logic (server-client), still 'belonging' to the court itself. There are plans for the complete centralisation of the hardware at ITIJ, while retaining each database's local control and autonomy.

Unlike H@bilus, Citius.Net and TribNet thus have a three-level architecture, which raises their security levels with regard to access to information. In order to

[46]Law no. 34/2009.

send pleadings (with 3 MB or less) and to access information about the proceedings through the internet, (1) lawyers or solicitors access Citius.Net which in this specific context works as an application server. Citius.Net makes available the routines necessary to send and to access pleadings. (2) Citius.Net then, connects directly to the central SGBD to save/store sent pleadings, or connects to the court's SGBD for direct access and consultation. (3) Pleadings submitted through Citius.Net are saved in the central server, and afterwards are delivered to the court of destination. (4) Common citizens may also use the application TribNet (also working as an application server) to access public information concerning the justice system (e.g. public sales and bankruptcies). In this case, when the citizens access the application, a connection to the SGBD is established to retrieve the relevant information (Critical Software 2009, 2010).

Nonetheless, both applications still have a couple of disadvantages, according to the results of the 2009 audit performed by Critical Software: (1) both Citius.Net and TribNet are exposed to the Internet and access the central SGBD for various actions, which implies that when application is compromised, such as an attack by SQL injection, the central server itself is also immediately compromised, thus causing a generalised fail of Citius functionalities; (2) Citius.Net directly accesses the courts' SGBD to download files, which implies that if the application is compromised, the local SGBD at the court may also be compromised, which may spread to the whole court.

6.3.2 *How to File a Payment Order Procedure*

The payment order procedure was conceived as a specific mechanism for the collection of debts arising from unpaid bills. It consists of a simplified pre-judicial procedure that allows for a swift enforceable title without the intervention of a jurisdictional organ (in the case of unchallenged claims).

As mentioned before, the payment order procedure is limited to money claims up to €15,000 for non-commercial transactions and has no value limitation for debts from commercial transactions.[47] A payment order can only be filled out in paper form when the creditor is not represented by a lawyer or solicitor. When the creditor is represented by a lawyer or solicitor, it is compulsory to deliver it electronically, via Citius.

Citius is thus only accessible to legal professionals. Lawyers can access Citius through a web portal (http://citius.tribunaisnet.mj.pt), using their user ID (professional email address) and password, and lodge the request electronically through the Internet, at the website, via form or computer file. User recognition is achieved

---

[47] Defined as 'transactions between undertakings or between undertakings and public authorities which lead to the delivery of goods or the provision of services for remuneration' (Article 2 of the Directive).

via digital certification, using PKI (Public Key Infrastructure), granting lawyers the necessary digital signature that enables access to the Citius-H@bilus platform.

The user can file a single claim for an unlimited number of unpaid bills and can also file a single claim against more than one debtor. The user must indicate the name, address and fiscal number of the debtor, the type and reference of the unpaid bills that justify the request, the date of issuance, the maturity and the amount in debt, stating also the amount of interest due and the competent court in case of statement of objection by the debtor. The amount of interest can be automatically calculated on the electronic form. In this phase and as long as the debtor does not present a defence, by means of a statement of objection, the user does not submit any documents supporting the claim.

With the delivery of the electronic form, the platform generates a unique identifying number, which allows for electronic payment of court fees by ATM or home banking. The court fees are substantially lower than in traditional procedural cases.

By filling in this electronic form, the creditor requests BNI to notify the debtor to pay, under penalty of said payment order becoming an enforceable title.

The procedure of the payment order by the BNI is fully electronic. Only the writ of notice to the debtor is sent by regular post. The notifications for lawyers are issued by email, but also by regular post. If no objection is stated by the debtor, i.e., in the case of unchallenged claims, an enforceable title that makes it possible to start an enforcement procedure is created, with absolutely no intervention by a judge.

If a statement of objection is lodged by the debtor or if it is not possible to notify the debtor, the proceeding must be presented to a judge and there is an electronic remittance of the payment order to the competent court. The statement of objection can be delivered by paper, email or via Citius. Nonetheless, the statement of objection can only be lodged via Citius if the debtor is represented by a lawyer, because the platform is only accessible to legal professionals.

Once the electronic remittance of the payment order to the competent court occurs, a new judicial case is created. Until the 1st of September 2013, after the statement of objection, lawyers were no longer obliged to communicate with the court electronically. If they choose to do so, they would benefit from a reduction in court fees. With the reform of the civil procedure, by means of Law 41/2013, from June 26, that came into force in September 1, lawyers are now obliged to communicate with the court electronically in all civil proceedings. Thus, if both parties to the case (debtor and creditor) are represented by lawyers the procedure, after the statement of objection, remain fully electronic.

6.3.3 Impact of Citius on Users: Roles and Satisfaction

The implementation of an electronic procedure brought significant changes to the daily practice of all judicial actors, as is patent in the everyday life of a court of law, after an initial period of adaptation. Both positive and negative aspects of Citius were more extreme as the habituation process was taking place.

With regard to the courts of law (in this case meaning judges and public prosecutors), the use of Citius became compulsory after a trial run of around 1 year, when intensive training courses were offered to those officers. The court clerks had the advantage of an application exclusively designed for their activity, providing them with an array of example-forms for the various acts to be undertaken, as well as an area for continuous training and problem-solving (H@bilândia).

Several positive aspects were immediately highlighted by users, of which the most unanimous were (1) simplified control of pending procedures waiting a decision and timely action on procedural acts by the registry; (2) simplification of the work at the registry; and (3) simplification of access to procedural acts by lawyers (GAIT/ASJP 2009). The broad scope of Citius was also pointed out by a CEPEJ report, which considered that 'these impressive efforts and the vision towards dematerialisation of justice by authorities have conducted Portugal to a very high level in the use of ICT, which places the State in the top rank of the European countries' (CEPEJ 2009).

As major pitfalls, security issues and work-form adaptations were the highest source of concerns back in 2009. The Judges' Association denounced the fact that, 6 months after Citius-Judges became compulsory, several judges reported health problems (posture, vision) directly connected with the systematic use of Citius (which meant using the computer almost all the time), and 79 % of consulted judges considered that there was an increase (up to 114 % in some cases) in the time spent on daily tasks. This increase was mostly due to inadequate equipment, slow actions (due to excess traffic) or the more prosaic multiplication of actions to fulfil a task that would otherwise be simple, such as an electronic signature, for which five different actions are required, instead of a simple handmade gesture (ASJP 2009).

In terms of security,[48] 60 % of the judges consulted by their trade union association back in 2009 did not trust Citius in terms of liability and security (ASJP 2009). However, the High Judicial Council (Communication no. 2/2009) and the Public Prosecution Office (Communication from 2 March, 2009) considered the system to be 'safe enough', both entities having cooperated with the Ministry of Justice and having been provided with guarantees deemed as sufficient; and the Bar Association officially declared that '[the Bar itself] guarantees the safety of the system, ensuring it is not possible to alter pleadings by anyone without said changes being thoroughly registered' (OA 2009, 12).

In spite of common worries about security still existing among users, it appears that the responsible entities still officially have faith in the system; minor breach reports conveyed by professional associations and media, and a bluntly negative audit in terms of security (Critical Software 2009, 2010) are overlooked as light and unavoidable in all systems. Security tends to be a lesser cause for concern among professionals, especially because Citius is mainly used for civil procedures and these kind of proceedings are, almost always, public in nature.

[48] For technical detail on the subject of security, see Sect. 6.4.

A few of the current conception problems that affect users' daily practice have persisted since Citius's introduction in 2009, such as (1) difficulties in consulting the dematerialised proceeding (i.e., opening several pdf documents is considered by some to be more complicated than browsing a single paper file); (2) the impossibility of consulting a proceeding during trial audiences; (3) the impossibility of working in Citius outside of court premises (i.e., taking work home to deal with more complex cases requiring additional time is not possible); (4) a basic word processor (that does not allow complex formatting, footnotes, grammar or spell checking, among other flaws); and (5) delays in technical support.[49]

On a more technical level, it was also noticed that the Citius applications were not fully communicating with one another, creating several difficulties in everyday practice, such as (1) feeble import–export of data (in terms of court fees, for instance); (2) failure to inform the judge/public prosecutor whether his/her order is actually enacted by the registry; (3) failure to inform the judge/public prosecutor when the proceeding was last accessed and altered; (4) inability of the judge/public prosecutor to qualify his/her own pleading or judicial order, so that the qualification by the court clerk may be incorrect; if this possibility existed in the Citius application, the court clerk would be freed from this task and the possibility of flawed classification would be eliminated.[50]

Changes in daily tasks undergone by the different actors can be classified as (1) automation—tasks that no longer require human intervention; (2) process reshaping—procedural flow from the tasks operated by different actors is altered by new functionalities of the system; and (3) redistribution of competences and intervention—task distribution altered by new functionalities of the system.

As evaluated in a mid-2009 diagnosis process (requested by the DGPJ of a private consultant), Citius had a high impact in terms of redistribution of competences with regard to the filing of the case and the subsequent exchange of pleadings (excluding trial); a similar degree of changes was observed in terms of automation and process reshaping for the same procedural moments. The trial phase was one where Citius had the lowest impact, mostly because it does not involve many written documents; nonetheless, light changes in terms of automation and process reshaping were still detected (KPMG 2009).

In terms of timesaving characteristics, this evaluation detected a net gain of up to 19 days per procedure. Most time was saved between phases and tasks, by reducing waiting time while one task is completed and the following started; in terms of beneficiaries, the majority of time gain was to the benefit of court clerks, while both pleading parties and judges experienced added time for most of their tasks (KPMG 2009).[51] This evaluation accords with the dissatisfaction with time-consuming tasks

---

[49] For further detail, see published stances and evaluation reports such as ASJP (2009), OA (2009), Vidal et al. (2009), Pereira (2010), Marçal (2011).

[50] For further detail, see, for instance, Marçal (2011) and Vidal et al. (2009).

[51] For further detail, see KPMG (2009).

expressed by judges, as reported above, and shows how the system was actually developed with the work of the registry as a matrix.

Applications were indeed designed *by* and *for* court clerks and registrars. Consequently, this design makes Citius-Judges and Citius-Public Prosecution less adapted to these professionals' activities. During fieldwork, the dissatisfaction of some actors was noted, which suggests that the applications, being based on H@bilus, are still more appropriate to the work of the registry than to the work of the judge and the public prosecutor. Nonetheless, some functionalities have been adapted to the judges and public prosecutors' activities more recently, in accordance with a series of requests and suggestions collected by the Ministry of Justice.

Since the implementation of Citius, practice in some registries has exhibited an evolution towards specialisation, benefiting both from the use of ICT in an increasingly dematerialised process and the surrounding climate of change. Court clerks from a registry observed during fieldwork divided tasks among them so that one individual or a small group would deal specifically with one, or a few, similar activities, thereby specialising in specific tasks. In this registry, teams specialised in specific activities (e.g., writs of summons and writs of notice, trials, etc.) operating according to a strict protocol of sequential actions. The end final result is a more efficient registry, resembling an assembly line of administrative and procedural acts that comprise a judicial proceeding. Nonetheless, said changes are not widespread. Furthermore, they are not grounded in legal norms: these registries do not just walk ahead of others, they run ahead of written law, thus making their practice de facto admirable but in practice not legally grounded.

All acts are made within the digital proceeding lodged in the Citius platform. In principle, both proceedings—digital and conventional/paper-based—are equal, one and the same: (electronic) pleadings and other procedural documents are printed; authentic documentation added as proof is scanned. Still, some minor administrative acts (such as re-scheduling) are considered by various actors to be unnecessary in paper form, thus making the digital version more complete. This practice, unveiled during fieldwork, is not homogenous, though.

The decision (to print or not to print) belongs to each judicial actor, although the Ministry of Justice (DGAJ-ITIJ) suggests that the following documents only exist in the digital proceeding: minor pleadings and other documentation related to work at the registry and similar doings, delivered by lawyers through the Citius platform; minor judicial orders related to work at the registry and similar doings, delivered by judges and public prosecutors; and acts of court clerks that do not require the signature of the parties, legal representatives or third persons. The aim is to reduce the paper documents used in proceedings, containing only the major pleadings and documents with odd formats/objects that cannot be digitalised, as well as the pleadings and documents considered to be most important for the judge's decision. A major aim is that the paper proceeding becomes easier to use, with coloured markers indicating the most important pleadings of the proceeding.

Another finding was that since some actors do not fully trust ICT, there is a practice—more common in the first years—of having everything in paper form 'just in case something happens', i.e., in an attempt to protect both the information within the proceeding and the solid proof of one's own actions and work.

Furthermore, since parties need a paper proceeding to consult, when not accompanied by a lawyer, total 'dematerialisation' looks like being a distant goal.

6.4 Concluding Remarks: Citius-Payment Order Procedure as a Simplified Application in a Complex System

The development of ICT in the Portuguese justice system constitutes an example of piecemeal development and cultivation of the installed base (Farrel and Saloner 1986; Contini and Cordella 2007; Hanseth and Lyytinen 2010; Lanzara 2009). The Citius project both benefited from and suffered the limitations of being a further development of H@bilus, an application used by court clerks and registrars in courts to manage the acts of registries. The cultivation of the installed base generated path-dependence in the later developments.

As major limitations, we can identify the following:

1. Technological limitations. The result of Citius being based on an outdated technology. Nonetheless, Citius Plus responded to this obstacle and could be expanded to all the courts of civil jurisdiction. A common platform for the judiciary, as foreseen by the Portuguese Action Plan for Justice in the Information Society, looks like a more realistic option for ICT systems in justice. Either way, in terms of institutional and normative frameworks, current legislation seems flexible enough to allow for change. It has been proven in the past that technological evolution does not actually need to be preceded by a heavy building of specific ruling institutions and laws. Norms describing how the system must operate are not detailed, which may also give latitude to further changes.
2. Lack of participation of the legal professions in the conception of the system. While H@bilus has not encountered visible resistance from court clerks and registrars, the same cannot be said about the Citius applications for judges and public prosecutors. The first were created and developed by the same professionals who were meant to use it, ensuring a great advantage in terms of both adequacy and accessibility. In terms of daily use, Citius-Judges and Citius-Public Prosecution appear to be less adapted to these professionals' activities than Citius-H@bilus. The different degree of participation of the various judicial actors in the building of ICT tools to the justice systems seems to play a significant role in the implementation of such tools by their users. Since the H@bilus was specifically addressed and conceived by court clerks, it was immediately acceptable to them. The lack of participation of judges and public prosecutors led to its rejection, at least initially. Lawyers, by contrast, were 'forced' to adapt to the new circumstances, mainly through the benefits in court fees.

3. Limited exchange of information on the technological functioning of the system. Citius was specifically developed by the Ministry of Justice with the same team of registrars and court clerks under the aegis of DGAJ, and currently inserted in ITIJ, that created and developed H@bilus. This resulted in an excessive reliance on a small team of experts to perform all the technological updates needed.

Nonetheless, the benefits brought by Citius, directly and indirectly, in terms of efficiency and effectiveness of judicial procedure appear to be indisputable.

The development of the payment order procedure shows how the design goal of functional simplification resulted in a solid system. The payment order procedure is an example of functional simplification (Carnevali 2009; Kallinikos 2009) within the Portuguese civil justice system at various levels. The 1990s saw the introduction of a non-jurisdictional process (so long as there was no opposition to a claim) and a reduced *iter processualis* providing an enforcement title on a short period of time; more recently, the installation of the BNI simplified the jurisdictional building of competences with clear benefits for all intervenients, thus providing for both centralisation and staff specialisation. Such an evolution was made possible by the flexibility of its legal framework, the last amendments of which have been made simultaneously and in direct connection with Citius-Payment Order Procedure and by the same development team. This integrated development process generated a set of procedural rules and a computer application that work as true symbionts, all made real in a tailored registry.

Thus, Citius-Payment Order Procedure benefited from the lessons learned in the construction of other Citius applications. Although there are a number of factors of simplicity present in Citius-Payment Order Procedure that are not present in the other applications (such as the use of updated technology, since it is conceived in VBNet format; the use of a central database; and the use of digital signature alone as a prerequisite to access the system), the most revealing difference one can identify is the integrated development process of the payment order procedure. In fact, what truly distinguishes Citius-Payment Order Procedure from the other Citius applications is that it has been designed as part of a more comprehensive project aiming at procedural simplification.

The other Citius applications have been designed to carry out a digital version of existing formal procedures on paper. That is, the major changes rely almost solely on the automation of some tasks. The development of Citius-Payment Order Procedure, by contrast, followed a different strategy, incorporating not only technological updates but also organisational and legal reforms. It is therefore an example of how the introduction of a technological component in an organisation generates the co-evolution and co-modification of organisational and technological systems (Migliarese and Corvello 2009). Citius-Payment Order Procedure has also proven that even a very simplified and digitalised proceeding requires paper, mainly when interaction with citizens is needed.

Nonetheless, Citius-Payment Order Procedure does not fulfil the purpose of broadening access to law and justice. Like the other Citius applications, Citius-Payment Order Procedure has been designed to work with legal professionals, thus excluding pro-se litigation. When a statement of objection is presented and the payment order procedure is remitted to a court, it embraces all the factors of complexity present in Citius-H@bilus: (1) outdated software (Visual Basic 6); (2) complexity in connection with other entities; (3) digital certification for lawyers, judges, public prosecutors and court clerks; and (4) more detailed and rigorous description of how technology must be used to meet the formal structure of the judicial system.

Moreover, although the design of Citius was intended to produce a tool for procedural management, the current version of the application does not allow its use for that purpose because it has been designed to reproduce pre-existing proceedings on paper and to accommodate the pre-existing organisational system. Consequently, it is unable to identify blockages in judicial proceedings.

References

ASJP. 2009. Primeiros Seis Meses de Utilização do Citius. Inquérito de Avaliação à Funcionalidade e Eficiência. Relatório Preliminar. http://72.29.69.19/~ejal/images/stories/arquivos/artigos/relatorio_preliminar_citius.pdf. Accessed 30 March 2012.

Boaventura de Sousa, Santos, and Conceição Gomes. 2006. *A geografia da justiça: Para um novo mapa judiciário*. Coimbra: CES/OPJ.

Carnevali, D. 2009. E-Justice and policies for risk management. In *E-justice: Using information communication technologies in the court system*, ed. A. Cerrillo and P. Fabra, 20–37. New York: IGI Global.

CEPEJ. 2009. Dematerialization and the use of ICT. A report approved by the CEPEJ at its 13th plenary meeting. https://wcd.coe.int/ViewDoc.jsp?id=1481171andSite=COE-P122_4757. Retrieved 24 Jan 2012.

Contini, F., and A. Cordella. 2007. Information system and information infrastructure deployment: The challenge of the Italian e-justice approach. *Electron J e-Government* 5(1): 43–52.

Critical Sofware. 2009. ACitius: Relatório de Auditoria ao Citius. http://72.29.69.19/~ejal/images/stories/arquivos/artigos/CSW-ACITIUS-2009-RPT-02393-relatorio-final.pdf. Retrieved 30 March 2012.

Critical Sofware. 2010. ACitius: Relatório de Auditoria—Aditamento. http://72.29.69.19/~ejal/images/stories/arquivos/artigos/CSW-2010-RPT-02371-aditamento-auditoria-acitius.pdf. Retrieved 30 March 2012.

Farrell, J., and G. Saloner. 1986. Installed base and compatibility: Innovation, product preannouncements, and predation. *Am Econ Rev* 76(5): 940–955.

GAIT/ASJP. 2009. Primeiros seis meses de utilização do Citius: Inquérito de avaliação à funcionalidade e eficiência. Relatório preliminar. http://www.asjp.pt/wp-content/uploads/2010/05/Estudo-Relatório-preliminar-sobre-o-citius.pdf. Retrieved 30 March 2012.

Hanseth, O., and K. Lyytinen. 2010. Design theory for dynamic complexity in information infrastructures: The case of building internet. *J Inf Technol* 25(1): 1–19.

Kallinikos, J. 2009. Institutional complexity and functional simplification: The case of Money Claim Online Service in England and Wales. In *ICT and innovation in the public sector: European studies in the making of e-government*, ed. F. Contini and G.F. Lanzara, 174–210. Basingstoke: Palgrave Macmillan.

KPMG. 2009. Diagnóstico à eficiência e eficácia processual nos tribunais judiciais antes e após implementação do suporte electrónico. http://72.29.69.19/~ejal/images/stories/arquivos/artigos/KPMG_Diagnostico.pdf. Retrieved 30 March 2012.

Lameiras, L.F.B. 2008. A informatização na justiça cível. In *Novos rumos da justiça cível*, ed. R. Brito, 115–129. Braga: CEJUR.

Lanzara, G.F. 2009. Building digital institutions: ICT and the rise of assemblages in government. In *ICT and innovation in the public sector: European studies in the making of e-government*, ed. F. Contini and G.F. Lanzara, 9–48. Basingstoke: Palgrave Macmillan.

Marçal, A. 2011. Informatização da "Justiça".' Proceedings of the 'Conferência informatização da justiça: problemas e soluções. Sintra, 24 Feb 2011.

Migliarese, P., and V. Corvello. 2009. Organizational relations and organizational routines in organizational and information systems design. Paper presented at IWODE'09—International Workshop on Organizational Design and Engineering, Lisbon, 11–12 Dec 2009.

Ministry of Justice. 2009a. Citius—Magistrados judiciais: Guia de consulta rápida.http://www.citius.mj.pt/portaldnn/LinkClick.aspx?fileticket=nTZaQoUKCzY=andtabid=59. Retrieved 30 March 2012.

Ministry of Justice. 2009b. Citius—Ministério público: Guia de consulta rápida. http://www.citius.mj.pt/portaldnn/LinkClick.aspx?fileticket=z+MPsogpXD8=andtabid=59. Retrieved 30 March 2012.

OA. 2009. Ordem garante segurança do Citius. *Boletim da Ordem dos Advogados* 51: 12–14.

Pereira, J., and R. Timóteo. 2010. A criação e gestão do sistema informático dos tribunais na computação das tecnologias da informação. Proceedings of the VII Encontro Anual do Conselho Superior da Magistratura. http://www.csm.org.pt/ficheiros/eventos/7encontrocsm_joelpereira.pdf. Retrieved 30 March 2012.

Vidal, R.M., J.F. e Cunha, M.P. Monteiro, J.P. Faria, L. Amaral, P.C. Henriques, and P. Gomes. 2009. *Relatório final comparativo e valorativo sobre os métodos de trabalho resultantes da introdução do processo electrónico do projecto Citius e da utilização das aplicações informáticas Citius e Habilus*. Oporto: FEUP/ITIJ.

Chapter 7
Pushing at the Edge of Maximum Manageable Complexity: The Case of 'Trial Online' in Italy

Davide Carnevali and Andrea Resca

Abstract Since 2000, Trial OnLine (TOL) is a typical nationwide e-filing project aiming at managing, in a comprehensive way, documents and communications of all civil trial proceedings through digital solutions. Even though it was expected that in 2005 more than 50 courts would have taken advantage of TOL's applications, at the end of 2006 only one application (payment order) was in use and only in one court: the Tribunal of Milan. Now the situation is changed and some other online civil proceedings are progressively spreading. In this chapter, the reasons behind this deep change are investigated. The understanding of the great complexity of legal, technological, organizational, and institutional domains involved in TOL project development has been the goal of our analysis. The simplification of the technological architecture, the modification of the legal framework for promoting legally viable ICT-based practices, and, above all, a close collaboration between courts and bar associations in facilitating user access to e-justice are considered the main factors for the revitalization of TOL when project failure was around the corner.

7.1 Introduction

In Italy, massive investments in ICT projects have been made to improve the 'quality of justice'. It was considered the only solution (but also the best way) to take justice out of a never-ending state of crisis, although this was not what happened in practice. The applications that currently work in judicial offices have not really changed or affected the judiciary and its functioning (such as structures, procedures, working practices, ways of thinking, etc.) (Contini and Carnevali 2010). Being considered

D. Carnevali (✉) • A. Resca
Research Institute on Judicial Systems, National Research Council of Italy (IRSIG-CNR), Bologna, Italy
e-mail: davide.carnevali@irsig.cnr.it

F. Contini and G.F. Lanzara (eds.), *The Circulation of Agency in E-Justice*, Law, Governance and Technology Series 13, DOI 10.1007/978-94-007-7525-1_7,

plug n' play tools (Fabri 2009), technology applications have been simply and usually 'superimposed' upon the current judicial environment, largely losing their potential to produce change and economic and social benefits (Contini and Cordella 2007; Contini 2008).

The ability to generate innovation through the adoption of new technology is a very difficult process. It is usually a long journey, marked by interruptions and twists, often plagued by unintended consequences and very costly in the early phases (Ciborra 2000). This is even more so if technological and institutional complexity is high, as in the development of e-justice (i.e., more technical specifications, more rules, more organisations and institutions involved, more interoperability requirements, etc.) (Carnevali et al. 2007; Carnevali 2009; Contini and Fabri 2003; Contini and Lanzara 2009; Velicogna 2008, 2011; Velicogna et al. 2013). The implementation of innovation requires committed involvement from institutions, organisations, judges, court staff, court users, etc. They must take care of and 'cultivate' (Dahlbom and Mathiassen 1993) the process of change in day-to-day operations, according to an incremental approach (Fabri 2009). Another important factor in the success of ICT adoption is the attainment of a 'critical mass' of users: 'As the number of users grows, technology tends to gain momentum and starts growing through a 'self-reinforcing process' (Hanseth and Aanestad 2003).

Taking up the predicament of ICT-based innovation, the present chapter reports on an e-justice development project in Italy. The Trial Online (TOL) project[1] is the most important ICT-based development programme undertaken over the last 10 years by the Ministry of Justice, and it has required the largest investment of resources. TOL is a project upon which great expectations were placed as regards its capability to be the 'ultimate engine of change' and to overcome the chronic crisis of civil justice in Italy. The results to date indicate that there is still a long way to go, however.

TOL aims to be a full e-filing system, that is, a complete electronic management system for any type of civil proceeding, from case filing to judgement to final enforcement. The system also provides public access (with some restrictions) to the data collected in the court (in case management systems, electronic case file, documents repository, judgements databases, statistics, etc.), electronic notification and communication to and from the court, payment of amounts due and of court fees (Contini and Fabri 2003; Carnevali 2006, 2010).

The whole story will be told in a chronological manner, using an in-depth analysis to better understand some specific problem areas. The data come from several interviews with key actors located at government and executive levels. Some data were collected during observations on-site. All this data collection was embedded in a solid literature produced in this field in the last 20 years, mainly by the IRSIG-CNR researchers, during the course of European Commission projects.

An overview of the environment in which TOL has been developed will be presented, from the technical infrastructure to the legal framework. Next, we will

[1]The word 'trial' is the conventional name given to the project even if the right word to be used is 'proceeding'.

introduce the situation before TOL, and then the TOL system will be described: its project, architecture, pilot experiments (i.e., 'laboratories in place' or TOL Labs) and various releases. Special attention will be given to the first operating case, the 'Tribunal of Milan', in a dedicated section. In the concluding section, we will try to understand the steps of TOL's evolution in light of the different capabilities of different information infrastructures to manage the complexity characterising technological development.

7.2 Legal Framework and Technical Infrastructure

In order to better understand the characteristics and the functioning of TOL, it is necessary to define the technical infrastructure and legal framework within which TOL was created and developed. In addition, it must be recognised that the environment keeps changing, mainly under the pressure of the dynamics of ICT innovation, highlighted by the TOL project itself.

The first issue to be considered for describing the TOL environment is the main technical infrastructures that characterise courts' and lawyers' information systems. Since 1995, the Italian public administration has had a public network infrastructure known as *Rete Unitaria della Pubblica Amministrazione* (RUPA) and the justice domain *Rete Unitaria della Giustizia* (RUG). In 2006, the architecture changed and was named *Sistema Pubblico di Connettività* (SPC). The ICT Department of the Ministry of Justice, facing serious budget cuts, decided to move the location of databases from the court to the judicial district level. In particular, this meant changing the server of each court of first instance with a new main district server divided virtually in each court-related database. Furthermore, the new configuration provided a replacement application server for each court. A web-based connection via the application server operated the link between the main district server and the thin-clients located in the court. Thus, it was possible to keep under control not only the costs of server maintenance and management but also the risks related to database protection and data transmission security. In this new framework, it was also necessary to improve the broadband connections while simultaneously reducing costs (Carnevali 2010).

By contrast, the ICT infrastructure available to external users, lawyers mainly, is not well known. Lawyers usually mediate electronic access for the general public. People access directly just the court web site to watch or download basic information related to the services provided by the office: timetable, map, chart, procedures, how-to information, etc.

There are 160,000 lawyers in Italy, of whom about 100,000 are thought to be practicing. The lawyers' offices are rather small organisations and there are few large law firms. Lawyers are organised in 165 fragmented local bar associations. Consequently, lawyers, law firms and bar associations developed their own ICT infrastructure in the most heterogeneous ways, even for electronic data interchange with the judiciary (Fabri 2009). As illustrated below, this heterogeneity affected seriously TOL deployment. Indeed, for a long time, only the bar associations were entitled to grant access to TOL, since the bars are the body entitled to issue practicing certificates, as will be discussed later on.

A further issue to be considered in order to understand the dynamics of ICT innovation in the Italian judiciary is the complexity and the level of detail of the rules that prescribe how technology has to operate (Contini and Mohr 2008).

Italy was the first country in Europe to have specific and complete legislation on the application of ICT for public administration, in particular electronic documents and digital signature (Fabri 2009). The proliferation of rules was also caused by the particular requirements relating to the 'sensitivity' and 'security' of judicial proceedings. Those requirements can be summarised as high data and proceedings sensitivity, high security needs and detailed formal regulations to avoid possible malfunctioning and misuse. This excess of risk anticipation often had the effect of paralysing the innovation itself (Hanseth 2007; Carnevali 2009) and led to hypertrophic regulation mainly driven by 'legal formalism' instead of 'legal pragmatism' (Fabri 2009). The unwieldy and constant regulations were introduced to make possible and legal the use of judicial electronic documents, electronic folders and the electronic data and documents interchange, but they were oversized with respect to practical needs even if coherent with formal concerns.

The first technical rules were introduced in 1999 (DPCM 8 February 1999), regulating the use of the 'strong' digital signature with a public key infrastructure (PKI) and setting out rules and standards for establishing certification authorities provided by a presidential decree (DPR 513/1997). In 2000, another presidential decree (DPR 445/2000) legislated for the reordering of all related prior regulation (including the DPR 513/1997) regarding documentation in public administration. This act seemed to be inapplicable to the regulation of the justice sector, so another regulation (DPR123/2001) allowed the use of such electronic means for civil, administrative and fiscal proceedings. In 2002, a legislative decree (D.Lgs.10/2002) changed the rules again, embedding the European Directive 1999/93/CE provisions that allow the use of a 'lighter' electronic signature instead of the digital signature (PKI). In addition, the so-called Privacy Code (DPR 196/2003) was enacted. It heavily circumscribed rules of access and security. It was meant to provide other specific ministerial regulations for the judiciary (DM 14 October 2004). In the same year, Parliament enacted the so-called Code of Digital Administration (D.Lgs.82/2005), which collects most of the previous dispositions related to the use of electronic means in public administrations (Carnevali 2010).

However, it was necessary to legislate another technical rule (DM 15 December 2005) with the document type definition model (DTD)[2] to give 'legal validity' to

[2] A Document Type Definition (DTD) is a set of mark-up statements that define a document type for a language (SGML-family), such as SGML, XML and HTML. A DTD provides a formal syntax that states precisely which components and positions can appear in the document, and how the elements' contents, attributes and entities may be used (source Wikipedia).

electronic transactions in the civil judiciary. Thus, it was only in 2006 that the legal conditions for using the TOL system in practice were finally established.

Less than a year later, a legislative decree (D.Lgs.40/2006) provided for the e-filing and sending of documents from external users to the court by 'certified email',[3] a formal communication system required for the entire public sector. Article 51 of Law L.133/2008 allowed court communication online in the same way, so it was necessary to provide a special provision for the application of these rules (certified email for document transactions and communications online) to the TOL system (DPR 193/2009). It was another big change in TOL's project story. The huge difficulties in applying this bundle of rules in the day-to-day operations of judicial offices are thus quite clear (Fabri 2009).

7.3 The Challenge of the Early e-Justice System

The origin of the TOL conception dates back to the end of the 1990s. The Bologna Bar Association was an early pioneer. Their idea was to set up a system to share online judicial decisions taken in civil procedures. This application, known as POLIS, supported judicial writings with various office automation tools. Once printed, signed and sealed, judicial decisions would have been scanned and made available in a repository accessible to lawyers and other judges (Jacchia 2000).

After the first stage of analysis, the study group better understood the broader potential of ICT in this area. Based on these considerations, a proposal was made to fully digitise civil proceedings and pursue the goal of the 'paperless office'. The exchange of any document and data in any type of civil proceeding would have allowed lawyers to do their job without having to commute daily to court and would have sped up the work of judges and clerks enormously.

In 1999, the Bologna Bar Association contracted a consulting firm to carry out an explorative study addressed to transform this vision into reality. The outcome of the study was that only a systematic digitisation of the entire body of civil procedures would allow the removal of the structural inefficiencies that characterise Italian courts (Jacchia 2000). Since then, the implementation of such a vision has been anything but easy.

Based on this study, the Ministry of Justice decided to finance the attempt to develop a new e-justice system based on a new Case Management System (CMS) as its backbone. Several CMSs were delivered step by step to the different branches of the judiciary (litigation, labour, insolvency, enforcement, etc.).

The most important component of this first wave of e-justice systems was the system for accessing the POLIS judgements databases (local case law) and CMSs of the court by the lawyers. This would allow the lawyers to better plan and

[3]The 'certified email' (CEM now on) is an email address given by a specific certification authority after a process of registration and validation.

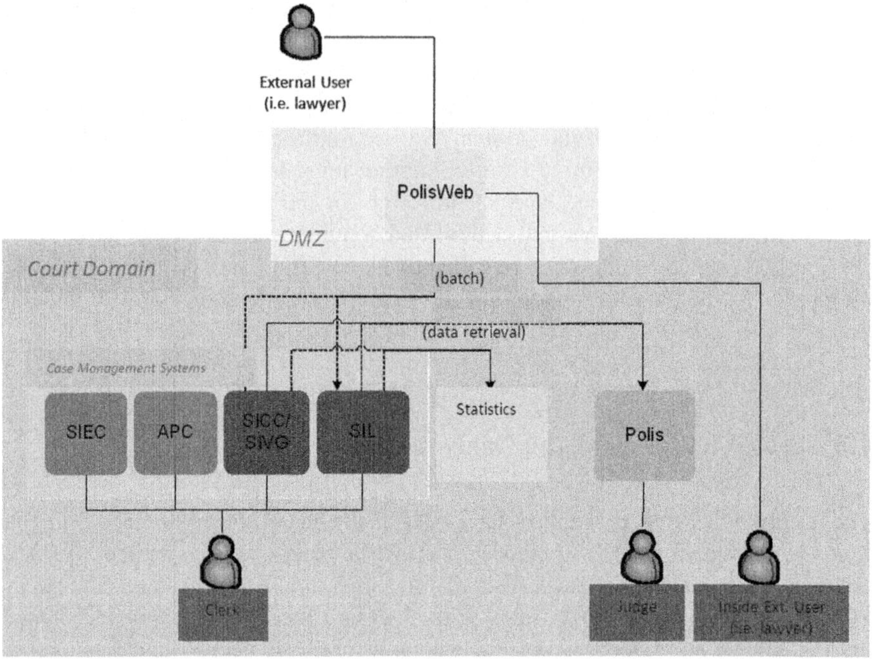

Fig. 7.1 The first e-justice architecture: PolisWeb (Source: Borsari and Baratta 2004)

schedule their activities, save time for accessing the court counter and thereby reduce travelling time and costs. Moreover, the Bologna Bar Association requested remote access to the CMSs database from the Ministry of Justice. Following this request, the Ministry of Justice contracted the software firm already engaged in the POLIS project to develop the so called PolisWeb service: a web-based application that allows remote access to court POLIS judgements databases (local case law) and CMS data[4] (see Fig. 7.1).

At the beginning of 2000, the technological installed base (architecture) of this first e-justice system consisted of the following components:

1. CMSs supporting different kinds of proceedings (litigation SICC, labour SIL, insolvency APC, enforcement SIEC);

[4]The system operated in this way. During the night, the databases of the court were replicated in batch mode on the PolisWeb server. The PolisWeb was placed on a so-called DMZ network (it means De-Militarized Zone in informatics) to preserve the LAN of the court from outside, protecting a piece of it. Once registered with the court, the user receives an ID and password to enable the service for the kiosks located inside the court. Otherwise, if the request for access came from a remote location, it was necessary for the user to acquire a piece of software to allow 'traceability' of the computer that was connecting and for the encryption of data exchange.

2. The POLIS system, supporting judicial writings for judges and generating case law collection;
3. The PolisWeb service for initial public access (mainly for lawyers) to courts' CMSs and the local case law collection.

Despite the very positive results reached by the PolisWeb service in allowing remote access to CMS data in the pilot courts, there has been no dissemination. Indeed, the success pushed the Ministry of Justice to start the development of a much more challenging project to create a 'paperless office', transforming conventional paper-based procedures into digital ones. This project, well known as Trial Online, became the key strategic plan of the Ministry of Justice's ICT development programme. Since then, the larger part of the available resources has been allocated to it (Carnevali 2006, 2010).

7.4 TOL: The System 'All-in-One'

As mentioned, it was during the development of the POLIS project that the Bologna Bar Association and the Ministry of Justice decided to explore the feasibility of TOL. In 2000, a 10-month feasibility study was launched at the Tribunal of Bologna and at the Tribunal of Rimini. The Ministry of Justice contracted the same consultant firm engaged in 1999. This study analysed the organisational features of the courts (organisation units, roles, functions, competencies, etc.) and mapped out the civil procedures 'in practice' to redesign the different roles, functions and working practices in light of TOL development. The results of this feasibility study were positive; the civil procedures would be fully digitised and the courts would become paperless offices (Jacchia 2000).

The technological solutions identified were considered as cutting edge. MS word processors would be used to generate XML documents to be uploaded automatically into courts' case management systems. XML files would be formatted using the brand new XSL specifications (including XSLT and XSL-FO)[5] to have also "digital documents" with layouts similar to the one of traditional paper documents. Simpler solutions as PDF were not considered adequate at this stage. However, as seen in Sect. 7.4.2.2, the implementation of such standard turned out to be a serious obstacle to the development of the project. SOAP would be adopted as the protocol to let applications exchange information over the secured network. Public Key Infrastructure would be used to improve the security of the information exchange, in particular authenticity, integrity and non-repudiation (Borsari 2004).

[5] Standards definitions are available at www.w3.org/Style/XSL/www.w3.org/TR/2001/REC-xsl-20011015 and www.w3.org/TR/xslt

In 2001, the ICT Department of the Ministry of Justice issued two competitive tenders, one for software development, the other for organisational support. In 2002, the Ministry of Justice assigned the organisational support contract to a consultancy firm. Support was provided through various committees and through the establishment of 'local laboratories' in seven pilot courts (TOL Labs). Support had to be provided, however, for the adoption of a technological system that was not ready yet. It was not until 2003 that the Ministry of Justice awarded the competitive tender for the hardware and software development (Carnevali 2010). Based on the tender, the assignee had to provide the following deliverables:

1. Reengineering of both automated CMSs of civil proceedings and a system for editing, collecting and sharing the court decisions based on POLIS experience;
2. Development of an application dedicated to lawyers and experts for the electronic data and document interchange with the court, in particular e-filing of legal documents and provision of a documents repository of electronic folders accessible online;
3. Creation of a 'model office' in the Ministry of Justice in which the TOL system could be developed and tested;
4. Installation of the TOL system in the seven TOL Labs (pilot courts and related bar associations) with maintenance and customer care services; and
5. Dissemination of the TOL system with a help desk service and training programme to an additional 50 courts.

7.4.1 A Fully Digital Information System: An Impossible Challenge (2000–2005)

TOL was born as a very ambitious project. Its original design outlined a full e-filing system intending the complete electronic management of any type of civil proceeding, from case filing to judgement to final enforcement. In particular, lawyers, experts, clerks and judges would be able to access data collected in the CMS databases (as with PolisWeb), but also to file cases and download and upload procedural documents to and from an electronic folder in the court. The project also provided electronic notification and communication to and from the court, including payments of amounts due and court fees (Contini 2006; Contini and Fabri 2003).

In particular, TOL's main focus was to manage, in a comprehensive way, every document and communication in any kind of civil proceeding through digital solutions. In other words, it should be possible to have paperless offices and procedures in which users would have:

1. Converted the larger part of the data related to civil proceedings (from filing to judgement) to digital;
2. Managed, on the basis of electronic means, all communications and information exchanges among the different players involved in a civil proceeding (judges, lawyers, clerks, bailiffs, advisors, expert witnesses, etc.);

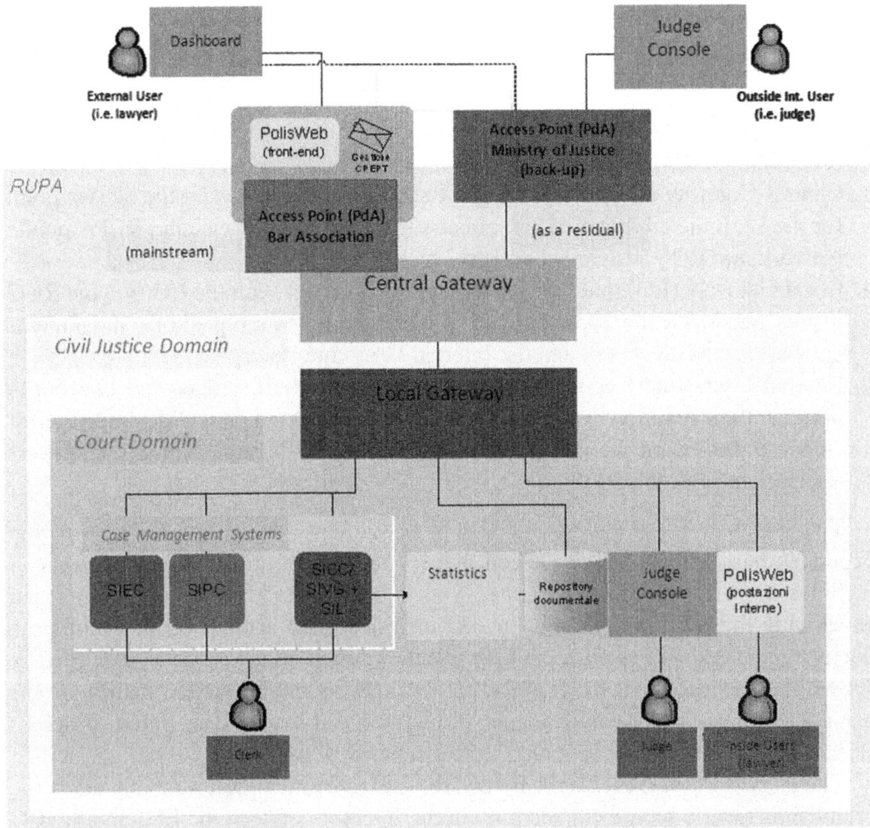

Fig. 7.2 The TOL system as a whole (Source: Borsari and Baratta 2004)

3. Simplified the activities of any player involved in civil proceedings; and
4. Promoted the proceedings' transparency and timeliness.

TOL's deployment was expected to be beneficial to judges because documents and information management would be streamlined. Taking advantage of electronic communication and electronic filing, the connection with clerks and lawyers would be facilitated and the entire digitisation would produce a wide spectrum of beneficial effects.

7.4.1.1 TOL Architecture

The system architecture designed by the Ministry of Justice to implement TOL is very complex. Components are placed in many different locations: local and central and internal and external to the justice system (see Fig. 7.2).

These components consist of:

1. External Users Interface (EUI), the dashboard and web service through which lawyers and experts can interact with the system from their own offices;
2. Access Point (PdA: Punto d'Accesso) that allow the connection between the EUI (outside) and the rest of the system (inside);
3. Central Gateway (CG) that manages the connections between the access point for the EUI, the civil justice domain and the court domain (via the RUPA public network and RUG justice network);
4. Local Gateway (LG) that manage the connections between the CG (via the RUG justice network), the court domain (CMSs, documents repository, judgements databases, statistics, etc.) and the Internal Users Interface;
5. Internal Users Interface (IUI) to be used by court staff, judges and lawyers to perform their functions from inside the court. It is based on a CMS interface for clerks, a dashboard for judges and the internal web service station for lawyers (Borsari and Baratta 2004).

The External User Interface (EUI) is a dashboard to allow the lawyer and expert witnesses to draft, sign electronically and serve procedural documents. It includes a word processor integrated with software for signing, encrypting and enveloping the document (based on PKI infrastructure) and a tool for e-filing the documents, based on a specific email application functioning just for TOL (CPEPT). As will be seen later on, the EUI has to be financed and developed mainly by the bar associations. The dashboard also provides a web-based connection to access selected data collected in the court CMS databases (front-end).

The Access Point (PdA) is the hardware, software and middleware that allow the establishment of a secure connection via the internet between the EUI and the CG (protecting access to the justice domain) and from there to local courts. In practical terms, it is the system that enables lawyers, through their dashboard, to access and interact with the systems of the Ministry of Justice. In legal and technical terms, the PdA has to solve the problems of secure access to the justice domain, of enabling digital signature and of correct identification of practicing lawyers. For this reason, as a rule, it has to be set up by each local bar association and 'certified' by the ICT Department of the Ministry of Justice. It is through registration to the PdA that lawyers get the above-mentioned specific mailbox called CPEPT and their smart cards for digital signature of procedural documents for identification and authorisation to access to the systems of the Ministry of Justice.

The Central Gateway (CG) manages the connections between the PdAs, the civil justice domain and the courts systems. The CG ensures the accuracy of the composition of the envelopes produced, routes the communications to the court systems and tracks all data flows. In practical terms, the CG executes the requests submitted by lawyers via PdA and addresses the communications to the court via the LG and vice versa. The CG also certifies the receipt of a case e-filing, providing a reply message addressed to lawyer CPEPT mailbox (time stamp). This is to be considered the date and time of legal filing.

The Local Gateway (LG) handles the connections between the court systems (CMSs, documents repository and internal users), the PdA and external users. It controls case filing delivery, manages levels of access and directs communications between the court and the external users. Since 2011, the LG handles the 'new' PolisWeb (TOL PolisWeb), the web service designed to provide access to the court databases (CMSs, documents repository, statistics, etc.) from the external court users within the TOL architecture.

The Internal User Interface (IUI) is the interface used by judges to work with TOL. Indeed, while the clerks and the court staff perform all their functions through the CMS applications, the judges needs a specific dashboard (the so-called Judges' Console)[6] to write judicial documents and support tasks such as calendaring. In 2004, the Ministry of Justice developed a new web-based application with similar functions, called Judge's Work Desk, and more recently a new simplified application called MagOffice. We will return to these difficult developments in Sect. 7.4.2.2.

The analysis of the difficult development of such technological components provides an interesting framework to discuss the peculiar features of the development of large techno-legal infrastructures and demonstrate how complexity can quickly reach the threshold of 'maximum manageable complexity' (see Chap. 1).

7.4.1.2 TOL in Place

TOL's technical system was released at the end of 2004 (Borsari and Baratta 2004) and completed in 2005 (Carnevali 2006). Alongside the development of the TOL architecture, the testing stage started in the seven pilot courts called TOL Labs. The aim of this testing stage was to develop a method to promote its organisational adoption and integration within the courts' working practices and to solve technical and organisational problems emerging at local level (Xilo 2004). The project milestones indicated the ending of the testing stage by 2004 and the start of the TOL deployment stage in a further 50 courts. The true story has been quite different, however.

First of all, there were delays with the adjudication of the bid for software development and with the issuing of normative components required by TOL. Just at the end of 2005, the so-called DTD (see footnote 2) were issued by a decree of the Ministry of Justice (DM 15 December 2005) and, from this point, proceedings and documents based on TOL acquired 'legal validity' (see Sect. 7.2). However, the lack of necessary legal components was not the only reason for the failure of the TOL Labs. Indeed, the involvement of lawyers and bar associations was more difficult to obtain than expected. As noted, part of the software required for the functioning of the TOL was to be developed by software houses hired by bar associations, as in the case of the PdAs, or bought by lawyers in the free market (such as the EUI). Moreover, lawyers had to buy digital signatures, thus incurring further costs.

[6]The Judges' Console is an evolution of the 'old' POLIS briefly introduced in Sect. 7.3.

Simply speaking, the quality and the costs of the products offered by the market did not match the demands of potential users: the software providers were too few and the costs of their products too high. The requirements of two smart cards for authentication and digital signature, a dashboard for editing documents and for accessing the system, and the construction of a PdA at each bar association—the result of the design choice of the Ministry of Justice—demanded far too much of individual lawyers and their associations.

Thus, due to the lack of legal validity of TOL operations—and the hard work of testing without real results and perspectives—the seven piloting courts began to disengage from the project. The costs for PdA development were too high and the benefits anything but clear. In 2006, the TOL Labs reached a dead end (Carnevali 2010). After almost 6 years, during which 12 million euro were spent in feasibility studies, software and organisational development and testing (Fabri 2009),[7] results were far from being achieved and TOL failure was a certainty.

7.4.2 *The System's Light Version: Starting to Operate for Payment Order (2006–2011)*

During those same years, however, the unexpected happened. The Tribunal of Milan—a court outside every TOL development programme—took the lead in a 'renewed' TOL project. Thanks to the remarkable investments made by the bar association of the rich financial city of Milan and the strong sponsorship of the court, the bar implemented the PdA and started to operate TOL, although limited to the payment order proceedings.

7.4.2.1 The 'Renewed' TOL Project

The TOL developed in Milan became the strongest chance for the Ministry of Justice to save the TOL programme from failure and the ICT Department of Ministry of Justice decided to support it strongly. However, it did not aim to digitise the entire set of civil proceedings and to push toward the 'paperless office'. It chose instead to downsize the project and focus on its simplest but routine and very bulky procedure: the 'payment order'. In Milan in December 2006, TOL's 'light version' for payment order became operational with 'legal validity', following the specific regulations and technical requirements (DTD) for the 'new' system (DM 15 December 2005). Since then, Milan has been the forerunner in TOL development and use, as better discussed in Sect. 7.5.

In 2008, the TOL Light Version also went online in the Tribunal of Catania (with its PdA developed through an inhouse solution), and in four other tribunals.

[7] About 84 % of the total investments in ICT projects in the civil sector (Fabri 2009).

In 2009, another ten courts went online. All these courts were using TOL just for payment orders. The development was not easy at all, with technical, financial and managerial problems persisting for years. The main problem associated with PdA development was the cost to be paid by each bar but the IT specialists engaged in the development of the PdA and dash board also pointed to interaction problems with the ICT Department of the Ministry of Justice, reporting a lack of clear and technical documentation and problematic access to the model office to simulate the functioning of the applications under development (Zanga 2008).

Thus, for several years, the system operated only in Milan. In 2010, almost 80 % of lawyers were entitled to the service. Payment orders online reached 12 % in 2007 and 40 % in 2010[8]. In those years, the ICT Department of the Ministry of Justice improved the system with court communications and then with the exchange of written statements (Sala 2010). This first successful and milestone experience will be discussed in detail in Sect. 7.5.

7.4.2.2 New Dashboard for Judges and XML Makeover

The judges' dashboard inside the court (IUI) has been the other technological component with a problematic track record. The implementation of TOL required the engagement of judges, who were obliged to write their procedural documents using tools integrated into the TOL system.

After 2004, the Judges' Console of the original TOL architecture—an evolution of the 'old' POLIS briefly introduced in Sect. 7.3—was changed to a web-based application called Judge's Work Desk (JWD). With the JWD, the judge, instead of using a commercial word processor, opens a web application integrated into the CMSs of the court. The document saved in XML format can be digitally signed and transmitted to the registry, which will take care of a distinct set of functions. Judges can also collect all the decisions and thus set up databases of local jurisprudence. JWD is expected to empower the managerial and bureaucratic capabilities of the judge who, by using this system, is much more and much better integrated into the organisational process. However, 4 years of development process and a number of releases to align the judges' needs resulted in low adoption of JWD. Judge Console and JWD were too complex for many judges, accustomed to working with standard word processors. Consequently, the Ministry of Justice decided to develop a simpler interface for judges called MagOffice, which was a simple customisation of MS Office integrated into the CMS SICID and a calendar management system based on MS Outlook (DGSIA 2011).

The original XML solution for editing the document was abandoned in favour of the simplest one provided by the use of a standard word processor to generate PDF files, albeit enclosed in an XML envelope, along with the most important data for identification (i.e., digital signature) and recording. As a consequence, various

[8] Source: Ministero della Giustizia (www.processotelematico.giustizia.it/pdapublic/index.jsp)

Table 7.1 Main changes introduced by law L.44/2011

Level	Before	After
Access point	The 'closed' TOL dedicated email (CPEPT) was used for communications and e-filing between court users (lawyers) and the court through Access point (PdA)	The 'open' certified email (CEM) for communication and e-filing is introduced between court users (lawyers) and the court
	The PdA allowed the connection between lawyers and the court-by-court users' identification and authorisation	The PdA is maintained to allow CEM use by CEM personal email identification and authorisation
		The PdA is maintained to access the current courts' CMSs at district level
Central	The Central Gateway (CG) in Naples was used to manage the connection (identification and authorisation) among the PdA, the civil justice domain and the court domain through the LG	The CG with the PolisWeb is abandoned
	The CG was also used to access the copy of courts' CMSs at central level (PolisWeb)	Central CEM System with Certified CEM Registry is introduced to identify and authorise access and data exchange by lawyers
		E-service Portal is planned to allow access by the general public

technical specifications, in particular those associated with the exchange of XML file based on XSL stiles, have been abandoned. This has simplified the technological implementations and made the system deployment and evolution less expensive.

7.4.3 *The System's Light Version Takes a 'New Shape': Opening the Door to Standard Certified Email (from 2011)*

As mentioned before, at the beginning of 2011 the Ministry of Justice issued a Ministerial Decree (DM 21 February 2011 n.44) entailing major changes to the TOL architecture. Particularly relevant for our analysis is the switch from the old ad hoc email application used by TOL (CPEPT) to a new one based on the standard of 'certified email' (CEM).

Thus, the TOL architecture had to undergo a major reconfiguration (see Table 7.1). In particular, the new rule changes the system of communication of the EUI component. The e-filing of the case is operated by the lawyer through standard personal CEM email procured from a broad set of private providers instead of the TOL dedicated email CPEPT given by the Ministry of Justice via PdA.

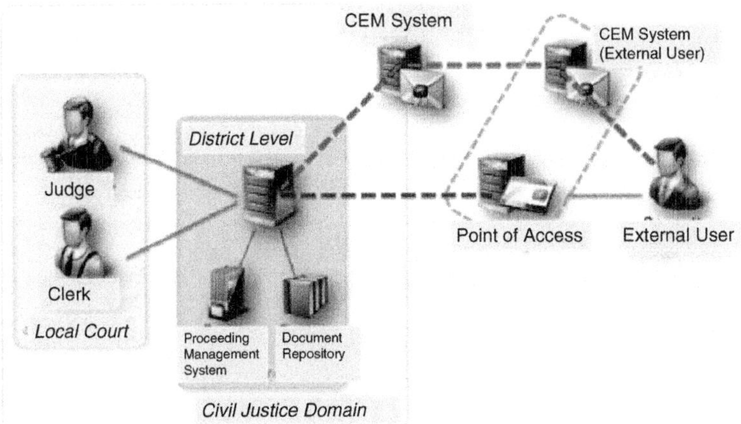

Fig. 7.3 TOL new architecture (Source: Borsari 2011)

The PdA is maintained solely to allow lawyers to access the CMS data, while case-related files are simply exchanged via the new standard of registered email. As a consequence, the Central CEM System with Certified CEM Registry (located in Milan) was introduced to control (identification and authorisation) access and allow the exchange of data and documents between court and lawyers (see Fig. 7.3).

This 'new shape' is the last in a long list of changes affecting TOL. In a few years, for several reasons, the system has been modified several times, forcing courts, bar associations, lawyers and other professionals to chase after this evolving situation. This continuous transformation produced an increase in costs (economic and organisational) to adapt the system to these different solutions but also represented an example of ex post facto simplification of the multiple entanglements between technological components, legal requirements and institutional and organisational constraints.

Indeed, after the introduction of CEM, the role of the bar associations is reduced significantly, since the PdA (developed by the bar) is not needed anymore for sending and receiving procedural documents. Nonetheless, the bars are still the guardians of the legitimacy of their members to practice law and without their authorisation, CEMs cannot be activated. In the meantime, however, the PdA continues to be used for accessing the court's CMS databases, also through the new district architecture. Therefore, it is expected that bar associations will continue to play a role in this respect, providing their members with software applications that integrate PdA and CEM functionalities.

To sum up, the full digitisation of civil proceedings pursued according to the original plans is still far from being reached. There are almost 150,000 CEM addresses in the Central CEM Registry. The TOL Light Version for payment order and court communications is present in 32 courts. About 130,000 communications

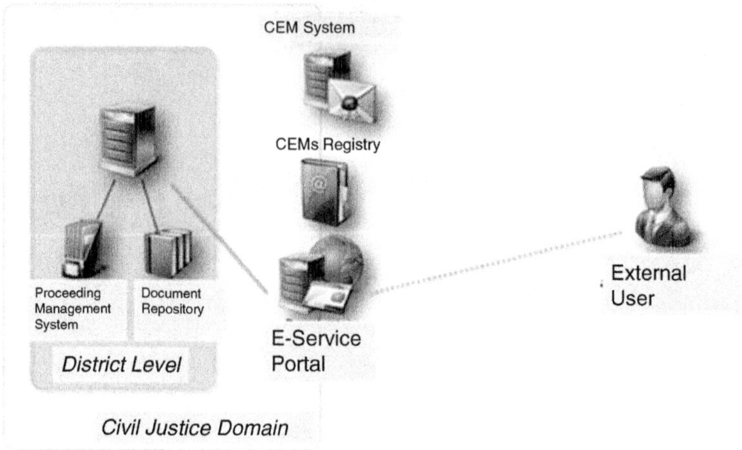

Fig. 7.4 E-Service Portal architecture (Source: Borsari 2011)

are transmitted electronically in those courts (up to 30 June 2011)[9]. The exchange of written statements between parties and the judge is limited, available in four courts. Only in the Tribunal of Milan is a large part of proceedings to be digitised by the TOL project already available in this form. Next, the system should be accessed also through an e-service portal (Fig. 7.4).

7.5 Implementing TOL at the Tribunal of Milan

7.5.1 Description of TOL's Proceedings Deployed in Milan

7.5.1.1 The Payment Order

The Tribunal of Milan started to use TOL for payment orders with legal validity on 11 December 2006. The rate of adoption of this solution was relatively slow, because in 2007 only 11 % of total payment orders were run online, although in 2010 the rate had risen to around 60 %. The lawyers decided to gradually relinquish consolidated practices in favour of new ones.

To file a case, a lawyer drafts the document required for filing through the software suite, attaches digital copies of original paper-based documents previously scanned and digitally signs the document using the smart card provided by the bar. In so doing, the lawyer also enters key data, including proof of payment of the court

[9]Data from http://www.processotelematico.it. The information includes data for enforcement and insolvency proceedings not considered by this study.

fee, and then the package can be sent to the court through the PdA made available by the Milan Bar Association, the gateway to the registry of the court.

At this point, the clerk opens the package, checks the data and transmits the case to the competent judge. The judge handles the case through his dashboard, studying the file then writing and digitally signing the decision. The decision is then sent to the records office where it is downloaded and digitally countersigned by the clerk. At this stage, an electronic communication is sent to lawyers to inform them that the decision has been issued. The digital copy of the document is attached. At this point, the electronic proceeding is considered over and the paper-based one begins. Indeed, the document, even if digitally signed and countersigned by the judge and the clerk, cannot be served to the defendant due to the lack of a legal framework authorising this procedural step in digital format. Consequently, the claimant has to collect the 'true copy' of the decision at the court counter and then serve it through the bailiff service.

To guarantee the performativity of the system, agency must therefore repeatedly circulate from conventional to digital and then return to conventional. The idea of a one-stop shop is still far away, and rather than consider such switches as a fault or a drawback, they should be regarded as the rule.

7.5.1.2 The e-Filing of Written Statements and Other Procedural Documents

Procedures for the electronic submission of written statements or other procedural documents are in line with those of the payment order. The lawyer prepares the document with the ad hoc application and digitally signs and sends it to the court via PdA. The document refers to the case number in order to attach it automatically to the right case file. From a legal perspective, the e-filing of some procedural documents (written statements mainly) online has had legal validity since 15 March 2010, and since 26 April 2010 the option to do so has increased. The adoption rate is relatively slow because the Tribunal of Milan and the local bar association consider a step-by-step approach to be a wise move. Indeed, in many cases some of the lawyers may use TOL, whereas others prefer to work on paper. The solution found tries to accommodate this hybrid situation.

Thus, a sort of two-way procedure takes place; the electronic way and the paper-based way overlap. Nevertheless, it is considered a useful preliminary phase that provides various advantages. In particular, the requirement to use paper-based documents and to visit the courts is restricted to specific moments of the process.

7.5.2 The Project Stakeholders

As stated in Sect. 7.5.1.1., the judicial district of the Tribunal of Milan has been the first to discover and implement a way to develop and use TOL. The point now is to investigate the reasons for its success by focusing on how ad hoc organisational arrangements have been able to buffer and manage the complexity associated with TOL.

7.5.2.1 The 'Innovation Office' and the Role of the Milan Bar Association

The 'Innovation Office' has certainly played a relevant role. Its mixed composition of judges, clerks, lawyers and ICT specialists from the Ministry of Justice provided a forum and the know-how to solve the many problems that affected development.

What does the Innovation Office do exactly? It promotes the use of the several software applications to court users and works as an information centre for other courts. Activities at the Innovation Office are not formalised and decisions made in the office are not converted into work orders or circulars that will be adopted at court or district level. Nevertheless, given its high reputation and its problem-solving capacity, the solutions suggested are regularly adopted.

The leadership role in innovation taken by a judge with high standing within the Italian judiciary is just one of many strengths. In addition, clerks have played a 'hidden' but pivotal role. Given their pivotal role in judicial proceedings, they have provided the knowledge required to debug the many administrative tasks associated with the handling of judicial proceedings and found viable solutions. The same applies to ICT specialists, who combined the experience and the solutions found by the Innovation Office with the ICT Department of the Ministry of Justice.

However, the moving engine for the introduction of TOL was the Bar Association, which has a long tradition in promoting ICT innovation between lawyers and judicial offices. In this endeavour, the Bar Association has developed partnerships with various institutions, including the University of Milan, which is involved in the training programmes. Thus, the Innovation Office and the Bar Association played key roles, founding smart mediations between the many constraints emerging from the entanglement of legal, technological, administrative and organisational factors. Besides the resourcefulness, however, resources are also important, and the wealthy Milan Bar Association financed, among other things, the development of the PdA and the training for its associates.

7.5.2.2 Tribunal and Bar Association Joint Venture: The 'Unified Front Office'

A 'Unified Front Office' run by clerks and staff hired by the Bar Association represents a good example of the mediations required by the adoption of TOL. It provides two main services: a help desk for lawyers without PdA access to collect case-related documents and information, and a help desk to provide information to lawyers about TOL. The court clerks run the former while staff hired by the Bar Association runs the latter. The intention is to provide both a service to users and to promote TOL.

At the basis of the creation of the Unified Front Office, there are the entanglements and the problems generated by the entry into force of the already mentioned art.51 Law 133/2008. According to this rule, it is the lawyer who has to check if procedural documents or communications have been issued on his/her behalf, whereas previously clerks were in charge of informing the parties. The new CMS sends communications to parties substantially by default, when a document is registered. This simplifies significantly administrative staff tasks.

This rule was also decisive in the process of spreading PdA adoption. Lawyers with access to these data through a PdA can keep under control all their cases remotely. Those without PdA access are forced to visit the court. If this regulation had come into effect with only a restricted number of PdA users, the front office would have been invaded by lawyers, thus putting normal operations at risk. For this reason, offering lawyers' queuing at the front office (to collect case-related information) the option of enrolling at the PdA and avoiding queues (thanks to the helpdesk) was a simple way to solve two problems at once.

A significant number of registrations with the PdA and the possibility of access to the Unified Front Office allowed the enforcement of the new provision with relatively no effort.

7.6 Concluding Remarks

TOL was originally developed as a full e-filing system with the goals of digitising the entire exchange of data and documents of Italian civil procedures and going online for summonses and the payment of court fees. Until 2006, the level of complexity involved in this approach proved unmanageable even in the TOL Labs, in which organisational experts were recruited to support staff, judges and bar associations in TOL development. This was due to a number of factors.

The development of 'technical' architecture was too complex due to the amount of legal, institutional and organisational constraints and to the complexity of the legal provisions to be inscribed into the system.

Technology had to deal with the detailed and massive regulations governing civil proceedings, regulations that, since 1997, were endlessly changing for reasons not connected with the TOL project. Moreover, technical rules prescribing the features of electronic documents required for their 'legal validity' were issued only in 2005. Thus, until 2005, software houses were not in a position to develop the access points, and TOL Labs have worked for years upon a shifting platform.

PdAs development has also been a key issue, for a number of reasons. At first, just a few software houses were providing this component and its costs were too high for bar associations and individual lawyers. Secondly, PdAs certify that the subject connecting to the court is a practicing lawyer in a given local bar, following in this way the current practices and regulations. According to the official explanation, it is for this legal rationale that the local bars had to be involved in the TOL architecture. A single PdA at the central level could have simplified the architecture, however, achieving significant economies of scale and complexity reduction, and without legal changes, but the Ministry of Justice resisted this option for reasons that are not yet clear.

The PdA case highlights the effects—in terms of complexity growth—of the design decision to inscribe a pre-set of civil proceedings rules into the systems and the technical rules into the law, furthermore, to outsource electronic access to courts to the bar associations (each of them). The decisions to embed the legal and technical rationale, and to leave to the market forces (software houses) the design and development of a part of the system (even a significant part of responsibility) built insurmountable barriers of adoption.

TOL development also required strict integration among different actors and institutions at local level: courts, software houses, lawyers and their bar association. The architecture implementation also required better integration between the central level (the ICT Department of the Ministry of Justice) and the local one (every court system and software house). This 'intricate' structure of relations calls into play a number of independent organisations and technological systems. Furthermore, it delegates to a number of actors (165 local bar associations, neither necessarily motivated or sufficiently wealthy) the key role in PdA deployment and adoption. To sum up, the decision of having the PdAs replicated all over the national territory has been a powerful complexity generator.

Finally, even when procedures had been digitised, some functions would have remained paper-based, such as summonses or payment of amounts and court fees. This entails the need to provide a system able to manage frequent switches from paper to electronic and vice versa.

These constraints show the existence of a number of 'cleavages' affecting TOL development, such as rules-based design vs. information infrastructure cultivation, paper-based procedures vs. digital ones, public vs. private and central vs. local. Such cleavages further generated complexity that has been non-manageable for many years (see Chap. 1). Indeed, after 6 years of development, the TOL project was 'locked in'.

Only at the end of 2006, in Milan, did the court and the local bar succeed in developing the PdA and in going digital with one specific civil proceeding: the payment order. This has been possible, mainly, thanks to the major reduction of complexity resulting from the switch from the digitisation of the entire civil proceedings to the digitisation of a relatively simple and straightforward procedure like the payment order. It was also thanks to the greater capacity of the Milan Bar Association in terms of financial, organisational and human resources, and to an increased capacity for managing complexity due to a local organisational arrangement, in particular the Innovation Office of the court. More particularly, the Milan Bar Association was not only strongly motivated but also wealthy enough to sustain the costs of PdA development and to promote its use among lawyers. This has been done in various ways, including specific training. Then the Innovation Office became, de facto, the management board of the project, involving all the main players. Within this office, lawyers, clerks, judges and ICT specialists, together with representatives of the bar, found viable solutions to the many problems posed by the implementation of this system.

The establishment of the Innovation Office and its day-to-day activity provides an example of how to increase institutional capacity to handle complexity. Here, the judge in charge of the office played an important role. In a context in which activities are not formalised and peer-to-peer relations prevail, he promoted a clear division of labour and responsibility and fostered the growth of a different working culture, a culture that is not only related to the interpretation of law typical of such a legal environment but also which addresses problem-solving and the implementation of ICT. Here, the use of TOL is promoted and the many problems that may hamper its use are analysed according to different perspectives and then solved. The Innovation Office offers a context in which new expertise can develop, so that some employees have literally changed jobs. Judges, clerks and lawyers have had the chance to operate in a situation that, thanks to the increased problem-solving orientation, has raised the capacity to manage complexity with a ‘cultivation’ approach (Dahlbom and Mathiassen 1993).

Like the Innovation Office, which can be considered a solution for increasing organisational capacity to manage complexity, the ‘Unified Front Office’ is an example of how to reduce it to a level that is manageable. Lawyers not enrolled in a PdA, who have to go to the Unified Front Office to get case-related information in person, can take advantage of the nearby PdA help desk, which is also promoting its diffusion among the legal professions.

The further switch from PdA to CEM as the means for filing cases is the last change in the architecture discussed in this chapter. Firstly, it represents an attempt by the Ministry of Justice to approach a standard and spread solutions (CEM is the standard technology used by public agencies for official exchanges of documents in the Italian public sector). According to information infrastructure theory, CEM is a step in the right direction because it is likely to produce a faster bootstrapping of the information infrastructure, as a critical mass of users have already adopted it (Hanseth and Aanestad 2003). It has been a long journey from an unmanageable system ready for the trashcan to a working one, but now it is time to change it again and it remains to be seen what price will have to be paid (perhaps too much) during this new adoption process. Care must be taken.

References

Borsari, G. 2011. Regole tecniche del funzionamento del PCT. Unpublished manuscript presented at the Conference “Processo Civile Telematico”, Florence, 21 Jan 2011.

Borsari, G., and A. Baratta. 2004. L’interoperabilità e gli strumenti per i soggetti esterni. In *Tecnologia, organizzazione e giustizia: L’evoluzione del Processo Civile Telematico*, ed. S. Zan, 227–237. Bologna: Il Mulino.

Borsari, G. 2004. Approfondimenti sull'interoperabilità e gli strumenti per i soggetti esterni. In *Technologia, Organizzazione e Giustizia: L'evoluzione del Processo Civile Telematico*, ed. S. Zan. Bologna: Il Mulino. CD-ROM with annexes.
Carnevali, D. (ed.). 2010. *Soggeti smarriti: Perché innovazione e giustizia non si incontrano (quasi) mai*. Milan: Franco Angeli.
Carnevali, D. 2009. E-Justice and policies for risk management. In *E-Justice: ICT in the court system*, ed. A. Cerrillo and A. Fabra, 19–35. Hershey: Information Science Reference.
Carnevali, D. 2006. L'Italia nel tunnel dell'e-justice. In *Tecnologie per la giustizia. I successi e le false promesse dell'e-justice*, ed. D. Carnevali et al., 83–132. Milano: Giuffrè Editore.
Carnevali, D., F. Contini, M. Fabri, and M. Velicogna. 2007. Technologies for the prosecution offices in Italy: The tensions between legacy and creativity. In *Information and communication technologies for the public prosecutor's offices*, ed. M. Fabri, 229–281. Bologna: Clueb.
Ciborra, C.U. (ed.). 2000. *From control to drift: The dynamics of corporate information infrastructures*. Oxford: Oxford University Press.
Contini, F. 2008. ICT, assemblages and institutional contexts: understanding multiple development paths. In *ICT and innovation in the Public Sector: European studies in the making of e-government*, ed. F. Contini and G.F. Lanzara, 244–271. Basingstoke: Palgrave Macmillan.
Contini, F. 2006. L'infrastruttura dell'informazione nei sistemi giudiziari. In *Tecnologie per la giustizia. I successi e le false promesse dell'e-justice*, ed. D. Carnevali et al., 43–82. Milano: Giuffrè Editore.
Contini, F., and D. Carnevali. 2010. The quality of justice: From conflicts to politics. In *Handbook on judicial politics*, ed. R. Coman and C. Dallara, 157–194. Iasi: Editura Institutul European.
Contini, F., and G.F. Lanzara (eds.). 2009. *ICT and innovation in the public sector: European studies in the making of e-government*. Basingstoke: Palgrave Macmillan.
Contini, F., and A. Cordella. 2007. Information system and information infrastructure deployment: The challenge of the Italian e-Justice approach. *The Electronic Journal of e-Government* 5(1): 43–52.
Contini, F., and M. Fabri. 2003. Judicial electronic data interchange in Europe. In *Judicial electronic data interchange in Europe: Applications, policies and trends*, ed. M. Fabri and F. Contini, 1–26. Bologna: Lo Scarabeo.
Contini, F., and R. Mohr. 2008. *Judicial evaluation, traditions, innovations, and proposal for measuring the quality of court performance*. Saarbrücken: VDM.
Dahlbom, B., and L. Mathiassen. 1993. *Computers in context: The philosophy and practice of systems design*. Cambridge: Blackwell.
Fabri, M. 2009. E-justice in Finland and in Italy: Enabling versus constraining models. In *ICT and innovation in the public sector: European studies in the making of e-government*, ed. F. Contini and G.F. Lanzara, 115–146. Basingstoke: Palgrave Macmillan.
Hanseth, O. 2007. Complexity and risk. In *Risk, complexity and ICT*, ed. O. Hanseth and C. Ciborra, 75–93. Cheltenham: Edward Elgar.
Hanseth, O., and M. Aanestad. 2003. Design as bootstrapping networks: On the evolution of ICT networks in health care. *Methods of Information in Medicine* 42: 385–391.
Jacchia, M. (ed.). 2000. *Il processo telematico: Nuovi ruoli e nuove tecnologie per un moderno processo civile*. Bologna: Il Mulino.
DGSIA. 2011. Rapporto ICT giustizia. Ministero della Giustizia.
Sala, M. 2010. Il processo telematico del 2010. *Immobili and proprietà* 3(2): 1–8.
Velicogna, M., A. Errera, and S. Derlange. 2013. Building e-Justice in Continental Europe: The TéléRecours experience in France. *Utrecht Law Review* 9(1): 38–59.
Velicogna, M. (2011). Electronic access to justice: From theory to practice and back, Droit et Cultures. 61/2011. http://droitcultures.revues.org/2447. Accessed 18 Jan 2013.
Velicogna, M., A. Errera, and S. Derlange. 2011. e-Justice in France: The e-Barreau experience. *Utrecht Law Review* 7(1): 163–187.

Velicogna, M. 2008. Use of Information and Communication Technologies (ICT) in European Judicial Systems, CEPEJ Studies No. 7. 1-64. Council of Europe.

Xilo, G. 2004. L'esperienza dei laboratori sperimentali del Processo Civile Telematico. In *Tecnologia, organizzazione e giustizia*, ed. S. Zan, 119–138. Bologna: Il Mulino.

Zanga, D. 2008. La PA e quei software senza licenza. Punto informatico. http://punto-informatico.it/2207688/PI/Commenti/pa-quei-software-senza-licenza.aspx. Accessed 18 Jan 2013.

Chapter 8
The Making of Pan-European Infrastructure: From the Schengen Information System to the European Arrest Warrant

Marco Velicogna

Abstract This chapter investigates how a complex EU criminal justice procedure, the European Arrest Warrant (EAW), has been implemented and is performing its function through the support of a pre-existing information infrastructure: the Schengen Information System (SIS). Below the apparently seamless surface of the enabling information infrastructure lays a world of complexity. The infrastructure supports the transmission of data as well as sensemaking and the solution of semantic, administrative and procedural micro-issues through its human 'intelligent' components operating in ad hoc organisational units. Complexity is embedded in the heterogeneous, loosely integrated, and time bounded components of SIS. The chapter also investigates how the attempt to introduce a more complete Schengen Information System (SIS II) in order to fully satisfy EAW requirements resulted in a never-ending normative and technological development phase. Building on this wealth of experience, the chapter provides an in-depth view of the dynamics affecting the development of large transborder information infrastructures supporting the circulation of legal agency.

M. Velicogna (✉)
Research Institute on Judicial Systems, National Research Council of Italy (IRSIG-CNR), Bologna, Italy
e-mail: marco.velicogna@irsig.cnr.it

F. Contini and G.F. Lanzara (eds.), *The Circulation of Agency in E-Justice*, Law, Governance and Technology Series 13, DOI 10.1007/978-94-007-7525-1_8,

8.1 Introduction

This chapter investigates the technological and institutional conditions that allowed the circulation of agency[1,2] in the European Arrest Warrant (EAW) procedure. The EAW is a judicial decision, based on a 2002 EU Framework Decision (FD) and national implementing laws, that can be issued by a member state judicial authority 'with a view to the arrest and surrender by another member state of a requested person, for the purposes of conducting a criminal prosecution or executing a custodial sentence or detention order'.

EAW performativity[3] is accomplished through an assemblage[4] of normative, technological and organisational components (Contini 2009; Lanzara 2009) allowing the interoperability of a judicial decision issued by an EU member state in relation to the arrest and surrender by another EU member state of a requested person. The chapter explores how the EAW is made performative and the process of development and change that characterised the information infrastructure[5] that

---

[1]The author wishes to express his gratitude to all the experts and informed participants who supported the data collection, and in particular to the personnel of the Italian SIRENE Bureau and of the Directorate for International cooperation (Ufficio II) within the Directorate General for Criminal Justice of the Italian Ministry of Justice. Special thanks go to Francesco Contini and Giovan Francesco Lanzara for very useful comments and support. The opinions expressed in this chapter are those of the author and do not necessarily reflect the positions of the aforementioned persons and institutions.

[2]'Agency is broadly defined here as the capacity of an entity—human or nonhuman, material or symbolic—to produce effects upon a state of affairs. By "circulation of agency" we mean the possibility for such capacity to be transmitted across multiple media, national borders and functional domains' (see Chap. 1).

[3]The communication exchange which takes place is not only passively describing a given reality but is also performative because it changes the social order it is describing and 're-establish(es) relations between citizens within a legal order' (Mohr and Contini 2011, 999).

[4]The concept of assemblage, derived by the definition provided by Lanzara (2009), allows the evocation of the heterogeneous and loosely integrated nature of the EAW, a system characterised by the presence of distinct components of a normative, technological and organisational nature, a system that is constituted by—and at the same time is the result of—a multiplicity of actors and authority structures that emerge and define their role over time, none of which is exercising full control over the system or its development. It is a net of situated interventions and design activities that are bounded in space and time; of intervention and activities that tend to be 'local' and fragmented, focused on maintaining, updating, adapting and patching together one or more technological, organisational and legal components, confronting unexpected events, drifts and deviations from the planned development path. Its components have been often designed for other scopes and are still performing other tasks. Its essence is continuously defined and redefined in a process that takes place through mediation and negotiation, in which governance structures are explored, experimented and temporarily adopted. In the assembling, existing administrative routines, interfaces and jurisdictions are more or less intentionally redesigned to reach a technical, functional and institutional compatibility.

[5]Hanseth and Lyytinen define information infrastructures as a 'shared, open, heterogeneous and evolving socio-technical system of Information Technology (IT) capabilities. … IIs [information infrastructures] are recursively composed of other infrastructures, platforms, applications and IT

allowed the EAW procedure to be so smoothly implemented and that is now enabling its functioning: the Schengen Information System (SIS).

The SIS is an EU Large Scale Information System that became operational in 1995 and which was 'created as a compensatory measure following the abolition of controls at internal borders within the Schengen area' (European Commission 2010c, 5). The SIS allows competent authorities in Schengen member states to exchange information that is used for performing controls on persons and objects at the external borders or on the territory, as well as for the issuance of visas and residence permits. From a normative perspective, if a person is 'wanted for arrest for extradition or surrender purposes [. . .] the alert in SIS is equivalent to a European Arrest Warrant or a request for provisional arrest'.[6] Until the SIS is capable of transmitting all the mandatory EAW information, however, the alert is the equivalent to an EAW only as a provisional measure awaiting the transmission of the official paper documents.[7] The attempt to develop a second generation SIS (SIS II) that should be capable of transmitting all such information has not been very successful so far.

At the same time, the role of the SIS in creating the conditions for the cross-border circulation of legal agency in the EAW procedure is not just that of a technological infrastructure allowing the transmission of information or of legally valid documents. The SIS itself is an assemblage of technological, normative and organisational components. The SIRENE Bureaus, the core organisational SIS units for each Schengen State, have an important role in the EAW procedure and were key in the implementation phase, providing the competences and resources needed to absorb part of the semantic, normative and organisational complexity.

The chapter also shows the tension between the EAW procedure and its enabling information infrastructure. Because the SIS predates the EAW FD, the fit between the two is not seamless. As an example, not all the elements provided for by the EAW form find their equivalent in the SIS database structure. Furthermore, the scope of the SIS is broader than that of the EAW. As a consequence, the SIS, while making the EAW 'performative', has changed in a not-always-parallel path to it. Indeed, over time, as the Schengen area expanded, institutional settings changed and risks and their public perception shifted, the SIS has evolved through a path characterised by strong drifts and deviations (Ciborra et al. 2000; Contini and Lanzara 2009; Carnevali 2009), not always 'EAW oriented'. Therefore, the case also presents an opportunity to reflect on the issue of not-necessarily convergent adaptability and evolvability of the information infrastructure in relation to the procedure being enabled.

Finally, as pointed out by Hanseth and Lyytinen, 'effective design of IIs [information infrastructures] holds considerable benefits for individuals, businesses

---

capabilities and controlled by emergent, distributed and episodic forms of control. II's evolutionary dynamics are nonlinear, path-dependent and influenced by network effects and unbounded user and designer learning' (Hanseth and Lyytinen 2010, 1).

[6]http://www.consilium.europa.eu/policies/council-configurations/justice-et-affaires-interieures-%28jai%29/sirene-schengen-information-system/sis.aspx?lang = en

[7]Art. 9 EAW FD, Council Framework Decision 2002/584/JHA

and society at large [. . .] Yet, failures to design IIs are more common incurring huge losses in foregone investments, opportunity costs, and political and social problems' (Hanseth and Lyytinen 2010, 1–2). From this perspective, the never-ending struggle of the heterogeneous actors involved in SIS I maintenance-and-evolution and in SIS II development, as well as the 'dynamic complexity' (technological, normative, organisational and institutional) (Hanseth and Lyytinen 2010, 2) these actors have confronted over the years, allow us to examine information infrastructures dynamics in depth and the conflict/competition between existing and emerging Information Infrastructures. In these dynamics, a key role is played by the combination of a number of factors, such as path dependencies; emerging needs, goals and opportunities; unexpected events, drifts and deviations; drives to change and tensions over ownership, management, control and access (Edwards et al. 2007); variations in Maximum Feasible Simplicity, Maximum Manageable Complexity design and operational requirements.[8]

While from a procedural perspective, the EAW is performing well, it should be noted that many relevant issues are still open from a human rights perspective, such as the lack of proportionality in the seriousness of the offences for which the EAW is issued between member states, the lack of proportionality checks and the lack of a structured organisation/procedure to address the improper use of the EAW (i.e., criminal investigation instead of prosecution).[9] However, since such issues are outside the scope of this work, they are not pursued further.

The rest of the chapter, after a description of the main relevant features of the EAW, analyses the SIS and its long evolution as the information infrastructure backbone that enables the EAW to operate. The conclusions provide some reflections on the EAW and SIS experience for interoperability at EU level.

8.2 The European Arrest Warrant

The EAW procedure was introduced with the purpose of replacing the extradition procedure between EU member states with a faster and simpler surrender procedure through the Council Framework Decision of 13 June 2002 on the EAW and the surrender procedures between member states (2002/584/JHA). Once issued, the EAW is valid throughout all EU member states. This new procedure removes some of the political and administrative phases from the decision-making process.[10] According to the Council of the European Union, 'In general, the EAW is operating efficiently. The basis for this conclusion is the increasing volume of requests, the percentage of them that result in effective surrender and the fact that the surrender

[8]See Lanzara, Chap. 1.

[9]On the topic see for example Kurtovic and Langbroek (2010).

[10]http://europa.eu/legislation_summaries/justice_freedom_security/judicial_cooperation_in_criminal_matters/l33167_en.htm.

deadlines are generally met. The improvement is even more striking when these variables are compared with those existing under the previous extradition regime' (Council of the European Union 2009b, 6).

Without going too much into the details of the political events that led to its introduction, it is important to mention that the EAW FD emerged as a response to the climate created by the terrorist attacks of 11 September 2001. By December 2001, the political decision to adopt the EAW legislation had already been taken. This provided a strong signal to the public that concrete actions were being taken. However, while promoted as an anti-terrorist measure, the EAW FD affects a much wider range of ordinary crimes (Impalà 2005, 59).

The implementation laws introducing and regulating the EAW in the member states' systems were often complex processes and took longer than anticipated. Only half of all member states complied with the time limit laid down in the FD.[11] Time delay was not the only issue. Several member states had to revise their constitutions in order to adopt specific legislation transposing the EAW FD.[12] In some cases, national implementing law failed to fully transpose the EAW FD and Parliaments and Constitutional Courts have been required to intervene, or courts jurisprudence has found viable compromises. Still, as noted by the practitioners involved in the procedure, not all problems and tensions have been solved yet.

The EAW stands on the assumption of a high level of mutual trust and cooperation between EU countries and of the existence of common minimum standards of rule of law. This is provided for the European Commission, by the fact that 'member states and national courts have to respect the provisions of the European Convention on Human Rights and to ensure that it is respected. Anyone arrested under an EAW may have a lawyer and, if necessary, an interpreter, as provided by the law of the country where he or she has been arrested.'[13] An EAW can be issued by a national judicial authority for the purposes of conducting a criminal prosecution (for offences carrying a maximum penalty of at least 12 months) or enforcing a custodial sentence (for sentences of 4 months or more). At the same time, an EAW cannot be issued for investigation purposes.

In comparison with the previous extradition system, the EAW FD introduced a number of functional simplifications, the main ones being the following[14]:

- The EAW is issued and executed directly by judicial authorities—the role of the executive branch (ministries, etc.) has been abolished or reduced to that of a transmission facilitator.
- The EAW is issued on the same simple form in all member states, so that it is easy to use and translate.

---

[11] http://ec.europa.eu/justice/doc_centre/criminal/doc/com_2005_063_en.pdf.

[12] http://ec.europa.eu/justice/doc_centre/criminal/doc/com_2005_063_en.pdf.

[13] http://ec.europa.eu/justice/policies/criminal/extradition/policies_criminal_extradition_en.htm.

[14] http://www.consilium.europa.eu/policies/council-configurations/justice-et-affaires-interieures-%28jai%29/sirene-schengen-information-system/sirene/european-arrest-warrant-%28eaw%29.aspx?lang = en.

- For a list of 32 categories of specified crimes, and under certain conditions, the offence must be punishable under the criminal laws of the requesting member state and not both the surrendering and the requesting State.
- Grounds for refusal are strictly limited by the EAW FD that distinguishes between mandatory and optional grounds. The surrender of member states' citizens can, for instance, no longer be refused on the grounds of their citizenship. However, some member states have added some grounds for refusal when implementing the EAW FD into their national law.
- The time limits for deciding on and executing an EAW are explicit, making the surrender procedure much faster than the previous extradition procedure.
- An SIS Alert has the same status as the original EAW, thereby simplifying the distribution of the warrants.

In spite of the difficulties that characterised both the adoption of the EAW FD and its initial implementation (of consistency between national norms and a lack of operative practices and a shared understanding of roles and competences of the relevant actors), legal interpretations have progressively stabilised and organisational and inter-organisational learning, both of national and of other member states' norms and practices, has taken place. At the same time, during the implementation process, both national norms and EAW FD have been amended to support the long-term functioning of the EAW mechanism and to reduce some of the tensions it introduced. Indeed, a high level of legal, organisational and technological adaptation has been required to keep the circulation of agency going through the assemblage. The result is a system that is technically and organisationally sound and which has proved to be a quite effective tool of criminal cooperation. The next section provides a description of the EAW in action in one country, namely, Italy. The description builds on the data collected through in-depth interviews, focus groups, literature and documents analysis within the projects "The European Arrest Warrant in Law and in Practice: a comparative study for the consolidation of the European law-enforcement area"[15] and "Building interoperability for European civil proceedings online".[16]

8.2.1 *The European Arrest Warrant in Action*

8.2.1.1 Issuing an European Arrest Warrant

In Italy, in order to issue an EAW both for the prosecution of a crime and for the enforcement of a sentence, there needs to be evidence that the requested

[15]Co-financed by the European Commission JLS/2007/JPEN/245; for more details see Velicogna (2010).

[16]Co-financed by the European Commission JLS/2009/JCIV/AG/0035.

person is, resides or is domiciled in the territory of one of the EU member states. The *Vademecum* drafted by the Ministry of Justice to support the EAW implementation suggests the application of the *principle of proportionality* to issue an EAW. The judge or the public prosecutor should assess the gravity of the crime, the personality of the perpetrator, the amount of the punishment and the duration of the precautionary measure, along with consideration of the expiry of the terms of the phase. They should also consider the large amount of resources that the enforcement of the arrest warrant requires. As a consequence of both normative restraints and *Vademecum* persuasive reasoning, Italian judges and public prosecutors typically issue EAWs only in 'serious cases', such as terrorism, organised crime, murder, rape, major drug smuggling, etc.

The competent authority to issue an EAW during the investigation and trial phases is the judge who issued the domestic arrest warrant (precautionary measure of prison custody or house arrest), while for the enforcement of a sentence it is the public prosecutor attached to the court that issued the arrest order. Once the EAW is issued, a copy of the EAW (with relevant supplementary documents attached) is sent to the Ministry of Justice and, frequently, also directly to the SIRENE Bureau (and Interpol for the diffusion to 'EAW Countries' that are not included in the SIS). While, according to the EAW FD, the issuing judicial authority can transmit the EAW directly to the executing judicial authority, this seldom happens but in this case, the EAW is usually transmitted through the Ministry of Justice too.

The Ministry of Justice has the task of assisting the competent judicial authorities and the responsibilities for the administrative transmission and reception of EAWs, as well as for all other official correspondence related to it.

After receiving the EAW (generally the first communication takes place by post or by fax), the Ministry of Justice faxes the EAW to SIRENE to issue an SIS Alert 95[17] and to Interpol. On a few occasions in the past, it happened that the request for the issuing of an SIS Alert 95 was sent by the issuing judicial authority to the SIRENE Bureau without informing the Ministry of Justice. For this reason, the SIRENE Bureau now alerts the Ministry of such events.

If the location of the person is not known and there is no suspicion that the person is outside the Italian border, often an SIS Alert 98[18] (or SIS Alert 99[19]) is filed to locate the person. If the person is located, an EAW and an Alert 95 are then issued. While an SIS Alert 98 (99) is filed at local level, Alert 95 s are issued only by the SIRENE Bureau. When receiving an EAW issued by an Italian judicial authority, the SIRENE Bureau in Rome completes the required SIS forms (A[20] + M[21]) and enters the data in the SIS, translating the required information from Italian to English.

---

[17] Persons wanted for extradition to a Schengen State.

[18] Article 98: persons wanted as witnesses, or for the purposes of prosecution or the enforcement of sentences.

[19] Article 99: persons or vehicles to be placed under surveillance or subjected to specific checks.

[20] Supplementary information.

[21] Miscellaneous information.

The translation is typically made by the operator entering the data. All SIRENE personnel typically speak English at a fair–good level as well as other languages. During the interviews, however, it was noted that the task of translating is both delicate and time-consuming, and this may generate problems with the growing number of cases that the Bureau is facing. Direct interaction between the public prosecutor/judge following the case and SIRENE may take place in order to better respond to the requirements of the case (i.e., particularly urgent, missing relevant information, ambiguities to be solved to allow a correct translation and the issuing of the alert, etc.).

Some discrepancies between the EAW and the SIS may need to be addressed. For example, while 'an EAW can be issued for several offences at the same time, as long as they are covered by the same domestic arrest warrant or conviction' (Council of the European Union 2009a, 12), the SIS Alert 95 must refer only to the main offence. This may generate problems for data entry. Moreover, if a requested person is wanted for the execution of more than one sentence, the public prosecutor must fill out one EAW form for each sentence and inform the SIRENE Bureau about which sentence to use in order to issue the alert, because the SIS allows the entry of just one alert per person. In general, the 'main' sentence is inserted. When the requested person is located/arrested, the SIRENE Bureau informs the executing member state of the existence of more than one sentence and of a plurality of EAWs. When more than one EAW exists for the same person, it is necessary that the executing judicial authority decides about the surrender on each one of them. When the surrender takes place, only the sentences for which the EAW has been approved can be enforced (Di Giorgio 2009).

The Italian authority issuing an EAW does not check the existence of other EAWs already issued by other Italian courts. Checks are made both by the Ministry of Justice and by the SIRENE Bureau. The SIRENE Bureau and the Ministry of Justice alert each other that the EAW has already been issued for the same person.

If the decision leading to the EAW is reviewed or retracted, the EAW and the SIS alert should be retired. It does happen, though, that SIRENE is not notified. As a consequence of such missed notifications, the alert originally inserted in the SIS appears to be valid. This may give rise to substantial problems because the person is still subject to arrest.

Foreign SIRENE Bureaus may ask to flag the Alert 95 in relation to their State. The flag is inserted by the SIRENE Bureaus that entered the alert. A flagged alert is considered as being issued for the purpose of communicating the place of residence of the person concerned.[22]

[22] An issue that has arisen in the EAW evaluation reports 'is the scrutiny and flagging in the SIS of alerts for arrest for surrender purposes without the matter being put before the competent executing judicial authority for consideration. This is a major issue for the operation of the EAW, since the flagging of an alert may de facto amount to non-execution of the underlying EAW' (Council of the European Union 2009b, 17).

After a person has been located/apprehended in another EU country, the SIRENE Bureau is typically alerted by the national SIRENE Bureau of the country in which the person has been located/apprehended. Additional information may be required by the foreign authority. If available, the Office directly provides it through the SIS. Furthermore, the SIRENE Bureau informs the Ministry of Justice and the issuing authority about the need to provide the translation of the EAW in one of the languages accepted by the executing authority, as well as the need to provide for relevant missing or additional information asked for by the foreign authority. The Ministry of Justice or the issuing judicial authority may also be contacted directly by the foreign authority once the requested person has been apprehended in one of the EU countries. The translation of the EAW is made by the Ministry of Justice. English, French, German and Spanish translators are available internally. For other languages, the Ministry of Justice must resort to the services of external translators. This may generate problems, especially in case of countries with very tight deadlines for the transmission of the official translation.

If the surrender is granted, Interpol organises the transfer of the person, who is arrested by the Frontier Police when passing the border or at the national airport. The Alert 95 is revoked. In case the surrender is not granted, the foreign authority requires the Italian SIRENE Bureau to flag the alert for that country. The alert is still valid for all other SIS countries, however. The issuing authority may issue a new EAW concerning the same person, which results in a new alert for the same person that is also valid in that country.

8.2.1.2 Executing an European Arrest Warrant

The execution of an EAW typically begins with the location/apprehension of the requested person by a local police unit following a check based on an Alert 95 (or on the basis of an Interpol alert-diffusion or red notice) or on a routine check from which the existence of an alert is discovered (e.g., passport control at an airport). If an Alert 95 is discovered when a check is made, the person is taken into custody straightaway. The local police immediately contacts the SIRENE Bureau, which verifies the consistency of the alert, notifies (through the SIS) the SIRENE Bureau of the issuing country and, if needed, requests additional information. This is particularly important in order to spot cases in which identity theft has occurred or in which details are so vague that no exact identification is possible.

The Italian SIRENE Bureau provides the local police office with a 'support kit' for the procedure the local police office has to follow according to the Italian EAW FD implementation law and the Court of Cassation adjourned case law. This kit has been specifically designed to be easy to use and contain both indications on the activities to carry out and electronic forms to fill out the documents the local police office needs to produce.

The local police office then proceeds with the arrest of the person. This is not necessarily an easy task because the person being arrested needs to be informed in a language that he or she understands about the EAW and its content, about the possibility of consenting to surrender, about the right to legal counsel and the right to be assisted by an interpreter. A local office may not have, for example, the availability of a translator with the right competences. The police office then notifies all the Italian authorities interested (the Court of Appeal of the District, the Public Prosecutor Office General attached to it, the Ministry of Justice and the SIRENE Bureau), providing a copy of the report of the procedural steps followed (including the steps taken to identify the requested person) and of the SIS Alert.

The Italian Ministry of Justice then notifies the requesting member state of the arrest, requesting the transmission of the arrest warrant and relevant additional documentation (in general, the issuing country has already been unofficially notified by the SIS) translated into Italian. The Ministry of Justice, upon reception of the EAW, examines it and, in the case of obvious problems such as missing parts or the EAW not being translated into Italian, contacts the issuing authority asking it to make the appropriate corrections/integrations. It should be noted that the lack of translation of the EAW into Italian is a common reason for the rejection of an EAW execution on formal grounds (Council of the European Union 2009a, 25). When the Ministry of Justice receives the EAW from the issuing authority, it then submits it to the Court of Appeal with territorial jurisdiction, which is the court in charge of the decision about the execution of the EAW.

The person held in custody is then made available by the police to the Court of Appeal in whose district the arrest has been made for the arrest to be validated. If it is evident that the wrong person has been arrested or the person was arrested on grounds other than those pursuant to the law, the release of the person is ordered. The SIRENE Bureau should be informed because if the SIS Alert is not flagged, the person may be arrested again. In case of problems concerning the content or the authenticity of the documents transmitted by the issuing judicial authority, the Court of Appeal can contact directly, or through the Ministry of Justice, the issuing authority.[23]

After the first examination by a judge of the Court of Appeal to validate the arrest, a panel of three judges of the Court of Appeal holds a hearing for the discussion of the surrender. Additional information is often requested from the issuing authority to comply with the additional requirements of the Italian law implementing the EAW FD. If relevant information is missing from the EAW, the executing authority may request it directly or through the Ministry of Justice. The Ministry of Justice translates the request into the language requested by the issuing country and submits it to the issuing authority. The Ministry of Justice routinely submits such a request to Interpol and SIRENE as well, asking them to

[23]If the competent issuing authority does not provide an Italian translation of the EAW (or the SIS alert) to the Italian Ministry of Justice or to the competent Judicial Authority within 10 days of the validation of the arrest by the Court of Appeal, the order imposing the coercive measures is null and void. If the EAW in Italian is delivered and there is still a danger that the person may abscond, new coercive measures can be ordered. The order can be challenged before the Supreme Court of Cassation. The appeal may be lodged by the legal counsel of the requested person or by the public prosecutor general of the Court of Appeal in the interest of the law.

inform the corresponding service in the issuing member state in order to ensure the transmission and reduce the possibility of errors through redundancy (Council of the European Union 2009a, 29).

If the issuing authority does not provide such information within the allowed timeframe, the court decides on the case anyway. While initially this was considered a reason for automatic refusal, the case law of the Court of Cassation has suggested that a favourable decision may be taken if enough information is available.

The Court of Appeal holds a hearing in the presence of the general prosecutor, the legal counsel of the requested person and the requested person if he or she wants to be present. Immediately following the hearing, the Court of Appeal discusses 'in camera' the decision regarding the execution of the EAW. At the conclusion of this discussion, the decision is read out immediately. The reading is regarded as notification to the parties, whether present or not. The parties are entitled to receive a copy of the decision.[24]

The decision should be issued within 60 days of the execution of the precautionary measures related to the EAW request. The decision is transmitted immediately to the Ministry of Justice, who informs the competent authorities of the issuing member state directly and through SIRENE. In the case of a positive surrender decision, the Ministry of Justice also informs Interpol, in order to organise the physical surrender.

If the Court of Appeal refuses the surrender request, it immediately revokes the relevant precautionary measure related to the EAW procedure and orders the release of the requested person. In this case, the SIRENE Bureau also needs to be notified so that the SIS Alert is flagged.

The decision of the Court of Appeal on the surrender request may be challenged before the Court of Cassation. The appeal may be lodged by the legal counsel of the requested person or by the public prosecutor general of the Court of Appeal and suspends the execution of the surrender decision.

The Court of Cassation holds a hearing within 15 days of receiving the documents of the case. The public prosecutor's office and the legal counsel are notified at least 5 days in advance. The Court of Cassation does not decide only on points of law, as it usually does in other cassation procedures, but also on the substance of the case. Moreover, contrary to the typical Court of Cassation procedure, the requested person can be present and is allowed to speak to the Court. This rarely happens, however. At the conclusion of the hearing, the Court of Cassation decides in chamber and immediately afterwards reads out its decision. The written decision of the Court of Cassation at the conclusion of the hearing should be accompanied by a specific statement containing the grounds underlying it.[25]

---

[24] Art. 17.6. of the Italian EAW FD implementing law. See also Council of the European Union (2009a, 31).

[25] If it is not possible to immediately deliver this statement, the Court of Cassation should deliver the statement within 5 days of reaching a decision.

A copy of the decision is immediately transmitted to the Ministry of Justice. The procedures that follow in the case of a surrender decision or acquittal are analogous to those described for a decision of the Court of Appeal. The Court of Cassation can also quash a decision with remittal, in which case the documents are transmitted by the Court of Cassation to the Court of Appeal where the remittal judge should decide the case within 20 days of receiving them.

There is a contact point for EAW matters at the Court of Cassation. The aim of the contact point is, on the one hand, to function as a centre of expertise for the benefit of the members of the Court of Cassation (and, as appropriate, for members of Courts of Appeal that may need information or assistance in EAW matters) and, on the other hand, to facilitate contacts with issuing authorities in the other member states.[26]

8.2.2 European Arrest Warrant Performativity

The practical application of the EAW has been the subject of in-depth mutual evaluations.[27] The information gathered during the mutual evaluation exercises show that 'in general, the EAW is operating efficiently. The basis for this conclusion is the increasing volume of requests, the percentage of them that result in effective surrender and the fact that the surrender deadlines are generally met. The improvement is even more striking when these variables are compared with those existing under the previous extradition regime.'[28] As the description of the EAW in action in Italy shows, performativity is ensured through two main dimensions:

- Across national judicial borders, when a judicial decision that is the result of procedures appropriate in the issuing country does not just 'say' something but instead performs a certain kind of action (activates an arrest, a surrender procedure, etc.) in another national judicial system;
- Across media as agency is translated (at least partially and temporarily) from paper to electronic to action. It is interesting how different channels and media provide redundancy and support one another (e.g., fax, telephone, SIS forms).

While the procedure seems to be working like a well-oiled machine, the reality is a bit more complex. The next section explores some of the complexity that lies behind the way in which performativity is ensured, looking in more detail at the features and evolution of the EAW information infrastructure (SIS).

[26] See also: Council of the European Union (2009a, 32).

[27] See for example: Council of the European Union (2009b).

[28] Council of the European Union (2009b, 6).

8.3 The Schengen Information System

While the SIS is an integral part of the EAW, SIS predates it and has a broader field of application. SIS is the Europe's 'largest shared database on maintaining public security, supporting police and judicial cooperation and managing external border control. Participating States provide entries, called "alerts", on wanted and missing persons, lost and stolen property and entry bans.'[29]

From a normative perspective, SIS finds its roots in the Convention on the Implementation of the Schengen Agreement signed on 19 June 1990 (Brouwer 2008, 1). When it took effect in 1995, the Convention on the Implementation of the Schengen Agreement 'abolished checks at the internal borders of the signatory states and created a single external border where immigration checks for the Schengen area are carried out in accordance with identical procedures. Common rules regarding visas, right of asylum and checks at external borders were adopted to allow the free movement of persons within the signatory states without disrupting law and order.'[30] The abolition of obstacles to the free movement of goods, persons, services and capital between Schengen States was coupled with the introduction of 'compensatory measures'—increased cross-border cooperation and coordination—in order to uphold security, fight against organised crime and ensure justice. Accordingly, the Schengen Implementing Convention of 1990 'created a multinational database (the Schengen Information System) for the use of immigration, border control, judicial and police authorities in any of the States which fully apply the Schengen Convention' (House of Lords 2007). The 1990 Convention on the Implementation of the Schengen Agreement dedicates 28 out of 142 articles to the SIS in its Title IV. Going into quite some detail, the Schengen Convention provides for SIS establishment (Arts. 92–93), operation and use (Arts. 94–101), for protection of personal data and security of data contained in it (Arts. 102–118) and for the apportionment of costs (Art. 119). In particular, 'Articles 94–100 divide the data entered in the SIS into a number of different categories of "alerts"' (House of Lords 2007). Alerts include people (wanted, to be controlled or with refusal of entry) and goods, with the objectives ranging from border control, to the 'issuing of visas, residence permits, driver's licenses, customs regime, police and judicial activities, and also to guarantee public order, national and European security'.[31] An alert is a set of data entered in the SIS allowing the competent authorities to identify a person or an object/vehicle with a view to taking specific action.

From a technical perspective, the countries participating in the 1990 Schengen Convention adopted a data-processing star architecture with a central site containing

---

[29]http://www.consilium.europa.eu/policies/council-configurations/justice-et-affaires-interieures-%28jai%29/sirene-schengen-information-system.aspx?lang = en.

[30]http://europa.eu/legislation_summaries/justice_freedom_security/free_movement_of_persons_asylum_immigration/l33020_en.htm.

[31]http://www.mvr.bg/en/shengen/sis.htm.

a reference database, the 'technical support function of the Schengen Information System', known as C-SIS, and 'national sections', known as N-SISs, containing a copy of the database.[32] The French Republic is responsible for C-SIS, which is located in Strasbourg. N-SISs are set up and maintained individually by each State. In theory, the national data file should be 'materially identical to the data files of the national sections of each of the other contracting parties'.[33] When setting up its national section, each State must observe the protocols and procedures, which have been jointly established for the C-SIS. Each national section's data file is used for searches in the territory of each State. It is not possible to search the data files of other N-SISs.[34] Maintenance and service level commitments for hardware and software must be provided for by each State to ensure the 24/7 operation of its N-SIS and to guarantee the data integrity of each N-SIS. Similar performance levels and guarantees needs to be provided for any national copies, where these exist (including real-time synchronisation of copies and regular database comparisons) (Council of the European Union 2002).

'All national systems are connected online with the central system via a secured communication network.'[35] The system was conceived with an architecture that should ensure that national databases contain identical information.[36] Altogether, C-SIS, N-SISs and the linking network constitute the SIS. The system became fully operational by the end of 1994, with the first technical link between the then seven participant States taking place on 30 November 1994 (Yung 2005, 8). While the technical assemblage has been running ever since, the components have changed over time. So, for example, the current network, SISNET, a virtual private network based on TCP/IP protocol,[37] was introduced between 2001 and 2002 to replace the previous network, the SIRENE Network Phase II, which was based on X.25,[38] one of the oldest packet-switched services,[39] developed by the

---

[32] http://en.wikipedia.org/wiki/SIRENE

[33] Art.92.2. of the Convention Implementing the Schengen Agreement.

[34] Ibidem.

[35] http://www.consilium.europa.eu/policies/council-configurations/justice-et-affaires-interieures-%28jai%29/sirene-schengen-information-system/sis.aspx?lang = en.

[36] In particular, according to Art 92.3. of the Convention Implementing the Schengen Agreement, C-SIS comprises a data file that will ensure via online transmission that the data files of the national sections contain identical information.

[37] Council of the European Union, (2004), Note 12465/04 LIMITE SIRIS 92 COMIX 557 from the Spanish delegation to SIS/SIRENE Working Party (EU-Iceland and Norway Mixed Committee) on 'Connection of new States to SISNET'.

[38] ITU-T (previously CCITT) Recommendation X.25: Interface between Data Terminal Equipment (DTE) and Data Circuit-terminating Equipment (DCE) for terminals operating in the packet mode and connected to public data networks by dedicated circuit (Geneva, 1976; amended at Geneva, 1980; Malaga-Torremolinos, 1984; Melbourne, 1988; Helsinki 1993; revised in 1996). For more information see http://www.itu.int/rec/T-REC-X.25/en

[39] The first edition of the X.25 Recommendation was approved in 1976, http://www.itu.int/en/ITU-T/studygroups/com17/Pages/history.aspx

International Telegraph and Telephone Consultative Committee.[40] Furthermore, the use of another network, s-TESTA (Secured Trans-European Services for Telematics between Administrations),[41] has been contemplated. As an example of the system in action, in case of the escape of a prisoner, the competent authority immediately reports that an SIS Alert needs to be issued on that specific individual and the relevant information is entered in the national SIS database. The N-SIS in turn transmits the data immediately to C-SIS. The central system will then send this data to the other N-SISs so that all N-SISs are updated in real time and (almost) simultaneously (Yung 2005, 9). While in theory everything should run smoothly and as provided for by the normative framework, this is not always the case. For example, in its first control mission in 1996, the Schengen Convention Joint Supervisory Authority (JSA) discovered that the databases of the N-SISs were not identical,[42] as provided for in Art. 92.2. of the Convention, and that due to design features never could be; the procedure for detecting differences currently followed was too infrequent[43] and too long[44]; the technical measures necessary to safeguard established security standards were not always applied; the set rules were too vague and had not been properly issued; too many people were granted super user access to the system[45]; tracing functions[46] were not satisfactorily applied; and security for the management and transport of the magnetic media containing the SIS data was lacking (JSA 1997).

Supplementary information, which cannot be inserted in SIS records but needs to be exchanged for allowing the appropriate action to be taken in case people and

---

[40]The network lines were leased by the French Government between C. SIS and the French border and by each Member States from the French border to the Member State. At the same time, each Member State had purchased and was the owner of the crypto devices (Kryptoguards) used on the network (Council of the European Union, (2002), Note 12436/1/02 REV 1 LIMITE SIS-TECH 137 COMIX 539 from SIS-TECH Working Group (EU-Iceland and Norway Mixed Committee) to SIS-SIRENE Working Group (EU-Iceland and Norway Mixed Committee) on 'Information about the SISNET'.

[41]s-TESTA is the European Community's own private, IP-based network dedicated to inter-administrative requirements and providing guaranteed performance levels. s-TESTA has been created to offer a telecommunications interconnection platform that responds to the growing need for secure information exchange between European public administrations. s-TESTA has been build on the experience of a preceding network (TESTA). Its kick-off was in mid 2007, and full migration was achieved by end of April 2008. http://ec.europa.eu/idabc/en/document/2097/5644.html

[42]A large number of disparities were detected between the databases of France and Luxembourg and those of other countries; these differences date back to April 1996 and had not been rectified 6 months later (JSA 1997).

[43]Approximately once every 6 months (JSA 1997).

[44]Taking up several months to be carried out (JSA 1997).

[45]'enabling them to access and change the contents of any file in the computer system (operating system, database and network) and to erase any trace of their action' (JSA 1997).

[46]'to verify in retrospect the operations carried out by the users, regardless of priority (date, time, terminal, user ID, type of operation)' (JSA 1997).

objects are found as a result of a search on SIS, is provided by a network of member state central authorities known as SIRENE Bureaus,[47] which are the human interface of the SIS.[48] SIRENE Bureaus are 'set up and designated as the single point of contact for each Schengen State in respect of SIS Alerts and post-hit procedure' (Council of the European Union 2002, 14), reducing the complexity of cross-border communication and coordination. They were not foreseen in the initial version of the Convention Implementing the Schengen Agreement but were introduced from the beginning as national responses to an organisational and coordination need for the SIS to operate (JSA 1997) and showed themselves to be 'an essential feature of the SIS system, without which it could scarcely function' (House of Lords 2007). Only 10 years after the Schengen Convention implementation, Art. 92.4 was added to it, providing a common legal basis for them to all Schengen States.[49] SIRENE Bureaus' 'missions and acts are defined in a concrete way in a common manual designated as "SIRENE manual"' (JSA 1997). The SIRENE manual is an important element of coordination, providing instructions to the SIRENE personnel and describing in detail the rules and procedures governing the exchange of information through the SIS. It is interesting to note that the document has needed to be frequently updated to continue supporting the uniformity of working procedures of the SIRENE Bureaus and ensure their alignment with changes of the relevant European Union law (European Commission 2011).

8.3.1 The Schengen Information System's Evolution

Although the SIS began officially to perform its tasks in 1995, this date should be seen more as the beginning of a long process of development than an end of it. This is due to several factors, including new contracting parties (States) to the Schengen Convention, changes in the political context (such as the rise of the terrorism issue in the European political agenda) and in the EU legal framework, the evolution of technologies and misalignments between components that needed to be worked on. The following sub-sections try to describe some of the main steps that characterised this process of development.

---

[47] SIRENE stands for Supplementary Information Request at the National Entry.

[48] http://europa.eu/legislation_summaries/justice_freedom_security/free_movement_of_persons_asylum_immigration/l33020_en.htm.

[49] Art 92.4 of the Schengen convention was added through Council Regulation (EC) No 871/2004 and Council Decision 2005/211/JHA: 'member states shall, in accordance with national legislation, exchange through the authorities designated for that purpose (Sirene) all supplementary information necessary in connection with the entry of alerts and for allowing the appropriate action to be taken in cases where persons in respect of whom, and objects in respect of which, data have been entered in the Schengen Information System, are found as a result of searches made in this system.'

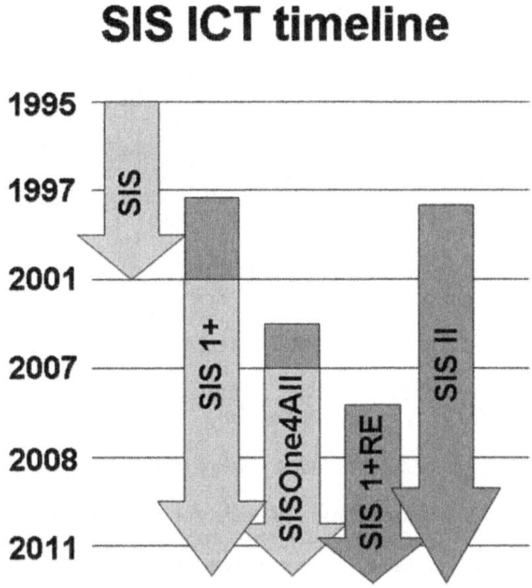

Fig. 8.1 SIS ICT timeline

8.3.1.1 The First Step, from SIS I to SIS I+

Beginning in 1998, a more up-to-date version of the SIS was developed (SIS 1+) to allow the Nordic countries to join Schengen (Denmark, Sweden, Finland, Norway and Iceland). SIS 1+ 'included the possibility of linking two or three additional countries to the system. The upgrade was also meant to improve the performance of the SIS and make it easier to manage and maintain' (Coelho 2006). SIS1+ became operational in 2001, at the end of SIRENE Network Phase II. The JSA considered SIS1+ to be an improvement on the previous system in so far as compliance with the relevant data protection principles was concerned (JSA 2003) (Fig. 8.1).

8.3.1.2 SIS II

Given some design limitations—the initial design of the SIS had not provided for the participation of more than 18 States—and as the Schengen area kept growing, the need emerged for a new version of the SIS to accommodate the inclusion of the EU's new member states. According to Hayes, 'The Schengen Executive took the decision to create SIS II in late 1996 after Italy, Austria and Greece joined the SIS. This took the number of participating states to ten—two more than originally planned—and with the prospect of up to 25 countries eventually joining it was agreed that the existing SIS simply could not cope' (Hayes 2004). This need was also seen as an opportunity to benefit from developments in the field of information technology and to allow for the introduction of new functionalities, such as the inclusion of biometric data (House of Lords 2007) (Fig. 8.2).

Timetable for SIS II development

June 2003 - Definite list of functionalities and decision on the architecture [document not publicly available],

August 2003 - Launch of the call for tender of SIS II,

Mid-May - June 2004 - Final agreement of functions and presentation to [Article 36 Committee], Council Conclusions as required,

June 2004 - Signature of the contract for the detailed design and the development of SIS II and subsequent draft of the detailed design,

January 2005 - Start of SIS II development,

Spring 2005 - Start of Schengen States/Member States national system adaptation,

Autumn 2006 - Start migrating current Contracting Parties,

End 2006 - Ready for integration of new Contracting Parties (the issue of whether acceding countries could integrate in parallel with present Parties is still under discussion).

[6387/02, 25.2.03 and 5117/04 , 7.2.04]

Fig. 8.2 SIS II timetable in 2003–2004 (Source: B. Hayes 2004)

The preparatory work on the concept of SIS II was carried out by the SIS Steering Committee and the Permanent Working Party at the end of the 1990s and the preliminary study was carried out by IBM (JSA 1999). The JSA become involved in it by mid-1998. Following this initial work, on 6 December 2001, the Council adopted two legislative instruments (Council Regulation [EC] No 2424/2001 and Council Decision 2001/886/JHA), making the Commission responsible for developing SIS II and providing for the related expenditure to be covered by the general budget of the EU.[50] The Commission published a communication on 18 December 2001 (European Commission 2001) examining ways of creating and developing SIS II. 'The Commission launched the technical implementation in October 2004 by signing a contract with a budget of up to €40 million for the development of the SIS II and the VIS (Visa Information System), which shares the same technical platform. The target date set for the delivery of the SIS II was March 2007. In parallel to the technical implementation, discussions on new requirements of the SIS have been on the agenda of the Council, which adopted a number of conclusions on the functionalities of the SIS II in 2003 and 2004. The European Parliament contributed also to the debate and expressed its views at the end of 2003' (Coelho 2006).

[50]These instruments were modified in 2006, extending the period of their validity until 31 December 2008.

To provide an appropriate legal framework describing SIS II operation and use, after studies and discussions relating to the architecture and functionalities of the future system, the Commission presented three proposals for legislative instruments in 2005. Two of the instruments in this package[51] were adopted on 20 December 2006. The third instrument[52] was adopted on 12 June 2007.[53] As a consequence of these instruments, whereas in SIS I a paper copy of the EAW has to be sent from the issuing country to the executing one following an arrest based on an Alert 95; this will become unnecessary under SIS II because an electronic one will be sufficient.

SIS II high-level architecture is similar to that of SIS I. This architecture has been normatively regulated in quite some detail from an early stage of development. SIS II is composed of a central system (Central SIS II), a national system (the 'N-SIS II') in each of the Schengen member states and a communication infrastructure connecting them. SIS II's secured private communications infrastructure is provided by the Secured Trans-European Services for Telematics between Administrations (s-TESTA). The cost of developing SIS II is a charge on the budget of the EU. By 2007, according to the House of Lords, a total of over €26 million had been committed to this project from the EU budget. At the time, 'according to the Commission's proposed SIS II legislation, the EU budget will be charged a further €114 million between 2007 and 2012 to get SIS II up and running' (House of Lords 2007). By December 2010, the total budgetary commitments made by the Commission on the SIS II project (2002–2010) amounted to over €133 million (European Commission 2010b).

8.3.1.3 Some New Functions for SIS I+

While SIS II was being developed, SIS I evolution continued. Following the emergency related to the terrorist attacks of 9/11, the Spanish Government proposed important changes to increase the scope of SIS I without waiting for the roll-out of SIS II.[54] In light of the possibility of using SIS to support the fight against terrorism, existing Schengen Convention provisions were modified and new SIS functions were introduced. While not evident from changes in the system nomenclature, this

---

[51]Regulation (EC) No 1987/2006 of the European parliament and of the Council of 20 December 2006 on 1st pillar aspects of the establishment, operation and use of SIS II and Regulation (EC) No 1986/2006 on access to SIS II by the services responsible for issuing vehicle registration certificates.

[52]Council Decision 2007/533/JHA determining 3rd pillar aspects of the establishment, operation and use of SIS II.

[53]http://europa.eu/legislation_summaries/justice_freedom_security/free_movement_of_persons_asylum_immigration/l33020_en.htm

[54]The Spanish initiative (OJ C 160, 04.07.2002, p. 5 and 7) resulted in Council Regulation (EC) No 871/2004 of 29 April 2004 and Council Decision 2005/211/JHA of 24 February 2005 'concerning the introduction of some new functions for the Schengen Information System, including in the fight against terrorism'.

step 'amounted to a fundamental departure from the basic principles of Article 102 of the Schengen Convention, which limits the use of Schengen data to the purposes laid down in each category of alert' (JSA 2003). The main amendments made to the SIS concerned access for Europol and the national members of Eurojust to the data stored in the SIS, and extension of the list of missing objects for which alerts can be entered.

In order to provide the authorities designated to exchange additional information with a legal basis and to establish rules applicable to deletion of data held by them, other amendments were introduced concerning access to the SIS for the national judicial authorities responsible for investigating and prosecuting crime, as well as the determination of a common legal basis for the existence and operation of SIRENE Bureaus.[55]

8.3.1.4 SIS One4All

After the introduction of new functions in SIS I, and due to delays in SIS II development and implementation, in October 2006 Portugal put forward a proposal for a temporary solution to allow the SIS to be adapted to allow for the participation of more than 18 States, thereby enabling the new EU member states (the Slovak Republic, Slovenia, Estonia, Hungary, Latvia, Lithuania, Malta, Poland and the Czech Republic) to join Schengen by October 2007. 'The proposal involved the "cloning" of the Portuguese national system, its integration in the new member states and subsequently their connection to the central system already in use.'[56] The system was called SIS one4All. The Commission believed that SIS one4All 'would add 9 months to the planning of SIS II. Nevertheless on 5 December 2006 the Justice and Home Affairs Council, after re-affirming that "the development of the SIS II remains the absolute priority", decided to implement SIS one4all [...], and invited the Commission to present yet another revised timetable for SIS II by February 2007' (House of Lords 2007).

The successful implementation 'of SIS one4all and the positive Schengen evaluations of the new MS allowed the lifting of internal border controls with these new countries at the end of 2007 for land and sea borders and in March 2008 for air borders. The lifting of internal border controls paved the way for implementing alternative and less risky approaches for migrating from SIS1+ to SIS II.'[57] At the same time, 'Following requests by the member states to allow more time for testing the system and to adopt a less risky strategy for migration from the old system to the new one, the Commission presented proposals for a regulation and a decision

[55] http://europa.eu/legislation_summaries/justice_freedom_security/free_movement_of_persons_asylum_immigration/l33198_en.htm.

[56] http://www.epractice.eu/cases/SISone4ALL.

[57] http://europa.eu/legislation_summaries/justice_freedom_security/free_movement_of_persons_asylum_immigration/l33020_en.htm.

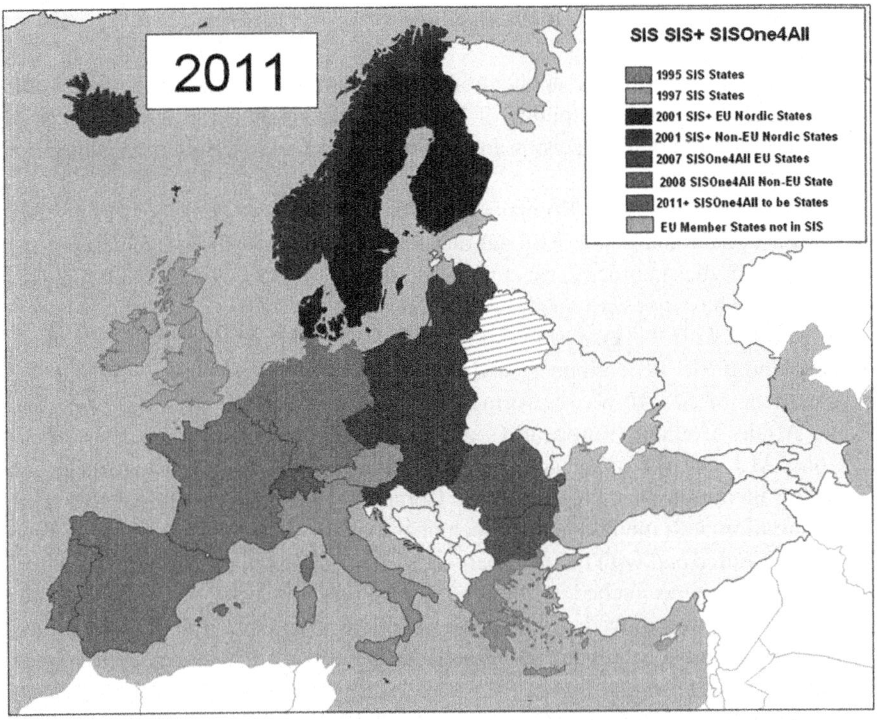

Fig. 8.3 SIS in 2011 (Source: The author)

defining the tasks and responsibilities of the various parties involved in preparing for the migration to SIS II (including testing and any further development work needed during this phase). These proposals were adopted by the Council on 24 October 2008.'[58]

As time went by, though, further delays characterised SIS II development and implementation. As a consequence, 'in June 2009, during JHA [Justice and home affairs] Council, Romania and Bulgaria presented a joint declaration regarding the common intention to connect to SIS through SIS one4ALL solution'[59] while continuing the parallel development of national SIS II systems in order to be ready to migrate from SIS1+ to SIS II together with the other migrating member states (Fig. 8.3).[60]

[58]http://europa.eu/legislation_summaries/justice_freedom_security/free_movement_of_persons_asylum_immigration/l33020_en.htm.

[59]http://www.schengen.mai.gov.ro/English/index07_01.htm.

[60]http://www.mvr.bg/en/Shengen/sis.htm.

8.3.1.5 SIS II and SIS I + R (Evolution)

The Council decision on the application of the provisions of the Schengen *acquis* relating to the SIS in the Republic of Bulgaria and Romania was adopted in June 2010. The adoption of the Decision enabled the Romanian and Bulgarian authorities to enter data into the SIS.[61]

As a consequence, both Romania and Bulgaria are now connected to the SIS and enter, update and delete national alerts in the SIS as well as undertaking the necessary activities in order to execute the alerts entered in the SIS by other States,[62] although they have not yet joined the Schengen area.

In parallel with the changes taking place to the functioning SIS I, the work on developing SIS II continued. At the same time, while absolute priority to the development of SIS II was reaffirmed on several occasions by the Justice and Home Affairs Council (European Commission 2007), the implementation of the SIS one4ALL project impacted on the SIS II schedule. As a consequence, and following invitation by the Council, the Commission drew up a revised timetable in consultation with member states' technical experts from the Council's informal SIS II Task Force and with the member states' delegations in the SIS II Committee. According to this new schedule, the operational date for SIS II for member states using SIS I + was moved to December 2008. Only then could the integration process for member states not connected to the SIS I + commence (European Commission 2007).

By the end of 2007, the legal provisions for the establishment, operation and use of SIS II and for the network requirements had been adopted. At the same time, a comprehensive test of SIS II needed to be set out, conducted by the Commission together with the member states and validated by the preparatory bodies of the Council, confirming that the level of performance of SIS II was at least equivalent to that achieved with SIS 1 +.[63] The test scope and organisation were specified by Council Decisions and Council Regulations,[64] which also foresaw the obligation for the Commission to draw up interim and final test status reports. Furthermore, a legal instrument to govern the migration from the SIS I + to SIS II environment was also required. This instrument, provided in October 2008,[65] required that an 'interim migration architecture' for the Schengen Information System be established and tested in order to better manage the potential difficulties brought about by the

---

[61] http://www.schengen.mai.gov.ro/English/index09.htm.

[62] http://www.mvr.bg/en/Shengen/sis.htm. Furthermore, 'On January 28, 2011, the meeting of the Schengen Evaluation Working Party took place in Brussels. On this occasion, the group adopted the Schengen evaluation report in the field of SIS/SIRENE for Romania, drafted after the last evaluation mission which took place in Romania during December 6–10, 2010. Thus, Romania successfully concluded the Schengen evaluation process' (http://www.schengen.mai.gov.ro/English/index09.htm).

[63] Regulation (EC) No 1987/2006 and Council Decision 2007/533/JHA.

[64] Council Regulation (EC) No 189/2008 and Council Decision 2008/173/EC.

[65] Council Regulation (EC) No 1104/2008 and by Council Decision 2008/839/JHA.

migration from SIS 1+ to SIS II. The interim migration architecture was to have no impact on the operational availability of SIS 1+. A converter (a technical tool to allow consistent and reliable communication between C-SIS and Central SIS II) was to be provided and kept updated by the Commission. The migration legal instrument had an expiration date of 30 June 2010.

While this normative implementation framework was being developed, the technological development encountered significant problems, in particular in the development of the SIS II central system (European Commission 2008). This resulted in a delay in the schedule and the need to prevent the expiry of the migration legal provisions.

Furthermore, in December 2008, the failure of the main development contractor to pass the Operational Systems Test (European Commission 2009a) triggered both an analysis-and-repair period and a comprehensive architectural review—which pointed out that the system components were 'over-engineered and capable of simplification' (European Commission 2009b)—as well as the exploration of 'an alternative technical scenario for developing SIS II based on SIS 1+, known as "SIS 1+ renewal and evolution" (SIS 1+ RE)' (European Commission 2009a).

In order to improve the involvement of the member states, 'as the project moved into a new phase, a global SIS II programme management approach was introduced in January 2009, as recognised by the Council on 26–27 February' (European Commission 2009b).[66] Furthermore, the Council on 26–27 February 2009 requested the Presidency and the Commission[67] to submit a report containing an in-depth assessment and comparison of both scenarios. As both projects were judged technically feasible, the Council concluded on 4–5 June that the development of SIS II was to continue on the basis of the SIS II project and that SIS 1+ RE was going to be retained as the contingency plan. The Council also agreed to two project milestones to test the stability, reliability and performance of the Central SIS II and the proper functioning of vital core functionalities after significant development phases of the SIS II project (European Commission 2009a). Contracts with SIS II contractors had to be renegotiated to include milestone non-compliance as resolutive conditions (European Commission 2009b). Furthermore, France negotiated a contract for the replacement of obsolete components of SIS 1+ (and optionally extendable for SIS 1 + RE), which could not be used beyond September 2010 (European Commission 2010a).

Another element that needed to be considered was the significant increase in the number of alerts. In 2009, 'From the 22 million alerts originally foreseen, the latest estimates predict[ed] 73 million alerts in the foreseeable future' (European

---

[66]Furthermore, 'the Council of 4–5 June invited the Commission to build upon the experience and lessons learned from this management structure and develop it further. These management changes have been consolidated in the legislative proposal for a Regulation to amend the migration instruments' (European Commission 2009b).

[67]In close cooperation with the SIS II Task Force and in consultation with the appropriate instances (European Commission 2009a).

Commission 2009b) and in 2010, when SIS II was supposed to be ready to go live, the number was estimated at 52 million alerts (European Commission 2010a). This required a new system capacity specification, an intensive work on requirements and the redefinition of the SIS II schedule. A new expiry date was therefore introduced by Council Regulation.[68] At the same time, the 'process of refining the requirements did not modify the core obligations stemming directly from the SIS II legal instruments' (European Commission 2010a). This further delay also resulted in secondary repercussions, such as the temporary suspension of the back-up local national interfaces (to be re-activated at a later stage, prior to go-live) to reduce costs (European Commission 2010a).

By the end of 2010, the Commission was confident that the technical and political uncertainties over the future of the SIS II project, which had characterised the beginning of 2010, had been addressed. The first milestone test had been successful, with the consensual definition of final requirements for the system to go live and the conclusion of the corresponding contractual framework. As the Commission stated, 'These positive developments all contributed to bringing the SIS II project back on track with a clear and shared vision on the remaining phases of the project, as well as a realistic schedule and an adequate budgetary plan to complete the work outstanding' (European Commission 2010b).

On a final note, Regulation (EU) No 1077/2011 of the European Parliament and of the Council of 25 October 2011 established a European Agency for the operational management of large-scale IT systems in the area of freedom, security and justice to be responsible for the operational management of Central SIS II and certain aspects of the communication infrastructure. At the time of writing, December 2012, the old SIS I is still running, the migration is scheduled to start in January 2013 and SIS II is expected to be operational from April onwards. Now, however, it looks like there will be further delays.[69]

8.3.2 Lessons from the Schengen Information System Story

The SIS story offers a number of lessons which may help to better understand the critical factors for system performance and for the creation and evolution of the transborder interoperability infrastructure at the EU level. Lessons concern norms, organisation, technology, semantics and governance.

---

[68]Regulation (EU) 541/2010 amending Regulation (EC) no 1104/2008 and Council Regulation (EU) 542/2010 amending Decision 2008/839/JHA.

[69]http://www.eppgroup.eu/press/showpr.asp?prcontroldoctypeid = 1andprcontrolid = 11535and-prcontentid = 19187andprcontentlg = en.

See also: http://news.bbc.co.uk/democracylive/hi/europe/newsid_9770000/9770730.stm.

8.3.2.1 Lessons About Norms

When dealing with large-scale interoperability infrastructures, agreements need to be ratified and norms and contracts created. The story of SIS is full of examples of Council Decisions and Regulations defining technical, organisational and functional features of the system, allowing contracts to be ratified and by which authorities, and imposing time limits to their validity. In this way, the norms that are introduced shape not only the features but also the development path of the system. At the same time, norms (and contracts) reveal themselves to be time bounded and occasionally time-limited. As a consequence of escalating complexity and unforeseen drifts and delays, norms need to be changed and new contracts stipulated. This process does not take place in a linear and well-ordered manner. It produces effects that are not considered when observing an information system performing its functions at a particular point in time, but which are a fundamental component of the life of the system and a key element to understand it. Indeed, the juridical maze that is needed to assemble a large-scale information system requires constant attention and cultivation. Indeed, the SIS story shows how legal interpretations can progressively stabilise through recursive interactions between the various actors and components that constitute the 'performative assemblage'. At the same time, the Sirene manual example, which keeps being updated and adapted over time, shows how this stabilisation is not in the direction of a static asset but of a dynamic one.

The story also shows how the assemblage is capable of performing its functions while tolerating (at least for a time) some discrepancies between the normative layer and its technological and organisational components. As an example, while the JSA in 1996 discovered that the databases of the N-SISs were not identical, as provided for by the Schengen Convention, the system remained functional. In some cases, such discrepancies are resolved ex post facto, recognising, for example, roles and functions that have imposed themselves in practice, as in the case of the SIRENE Bureaus, formally introduced in the Schengen Convention[70] 10 years after they started to perform their essential tasks (House of Lords 2007).

8.3.2.2 Lessons About Organisation

While some organisational structures are conceived ex ante, e.g., N-SIS units, others impose themselves as a functional requirement and only afterwards become formally recognised, as in the SIRENE Bureaus case. Indeed, the SIRENE Bureaus, while adding one layer of organisation, reduced the complexity in several other layers of the system, providing a single gateway/interface at a national level capable of reducing and translating meanings and actions between different organisations, such as the various police forces. The role of the SIRENE Bureaus has proved to be paramount not only in the everyday functioning of SIS, supporting cross-training,

[70] By Council Regulation (EC) No 871/2004 and Council Decision 2005/211/JHA.

standardisation and sharing of practices, but also in its extension to new member states, with the training and assessment of the new units before they were connected. It is indeed due to the existence of the SIRENE Bureaus that appropriate competences and resources were provided in order to interface the existing SIS with the somewhat different requirements of the EAW FD. The SIRENE Bureaus have also absorbed part of the complexity of the EAW procedure, supporting communications between issuing and executing authorities or, as in the Italian example, providing a regularly updated 'support kit' for the EAW arrest procedure to the local police offices.

The SIS story also shows how, in the long run, the organisations involved may change, how their role may change and how new organisations can be created and begin to play a role. Eurojust and Europol are two examples from the 'user' perspective, but the changes in the governance component as EU governance structure changed over time is even more relevant.

8.3.2.3 Lessons About Technology

Perfect fit is not always required in order for the technology to be performative. Predating the EAW, SIS is not perfectly aligned with it (i.e., it does not provide for the 32 categories of crime for which the double criminality principle does not apply). At the same time, SIS performs its function 'well enough' for the EAW FD to be successfully implemented.

As already mentioned in the section on norms, problems of compatibility between technology and norms may emerge. The SIS showed itself to be able to tolerate some inconsistencies while still performing its functions.

Size and size growth, both in terms of stored data and from a geographical perspective, generated significant technical issues. The SIS updates, such as SIS I + and SIS one4All, were triggered by such needs. Between the results of this need to extend and keep SIS operational, there has been on the one hand a reduction in the resources that could be allocated SIS II, and on the other hand a growing misalignment between the SIS II technological and organisational components, which caused additional delays in the development and implementation of the system.

8.3.2.4 Lessons About Semantics

The way in which semantic issues have found solutions in the SIS case provides some useful hints for the development of other interoperability infrastructures; the key role of the SIRENE Bureaus in the translation of meanings and actions, for example. Furthermore, the capability of the system to allow some flexibility concerning 'where' the translation takes place increases the ability of the system to perform. The presence in the SIS Bureaus of personnel speaking several languages also allows the system to perform in many cases in which SIS Alerts are not in English. Furthermore, their specialised competences and their understanding of other States' EAW FD implementation laws and practices have also reduced the complexity of communication and finding a common understanding between issuing and executing authorities, helping to solve semantic impasses that are generated not only by the use of different languages but also from seeing and understanding the world from different, nationally bound, legal perspectives.

A final aspect, also related to semantics is that the definition of what SIS is, and therefore which procedures and practices it can support, has shifted with time. While initially SIS was created only for alerting authorities of other Schengen countries on certain categories of people and goods in order for them to take 'concrete measures' and 'compensate' for the removal of internal borders, over time its nature and scope have shifted in order to support new instruments, such as the EAW, but also to include investigative functions.

8.3.2.5 Lessons About Governance

Not only do governance structures need to be created and equilibrium achieved: as time goes by, they need to be able to change. This was the case for the events related to the decision to adopt SIS one4All but also for those related to the SIS I + RE alternative to SIS II.

Another element worth considering is that at least one 'great pressure source' seems to be linked to each relevant policy action/change. Such pressures have gone, on the one hand, in the direction of making SIS I evolve to remain operational and 'do more'. On the other hand, they seem to have resulted in a greater delay in SIS II development and implementation. As SIS II experience shows, the tighter the coupling attempted, the stronger become the drifts and time delays and the greater the level of coordination required. Given all these elements, it looks like the governance capability and drive were not enough for the complexity of the SIS II project.

8.4 Conclusions: The Critical Role of Infrastructure

This chapter has attempted to convey a flavour of how a complex EU criminal justice procedure has been implemented and is performing its function through the support of an existing information infrastructure: the SIS. As the description of the EAW in action has shown, the role of the infrastructure is not limited to the transmission of data and information but also supports sense making in cross-border communications and the solution of semantic, administrative and procedural micro-issues (Chap. 1) through its 'intelligent' human components. Particularly in the initial phases of EAW implementation, the existence of the SIS organisational infrastructure supported the national legal and administrative systems' process of learning how 'to communicate with one another and engage in cooperative action' (Chap. 1). In other words, SIS played—and still plays—a key role in allowing the cross-border circulation of EAW agency, absorbing and concealing from justice system users (judges and public prosecutors) most of the complexity involved in the procedure (Chap. 1).

The chapter has also shown the complexity that is below the surface of the enabling information infrastructure. It is a complexity that is embedded in the heterogeneous and loosely integrated nature of the assemblage, which, once 'in action', manages to perform its tasks and support the circulation of legal agency. At the same time, the reconstruction of the SIS and SIS II stories allows us to see how the assemblage components (normative, technological and organisational) change with time. It allows us to see how the trajectories these components follow are not always convergent and subject to drifts. In addition, it shows how external events and the broader political context (e.g., terrorism attacks, new EU Member accession) play a relevant, if ex ante unpredictable, role in determining the evolution of the system. Indeed, while the SIS is still there after almost 20 years from its implementation, it has changed over time in purpose, size and components (i.e., network, norms, etc.). While all these changes have taken place, the capability of the SIS to allow the circulation of EAW agency has been kept and maintained. At the same time, it also shows how the attempt to introduce a much more complete second generation SIS resulted in a never-ending normative and technological development phase of a system that exceeded the maximum manageable complexity.

The chapter provides, therefore, an opportunity to reflect on the implicit assumptions about how information systems are developed, should evolve and are made interoperable to support services provision. Indeed, in the last decade, much progress has been done, understanding that technology is just one of the components to be considered. For example, in the Commission's 'European Interoperability Strategy for European public services', it is recognised that 'Interoperability issues are not only technological, but also cover a wide range of aspects, such as: lack of a cross-border and cross-sector legal basis for interoperability, insufficient awareness and political will, or lack of agreement on the governance structures required' (European Commission 2010d).

At the same time, the same vision shows how information systems and interoperability between systems are still perceived as well-defined objects that can be designed, developed and implemented through linear processes. Indeed, the European Interoperability Framework (EIF) definition of interoperability as 'the ability of disparate and diverse organisations to interact towards mutually beneficial and agreed common goals, involving the sharing of information and knowledge between the organisations, through the business processes they support, by means of the exchange of data between their respective ICT systems' (European Commission 2010d), in its generality and inclusiveness miss the messiness of a reality characterised by multiple and conflicting objectives, unintended effects and time-bounded decisions. The SIS story shows the relevance of all these elements when the temporal dimension is added to the equation. More importantly, it shows how a system with all this messiness managed to support the circulation of agency for the EAW, while the attempt to develop a more tidy second generation system resulted in a never-ending sequences of accidents, delays and postponements.

While all this shows some of the limits of the present EU vision in relation to European Interoperability, it nevertheless remains the case that 'Interoperability between public administrations is crucial for achieving European integration and concerns core aims of the European Union' (European Commission 2010d). At the same time, as Hanseth and Lyytinen point out, one of the challenges in the research on information infrastructure 'has been in the difficulty of translating vivid empirical descriptions of IIs [information infrastructures] evolution into effective socio-technical design principles that promote their evolution, growth and complexity coordination' (Hanseth and Lyytinen 2010, 2). From this perspective, SIS lessons provide a significant contribution regarding what needs to be considered when attempting to maintain, adapt, evolve and replace information infrastructures and their technological, normative, organisational and institutional components.

References

Brouwer, E. 2008. *Digital borders and real rights: Effective remedies for third-country nationals in the Schengen information system*. Leiden: Brill.

Carnevali, D. 2009. E-Justice and policies for risk management. In *E-Justice: ICT in the court system*, ed. A. Cerrillo and A. Fabra, 19–35. Hershey: Information Science Reference.

Coelho, C. 2006. Report on the proposal for a council regulation amending Regulation (EC) No. 2424/2001 on the development of the second generation Schengen Information System (SIS II). Committee on Civil Liberties, Justice and Home Affairs.

Ciborra, C.U., K. Braa, A. Cordella, B. Dahlbom, A. Failla, O. Hanseth, V. Hepsø, J. Ljungberg, E. Monteiro, and K.A. Simon. 2000. *From control to drift: The dynamics of corporate information infrastructures*. Oxford: Oxford University Press.

Contini, F. 2009. ICT, assemblages and institutional contexts: understanding multiple development paths. In *ICT and innovation in the public sector: European studies in the making of e-government*, ed. F. Contini and G.F. Lanzara, 244–271. Basingstoke: Palgrave Macmillan.

Contini, F., and G.F. Lanzara (eds.). 2009. *ICT and innovation in the public sector: European studies in the making of e-government*. Basingstoke: Palgrave Macmillan.

Council of the European Union. 2002. Schengen information system, Sirene: Recommendations and best practices. EU Schengen Catalogue 2, December.

Council of the European Union. 2009a. Evaluation report on the fourth round of mutual evaluations: The practical application of the European arrest warrant and corresponding surrender procedures between member states. Report on Italy, 5832/1/09 REV1.

Council of the European Union. 2009b. Final report on the fourth round of mutual evaluations: The practical application of the European arrest warrant and corresponding surrender procedures between member states. 8302/4/09 REV4. http://www.statewatch.org/news/2009/jul/eu-eaw-evaluation-8302-rev4-09.pdf. Accessed 22 Jan 2013.

Di Giorgio, G. 2009. Le attribuzioni del Pubblico Ministero in tema di esecuzione delle pene detentive e di Mandato di Arresto Esecutivo. Training seminar 'Problemi aperti in materia di esecuzione della pena'. Appeals Court of Bologna, Accessed 30 Nov. 2009.

Edwards, P., S. Jackson, G. Bowker, and C. Knobel. 2007. Report of a workshop on 'History and theory of infrastructures: Lessons for new scientific infrastructures'. University of Michigan, School of Information. http://pne.people.si.umich.edu/PDF/ui.pdf. Accessed 22 Jan 2013.

European Commission. 2001. Communication from the commission to the council and the European parliament: Development of the Schengen Information System II.

European Commission. 2007. Revised global SIS II schedule in light of the SIS one4ALL implementation. Brussels. Accessed 29 Jan. 2007.

European Commission. 2008. Report from the Commission to the European Parliament and the Council on the development of the second generation Schengen Information System (SIS II): Progress report, July 2008–Dec 2008.

European Commission. 2009a. Report from the Commission to the European Parliament and the Council on the development of the second generation Schengen Information System (SIS II): Progress report, Jan 2009–June 2009.

European Commission. 2009b. Report from the Commission to the European Parliament and the Council on the development of the second generation Schengen Information System (SIS II): Progress report, July 2009–Dec 2009.

European Commission. 2010a. Report from the Commission to the European Parliament and the Council. Progress report on the development of the second generation Schengen Information System (SIS II): Jan 2010–June 2010.

European Commission. 2010b. Report from the Commission to the European Parliament and the Council. Progress report on the development of the second generation Schengen information system (SIS II): July 2010–Dec 2010.

European Commission. 2010c. Communication from the Commission to the European Parliament and the Council: Overview of information management in the area of freedom, security and justice.

European Commission. 2010d. European Interoperability Strategy (EIS) for European public services: Annex 1 to the communication from the Commission to the European Parliament, the Council, the European Economic and Social Committee and the Committee of Regions 'Towards interoperability for European public services'.

European Commission. 2011. Commission implementing decision of 1 July 2011 amending the Sirene manual (2011/406/EU).

Hanseth, O., and K. Lyytinen. 2010. Design theory for dynamic complexity in information infrastructures: The case of building internet. *Journal of Information Technology* 25(1): 1–19.

Hayes, B. 2004. From the Schengen Information System to SIS II and the visa information (VIS): The proposals explained. Statewatch Report, February

House of Lords. 2007. Schengen Information System II (SIS II). Report with evidence.

Impalà, F. 2005. The European arrest warrant in the Italian legal system: Between mutual recognition and mutual fear within the European area of freedom, security and justice. *Utrecht Law Review* 1(2): 59.

JSA (Schengen Convention Joint Supervisory Authority). 1997. First annual activity report: March 95–March 97.

JSA (Schengen Convention Joint Supervisory Authority). 1999. Third annual activity report: March 98–Feb 99.

JSA (Schengen Convention Joint Supervisory Authority). 2003. Sixth annual activity report: Jan 2002–Dec 2003.

Kurtovic, E., and P. Langbroek. 2010. The EAW in the Netherlands. In The European arrest warrant in law and in practice: A comparative study for the consolidation of the European law-enforcement area, B. de Sousa Santos and C. Gomes, coords. 245–347. http://opj.ces.uc.pt/pdf/EAW_Final_Report_Nov_2010.pdf. Accessed 22 Jan 2013.

Lanzara, G.F. 2009. Building digital institutions: ICT and the rise of assemblages in government. In *ICT and innovation in the public sector: European studies in the making of e-government*, ed. F. Contini and G.F. Lanzara, 9–47. Basingstoke: Palgrave Macmillan.

Mohr, R., and F. Contini. 2011. Reassembling the legal: 'The wonders of modern science' in court-related proceedings. *Griffith Law Review* 20(4): 994–1019.

Velicogna, M. 2010. The EAW in Italy. In The European arrest warrant in law and in practice: A comparative study for the consolidation of the European law-enforcement area, B. de Sousa Santos and C. Gomes, coords. 119–243. http://opj.ces.uc.pt/pdf/EAW_Final_Report_Nov_2010.pdf. Accessed 22 Jan 2013.

Yung, R. 2005. Legislative report to the French Senate: 'Proposition de résolution Le système d'information Schengen'. Annex to the procès-verbal of the meeting of 25 January 2006. http://www.senat.fr/rap/l05-174/l05-1740.html. Accessed 22 Jan 2013.

Laws and Regulations

Commission Implementing Decision 2011/406/EU
Council Decision 2001/886/JHA
Council Decision 2005/211/JHA
Council Decision 2007/533/JHA
Council Decision 2008/173/EC
Council Decision 2008/839/JHA
Council Framework Decision 2002/584/JHA
Council Regulation (EC) 1104/2008
Council Regulation (EC) 189/2008
Council Regulation (EC) 2424/2001
Council Regulation (EC) 871/2004
Council Regulation (EU) 542/2010
Regulation (EC) 1986/2006
Regulation (EC) 1987/2006
Regulation (EU) 541/2010

Chapter 9
Searching for Maximum Feasible Simplicity: The Case of e-Curia at the Court of Justice of the European Union

Francesco Contini

Abstract The chapter analyses the successful development of e-Curia, the e-justice platform of the Court of Justice of the European Union. Due to the institutional and procedural features of the Court, who deals with high profile transborder cases, complex multilingual procedures, and bulk procedural documents, development has presented new challenges to e-justice and e-government. To stay below the threshold of maximum manageable complexity, the project team has followed a development strategy pursuing the principle of maximum feasible simplicity by different means. The chapter analyses the strategy, the current functioning of the system, and the means used to reduce complexity, among which: 'black-boxing' through organisational or technological arrangements; building on the installed base of the users; avoiding techno-legal solutions that generate complexity; providing for smart switches between online and offline procedures. A light legal framework has established the ground for developing a platform. Once successfully tested by the Court and qualified users, its use has been made legal by a decision of the Court.

The author wishes to thanks the entire project team and the staff of the registries for their openness and encouragement, for the time spent in discussing the many areas of the project, and for their commitment in the development of e-Curia. Special thanks go to Lynn Hewlett and Henrik von Holstein for having offered the unique opportunity to study the project since its conception.

F. Contini (✉)
Research Institute on Judicial Systems, National Research Council of Italy (IRSIG-CNR), Bologna, Italy
e-mail: francesco.contini@irsig.cnr.it

F. Contini and G.F. Lanzara (eds.), *The Circulation of Agency in E-Justice*, Law, Governance and Technology Series 13, DOI 10.1007/978-94-007-7525-1_9,

9.1 Introduction

The institutional and procedural features of the Court of Justice of the European Union make its e-Justice programme particularly challenging. The Court is the judicial authority of the European Union. It reviews the legality of the acts of EU institutions, ensures that member states comply with the Treaties and interprets European Union law at the request of the national courts. Since its foundation, it has played a key role in building the European Union (Shapiro 2001; Stone Sweet 2005). It handles high-profile transborder cases, using a composite set of different judicial proceedings that can be held in the 23 official languages of the Union. Since its establishment in 1952, the Court has developed a well-run practice of transborder litigation based on conventional paper-based tools and procedures but the complexity generated by the entanglements between legal, administrative and linguistic factors is very high and may become even higher when such transborder proceedings have to go digital (see Sect. 9.2.2). The Court has to guarantee the performativity of the data, documents and utterances exchanged in the new digital channel. Case parties have to be properly summoned, the authenticity of procedural documents must be checked and users must be identified without ambiguity, just to mention a few key requirements to be fulfilled by the system. The translation of transborder proceedings from conventional to digital may easily reach the threshold of maximum manageable complexity (see Sect. 9.1.3). The challenge is to move such procedures from the conventional to the digital domain without reaching levels of complexity that are unbearable for the Court and for the external users. Consequently, e-Curia, the e-justice application of the Court, has been developed in a narrow design space squeezed between such multifaceted complexity sources and the tough search for simple solutions. Its successful deployment and smooth running demonstrate that e-justice can be developed not just for simple and streamlined procedures such as injunctive orders but also for complex procedures, including cross-border cases.

From a user perspective, the functioning of e-Curia is surprisingly simple. The representatives of the case parties, such as lawyers and agents of the member states and European institutions, can submit a ‘request of access’ to the Court to get enrolled into e-Curia. The representatives must also accept the terms of use of the system.[1] Once having checked the credentials, the Court sets up a user profile and sends a user name and password to the representative. Afterwards, the representative can log in with their user name and password and, following the instructions provided by the e-Curia website, upload procedural documents and annexes in electronic format (pdf). E-Curia is also used by the Court to serve procedural documents to the parties. Launched in November 2011, the system has been adopted by a growing number of users (Hewlett 2012). E-Curia

[1] https://curia.europa.eu/e-Curia/term-of-use.faces?conversationContext=2. Last visited 15 December 2012.

is the first transborder and multilingual e-filing application running in Europe and is therefore particularly relevant for the development of transborder civil proceedings.

IRSIG-CNR researchers, including the author of this chapter, have been informally involved in e-Curia development since 2005, first meeting with the Court registries, followed by a workshop on e-Curia development plans in 2008. After these meetings, information was collected through informal talks with the registries and two fact-finding visits to the Court. The first visit was paid in June 2011, during the piloting of the system, the second in March 2012 when e-Curia was online. The meetings provided room for open-ended interviews with Court staff and ICT specialists, demos of the application and direct observation of the functioning of e-Curia in real proceedings. Other information was collected through analysis of the official documentation of the project made available by the project leaders since 2008. After March 2012, updates have been provided mainly through telephone interviews with one of the project leaders.

This chapter investigates the development strategy and the functioning of e-Curia, focusing on the ways in which maximum feasible simplicity has been pursued without hampering the performativity of procedural documents exchanged electronically. Section 9.2 briefly introduces some of the peculiarities of the Court to identify the main complexity sources and map out the design space. Section 9.3 discusses the development history of e-Curia and singles out the design principles followed by the project team. Sections 9.4 and 9.5 present the current functioning of the application, looking at the Court and at the user's perspective. The last section analyses how complexity has been dealt with and simplicity pursued, but also at how some of the design choices may hamper future developments.

9.2 The Court of Justice of the European Union

The Court of Justice is the judicial authority of the European Union. It reviews the legality of the acts of EU institutions, ensures that the member states comply with the Treaties and interprets European Union law. The parties of the cases can be member states, European institutions, large companies or national courts but also companies and, in some cases, 'normal' European citizens. The Court often handles high-profile cases, and decides on sensitive topics such as privacy, EU competition and EU integration (Tallberg 1999; Di Federico 2011; Stone Sweet 2010), but it is also the labour court of the employees of European institutions. The Court is multilingual and each of the 23 official languages of the Union can be the language of a case. To grant smooth internal operations, French has been chosen as the working language.

The Court of Justice of the European Union is composed of three courts: the Court of Justice (established in 1952), the General Court (since 1988) and the Civil Service Tribunal (2004). Since 1952, the three courts have issued about 15,000 judgements.

Its organisation and its proceedings have been the subject of many scholarly works analysing legal and institutional features, judicial procedures and jurisprudence. For the purpose of this chapter, such a bold set of contributions remains in the background. Nevertheless, we should introduce some key information about Court organisation and Court procedures, eliciting the key elements required to understand the development and functioning of e-Curia.

9.2.1 Jurisdiction, Organisation and Procedures of the Court

The Court of Justice is composed of 27 Judges (one per each member state) and eight 'Advocates General', appointed for a renewable 6-year term. The General Court (previously known as the 'Court of First Instance') has a similar composition, with 27 judges, while six judges deal with the caseload of the European Union Civil Service Tribunal. A chamber composed of various staff units supports the work of each judge.

The Court of Justice deals mainly with References for preliminary rulings and direct actions. References for preliminary rulings are the most frequent cases brought before the Court (423 out of 688 in 2011).[2] In each member state, national courts must apply and enforce European Union law. Pursuing such a mandate, they may refer to the Court of Justice, asking it to clarify the interpretation of EU law in specific areas, to ensure its effective and uniform application and to ascertain if a given national legislation complies with EU law or if an act of EU law is compliant with the treaties.[3] The applicant is a court of a member state but a number of parties must be informed and can take part in the proceedings, such as other member states and the institutions of the European Union. The applications filed must be served to the agents (lawyers) representing member states and EU institutions that have the right to intervene. The Court also has jurisdiction over 'direct actions' (namely actions for failure to fulfil obligations, for annulment and for failure to act) between European institutions and member states, between member states themselves, and between European institutions relating to the Communities' legislative activities. It also deals with appeals to decisions of the General Court.[4] Through the direct actions, the Court establishes if a subject has fulfilled its obligations under European Union law.

---

[2] http://curia.europa.eu/jcms/jcms/P_91551/. Last visited 13 November 2012.

[3] The Court of Justice's reply (decision) is binding for the national court and for the other courts in which the same problem is raised.

[4] The Court of Justice may also act as appeal judge on points of law against judgements and orders of the General Court, and in special circumstances, it can review as the court of third instance an appeal decision of the General Court against judgements of the European Union Civil Service Tribunal.

The General Court has first-instance jurisdiction over actions brought by natural or legal persons against acts (or failure to act) of the institutions, bodies, offices or agencies of the European Union. Actions can be taken by natural or legal persons seeking compensation for damage caused by the institutions of the European Union or based on contracts made by the European Union or relating to Community trademarks. Actions can be also promoted by member states against the Commission or against the Council, or by member states against the Council.[5]

Established in 2005, the European Union Civil Service Tribunal decides disputes about working relations and social security of the employees of the European Union.

Each one of the three courts is supported by a registry, which takes care of typical case-related work: receiving, sending and keeping procedural documents; corresponding with the parties; keeping case-files and court registers (originally paper dockets), etc. The Tribunal has its own registry, but being smaller it may have to take advantage of some of the services offered by the Court of Justice. The three courts are also supported by the Central department, which provides a variety of services, such as translation, ICT and personnel administration.

Three main procedural peculiarities have to be considered for the purposes of e-Curia development. First, once an application is lodged, it has to be completely (or partially) translated into the official languages of the Union. Second, it has to be served not just to the case parties but also to EU institutions and member states that have the right to be informed and to consider whether they should intervene in the case. Third, procedural documents to be lodged and exchanged are often long and complex and procedures are mainly written, even if there is also a final oral stage.

9.2.2 *The Design Space*

E-justice and e-government development are deeply affected by the variety of procedures, documents and actors, and more generally by the multiplicity of components that have to be translated into the digital medium (see Chaps. 1 and 2). From this perspective, e-Curia had to face great heterogeneity caused by the number of procedures, the multiple procedural steps affecting each procedure, the different time limits of specific actions, the different types of document to be used in each procedure, the different linguistic rules to be applied and the translation of procedural documents, sometimes in the 23 languages of the Union.[6] Since its foundation in 1952, the Court of Justice of the European Union has operated with the legal systems of the member states: lawyers practicing in different national jurisdictions, different institutional settings and different legal frameworks.

---

[5]In addition, the Court deals with appeals, limited to points of law, against decisions of the European Union Civil Service Tribunal and actions brought against decisions of other EU bodies.

[6]For a more detailed analysis, see Contini (2012), available at: http://www.irsig.cnr.it/images/stories/biepco_documents/case_studies/eCuria13june12_ConferenceDraft%20_1_.pdf.

The variety to be inscribed into the digitally enabled workflow is therefore higher than in any other e-justice project. MCOL, COVL and CITIUS deal mainly with money orders; TOL, despite the original goal of digitising the entire set of civil proceedings, had to be simplified and for a long time has handled just money orders.

In this case, complexity sources are multifold. The Court deals mainly (even if not exclusively) with complex and high-profile cases. This often entails the production of a number of different procedural documents and massive annexes. As a rule, lawyers are experts in the field. Specialised state lawyers called 'agents' represent member states and European institutions in the proceedings dealt with by the Court. In some EU institutions or member states, agents operate in large State lawyers organisations, whereas in others they work in small legal offices. At the same time, some procedures are open to citizens, and the Tribunal handles labour and social security cases for civil servants working for EU institutions. The development of an e-justice application such as e-Curia has therefore to consider this heterogeneous set of procedures, potential users and types of documents exchanged that is difficult to simplify.

In addition, the frequency of the transactions is variable. Agents of member states and EU institutions are frequent players. They receive references for preliminary rulings almost every day. Therefore, both the Court and this group of users can immediately benefit from the development of an application providing the electronic exchange of procedural documents. They represent, then, the first target to create a 'critical mass of users' or, more precisely, a small number of users doing a 'critical mass of transactions' needed to bootstrap the infrastructure (Hanseth 2003).[7] At the same time, e-Curia must be easily accessible to all the potential users and not create problems of access to justice. As noted by one of the deputy registrars, the conditions of access should not create obstacles to a lawyer working in the most remote rural area of the Union.

To sum up, high-profile litigations sometimes coupled with the confidential data exchanged, multilingualism, users parties ranging from member states to simple citizens, complex judicial procedures and a relatively low number of cases outline a demanding framework for e-justice development. The task environment and the procedures to be handled by the Court are certainly complex in terms of the number of distinct elements to be considered, and in terms of their interconnections. The level of complexity to be faced by project developers and inscribed into the new digitally enabled system is certainly high.

At the same time, there are factors that contribute to reducing or increasing the level of complexity that can be managed by the Court. The Court has a unique location in Luxembourg. For this reason, procedures are mainly written and based on exchanges of documentations traditionally carried out through postal services, without the involvement of national bailiffs. Consequently, the entire set of tasks associated with the preparation of procedural documents and annexes—and their

[7]Bootstrapping is a process through which it is the same system that is loading and starting itself (as an operating system in a computer). The topic is broadly discussed in Chap. 2.

distribution—can be digitised, without the need of mediations with national judicial systems. Furthermore, procedures and data to be collected are well standardised and firmly controlled by the Court and by the registries.

The Court regularly works with the 23 official languages of the European Union, and even if not all the procedural documents have to be translated in all the languages, this semantic issue further increases procedural complexity. This source of complexity is black-boxed by a Directorate of Translation in which several hundreds specialists operate. In addition, a well-routed workflow is needed to keep control and facilitate the routing of documents within the Court and sending the right document to the right subject at the right time. At the same time, a typical source of complexity of judicial proceedings—the payment of court fees—is absent.

The Court has therefore developed a well-established interoperability with legal and judicial systems of member states based on conventional tools such as letters, post, fax and telephone, and on the capacity to acknowledge legal instruments used by the jurisdictions of the member states, such as the practicing certificates or the powers of attorneys. Court personnel mainly take care of procedural and organisational complexities, such as the need to operate with different languages or with multifaceted judicial procedures. The same may apply to the specialised law firms and agents of the member states and European institutions. Therefore, if the complexity to be faced remains high, so also is the level of complexity manageable by internal and external users. This background has eased the design and the adoption of e-Curia in various ways.

A different set of question is associated with the transfer of this well-managed but complex system from a paper-based to a new digital environment. The questions of how to provide access, identification, secure transmission and non-repudiation of sensitive data and documents, and how to bootstrap the system moving a high number of transactions from conventional to digital procedures, become particularly challenging. Complexity can easily become unmanageable, with unending requirement lists, a number of ICT applications to be made interoperable and difficult adaptations of the procedural rules, just to mention a few well-known problems affecting large-scale e-justice and e-government developments. Functional and administrative simplification (Kallinikos 2009a) is difficult to achieve, because judicial procedures cannot be easily streamlined, nor linguistic rules abolished or simplified, and procedural documents are too complex to be transformed into web forms. In comparison with other e-justice applications, the only advantage is that the Court does not have to develop an e-payment engine, since court fees are not required.

If the design space in which e-justice has to be developed is particularly narrow, the European Court of Justice has developed and successfully deployed e-Curia, an e-justice platform providing external and internal users with a range of functions, including easy access, secure identification, transmission of data and documents, e-filing, online notification and access to procedural documents. This has been done thanks to a systematic effort addressed to pursuing the goal of maximum feasible simplicity, as discussed in the next section.

9.3 History and Development of e-Curia

9.3.1 Project Background and the Installed Base

The development of e-Curia can be divided into the three main stages. In 2003, the Deputy Registrar and one of the principal administrators of the Court of Justice began to explore how the Court could benefit from e-justice. Back then, there were a few well-run experiences in Europe: the Finnish systems called Tuomas and Santra (Kujanen and Sarvilinna 2001), ERV (Elektronischen Rechtsverkehr) in Austria (Koch and Bernoider 2009) and Money Claims OnLine (MCOL) launched in 2001 in England and Wales (see Chap. 4). At the same time, many ambitious projects were stuck in the design or piloting stage, trying to address the issue of identification, signature, secure transmission and non-repudiation with state-of-the-art techno-legal solutions as PKI infrastructure based on the EU directive on digital signature.

It was clear that one of the main obstacles to the development of any e-filing applications was their high technological and legal complexity (Fabri and Contini 2003), and that the institutional and procedural features of the Court of Justice would make the e-justice implementations even more difficult.

In 2005, an amendment to the rules of procedure established that the Court might determine the criteria to exchange procedural documents with the registry in electronic format (see Sect. 9.6). This was the green light for the establishment of the e-Curia project team that began in 2005 with the identification of high-level requirements. Their work was guided by the idea of keeping the system as simple as possible, especially in terms of identification requirements, avoiding the complexity traps in which various European Judiciaries were locked.[8] Indeed, while simple identification mechanisms such as those used in England, Finland and, to a lesser extent, Austria were leading to running applications, the complex ones, and in particular those based on digital signature and public key infrastructures, were still facing overwhelming problems (Fabri 2009). From 2005 to 2008, the project leaders and the project team outlined the architecture of the application and how it should have been made interoperable with the installed base of the Court.

In 2008, in a presentation of the system architecture,[9] they unveiled goals and design principles. The main goal of e-Curia was the establishment of a digital channel of communication to exchange procedural documents between the Court and the parties of the cases. The design principle stated that the system had to be simple,

[8]Information on this first part of the e-Curia development has mainly been collected in two meetings in which IRSIG-CNR researchers and e-Curia project leaders shared ideas about e-justice development. The first informal talks occurred during the conference 'Judicial Electronic Data Interchange in Europe', held in Bologna in 2003. In 2005, e-Curia project leaders joined the IRSIG-CNR for a workshop to discuss the general architecture of the system in light of current e-justice development.

[9]IRSIG-CNR researchers also attended this meeting.

accessible and free of charge for users. No less important, the security level had to be equivalent to the level offered by conventional court proceedings based on exchange of documents through European postal services (Hewlett, Lombaert et al. 2008).

It was clear that the 'standard PKI solution', envisaged by the EU directive[10] and by various e-Government frameworks would never have worked for a Court operating with legal representatives coming from the 27 member states and even more legal systems. It would have required a European Certification Authority or seamless interoperability between the certification authorities of the various member states, or else a circle of trust between the various 'digital identity' providers operating within the justice domains of the member states. This infrastructural component was neither ready nor running at the European level and it was unreasonable to wait for its deployment.[11] From a design perspective, they decided to build e-Curia relying on the technological components already in place at the Court. In addition, e-justice development should not require security levels higher than those already adopted by Court proceedings. The authenticity of a hand-written signature is seldom checked, certified postal services are not foolproof and despite everything, the methods used by courts to grant authenticity and non-repudiability to procedural documents have worked quite well for 200 years. In contentious proceedings, false documents or false signatures can be easily discovered and severely sanctioned. Most importantly, the goal of e-Curia is not to reduce the risks of malfunctioning of judicial procedures to zero but to provide a handy system to exchange procedural documents and annexes in electronic format. Malfunctioning can be solved in various ways, and conventional proceedings will remain fully available should problems arise or to deal with specific issues that cannot be easily handled in the new digital environment.

Therefore the solution had to be self-contained, developed and managed by the Court, tailored to the specific procedural and institutional features described above but also based on technological and infrastructural components already available or easily accessible by potential users (Groupes de travail du greffe de la Cour 2008).

One of the issues discussed in the 2008 meeting was the development strategy. A first option was to start with the e-filing application, i.e., the external component of e-Curia (hereinafter 'External e-Curia'). This would have immediately improved access to justice and established the digital channel of communication, but it would have built additional work for the registries and meant limited benefits for the Court. Indeed, once it had received the documents in digital format, the Court would have had to print and process them with the traditional paper-based workflow, not being in a position to take advantage of their digital format. In addition, the Court would have been forced to scan the procedural documents to be served to the parties in electronic format. Therefore, the internal workflow also had to be made digital in order to be of any benefit. This second option would have had several advantages. At the development level, the main advantage was the possibility of

[10]Directive 1999/93/EC of the European Parliament and of the Council.

[11]It is e-Codex that is currently attempting to develop a similar infrastructure.

testing the technological components within the registries and opening the system to the external parties (users) just when Internal e-Curia was running smoothly. The registries would have had more time to test technological components and set up smooth running routines without external pressures. Given the procedural and linguistic complexity to be inscribed into the applications, the development of the digital workflow was expected to be long and difficult. Therefore, the project leaders decided to start by developing the internal systems.

The design of the technological architecture was based on assumptions just illustrated. External users do not need to get any particular software application. All the functions required to access and exchange documents can be carried out using a combination of SMTP email and web forms made available and exchanged through a secure https website.

Technological complexity has been faced at Court's systems level (i.e. the internal e-Curia), due to the features of the workflow and the need of making interoperable a number of pre-existing applications and data bases.

The new document management system is built on GED Alfresco, an open source package designed for content intensive process as those managed by the court. GED Alfresco provides document management facilities, the management of the users' profiles, indexing, data and document search. The document workflows, with all the rules required for processing, approving, signing and serving documents (see Sect. 9.2.1) is managed through a JBPM engine that has been integrated into Alfresco. e-Curia intranet uses also other standards such as LDAP while security has been improved through the use of the hashing procedure (based on SHA-512 standard) that generates a unique value for any specific set of data or document, thus avoiding risks of alteration of the procedural documents.

9.3.2 System Development and Internal Adoption

Between 2008 and 2011, the project team and the registries developed, tested and adopted the various technological components. New applications, in particular Internal e-Curia and Prodoc, were integrated with the pre-existing systems namely Registre and Litige, providing various case management functionalities described below.

The use of this system has contributed to developing the skills (technological and administrative) required to handle complex electronic workflow and to get the Court ready to handle the External e-Curia.

During the fact-finding visit carried out in June 2011, the three registries of the Court tested and tuned the system. The technological platform provided high-level case management functions and document management facilities, but there were still problems to be solved. The new digital workflow did not run smoothly and the control of the procedure through the new electronic applications was still difficult.

The digital leap, i.e., the switch from a paper-based to a digital workflow, entails the translation of tools, actions and procedural checks from one medium to another.

Routines that are simple in conventional procedure, such as the checking of the addresses of the parties that have to be summoned, may, surprisingly, become complex in the new digital environment. The registry staff identified the risk of mistakes with consequences for the judicial procedure such as not sending the right document to the right parties or the sending of a document in the wrong language. One example can clarify the point. In conventional proceedings, the registry staff works with the case folder (in paper form) and the electronic case management system. A typical task is to take data and information from procedural documents (collected in the case folder) and enter them into the electronic case management system (and vice versa). As they do this, the staff can see the two artefacts at the same time, the procedural document on the desk and the case management system on the computer screen. This supports double-checks and control routines. In the new digital environment, however, the computer screen provides just one artefact at a time, the case management or the electronic folder. To do this simple job, one is required to switch between different computer windows, making the task more complex than it was previously. Thus, the registry gave consideration to the possibility of working with two computer screens or with wider ones.

From a technological perspective, there were still some system breakdowns and slow system response time. As discussed with the project manager, one of the reasons for this malfunctioning was the number of different applications to be made interoperable to enable the digital workflow. Thus, a simple delay in the response time of one of the applications of the installed base slowed down the entire workflow. We will return to this analysis of the technological components (Sect. 9.4.1).

While the registries were testing, tuning and adopting the Internal e-Curia, the project team fixed the technical problems and developed the application for external users. A first release of the External e-Curia was tested with experienced case parties to make a systematic check of the functionalities offered and of the robustness of the exchange of data and documents. During the test, various suggestions were collected, and some of them implemented. Particularly important was the creation of new types of user profiles to meet the need of agents and large law firms.

At this point, new legal steps were needed to make performative the use of e-Curia for exchanging procedural documents. On 13 September 2011, the Court of Justice published the decision on the lodging and service of procedural documents by the use of e-Curia. The decision authorised the use of e-Curia in accordance with the amendment to the procedural rules of 2005. A few weeks later, the Chief Registrars of the three courts approved the conditions of use to be accepted by expected users, the last normative component required for making fully legal the use of e-Curia to exchange procedural documents.

In the same period, the project team prepared a communication strategy to inform the public and reach potential users. It included general information for agents and lawyers, as well as visits to EU institutions and some of the member states' agents. As stated, one of the first goals to achieve was the involvement of those users who, for institutional and procedural reasons, intervene more frequently in the procedure, in order to get a critical mass of transactions as soon as possible, with notifications and procedural documents exchanged through e-Curia.

9.3.3 The Launch of e-Curia for External Users

The Court opened the registration procedure 15 days before the launch of the External e-Curia. The registration process took some time and the Court wanted to check if applicants had the prerequisites to get enrolled. This required various checks including controls with local bar associations to verify applicants' legal qualifications. On 21 November 2011, the Court opened e-Curia to external users.[12] As in any real e-justice novel, a breakdown affected the first day of functioning, but since then e-Curia has run smoothly. The communication strategy and the promotion of e-Curia went ahead, with a progressive increase in the number of users. In June 2012, the majority of member states as well as various European institutions and agencies, were already using e-Curia, with a significant impact on the functioning of the registries (Hewlett 2012).

9.4 The Functioning of e-Curia Within the Registries of the Court

9.4.1 The Digitally Enabled Workflow

The idea of the project team was that the digitisation of the activities carried out by the registries should provide an easier workflow, particularly in the internal processing of procedural documents such as those needed for the translations. To face this challenge, the Court developed a complex technological architecture made of a set of different applications. Their functions are briefly described in Table 9.1.

The procedural documents received by the court are recorded into the case management systems, called 'Litige', and 'Registre'. Such case management systems have been made interoperable with a digital repository of the procedural documents (and their annexes) called the 'Fond Documentaire'. A document management system called Prodoc has been developed to prepare the accompanying letters, attach the documents and control the workflow. Prodoc is thus the backbone of the entire technological architecture. Internal and External e-Curia are just the final components of the architecture, enabling the exchange of documents with external parties.

This high number of applications has suggested the creation of another system (ASP) working as an entry point or a portal to access to the various applications. E-Curia thus relies on a number of systems to be well maintained and interoperable. A problem in one of the systems may generate malfunctioning in other systems, especially when Prodoc or Internal e-Curia check and assemble the documents to be served.

---

[12]Court of Justice of the European Union, press release No. 125/11, Luxembourg, 23 November 2011.

Table 9.1 Technological applications currently used by the European Court of Justice

Applications	Functions
ASP: portal	This is a kind of 'portal' that allows access to various applications of the Court of Justice. The entire staff of the Court uses it
Litige: procedural case management	This is the Case Management System collecting all procedural data. It is managed by the Equipe Litige (4 units)
Fond documentaire: digital archive	This is the digital archive collecting all the procedural documents scanned or transferred in digital format through e-Curia
Registre electronique: document registration	This is the registration system of every document received or served through various channels by the Court. It also provides a unique ID number to each document. It is managed by the Equipe Litige
Prodoc: document management	This is the document management system. It allows the preparation of the documents based on templates of standard letters available in all recognised languages
	It generates the letter by browsing the required data from Litige and from the Registre Electronique and prepares the list of documents to be annexed to the letter and to be served. It is managed by the assistants and by their supervisors (administrators)
Internal e-Curia	With this tool, the assistants prepare the 'packages' to be served. Attached to the letter prepared with Prodoc are the procedural documents collected in the Fond Documentaire. It facilitates controls and enables the validation and the signature by the 'administrators' of the registries. Finally, it serves the packages to the various case parties
External e-Curia: registered agents and lawyers	With this application, registered users can lodge procedural documents and can access and download procedural documents served by the Court

9.4.2 Handling Procedural Documents Received by Post and Fax

The Equipe Litige is the first unit in handling cases. Once it receives a procedural document (in paper form) it registers the date of deposit and makes an entry in Litige, the procedural case management system. This first record is not the filing because the document can be filed only after checking and on the instruction of the Administrator, which may require clarifications or integrations to the party, i.e., the delivery of a new amended procedural document or new annexes.

Once the Administrator gives the 'green light', the Equipe Gestion Affaires registers the required procedural data in Litige and indexes the documents with unique identification numbers using the Registre Electronique.

At this stage, the unit called Archive scans the document, stores the paper copy into the traditional paper file of the case and saves the scanned copy (in pdf format) into the Fond Documentaire, the digital document repository of the Court.

This first procedural stage reflects three main functional and legal needs: guarantee of procedural fairness, assure the respect for all the legal provisions, and generate the digital copies of paper-based documents. Once scanned, the document will be transferred within the Court in digital format, including its transmission to the Department of Translation. If the scanning requires additional work by the Court staff, it leads to various advantages that will be better appreciated later on.

9.4.3 Handling Procedural Document Received by e-Curia

As noted above, the development and the adoption of the digital workflow have taken a long time and have required the inscription of a number of procedural rules, documents, languages and organisational arrangements into the ICT applications (Lanzara 2009). The know-how of the Court staff facilitated this effort. Once the systems and the registries were ready and the digital workflow was precisely tailored to the Court's requirements, the launch of External e-Curia was quite simple. Indeed, at that point, e-Curia was just another channel to receive (and send) procedural documents.

From a registry point of view, the filing of a procedural document with e-Curia entails a procedure very similar to the one already described. The document is recorded in Registre, the administrator makes the juridical checks, then Equipe Gestion Affaires manages the procedure with Litige, Prodoc, etc., as described above. The advantage is that the document does not have to be scanned and can be directly archived in the Fond Documentaire. At the same time, the document is also printed to keep the paper file of the case in the archive.

9.4.4 Preparing and Serving the Documents

The filing channels (by postal service or e-Curia) do not affect the procedure to be followed to send the documents. For this purpose, the Equipe Gestion Affaires works with two different applications: Prodoc and Internal e-Curia.

Once the translations have been received, the Equipe Gestion Affaires is ready to serve (or 'signify', using the jargon of the Court) the procedural documents and the various annexes in the requested languages. Typically, the 'package' to be served consists of a letter—prepared by the Equipe Gestion Affaires and signed by the administrator—the procedural documents and other attachments.

The assistant logs in and opens the ASP, the internal 'web page' that grants access to all the different applications of the Court (see Fig. 9.1). From ASP, the assistant opens Prodoc to prepare the letters and identify procedural documents to be attached. Prodoc uploads data previously entered into Litige, such as the name and the addresses of the representatives and the language in which they want (or are entitled) to receive the documents, and data from the Registre Electronique,

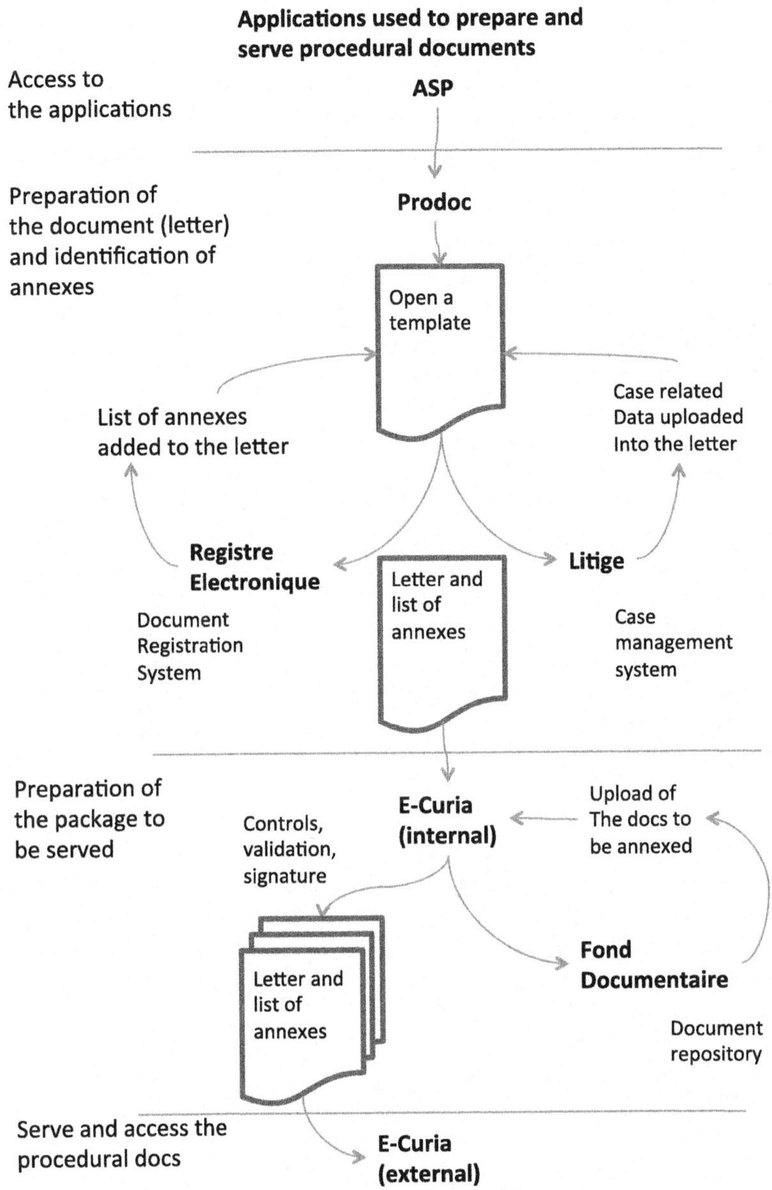

Fig. 9.1 Serving procedural documents

creating the list of annexes to be served. Prodoc automatically merges these data into the letters in preparation. Since Curia is multilingual, Prodoc automatically produces the documentation in all the languages required by any specific procedural step. Without entering into details, the linguistic rules of the Court are consistently inscribed into the system. Therefore the system 'knows' in which languages the documents must be produced and the assistant can work and control the workflow solely in French (or in his/her preferred language). The Equipe Gestion Affairs can use Registre to make various controls, enter interim decisions taken by the judges or register the letter; through Prodoc, it can check the addresses of the parties and the means of notification.

If necessary, the letters prepared using Prodoc can be modified with a word processor and saved in a common repository.

At this stage, the additional work done to digitise case documentation starts to generate positive returns because the handling of a multi-language procedure is much easier and faster with the new procedure.

As stated, this application comprises two main components: the Internal e-Curia is used by the registry of the Court, while lawyers and agents use the External e-Curia to lodge and access procedural documents.

In e-Curia, the assistant and the administrators finalise the preparation of the 'package' of documents to be served and serve such documents in paper or digital format. Once these documents are ready, the assistant 'assembles' the full package. E-Curia uploads the various documents to be served from the Fond Documentaire, then the assistant checks the procedure, the letters and the annexes. Once the package is ready, the assistant saves it and passes it to the Administrator. E-Curia communicates to the administrator the pending tasks. The administrator controls the full package, signs the letter and validates the procedure. At this point, the package is ready to be served and comes back to the Equipe Gestion Affaires.

Until November 2011, i.e., before the launch of the External e-Curia, the 'package' was printed out and sent by post to all the case parties. Since the launch, however, the package is served in paper form to the parties not enrolled in e-Curia and through e-Curia to the parties enrolled. The three registries are therefore particularly active in promoting the use of e-Curia among 'frequent users', such as European institutions and member states. It is worth noting that at the Civil Service Tribunal, which mainly operates with a limited number of specialised lawyers, some proceedings have been already handled exclusively in digital format.

9.5 The Functioning of e-Curia for External Users

Since November 2011, lawyers and agents have been able to use the External e-Curia to lodge and receive procedural documents online. The simple technical requirements to use the e-Curia area are a valid email address and an Internet connection to access the secure website https://curia.europa.eu/e-Curia. Access to e-Curia is free of charge and does not require any particular software application.

9.5.1 Users' Registration and Personal Data Management

The first step is enrolment as a user of the system. In order to get an account, the applicant must follow the instructions provided by the web application and, basically, enter personal identification data into web forms. Once this information has been entered, the system sends a pdf with the request of registration to the email address entered during the application. The pdf has to be printed, signed and sent by post to the registry of the Court with supporting documentation, such as a copy of the applicant's ID card/passport, of their practicing certificate, etc. In supplying these, the applicant declares his/her acceptance of the conditions of use of e-Curia. The hand-written signature on the application is the only signature required in the entire process.

In this enrolment stage, e-Curia is just guiding the preparation of the request for an account, and the procedure reflects those already required for representing a case party before the Court.

The approach is similar to that followed by many e-banking services, in which 'contractual' documentation has to be provided on paper, with a hand-written signature and copies of documents providing proof of identity. Once the account has been granted, the digital identity is associated with the physical one, and the lodgement of procedural documents becomes digital.

It must be observed that the legal principle of mutual recognition works effectively with the Court. Indeed, Article 6 of the 'conditions of use' states that, 'Agents and lawyers authorised to practice before a court of a member state or of another State party to the Agreement on the European Economic Area may apply for an account to be opened giving them access to all the functionalities of e-Curia. Once such an account has been opened, they may use e-Curia in every case in which they have been appointed as a representative.' This criterion solves the many problems associated with identifying basic standards to access legal practice in the European Union judiciaries. Indeed, the definition of what a lawyer is and what the professional qualifications to practice in court should be are not yet univocal (CEPEJ 2010), and the minimum standard accepted by the Court shows how legal interoperability may work.

As with conventional proceedings, the registries will next check the enrolment request. The procedure could require several days. If the request is approved, the new user will receive an ID and a temporary password (in separate emails) to be changed at the first login, and then at least every 6 months (Article 8 of the terms of use). Once the temporary password has been changed, the user profile is operative and can be used to lodge, receive and check procedural documents. Since e-Curia is common to the three registries of the Court, an account opened by one of the three registries is also valid for the other two.

Before the piloting stage, the External e-Curia provided just the profile of the agent/lawyer, i.e., the authorised representative of case parties. The pilot scheme highlighted the need, however, to better shape the type of user to tune up the functionalities offered by the application with the organisational features of the legal offices working with the Court. As a result, two new profiles were established in addition to the original profile of the representative. One is the profile of the Assistant partie, the other the profile of the Assistant. Each profile is regulated by specific conditions of use.[13]

As noted, in the written stage of the proceeding, member states and EU institutions have the right to be informed of new cases brought before the Court, and the Assistant partie is the subject that receives the notification of new plaints in each member state or European institution. As a rule, he/she is an employee working on a specialised board of state lawyers or in a department within the Ministry of Foreign or of European Affairs.

The assistant partie is therefore the gateway user who receives the case and transmits it to the state lawyer competent for that particular matter. The state lawyer does not therefore have to lodge new procedural documents or to prepare such documents.

The other two roles are the representative (i.e., the lawyer or agent representing a party in a case) and the assistant(s) of the representative. While the representative has access to the full functionalities of e-Curia, including the possibility to set up profiles for the assistants, the latter has just the options of accessing and preparing the documentation, and cannot lodge procedural documents.

The two profiles reflect the division of labour within large law firms (and state lawyers' offices), in which the lawyer (representative) is responsible for the case and the handling of it is supported by several activities, mainly administrative, carried out by assistants. It allows the assistant to receive the documents served, to consult procedural documents lodged or served by means of e-Curia and to prepare the lodgement of a document. The assistant must involve the representative to 'validate' the lodging and delivering the documents to the court, however. The representative is responsible for the use of this account and is required to update the list of assistants and, in particular, in the event of a change in professional responsibilities or termination of activity, to cancel any account assigned to assistant(s).

9.5.2 *Lodging a Procedural Document with e-Curia*

The lodgement of a procedural document is a two-step procedure well described in the users' manual (Court of Justice of the European Union 2011). The first step entails the preparation of the documentation to be sent. As noted, it can be done by the representative of the party (i.e., the lawyer or the agent with the mandate) but more frequently by the 'assistant'. All the procedural documents and annexes must be prepared following the practice directions of the Courts at which the document

[13]http://curia.europa.eu/jcms/jcms/P_81900/ and http://curia.europa.eu/jcms/jcms/P_81905/.

has to be lodged.[14] The three Courts have not changed the practice directions in this regard. Basically, the user prepares the documents following the traditional paper-based procedure. The difference is that users do not have to print and sign the documents and send them by post with all the annexes; instead, they just log in, upload the documents and the annexes and send them to the Court in pdf format via e-Curia.

Here, we can observe a relevant example of functional simplification, because the 'original signature in manuscript' is not needed. As in the US Federal Court, it is sufficient to type the name of the lawyer/agent. In this way, the user does not have to print, sign and scan the document signed. Identification and non-repudiation are granted by the login into the system.

The user must select the function 'Lodge a document' in the menu, then select the Court at which the document is to be lodged, the type of procedural document, the language, the name of the party on whose behalf the document is being lodged and the case number (if the document has to be lodged in a case already filed). In the subsequent web form, the user must specify the types of documents to be attached (procedural document and annexes, covering letter, practicing certificate, mandate, etc.) and their number.

The legal qualification of the representative and of his/her capacity to act in the name of a given party are provided at this stage through scanned copies of certificate to practice, proof of the existence in law of a legal person governed by private law and proof that the authority has been properly conferred by someone authorised for that purpose. Then the files have to be selected from the computer systems (document repository) of the representative, uploaded and sent to the Court. Additional information, such as the size of file, number of pages and Hash code can be checked. The Hash code is generated automatically by the system through an algorithm that reduces the document to a unique code (or function). If the document is changed by someone and for any reason, the Hash code will change, thereby allowing the identification of alterations to the original document. In this way, it becomes easy to establish the authenticity of the document filed and stored in the digital archives of the Court.

If the lodgement has been prepared by an assistant, the representative must enter his/her password and validate the transaction to send the procedural document to the Court, because the assistant cannot deliver the document. A summary of the activity carried out is sent by email to the representative and to the assistant (if the assistant prepared the lodgement). The users can also lodge other procedural documents following the same procedure.

[14] Files must be in PDF format and no file may exceed 30 MB. It is possible to lodge up to 50 files of annexes.

9.5.3 *Receiving Procedural Documents by e-Curia*

In this case, e-Curia displays the list of the documents served, (i.e., which have been sent to the user) and their status: awaiting acceptance, accepted (with an indication of the name of the person who accepted service and the date of acceptance) and acceptance presumed (when it has been served but not yet downloaded). Based on the conditions of use, the documents served and not accepted by users are 'presumed as accepted' 7 days after their delivery.

This techno-legal arrangement requires a comment. One of the lasting problems of e-justice is the so-called issue of 'non-repudiation' of the documents exchanged. Indeed, in any judicial procedure there is the risk that a party could make a complaint stating that a document has not been properly delivered or not been delivered at all, thereby hampering the fairness of the proceedings. Public Key Infrastructure and digital signature are usually justified with the need to solve the problem of non-repudiation (Poullet 2008; Fabri 2009; Velicogna et al. 2011). With e-Curia, however, it is the user who, accepting the conditions of service, acknowledges that he/she is responsible to check e-Curia, verify the delivery of the documents and 'accept the service' of the documents. The acceptance of the conditions of use is the legal (contractual) solution that has made possible the development of a relatively simple technological solution. In this as in many other cases, changes in formal regulations can reduce the complexity of the technological system.

9.6 E-Curia: Performativity Through Maximum Feasible Simplicity

As seen, the complexity of transborder procedures handled by the Court is great from many points of views, but unlike many other examples of e-justice (Fairchild and De Vuyst 2008; Langbroek and Tjaden 2009), the Court succeeded because the inscription of such variety into an e-justice platform has been fruitful. The digital leap has not magnified the complexity to be faced by the persons involved in judicial proceedings. External and internal users are finding a number of advantages from a system that has been running smoothly since its launch. It is interesting, then, to explore why the Court of Justice succeeded where others failed.

E-justice development at the Court of Justice is a story about how maximum feasible simplicity can be pursued without hampering the performativity of documents exchanged. Minimal—but radical—changes to the rules of procedure of the Court played a major role. Legal changes eased the cultivation of an information infrastructure that may appear unconventional in comparison to other European initiatives but which is growing and working well. So far, the digital exchange of procedural documents has been smooth and uncontested, meaning that legal and functional requirements have been met with proper identification of users, non-repudiation and authenticity of documents exchanged. In addition to legal changes, however, organisational arrangements and valuable design principles also played a role worth analysing.

The first legal change dates back to 2005, an amendment to the rules of procedure of the Court of Justice. Up to that point, the rules prescribed the typical paper-based means, including hand-written signature of the party's agent or lawyer in the original of every pleading (Article 37 paragraph 1), a typical requirement difficult to translate into digital form.

The 2005 amendment introduced a new paragraph, (7), stating that

> [...] the Court may by decision determine the criteria for a procedural document sent to the Registry by electronic means to be deemed to be the original of that document [...].[15]

The paragraph provides a good starting point for the development of the system. Rules provided a broad framework in which various technological options could have been explored rather than pre-established technological solutions as in the case of the advanced electronic signature in the European Payment Order or in Italy with TOL (see Chaps. 10 and 7).

Such a broad mandate may entail problems of accountability. Is the project team inscribing the right procedural safeguard in the technological application? Are the security measures adequate? Is the system under-performative for the high-profile cases dealt with by the Court? Such questions found an answer in the dialogue between the Court and the stakeholders in the 'Working Party of the Court of Justice'. The party deals with rules concerning proceedings in the Court of Justice, including the rules of procedure. The working party did not ask for more detailed regulations about e-Curia but expressed an interest in being regularly informed about the development process. This was sufficient to give the green light to the project. As a consequence, e-Curia was developed without having to consider pre-existing legal requirements dictating the technological features of the application. Thanks to this broad regulative framework, technology was developed that considered organisational settings and technological standards and constraints (including those of the installed base) rather than formal rules establishing which specific technology had to be adopted as the digital signature, as in TOL and EPO. The interplay between law and technology is often surprising. Technology and the law are two distinct but entangled regulative regimes (Lessig 2007; Kallinikos 2009b), each one with its own normativity (Hildebrandt 2008), dynamic and logic of evolution (Czarniawska and Joerges 1998). The constraints established by a narrow legal framework often create adverse conditions for technological innovation, especially when they fix in advance the technological solutions to be adopted.

The project team began work on the identification of the high-level specification of e-Curia in the same year (2005). After 6 years of systems and organisational development, meetings with the 'Curia working group' and successful tests of the applications, the Court was ready for the next step. On 13 September 2011, the

---

[15] http://curia.europa.eu/jcms/upload/docs/application/pdf/2011-07/rp_cjue_en.pdf.

Official Journal of the EU published the 'Decision of the Court of Justice on the lodging and service of procedural documents by means of e-Curia',[16] which made e-Curia a valid means for lodging and serving procedural documents. It was a legitimation of an existing and successfully piloted application. The decision states (among other issues) that, 'The information technology application known as "e-Curia" [...] allows the lodging and service of procedural documents by electronic means under the conditions laid down by this Decision' (Art. 1). In addition, 'This application, which is based on an electronic authentication system using a combination of a user identification and a password, meets the requirements of authenticity, integrity and confidentiality of documents exchanged'. Article 3 solves the problem of the signature: 'A procedural document lodged by means of e-Curia shall be deemed to be the original of that document [...] where the representative's user identification and password have been used to effect that lodgement. Such identification shall constitute the signature of the document concerned.'

In a conventional procedure, the signature is a way to check the identity of the signatory and to ascertain that the signatory assumes the will of the contents of the document.[17] The rule acknowledges that a login into e-Curia based on user name and password, along with the subsequent lodgement of procedural documents verified by the same credentials, fulfils such functional and legal requirements. Thanks to this techno-legal solution, and the pre-existing procedural arrangements, the project team was able to set up a self-contained identification mechanism accessible to the potential users with different organisational support, spread all over Europe and speaking 23 different languages, and authorised to practice law by a multitude of bar associations.

No less important is the subsequent approval of the conditions of use of e-Curia applicable to parties' representatives[18] and to assistants.[19] On 11 October 2011, the chief registrars of the three Courts approved the conditions of use that have to be accepted by expected users. Only if they explicitly accept these terms of use will they be authorised to lodge procedural documents with e-Curia.

Precise legal changes have been able to keep the architectural (and procedural) complexity of e-Curia near the threshold of maximum feasible simplicity. The technologies required (Internet connection, web browser and valid email) are really the minimum functional standard to exchange procedural documents. The functional simplification and closure of the procedure to be followed by external users should ease the lodgement of documents. So, as noted by Kujanen and Sarvillina (2001), procedural changes can also work as powerful means of simplification in e-justice (see also Chap. 3).

Performativity is also granted by the conventional paper-based mechanisms for lodging procedural documents that is still fully operational. Consequently, a user

---

[16] http://eur-lex.europa.eu/LexUriServ/LexUriServ.do?uri=OJ:C:2011:289:0007:0008:EN:PDF.

[17] http://www2.warwick.ac.uk/fac/soc/law/elj/jilt/2000_3/reed.

[18] http://curia.europa.eu/jcms/jcms/P_81900/.

[19] http://curia.europa.eu/jcms/jcms/P_81905/.

dissatisfied with the features of the digitally enabled procedure is free to follow the conventional one. This reveals another finding: instead of following the mantras of paperless procedures or one-stop shops,[20] e-Curia takes advantage of the circulation of agency between digital and conventional domains. In various procedural steps, the users must (as during the application) or can (in many other steps) switch from one medium to another. It is this circulation of agency that makes the system effective and performative. It would have been very complex to enrol lawyers without receiving paper copies or to handle procedural documents exclusively in digital format. Instead, agency is channelled through the medium that can best support its transmission, and the possibility of using two different media is an advantage, not a weakness.

Simplicity has also been pursued through procedural standardisation, proper organisational settings and technology design.

As noticed in Sect. 9.3.2, the development of Prodoc and Internal e-Curia was long and difficult. Indeed, a number of multifaceted procedures and thousands of document forms in 23 languages—just to mention two of the sources of procedural complexity—had to be inscribed into the two applications. Two factors have contributed to make this exercise fruitful: on the one hand, the high procedural standardisation, on the other, the staff of the registry had a full and detailed map of the procedures. In addition, the ICT specialists being employed by the Court had a sound knowledge of procedural flows. This know-how facilitated system modelling and the inscription of rules, procedures and workflow. The administrative and procedural complexity they have been able to inscribe into Prodoc and e-Curia is much higher that the one observed in other case studies (Lanzara 2009). Once this result was achieved and users got familiar with these applications, they black-boxed complexity. Users are guided by a system that becomes a powerful regulative means.

This results in great capacity to run complex procedures and even more complex projects. The threshold of maximum manageable complexity in the case of the Court is very high, as is the capacity of the Court to absorb procedural complexity.

As noted, e-Curia has been developed by taking advantage of the installed base of the users, and therefore adopting standards currently used in e-commerce and e-banking, such as individual users' registration, SSL and HTTPS. In line with the theoretical expectations about information infrastructure cultivation and growth (Ciborra 2002; Hanseth and Lyytinen 2010), this has simplified access to the system, the growth of the number of users and the bootstrapping of the information infrastructure. A well-designed set of tracking mechanisms, such as Hash codes and unique identification numbers attached to electronic documents, has resulted in the robust security of the system. The combination of simple identification mechanisms and well-tailored tracking mechanisms has not created problems of security, identification and repudiation of procedural documents. Users are satisfied with a system that is not too simple to be performative.

[20] http://eur-lex.europa.eu/LexUriServ/LexUriServ.do?uri=COM:2010:0743:FIN:EN:PDF.

E-Curia and Prodoc have also taken advantage of the installed base of the Court, in particular Registre and Litige, running for many years and tailored to the procedures of the Court. At the time of writing, interoperability between old and new systems is one of the problems affecting e-Curia, and ICT specialists based in the Court express some concerns about the evolvability of this maze of interoperable systems. This will be happen as the need arises to implement procedural changes recently entered into force. On 24 September 2012, new procedural rules were published and will enter into force within 2 months.[21] This will require adaptations in e-Curia, posing problems for the evolvability of the system. The tight coupling between the Court procedures and the digitally enabled workflow may create problems and highlight a design dilemma. Since the templates available in Prodoc are full of references to the rules of procedures,[22] all the templates have to be modified. If procedural complexity is reduced when it is black-boxed into the digital workflow, the black-box will have to be reopened when procedures change. It would be possible to keep the procedure and the workflow decoupled, but this increases the complexity associated with the use of the system. Coupling and black-boxing reduce the complexity faced by users but makes the evolution of the system more expensive.

In addition, the design principle of 'building on the installed base' seems to have a dual effect. In the short term, it can speed up and ease development and adoption. In the mid to long term, it may slow down or hamper the evolution of the technological platform.

The Court is a well-developed organisation, with extensive know-how in legal, technological and organisational domains. The registry provides high-level support to court proceedings. It is common that, in case of problems, the same registry calls the case parties to address the issue. This can be done thanks to the organisational features of the Court, but also because of the number of cases to be dealt with, which is relatively low in comparison to other courts. As noticed when discussing EPO and ESCP (Chaps. 10 and 11), linguistic diversity is one of the major obstacles in transborder cases. At the Court, the Directorate-General for Translation, which employs almost half of the staff of the Court, reduces this variety in a way that can be processed by users. Even if not necessarily efficient, it is effective in solving the problems of semantic interoperability. Thus, the organisational features of the Court are very effective in absorbing procedural and semantic complexity and facilitating the transmission of performative utterances. This certainly has relevant financial costs, but it suggests that without organisations in charge of handling and black-boxing the complexity affecting transborder proceedings, it is difficult to have an effective transmission of performative utterances. This is an argument to be considered when designing other transborder proceedings such as the EPO and the ESCP.

[21] http://curia.europa.eu/jcms/upload/docs/application/pdf/2012-10/cp120122en.pdf.

[22] On 25 May 2011, the president of the Court submitted to the president of the Council of the European Union the draft Rules of Procedure of the Court of Justice. http://curia.europa.eu/jcms/upload/docs/application/pdf/2011-05/en_rp_cjue.pdf.

References

CEPEJ. 2010. *European judicial systems: Efficiency and quality of justice. CEPEJ Studies 12.* Strasbourg: Council of Europe.

Ciborra, C. 2002. *The labyrinths of information: Challenging the wisdom of the system.* Oxford: Oxford University Press.

Contini, F. 2012. *e-Curia.* Bologna: IRSIG-CNR.

Court of Justice of the European Union. 2011. *e-Curia: User manual.* Luxembourg: Court of Justice of the European Union.

Czarniawska, B., and B. Joerges. 1998. The question of technology, or how organizations inscribe the world. *Organisation Studies* 19(3): 363–385.

Di Federico, G. 2011. Public enforcement of EU competition law and the principle of ne bis in idem. *European Public Law* 17: 241–260.

Fabri, M. 2009a. E-justice in Finland and in Italy: Enabling versus constraining models. In *ICT and innovation in the public sector: European studies in the making of e-government*, ed. F. Contini and G.F. Lanzara, 115–146. Basingstoke: Palgrave Macmillan.

Fabri, M. 2009. The Italian style of e-justice in a comparative perspective: Information and communication technologies in the court system. In *E-justice: ICT in the court system*, eds. A. Cerrillo and P. Fabra, 1–19. Hershey: Information science reference.

Fabri, M., and F. Contini, eds. 2003. *Judicial electronic data interchange in Europe: Applications, policies and trends.* Bologna: Lo Scarabeo.

Fairchild, A, and B. De Vuyst. 2008. From the ashes of phoenix: e-justice in a surreal country. 7th European Conference on e-Government, Lausanne, 235–240. Academic Publishing Limited.

Groupes de travail du greffe de la Cour. 2008. *e-Curia 0.3: Spécifications fonctionnelles.* Luxembourg: Court of Justice of the European Union.

Hanseth, O., and M. Aanestad. 2003. Design as bootstrapping networks: On the evolution of ICT Networks in health care. *Methods of Information in Medicine* 42: 385–391.

Hanseth, O., and K. Lyytinen. 2010. Design theory for dynamic complexity in information infrastructures: The case of building internet. *Journal of Information Technology* 25(1): 1–19.

Hewlett, L. 2012. e-Curia. Presentation at the 'Building Interoperability for European Civil Proceedings' online conference. Bologna. Available at http://www.irsig.cnr.it/biecpo. Accessed 10 Jan 2013.

Hewlett, L., M. Lombaert, and G. Lenvers. 2008. *e-Curia: Dépôt et notification électronique des actes de procédures devant la Cour de justice des Communautés européennes.* Paris: Journées européennes d'informatique juridique.

Hildebrandt, M. 2008. Legal and technological normativity: More (and less) than twin sisters. *Techne: Research in Philosophy and Technology* 12(3): 169–183.

Kallinikos, J. 2009a. Institutional complexity and functional simplification: The case of money claim onLine service in England and Wales. In *ICT and innovation in the public sector: European studies in the making of e-government*, ed. F. Contini and G.F. Lanzara, 174–210. Basingstoke: Palgrave Macmillan.

Kallinikos, J. 2009b. The regulative regime of technology: ICT and innovation in the public sector. In *ICT and innovation in the public sector: European studies in the making of e-government*, ed. F. Contini and G.F. Lanzara, 66–87. Basingstoke: Palgrave Macmillan.

Koch, S., and E. Bernoider. 2009. Aligning ICT and legal frameworks in Austria's e-bureaucracy: From mainframe to the internet. In *ICT and innovation in the public sector: European studies in the making of e-government*, ed. F. Contini and G.F. Lanzara, 147–173. Basingstoke: Palgrave Macmillan.

Kujanen, K., and S. Sarvilinna. 2001. Approaching integration: ICT in the Finnish judicial system. In *Justice and technology in Europe: How ICT is changing judicial business*, ed. A. Fabri and F. Contini, 29–44. The Hague: Kluwer Law International.

Langbroek, P.M., and M.I. Tjaden. 2009. Organising data exchange in the Dutch criminal justice chain. *Transylvanian Review of Administrative Sciences* 28: 8–26.

Lanzara, G.F. 2009. Building digital institutions: ICT and the rise of assemblages in government. In *ICT and innovation in the public sector: European studies in the making of e-government*, ed. F. Contini and G.F. Lanzara, 9–48. Basingstoke: Palgrave Macmillan.
Lessig, L. 2007. *Code and other laws of cyberspace: Version 2.0*. New York: Basic Books.
Poullet, Y. 2008. The Belgian case: Phoenix or how to design e-justice through privacy requirements. In *E-justice: ICT in the court system*, eds. A. Cerrillo, and P. Fabra, 186–195. Hershey: Information Science Reference.
Shapiro, M. 2001. The European court of justice. In *Judicial independence in the age of democracy: Critical perspectives from around the world*, ed. P.H. Russell and M. O'Brien, 273–300. Charlottesville: University Press of Virginia.
Stone Sweet, A. 2005. *The judicial construction of Europe*. Oxford: Oxford University Press.
Stone Sweet, A. 2010. The European Court of Justice and the judicialization of EU governance. *Living Review on European Governance* 5(2): 5–50.
Tallberg, J. 1999. *Making states comply: The European commission, the European court of justice, and the enforcement of the internal market. Lund political studies 109*. Lund: Lund University.
Velicogna, M., A. Errera, and S. Derlange. 2011. E-justice in France: The e-Barreau experience. *Utrecht Law Review* 7(1): 163–18.

Part III
Complexity and the Circulation of Agency in Transborder Civil Proceedings

Chapter 10
Legal Interoperability in Europe: An Assessment of the European Payment Order and the European Small Claims Procedure

Marco Mellone

Abstract EC Regulations No. 861/2007 on the European small claims procedure and No. 1896/2006 on the European payment order represent a significant example of the action of the EU in the field of civil proceedings. Indeed, for the first time, the EU legislature has proposed an autonomous model of rules governing civil proceedings with the purpose to facilitate European citizens to autonomously access to justice in cross border disputes. To this purpose the Regulations entail high levels of legal interoperability between all the subjects involved (courts, citizens, judiciary functionaries). In this chapter I focus on the mechanisms of legal interoperability and assess the problems which, at the present state, prevent a fast and effective communication between the above mentioned subjects. I then propose a wide range of solutions in order to facilitate the practical application of these European instruments.

10.1 Introduction

On 12 December 2006, the European Union (EU) adopted the regulation creating a European Payment Order (EPO) procedure,[1] applicable from 12 December 2008, and on 11 July 2007, it adopted the regulation on the European Small Claims

[1]Regulation (EC) No. 1896/2006 of the European Parliament and of the Council of 12 December 2006 creating a European order for payment procedure, in OJ L 399, 30.12.2006, pp. 1–32.

M. Mellone (✉)
Interdepartmental Research Centre on European Law, University of Bologna, Bologna, Italy

Research Institute on Judicial Systems, National Research Council of Italy (IRSIG-CNR), Bologna, Italy
e-mail: marco.mellone@irsig.cnr.it

F. Contini and G.F. Lanzara (eds.), *The Circulation of Agency in E-Justice*, Law, Governance and Technology Series 13, DOI 10.1007/978-94-007-7525-1_10,

Procedure (ESCP),[2] applicable from 1 January 2009. Both regulations represent a significant example of the action of the EU in the field of civil proceedings. Indeed, for the first time, the EU legislature not only regulated certain aspects related to civil proceedings in cross-border cases (e.g., the jurisdiction, the serving of documents, the gathering of evidences, etc.) but also tried to propose an autonomous model of rules governing civil proceedings.

These regulations generated an intense debate among European scholars and practitioners: in fact, the national jurists' comments on the new rules were sceptical, whereas European voices, although acknowledging some critical aspects, highlighted the wide and effective application of the EU rules throughout the territory of the EU (Lopez de Tejada and D'Avout 2007; Fiorini 2008; Tsikrikas 2009; Campeis De Pauli 2007; Défossez 2008; Guinchard 2008; Kramer 2010; Mellone and Pancaldi 2008).

It must be added that, at present, there are very few works or reports on the practical application of Regulations No. 861/2007 and No. 1896/2006 in Europe (ECCS 2011, 2012). For this purpose, according to both regulations, the Commission will publish an official report on the practical application of these procedures in Europe.[3]

Notwithstanding that, many issues come out of the practical application of these procedures: one of these issues concerns the lack of legal interoperability between the member states. Both the EPO and ESCP should be based on a tight and effective mechanism of legal interoperability between all the subjects involved (courts, citizens, judiciary functionaries) in order to speed up the functioning of these procedures. It should not be forgotten that the goal of these procedures is to simplify international litigation in Europe by reducing the costs in cross-border cases and by helping citizens to file claims autonomously before a court of another member state.

For this purpose, this chapter focuses on the levels and on the mechanisms of legal interoperability that both European procedures entail. It is based on some preliminary assumptions.

First, the object of this chapter is limited to the levels of interoperability that both the EPO and the ESCP entail. More precisely, this chapter aims, on the one hand, to determine which mechanisms of interoperability would be necessary at the moment for the good functioning of these European procedures; on the other, to propose possible solutions to improve interoperability between those actors who are involved in the application of these European procedures (EU, member states, national courts, citizens).

Second, the analysis of the levels of interoperability necessarily entails the description of some juridical aspects. These aspects are not exhaustively described,

[2] Regulation (EC) No. 861/2007 of the European Parliament and of the Council of 11 July 2007 establishing a European small claims procedure, in OJ L 199, 31.7.2007, pp. 1–22.

[3] See, on the one hand, Article 28 of Regulation No. 861/2007 and, on the other, Article 32 of Regulation No. 1896/2006.

since this is not a strictly juridical chapter. Instead, these aspects are examined with the purpose of facilitating the determination of the levels and mechanisms of interoperability of both the EPO and the ESCP.

Third, the chapter uses the term 'legal interoperability' in a broad sense: it not only refers to legal interoperability as such but also entails many levels of 'judiciary interoperability'. For this reason, the chapter also uses synonyms for the term 'interoperability', such as 'cooperation', 'coordination' and 'dialogue'. All these terms make reference to the concept of 'interoperability' and to the need for mechanisms of coordination between the actors of the European judiciary space.

That done, we will briefly describe these European procedures, then we will analyse the possible levels of interoperability and finally we will formulate some brief conclusions.

10.2 The ESCP

The ESCP applies in cross-border cases to civil and commercial matters, whatever the nature of the court or tribunal, where the value of a claim does not exceed 2,000 euro. The aim of the procedure is to allow European citizens to file autonomously a low-value claim with a member state court without having to ask for legal or technical assistance, and to reduce the applicable costs.

In order to achieve this goal, the European Small Claims Regulation provides for a very fast and easy procedure. The plaintiff is required to file the claim before the competent court using a standard claim form, Form A, as set out in Annex I of the European Small Claims Regulation.[4] This form must be duly filled out and must be filed along with the appropriate documents attached. The competent court makes a first assessment on the admissibility of the claim according to the scope of the regulation (for instance, if the value of the claim is higher than 2,000 euro): if the claim is outside the scope of the regulation, the court informs the claimant accordingly.[5] At the same time, if the claim is not clear or the information provided by the claimant is inadequate, the court informs the claimant by using another standard form, Form B, as set out in Annex II of the European Small Claims Regulation.[6] The claimant can complete or rectify the claim within the period of time indicated by the court. If the claim is admissible and does not need any integration, then a copy of it, together with the attached documents, is served upon the debtor.[7] Regulation No. 861/2007 does not clearly state whether the court or the claimant is required to serve the claim and the attached documents upon the

[4] See Art. 4, n. 1 of Regulation No. 861/2007.

[5] See Art. 4, n. 3, ibidem.

[6] See Art. 4, n. 4, ibidem.

[7] See Art. 5, n. 2, ibidem.

counterparty, but the goal of the regulation suggests that the court should do it, otherwise the claimant would be obliged to bear the costs related to the service.

The defendant has 30 days, starting from the service of the claim, to prepare a response and to file it before the court seized, by filling in Part II of the standard answer form, Form C—or another appropriate answer document—accompanied, where appropriate, by any relevant supporting documents.[8] The defendant's response must be dispatched, together with the relevant documents, to the claimant: in this case, the regulation clearly says that the seized court must do it.[9] Moreover, if the defendant raises a counterclaim, then the plaintiff can file a response to the counterclaim before the court seized within 30 days of service on the defendant's response.[10]

After this initial exchange of documents from both parties, the court will assess if the final decision can be taken or if further judicial activity is required. More precisely, the court can demand further details from the parties, take specific evidences or summon the parties to an oral hearing.[11] In such a case, the court will give the judgement either within 30 days of any oral hearing or after having received all information necessary for giving the judgement.[12] This final decision is then served upon both parties.

The European small claims decision is immediately enforceable in all the European member states because it is considered to be a European enforcement order: member states cannot refuse its enforcement unless it is demonstrated that it is irreconcilable with an earlier decision given in any member state or in a third country.[13]

The European small claims judgement can be challenged before the competent courts at a national level: time limits for the appeal, as well as all the other conditions for it, will be regulated by the rules of procedure of the country, but according to Regulation No. 861/2007, a review of the European small claims decision will be guaranteed if the defendant was unable to participate in the European procedure.[14]

[8] See Art. 5 n. 3, ibidem.

[9] See Art. 5, n. 4, ibidem.

[10] See Art. 5, n. 6, ibidem.

[11] See Art. 7, ibidem.

[12] See Art. 7. n. 2, ibidem.

[13] See Art. 22, ibidem.

[14] More precisely, according to Article 18 of the regulation, the defendant will be entitled to apply for a review provided that: '(a) (i) the claim form or the summons to an oral hearing were served by a method without proof of receipt by him personally, as provided for in Article 14 of Regulation (EC) No. 805/2004; and (ii) service was not effected in sufficient time to enable him to arrange for his defense without any fault on his part, or (b) the defendant was prevented from objecting to the claim by reason of force majeure, or due to extraordinary circumstances without any fault on his part, provided in either case that he acts promptly'.

10.3 The EPO

The EPO applies in cross-border cases related to civil and commercial matters with no value limits. It aims to simplify, speed up and reduce the costs of litigation in cross-border cases concerning uncontested pecuniary claims. In order to achieve this goal, Regulation No. 1896/2006 sets up a fast and simple procedure essentially based on the 'behaviour' of the debtor. Indeed, an EPO is issued by the competent court on the exclusive basis of a creditor's statement: if this order is challenged by the debtor within a 30-day limit, then an ordinary procedure will start. If this order is not challenged by the debtor within the above deadline, then the EPO becomes definitive and enforceable in all the European member states. More precisely, the creditor/claimant will file the claim using Form A as set out in Annex I of Regulation No. 1896/2006: this form must be properly filled out with all the information concerning the claim.[15] No documents should be attached, however.

The court will immediately assess if the claim falls within the scope of the regulation: if not, the court will immediately dismiss the claim. The court will also assess if the claim is clear and complete. If not, the court will give the claimant the opportunity to complete or rectify the application: for this purpose, the court will use Form B as set out in Annex II of the regulation.[16] If the claimant fails to send his reply within the time limit specified by the court or if the claim is clearly unfounded, then the court will reject the claim by using Form D, as set out in Annex IV.[17] If the claim is admissible, it meets all the requirements indicated by the regulation and it is not clearly unfounded, then the court will issue an EPO by using Form E as set out in Annex V of the regulation.[18]

The court can also issue an EPO for a part of the credit claimed: in this case, the claimant/creditor will be informed by Form C as set out in Annex III of the regulation and will be invited to accept or refuse the issuing of such an EPO.[19] If the claimant/creditor refuses an EPO for the amount specified by the court or does not reply within the time limit specified by the court by returning Form C, then the court will reject the claim, once again by means of Form D as set out in Annex IV of the regulation.

The EPO will be served upon the defendant together with the creditor's claim: Regulation No. 1896/2006 does not clearly state whether the court or the claimant should serve the EPO. Article 12.5 just states that, 'The court shall ensure that the order is served on the defendant in accordance with national law by a method that shall meet the minimum standards laid down in Articles 13, 14 and 15'. However,

---

[15] See Art. 17 of Regulation No. 1896/2006.

[16] See Art. 9, ibidem.

[17] See Art. 11, ibidem.

[18] See Art. 12, ibidem.

[19] See Art. 10, ibidem.

in the light of the goals of the regulation, the court should serve the EPO upon the debtor in order to avoid any cost or inconvenience related to the service.

The debtor/defendant has 30 days from the receipt of the EPO to challenge it. The opposition must be lodged before the court issuing the order by using Form F as set out in Annex VI of the regulation. As for the initial claim, no documents need to be attached to the opposition. In the case of opposition, the proceedings will continue before the courts issuing the EPO in accordance with their internal rules of procedure. Accordingly, the claimant will be informed whether the defendant has lodged a statement of opposition.[20] If no opposition has been lodged within the 30-day time limit, then the court of origin will declare the EPO enforceable using Form G as set out in Annex VII: this standard form will be sent to the claimant.[21]

Once the 30-day time limit has expired, the European enforcement order can no longer be challenged except in a very few cases: more precisely, the debtor must demonstrate that he/she was prevented from lodgement the opposition by circumstances that were not his/her fault.[22]

The EPO is immediately enforceable in all the European member states because it is considered to be a European enforcement order: member states cannot refuse its enforcement unless it is demonstrated that it is irreconcilable with an earlier decision given in any member state or in a third country.[23]

10.4 Legal Interoperability and the Preliminary Aspects of the EPO and ESCP

The EPO and ESCP proceed before the national court that is jurisdictionally competent according to the rules of international jurisdiction established by Regulation (EC) No. 44/2001.[24] At the moment,[25] this regulation, which has taken the place of the former Convention of Brussels of 1968, determines the court that has competence to bring proceedings related to civil and commercial matters.[26] These

[20] See Art. 17, ibidem.

[21] See Art. 18, ibidem.

[22] See Art. 20, ibidem.

[23] See Art. 22, ibidem.

[24] Council Regulation (EC) No. 44/2001 of 22 December 2000 on jurisdiction and the recognition and enforcement of judgments in civil and commercial matters, in OJ L 12, 16.1.2001, pp. 1–23. A huge number of doctrinal contributions exist on this subject: see mainly, Stadler, Astrid. 2005. From the Brussels Convention to Regulation 44/2001: Cornerstones of a European law of civil procedure, in Common Market Law Review 42(6): 1637–1661.

[25] It must be remembered that, starting from the 10th of January 2015, Regulation No. 44/2001 will be replaced by Regulation No. 1215/2012 of 12 December 2012, in OJ L 351, 20.12.2012.

[26] There are other Regulations that set up rules on jurisdictions in international civil claims, such as Council Regulation (EC) No. 2201/2003 of 27 November 2003 concerning jurisdiction and the recognition and enforcement of judgements in matrimonial matters and the matters of

rules aim to avoid conflict of jurisdiction and, thereby, those situations in which more than one court brings proceedings on the same issue, because that would create a waste of human and economic resources inside the European judiciary space.

If a court of a member state brings civil proceedings in violation of the jurisdiction rules of Regulation No. 44/2001, it is possible that the final decision adopted by that court will not have any legal effect in any other member state. That happens in the case of infringement of rules of jurisdiction relating to 'exclusive fora'[27] and those relating to 'protective fora'.[28]

The courts of the member states of the EU are requested to unanimously and correctly apply these rules in order to avoid any conflict of jurisdiction. The system of jurisdiction in civil matters set up by Regulation No. 44/2001 is not so easy to apply, however: it is sometimes based on quite complicated criteria of connection, whose interpretation can often differ according to the court seized.[29] Moreover, this system of jurisdiction is not very well known to the courts of the member states.

In addition, except for the rules on exclusive fora, there are no duties for the court seized to check automatically ('ex officio') its competence to deal with the case. In other words, if parties do not raise any exception of jurisdiction, the court seized can declare its competence to deal with the case even though it is not actually competent to do it.

All these circumstances show that the existence of common rules on jurisdiction does not avoid the risk that two civil proceedings on the same issue can be brought before two different European member states' courts. This is the reason why Regulation (EC) No. 44/2001 provides for a mechanism the aim of which is to avoid a situation in which two different courts declare their competence to deal with the same issue on the basis of different interpretation or application of the rules of jurisdiction. This is the *lis pendens* mechanism.

---

parental responsibility, repealing Regulation (EC) No. 1347/2000, in OJ L 338, 23.12.2003, p. 1–29; Council Regulation (EC) No. 4/2009 of 18 December 2008 on jurisdiction, applicable law, recognition and enforcement of decisions and cooperation in matters relating to maintenance obligations, in OJ L 7, 10.1.2009, pp. 1–79; Council Regulation (EC) No. 1346/2000 of 29 May 2000 on insolvency proceedings, in OJ L 160, 30.6.2000, pp. 1–18. These regulations deal with subjects not covered by the scope of the EPO and ESCP, however.

27 Article 22 and 23 of Regulation No. 44/2001.

28 Sections No. 3, 4 and 5 of Regulation No. 44/2001. These rules on jurisdiction refer to the 'weak' parties of a civil relationship, such as consumers, employees or persons who joined an insurance agreement: in such cases, these 'weak' parties can bring civil proceedings before the court of their residence, instead of the court of the counterparty's residence.

29 It must be added that the European Court of Justice is competent to deal with preliminary references concerning the interpretation of these rules (starting from the Treaty of Lisbon, it is also competent for preliminary references coming from European courts not of last instance). The case-law of the European Court of Justice is huge: just for the latest (but not less important) decisions on Regulation No. 44/2001, see: 11.03.2010, C-19/09, Wood Floor Solutions, in Rep. 2010 I-02121; 25.02.2010, C-381/08, Car Trim, in Rep. 2010 I-01255; 07.12.2010, Joined cases C-585/08 and C-144/09, Pammer and Hotel Alpenhof, not yet published; 23.04.2009, C-533/07, Falco, in Rep. 2009, I-03327; 16.07.2009, C-189/09, Zuid-Chemie, in Rep. 2009, I-6917; 19 April 2012, C-523/10, Wintersteiger, not yet published. 17.11.2011, C-327/10, not yet published. 15.03.2012, C-292/10, G, not yet published; 12.05.2011, C-144/10, Berliner not yet published.

According to Regulation No. 44/2001,[30] if two European Courts are seized on the same issue, the second court seized from a temporal point of view must stay the proceedings in order for the first court seized to assess which court is the competent one. In other words, only the first court seized from a temporal point of view is competent to examine and apply the rules on jurisdiction of Regulation No. 44/2001 and, therefore, to assess which court is the competent one to deal with the issue (this is the so called 'competence on competence'). The second court seized, even if competent according to the common rules of jurisdiction, must always stay the proceedings, unless its competence is based on an exclusive forum according to Article 22 of Regulation No. 44/2001.[31]

The mechanism of *lis pendens* is fundamental for the functioning of the European judiciary space (Bogdan 2007; Gallagher 2006; Gebauer 2007; Marongiu Buonaiuti 2010; McLachlan 2009): indeed, if the second court seized does not stay the proceedings and declares its competence and if the first court seized does the same, there is the high risk that two different decisions on the same issue can be adopted. In this case, those decisions cannot have any legal effect in the territory of the member state where the other decision has been issued and, in some cases, neither in all the other member states.[32]

In both the above cases, it is crucial to understand when and how the first document of the process has been served upon the counterparty. For this purpose, the EU adopted Regulation (EC) No. 1393/2007[33]: this regulation establishes how a document can be served upon an addressee located in a European member state and, in specific cases, determines when the service must be considered completed.

Regulation No. 1393/2007 is based on two main levels of interoperability, both based on the mechanism of 'transmitting and receiving agencies', which are national authorities charged to deal with the service of documents abroad: a 'high level of interoperability', in which the transmitting agency sends the document to the receiving agency, which serves it upon the addressee, and a 'low level of interoperability', in which the transmitting agency serves the document directly upon the addressee by postal service.

---

[30] See Article 27 of Regulation No. 44/2001: 'Where related actions are pending in the courts of different member states, any court other than the court first seized may stay its proceedings.'

[31] European Court of Justice, 8.12.1987, C-144/86, Gubisch; 27.09.1988, C-189/87, Athanasios; 19.05.1998, C-351/96, Drouot Assurances; 8.05.2003, C-111/01, Gantner; 9.12.2003, C-116/02, Erich Gasser GmbH; 27.04.2004, C-159/02, Turner; 14.10.2004, C- 39/02, Maerks Olie; 11.10. 2007, C-98/06, Freeport. It must be added that Regulation No. 1215/2012 will partially modify these rules, introducing some elements of flexibility.

[32] See Article 34 of Regulation No. 44/2001.

[33] Regulation (EC) No. 1393/2007 of the European Parliament and of the Council of 13 November 2007 on the service in the member states of judicial and extrajudicial documents in civil or commercial matters (service of documents), and repealing Council Regulation (EC) No. 1348/2000, OJ L 324, 10.12.2007, pp. 79–120. This regulation replaces Regulation (EC) No. 1348/2000.

Particularly at the first level of interoperability, national authorities are requested to 'dialogue' with one another in order to correctly and speedily carry out the international service of documents. This dialogue between these authorities is based on the functioning of specific standard forms provided for by Regulation No. 1393/2007: these forms contain all the elements related to the nature of the document to be served and the date of service of the document. If the dialogue does not work properly, the court seized will not receive the correct information on how and when the service has been carried out and, therefore, cannot correctly assess the moment and the full validity of the seizure. Hence, there is the risk that a national court can consider itself to be the first court seized even if the service of the act of summons or of the other initial document of the process has not actually been served upon the defendant or the service has not been correctly carried out.

In light of the this juridical framework, legal interoperability can be very important in order for the EPO and ESCP procedures to be correctly initiated: by the way, it is important that all the subjects involved in the initial part of these procedures can fully and efficiently cooperate, by exchanging the relevant information and data.

The seized court for an ESCP must determine if it is competent to deal with that case and if there is another court that has been already seized on the same issue. At the moment, there are no mechanisms of cooperation/interoperability between the courts of the member states, both at European and intergovernmental levels: therefore, a court of a member state cannot know if a court from another member state has been seized on the same matter and, if so, when exactly it was seized and if the latter declared its competence to deal with the case.

It is up to the parties to raise the exceptions of *lis pendens*: in other words, parties have a duty to 'warn' the courts about the fact that the same claim has been already filed with another court that is supposed to be competent to deal with the case. If parties fail to do so, then the court seized can declare its competence, even if another court would be competent to assess the competence and even if the latter is actually competent to deal with the case.

In light of the above, if European courts had a direct dialogue, the *lis pendens* mechanism would work properly and the risk of parallel proceedings would be avoided. Hence, courts should be able to transmit to each other the information concerning the date of the seizure and the jurisdiction grounds of the seizure; they would then know if a decision on the jurisdiction has been already adopted. By acting in this way, just one EPO or ESCP would run on a matter. As mentioned earlier, *lis pendens* and jurisdiction mechanisms depend on the good functioning of the European system related to the service of documents.

This system is based on the competent national authorities, who should have a constant and efficient dialogue: according to Regulation No. 1393/2007, this interoperability is ensured by the use of some specific forms that are annexed to the above regulation.

Undoubtedly, these forms play an important role for this kind of cooperation, but at the same time, a narrower and more efficient interoperability is absolutely necessary. These authorities should be able to exchange information and data concerning the service of documents on a common electronic platform. That would allow single authorities—and citizens—to check at any time the status of the service, whether there is a problem concerning the procedure of service of documents and, thereby, to carry out a faster and more efficient service for citizens and the courts.

10.5 Legal Interoperability and the Running of the EPO and ESCP

10.5.1 The Use of Standard Forms

In both European procedures, the court should play a role of 'centre of deposit and transmission' of the documents lodged by the parties. This intense dialogue between the seized court and parties runs through specific standard forms, which are annexed to Regulations No. 861/2007 and No. 1896/2006. The content of these forms was hardly discussed during the negotiations of the regulations with regard to achieving an efficient exchange of information regarding the dispute.

There is no doubt that the level of interoperability based on these forms can be improved. First of all, pursuant to the European Regulations, the use of the standard forms is not always mandatory and parties are free to use all the appropriate ways to participate in the procedures: for instance, according to Article 5, n. 3 of Regulation No. 861/007, 'The defendant shall submit his response in any other appropriate way not using the answer form'. The non-binding nature of these standard forms does not facilitate dialogue between parties and the court. Parties could use unilaterally prepared claim forms the content of which content could differ from that provided in the standard forms set up by the EU. Instead, the dialogue should be based on a common language.

Second, these forms are not very clear in most parts and often both citizens and courts do not know exactly how to deal with them.[34] According to the spirit of the European legislator, these forms should allow European citizens to autonomously file a claim with a member state court without having to ask for legal or technical assistance. However, their content is sometimes very complicated and difficult for the average reader to understand. An example should clarify this statement.

As mentioned earlier, both the ESCP and EPO run before the competent national court according to jurisdictional rules established by Regulation No. 44/2001. Standard forms for both procedures oblige the claimant to indicate the jurisdictional grounds for seizing the court of the specific member state: in this respect, it must be remembered that international jurisdiction is a complicated matter and it is not

[34] For this purpose, it must be remembered the first judgment issued by the European Court of Justice on the interpretation of Regulation No. 1896/2006, 13.12.2012, C-215/11, *Szyrocka*, not yet published.

hard to imagine the average citizen having difficulty in interpreting and correctly applying the rules of conflict (such as 'the place of performance of the obligation in question' or 'the place of harmful event', etc.) established by Regulation No. 44/2001.

Both regulations actually oblige member states to provide information on these issues and, more generally, on how the forms must be filled out,[35] but this obligation has not been met in practice: member states simply did not set up a system of information and instructions for citizens on how to fill out the forms.[36]

This dialogue can be built both at vertical and horizontal levels: at the moment, the Judicial Network in Civil and Commercial Matters uses mostly the vertical level (European Commission—member states). Indeed, member states are invited to transmit data and information to the Commission, the latter being charged with classifying all the data and disclosing them to the citizens. In the future, a more horizontal approach could be adopted: member states should dialogue between themselves as much as they can, using a common platform and/or communication systems.

To sum up, there is still a 'gap' between the courts and the citizens concerning the use of the standard forms set up by Regulation No. 861/2007 and No. 1896/2006: a more effective interoperability between the court and the citizens is absolutely needed.

10.5.2 The Means of Transmission of the Documents

A fast and efficient system of transmission of documents between the subjects involved in the both the ESCP and EPO (court and parties) is crucial for the correct functioning of these procedures. The goal of these procedures is to allow citizens to autonomously file a claim with a court located in a member state other than the state of habitual residence or domicile. In order to achieve this goal, European legislature aims to overcome the need for the personal lodgement of documents before the competent court. The personal lodgement of documents would mean an increase in costs for both parties involved in these procedures. member states' national rules on this point differ greatly, however. Some member states allow lodgement of claims (both coming from the national territory or outside) by post or by electronic means, whereas other member states accept only the personal lodgement of claims before the competent court.

---

[35] See Article 11 of Regulation No. 861/2007 and Article 29 of Regulation No. 1896/2006.

[36] In particularly, member states should cooperate via the European Judicial Network in Civil and Commercial Matters: the European Judicial Network in Civil and Commercial Matters is a network established in accordance with Council Decision of 28 May 2001 establishing a European Judicial Network in civil and commercial matters, OJ L 174, 27.6.2001, pp. 25–31, the goal of which is to ensure a narrow coordination between the EU and the member states in matters related to the application of EU Regulations of civil judiciary cooperation.

The filing of claims by means other than personal lodgement creates the juridical problem of 'identifying' the party who is acting. Identification normally is ensured by the physical signature of the party. Incidentally, given the nature of these European procedures, at least one of the parties is inevitably not physically resident in the state where the court is located. Therefore, other means of transmission of documents must be examined, such as the electronic transmission of documents. This could actually be helpful for the good functioning of European procedures because it would allow parties to easily file a claim with a court located in another member state.

According to this system of transmission, the physical signature does not exist: it is replaced by an electronic signature. Not all the member states have implemented efficient and common systems of identification of parties, however, the European legislature has adopted an intermediate approach on this point: claims can be filed with the competent court directly, by post or by any other means of transmission of documents, including electronic ones, that are accepted by the specific member state in which the procedure is commenced. This is the so-called 'court seized approach'.[37] This approach still limits a broad and uniform application of these procedures among the member states: cross-border cases can be facilitated only in those member states where efficient and safe systems of transmission of documents have been implemented. In the other member states, citizens are still obliged to directly file their claims with the competent court.

If a document has been transmitted to a member state that accepts this kind of transmission, the member state will also recognise the (electronic) signature incorporated in that document. In other words, member states will mutually accept and recognise the systems of identification of parties set up in an another member state, under one condition: the electronic signature must be carried out according to the common framework for electronic signature set up by EU Directive 1999/93/EC.[38]

According to the above directive, an electronic signature will be recognised in so far as it fulfils specific requirements such as, '(a) it is uniquely linked to the signatory; (b) it is capable of identifying the signatory; (c) it is created using means that the signatory can maintain under his sole control; and (d) it is linked to the data to which it relates in such a manner that any subsequent change of the data is detectable'. This kind of signature is defined as an 'Electronic Advanced Signature'.[39] European Regulation No. 1896/2006 goes further on this point. The electronic signature of the document will not be required if 'the member state of origin' has set up a system that permits the identification 'a priori' of the users in a secure manner.

---

[37] See Article 4 of Regulation No. 861/2007 and Article 7.5 of Regulation No. 1896/2006.

[38] Directive 1999/93/EC of the European Parliament and of the Council of 13 December 1999 on a Community framework for electronic signatures, Official Journal L 013, 19/01/2000 pp. 0012–0020.

[39] Article 2.2 of the directive.

It must be underlined that the wording 'member state of origin' included in Article 7.6 of Regulation No. 1896/2006 does not refer to the member state in which the document has been issued (the state of transmission) but to the member state where the proceedings are commenced (the state of destination).[40]

Therefore, taking into account that normally the claimant is resident in a member state other than the state where the court is located, it is difficult to imagine a foreign claimant being able to join a non-national system of identification of users. At the moment, the issue of electronic transmission of documents is being examined by important research projects in the EU: in particular, the E-CODEX project,[41] a co-funded project the aim of which is to improve the efficiency of cross-border judicial processes through standards and solutions that ease and facilitate cross-border case-handling activities.

10.5.3 The Issue of the Language

The EPO and ESCP are European civil proceedings running before national courts and between parties of different nationalities. As has been shown above, courts and parties need to communicate constantly between one another, but they cannot use the same language. This can entail some important problems. In addition, juridical language is itself a technical language and depends heavily on the national law. Therefore, it cannot be easily or automatically translated into a different language. High risks of discrepancy with the original meaning will occur.

It is not my intention to examine here a very deep and complicated matter, such as the relationship between law and language (Visconti 2010; Morawetz 2000). Many studies have been already carried out on such subjects. I would just like to point out that, within the context of European regulations in the field of civil proceedings, this problem becomes more and more important.

Since its foundation, the EU's principle has been multilingualism: this means that all the regulations and other documents of general application must be drafted in all the official languages of the EU.[42] Initially, this principle did not entail much complexity because at the time of its foundation, the EU was composed of only six member states and so only four official languages were required, but many other countries joined EU subsequently, with the result that the total number of official languages is now 23. All the official languages have the same dignity and no linguistic primacy is admitted: this means that all the national versions of EU

[40] Indeed, according to Article 5.4 of Regulation No. 1896/2006, '"court of origin" means the court which issues the EPO'.

[41] Fourteen member states do take part in it, plus a non-member state and some professional and scientific associations.

[42] See Regulation No. 1 determining the languages to be used by the European Economic Community, OJ 17, 6.10.1958, pp. 385–386.

documents are equally considered, as affirmed by the Court of Justice on many occasions.[43] Thus, the principle of multilingualism has generated more and more complexity (Sacco 2005; Abba 1988), above all when it is applied in a juridical context.

At the moment, European regulations in this field are internally negotiated and elaborated in all the official languages of the EU and the adopted text is then adapted to the linguistic and juridical characteristics of all the official languages of the EU. For this purpose, specific meetings at the European institutions take place in order to ensure that the different 'national' versions of the text negotiated reflect the original meaning of the European legislature. Nonetheless, it often happens that some adaptations to the national language can differ from the original meaning or, at least, can lead to different interpretations or applications.

Several examples can be given: for instance, Article 4 of Regulation No. 593/2008, dealing with the applicable law in international contracts of selling, states that the applicable law to the contracts of sale of goods shall be the law of the state where the seller has his/her habitual residence. This rule is applicable to the sale of goods, it being understood that the European legislator intended to apply this rule to material goods and not to immaterial goods.[44] However, the Italian and the French versions use the wordings *beni* and *biens*, respectively, words that generally include immaterial goods as well, whereas the Spanish version, more correctly, uses the word *mercaderia*, which excludes immaterial goods (Franzina 2009). Therefore, the scope and the meaning of Article 4 of Regulation No. 593/2008—which is a crucial rule within the context of the above regulation—changes according to the different versions.

Sometimes, the translations into the national languages are manifestly wrong and completely modify the original meaning of the text. The wrong translation of even one word[45] is enough to completely change the meaning and the *ratio legis* of a rule or of the entire legislative text. A simple example can demonstrate this. Article 22 of Regulation No. 2201/2003, concerning the international jurisdiction and recognition of decisions in matrimonial matters as well as matters related to parental responsibility,[46] establishes common rules on recognition and enforcement of foreign decisions in matrimonial matters. The *ratio legis* of this regulation is that decisions coming from a European member state shall be normally executed across the entire EU territory (the principle of mutual recognition of European decisions). Few exceptions to this principle are provided: in particular, European decisions shall

[43]European Court of Justice, 20.11.2011, C-268/99; 20.11.1993, C-152/01.

[44]See the positions of the delegations at the Council in doc. n. 14708/06 of the Council at http://register.consilium.europa.eu, p. 43 e p. 49.

[45]Let me mention Nobel Prize winner José Saramago and his work 'Historia do cerco de Lisboa', in which he describes the power of the word and how even a single word can completely change the meaning of human history.

[46]Council Regulation (EC) No. 2201/2003 of 27 November 2003 concerning jurisdiction and the recognition and enforcement of judgements in matrimonial matters and the matters of parental responsibility, repealing Regulation (EC) No. 1347/2000, O.J. 23.12.2003, L 338/1.

not be recognised 'where it was given in default of appearance, if the respondent was not served with the document which instituted the proceedings or with an equivalent document in sufficient time and in such a way as to enable the respondent to arrange for his or her defence unless it is determined that the respondent has accepted the judgement unequivocally'.

The *ratio legis* is to avoid the circulation of decisions in Europe if this decision comes from a judiciary procedure that did not respect the right to a fair trial. However, the Italian translation of this article is worded in the following way: 'A judgement shall not be recognised where it was given in default of appearance or if the respondent was not served with the document which instituted the proceedings or with an equivalent document in sufficient time and in such a way as to enable the respondent to arrange for his or her defence unless it is determined that the respondent has accepted the judgement unequivocally'.

The Italian translation completely changes the meaning of the rule and of the *ratio legis*[47] (Mellone 2011): according to the Italian version, a European decision will not be recognised each time it has been given in default of appearance. However, default of appearance does not automatically mean violation of the principle of a fair trial: each person is free to decide to appear or not in a process. If he or she does not, that decision must be in any case executed in the country where it has been issued, as well as across Europe: otherwise, each person will decide not to appear in order to automatically block the execution of the final decision.

Incorrect translations are also present in the national versions of the EPO: for instance, in the Italian version of this regulation, the defendant is sometimes called *imputato*, which is actually used to make reference to defendants in criminal matters (the 'accused person') and not in civil matters. In order to solve the linguistic issue, EU legislators set up a common linguistic platform, the European Judicial Atlas in Civil Matters: this platform helps parties to automatically translate the standard forms of both the EPO and ESCP into the required language by using a specific software. It also allows citizens to fill out the European Small Claims forms directly in the language required: citizens fill out the forms in their own language and the software automatically translates the forms into the language required.

This software is undoubtedly very helpful for European citizens aiming to access European civil procedures: until now, it has played an important role in the good functioning of other European instruments of civil judiciary cooperation, such as European regulations on service of documents, European regulations on the taking of evidences, etc. Indeed, it can greatly reduce the problem of the translation of the

[47] Art. 22, lett. b of the Italian version of Regulation No. 2201/2003: 'La decisione di divorzio, separazione personale o annullamento del matrimonio non è riconosciuta nei casi seguenti: (...) (b) quando è resa in contumacia, ovvero la domanda giudiziale o un atto equivalente non è stato notificato o comunicato al convenuto contumace in tempo utile e in modo tale da poter presentare le proprie difese, salvo che sia stato accertato che il convenuto ha accettato inequivocabilmente la decisione.'

documents[48] in cross-border cases, especially if the claim has a very small value (such as in the ESCP). Otherwise, the citizen can be discouraged from applying for this procedure and initiating any lawsuit due to the huge costs of translation of documents.

However, it cannot solve all the problems arising from the practical application of these regulations. First of all, the mechanism of translation of the European Judicial Atlas is based on the fact that the forms of the ESCP are 'standard' or, in other words, they have the same 'fixed' content for all member states. Consequently, the translation of the Atlas is limited to these 'standard' parts of the forms: no translation is provided for the parts of the forms that must be filled out by the parties. For instance, no translation is provided for the part where the claimant describes the nature of the issue and the object of the claim (Part 8 of the Claim form—Annex 1). Thus, citizens are obliged to ask for the help of a translator.

Second, the software of the European Judicial Atlas does not provide for the translation of attached documents, such as an invoice, an agreement, a letter of intent, etc. It must be remembered that both claimant and defendant are called not only to respectively file the claim and the response by using the standard forms—and therefore, translating them by using the Atlas platform—but also to file the documents related to the claim or to the response. These documents must be translated[49] into the language of the seized court or to the language of the counterparty. At the moment, there are no other mechanisms—at the European level—for the translation of documents that are filed together with the claim. This is an issue that is under the competence of the member states.

The need for translation of the documents seriously risks jeopardising the goal of the ESCP to reduce the costs for international disputes for small value claims. Moreover, it must be underlined that the claimant could be obliged to translate the claim and the attached documents not only into the language of the court but also into the language of the defendant. More clearly, according to the rules of jurisdiction set out in Regulation No. 44/2001, it can occur that the ESCP runs before a court of a state (state C) other than the state of the claimant (state A) and other than the state of the defender (state B). This happens, for instance, when the object of the claim is a right on an immovable property and the parties are domiciled in two European countries other than the country where the property is located.[50] In these cases, the claimant and the defendant must bear a 'double' cost of translation. Moreover, the translation of the documents is required not only for the forms and for the attached documents but also for the European Small Claims judgement.[51]

---

[48] It must be remembered that the term 'documents' in the 'European meaning' refers to the claim and to the attached documents. See European Court of Justice, 08.05.2008, C-14/07.

[49] See the European Court of Justice, 8.11.2005, C-443/03; 09.02.2006, C-473/04; 08.05.2008, C-14/07.

[50] Indeed, according to article 22 of Regulation No. 44/2001, the Court of the member state where the immovable property is located shall be competent to deal with the case.

[51] See article 21 of the Regulation No. 861/2007.

Finally, it must be not forgotten that European Judicial Atlas is an online mechanism of translation and as such is not available for a (still) large number of European citizens. Therefore, a 'point of access' to the European Judicial Atlas and the necessary assistance in using it should be provided in any court of the EU.

10.5.4 The Taking of Evidences

Taking of evidences can be a crucial point for the good functioning of the European regulations dealing with civil proceedings, especially for the ESCP. In the EPO, the claimant is not called to attach evidences of the credit, only to indicate them in the form. By contrast, the ESCP is an 'ordinary' procedure in which both claimant and defendant must prove their respective statements. Therefore, it is possible that the parties—or the court—will need to take evidence that is not physically located within the national territory of the court seized, but in another European state. For instance, the hearing of an important witness who is resident in a European state other than the state of the court seized, which can be important for the final decision, or a relevant document registered by a body or owned by a person physically located in a foreign state.

In all these cases, the taking of evidence can entail some supplementary expenses that can strongly impact on the total amount of the costs for a cross-border claim. For this reason, the ESCP does not entail any hearing, because that would oblige the parties (and above all the claimant) and/or the witnesses to bear huge costs of transfer. Hearings take place only in exceptional cases: more precisely, a hearing takes place if the court considers it necessary or if a party so requests.[52]

From a European perspective, the issue of the taking of 'foreign' evidences has been already examined and faced in the past. Indeed, the EU adopted Regulation No. 1206/2001,[53] which provides for an important mechanism of cooperation/interoperability between the courts of the member states in the taking of evidences. Regulation No. 1206/2001 provides for two different systems of interoperability. According to the first level of interoperability, the seized court requests that a court of another member state takes the evidence, for instance, hearing a witness: this is a high level of interoperability based on the mechanism of the delegation of the taking of evidences. Courts dialogue between one another—once again through specific forms attached to the above regulation—in order to exchange information and instructions on the practical application of the requests for taking of evidences. Cooperation is strengthened by the presence of 'central bodies', national authorities charged to deal with the application of this regulation.

---

[52] Article 5 and Article 9 n. 2of Regulation No. 861/2007.

[53] Council Regulation (EC) No. 1206/2001 of 28 May 2001 on cooperation between the courts of the member states in the taking of evidence in civil or commercial matters, OJ L 174, 27.6.2001, pp. 1–24.

The second level of interoperability is based on the direct taking of evidences: the seized court physically moves to the other member state and directly takes the evidence (i.e., hears the witness). This is a lower mechanism level of interoperability, since the seized court directly carries out the judiciary activity needed, although under the express authorisation of the host state.

European Regulation No. 1206/2001 does not ‘close the doors’ to the use of videoconferences for hearing ‘foreign’ parties or witnesses but this system of communication must be available at both the courts involved,[54] so the practical application of these technological means actually depends on national realities.

The same approach is adopted by the ESCP: the court seized can use videoconferences in order to reduce costs of transfer for the parties and/or witnesses.[55]

However, the European legislature did not impose on the member states the obligation to provide for video conferences in their national courts. It would have not been a workable solution because these technological means are very expensive and, at the moment, are only present in some of the courts in some member states.[56] Consequently, as mentioned earlier, the European legislature adopted an approach based on the single court seized: if the court seized is equipped with the technological means for a video conference, the oral evidence can be taken that way. Otherwise, parties and/or witnesses are obliged to bear the costs for the transfer.[57]

Although the hearing has a residual role in the ESCP, the interoperability between courts and citizens based on video conferences should be encouraged. Indeed, that would greatly reduce costs for European citizens to participate in the hearing before a foreign court and, at the same time, would allow the court seized to personally hear the parties and/or the witnesses.

10.6 Conclusions

This chapter has demonstrated that the EPO and the ESCP need a high level of interoperability among the national actors involved in their application. More precisely, different levels of interoperability have been identified.

First of all, these procedures entail efficient forms of cooperation at a vertical level, that is to say, between national authorities and users and between European institutions and member states. The exchange of documents and communications between seized courts and users is a good example of this: in the view of the European legislature, the national seized court plays a crucial role in both

[54] See Article 10.4 of Regulation No. 1206/2001.

[55] Article 8 of Regulation No. 861/2007 states that, ‘The court or tribunal may hold an oral hearing through video conference or other communication technology if the technical means are available’.

[56] See recital No. 20 of Regulation No. 861/2007.

[57] It must be added that, in some cases, parties can ask for legal aid. member states are obliged to grant this aid within the common framework set up by Decision 2005/630/EC.

procedures, being called not only to adopt a decision on the issue ('jurisdictional function'), but also to constantly dialogue and 'interoperate' with parties for the correct functioning of the procedure. As a matter of fact, parties do not have a 'direct dialogue' and thus are not called on to directly exchange documents between them, but only through the seized court.

A vertical level of interoperability is also needed between member states and European institutions: member states should provide the European Commission with all the relevant information for the practical application of these European rules in the national courts in order for the latter to make possible a common platform of exchange of information, such as the European Judicial Atlas in Civil Matters. For this purpose, it should be added that both Regulations No. 1896/2006[58] and 861/2007[59] establish that European member states must transmit to the Commission this information. Sometimes, however, member states do not transmit very clear responses and this sometimes does not help the user.

Second, these procedures entail important levels of horizontal interoperability, that is to say, mechanisms of cooperation between member states and their national authorities. This level of interoperability operates, for example, for the exchange of information between the national competent authorities (seized courts, judicial functionaries, etc. . . .) concerning international civil cases. As demonstrated above, this level of interoperability could solve many problems concerning many aspects of an international civil case, such as the issues of international jurisdiction or *lis pendens*, the need to serve a document abroad or to take evidence in a state other than the state where the proceedings are brought.

Both vertical and horizontal level of interoperability should be efficient so as to actually contribute to the good functioning of the European procedures in civil proceedings.

In other words, the analysis made in this chapter has showed that the construction of a European judiciary space does not only depend on the individuation of common rules but also on the functioning of common mechanisms of interoperability. All the actors involved in these procedures are required to cooperate and dialogue as far as possible: otherwise, these European procedures risk failure due to their high complexity and to their 'distance' from the national users. Legal interoperability can avoid this risk.

References

Abba, L. 1988. *Computer e linguaggi settoriali: Analisi automatica di testi giuridici e politici.* Milan: Angeli.

Bogdan, M. 2007. The Brussels/Lugano lis pendens rule and the 'Italian torpedo'. *Scandinavian Studies in Law* 51: 89–97.

---

[58] See Article 29 of Regulation No. 1896/2006.

[59] See Article 25 of Regulation No. 861/2007.

Campeis, G., and A. De Pauli. 2007. Prime riflessioni sul procedimento europeo di ingiunzione di pagamento (regolamento n. 1896/2006/CE). Giustizia Civile 355–365.

Défossez, M. 2008. *Titre exécutoire européen, injonction de payer européenne et procédure européenne de règlement des petits litiges. In Enforcing contracts: Aspects procéduraux de l'exécution des contrats transfrontaliers en droit européen et international, dir. M. Défossez and J. Sénéchal*, 105–116. Brussels: Larcier.

ECCS European Consumer Centres Network. 2011. Procédure de règlement des petits litiges et injonction de payer européenne. http://www.cec-zev.eu/fileadmin/user_upload/eu-consommateurs/PDFs/publications/etudes_et_rapports4.4.3_procedure_de_reglement_des_petits_litiges.pdf. Accessed 29 Nov 2012.

ECCS European Consumer Centres Network. 2012. European small claims procedure report. http://ec.europa.eu/consumers/ecc/docs/small_claims_210992012_en.pdf. Accessed 29 Nov 2012.

Fiorini, A. 2008. Facilitating cross-border debt recovery: The European payment order and small claims regulations. *International and Comparative Law Quarterly* 57(2): 449–465.

Franzina, P. 2009. *Commentario al regolamento (CE) N. 593/2008 del Parlamento europeo e del Consiglio del 17 giugno 2008 sulla legge applicabile alle obbligazioni contrattuali. In Le nuove leggi civili commentate*. Milan: Cedam.

Gallagher, N. 2006. Parallel proceedings, res judicata and lis pendens: Problems and possible solutions. In *Pervasive problems in international arbitration*, ed. A. Loukas and J.D.M. Lew, 329–356. Alphen aan den Rijn: Kluwer Law International.

Gebauer, M. 2007. Lis pendens, negative declaratory-judgment actions and the first-in-time principle. In *Conflict of laws in a globalized world*, ed. A.T. von Mehren and E. Gottschalk, 89–100. Cambridge: Cambridge University Press.

Guinchard, E. 2008. L'Europe, la procédure civile et le créancier: l'injonction de payer européenne et la procédure européenne de règlement des petits litiges. In: Revue trimestrielle de droit commercial et de droit économique. Afl. 3: 465–483//2008.

Kramer, X.E. 2010. Enhancing enforcement in the European Union: The European order for payment procedure and its implementation in the member states, particularly in Germany, the Netherlands, and England. In *Enforcement and enforceability: Tradition and reform*, ed. C.H. van Rhee and A. Uzelac, 17–39. Anvers: Intersentia.

Lopez de Tejada, M., and L. D'Avout. 2007. Les non-dits de la procédure européenne d'injonction de payer. *Revue critique de droit international privé* 96(4): 717–748.

McLachlan, C. 2009. *"Lis pendens" in international litigation*. Nijhoff, Leiden/Boston.

Marongiu Buonaiuti, F. 2010. Lis alibi pendens and related actions in civil and commercial matters within the European judicial area. *Yearbook of Private International Law* 11: 511–564.

Mellone, M. 2011. Brevi considerazioni in merito all'impatto del diritto internazionale privato e processuale europeo sulla prassi giudiziaria italiana. In *Il diritto internazionale privato e processuale dell'unione europea*, ed. L.S. Rossi and M. Mellone. Napoli: Editoriale Scientifica.

Morawetz, T. 2000. *Law and language*. Aldershot: Ashgate/Dartmouth.

Mellone and Pancaldi. 2008. Il nuovo regolamento comunitario sulle controversie di modesta entità. Rivista di Diritto dell'Unione europea 281–317.

Sacco, R. 2005. Language and law. In *Ordinary language and legal language*, ed. B. Pozzo, 1–21. Milan: Giuffrè.

Tsikrikas, D. 2009. L'injonction de payer européenne. *Zeitschrift für Zivilprozess international: Jahrbuch des internationalen Zivilprozessrechts* 14: 221–237.

Visconti, J. (ed.). 2010. *Lingua e diritto: livelli di analisi*. Milano: LED.

Chapter 11
Testing Transborder Civil Procedures in Practice: Findings from Simulation Experiments with the European Payment Order and the European Small Claims Procedure

Gar Yein Ng

Abstract This chapter reports about the findings of a simulation experiment that we conducted on the practical functioning of the European Payment Order and the European Small Claim Procedure. It focuses on one actor in particular, namely the claimant, and on the specific problems s/he may encounter in completing the forms and what to expect from the final outcome itself. The experiment allows the identification of a set of bottlenecks and micro-problems that may affect the circulation of agency in real proceedings. Based on the findings I argue that building adequate transborder interoperability levels requires not just the assessment of the legal infrastructure established by the EU, but also a thorough understanding of the fine grain legal and administrative practices within and across specific jurisdictions.

11.1 Introduction

The assessment of the legal, technological and semantic conditions needed to support transborder civil proceedings requires not just the assessment of the legal infrastructure established by the European Union (EU) and analysed by Marco Mellone in Chap. 10, but also the identification of the broader set of problems that may affect the circulation of agency in real proceedings. Gaining some initial insights into how well transborder civil claims at the EU level operate has been difficult, however. The EU and the judiciaries of the member states do not collect statistical data about such procedures. Experts interviewed in various courts agreed on the low frequency of such cases, and when few cases are assigned to courts and judges spread all over Europe, experience about the functioning of the procedure is dispersed and not easily accessible. This has also been confirmed in a recent report published by the European Consumer Centres Network in September 2012

G.Y. Ng (✉)
Central European University, Budapest, Hungary
e-mail: Garyeinng@gmail.com

F. Contini and G.F. Lanzara (eds.), *The Circulation of Agency in E-Justice*, Law, Governance and Technology Series 13, DOI 10.1007/978-94-007-7525-1_11,

(ECC-Net 2012, 23). The decision to organise a simulation of a European Payment Order and of a European Small Claim Procedure, the results of which are presented in this chapter, stems from these methodological difficulties.[1]

The first simulation was for the European Small Claims Procedure (ESCP) and the second was for the European Payment Order (EPO).[2] Both of these procedural regulations[3] have been described in some detail by Marco Mellone in the previous chapter. This essay focuses on one actor in particular for both simulations, namely, that of the claimant in relation to either one of the proceedings, in terms of specific problems encountered in completing the forms and what to expect from the final outcome itself.

After the simulations and reports were completed, the European Consumer Centre (ECC) published its report on the ESCP and the EPO. Whilst I shall refer to this to underscore the main problems found by this simulation, two things need to be kept in mind. One is that the ECC is not a body of legal experts, and the other is that its report is restricted to consumer issues only, not to broader issues of private law. The methodology was also different, in that the ECC conducted surveys more broadly across the EU, using direct contact with courts to learn more about the procedures and experiences of the courts and the users of these claims. However, at the end of the day, the results of our simulation and those of the ECC report are very similar. The French branch of the ECC also published a report, following the experiences of consumers who chose to use the online procedures of the EU and the branch's own experiences advising consumers to use the online procedures (ECC-NET 2011). The French report also took a methodological approach different from that used by this simulation and the other ECC report, but again the conclusions are similar.

11.2 Methodology

The simulations followed flow charts that were designed to lay out the steps provided by the two regulations. This was done by going through each step described by the e-Justice website for the EPO and ESCP proceedings and by the two European regulations. The flow charts provide a picture of how the steps should work and the simulation describes how it actually works (see Figs 11.1 and 11.2).

---

[1]This essay is based on two earlier reports produced by Gar Yein Ng and Marco Mellone. With thanks to Marco Mellone and Francesco Contini for comments. One of these reports is available for download at www.irsig.cnr.it/biecpo

[2]This was conducted in February 2012, moving from the information available at https://e-justice.europa.eu/content_european_payment_order-41-en.do. Since both simulations, the websites have had some slight alterations made to them but do not actually affect the insights in this essay.

[3]Regulation (EC) Nos. 1896/2006 and Regulation (EC) No. 861/2007.

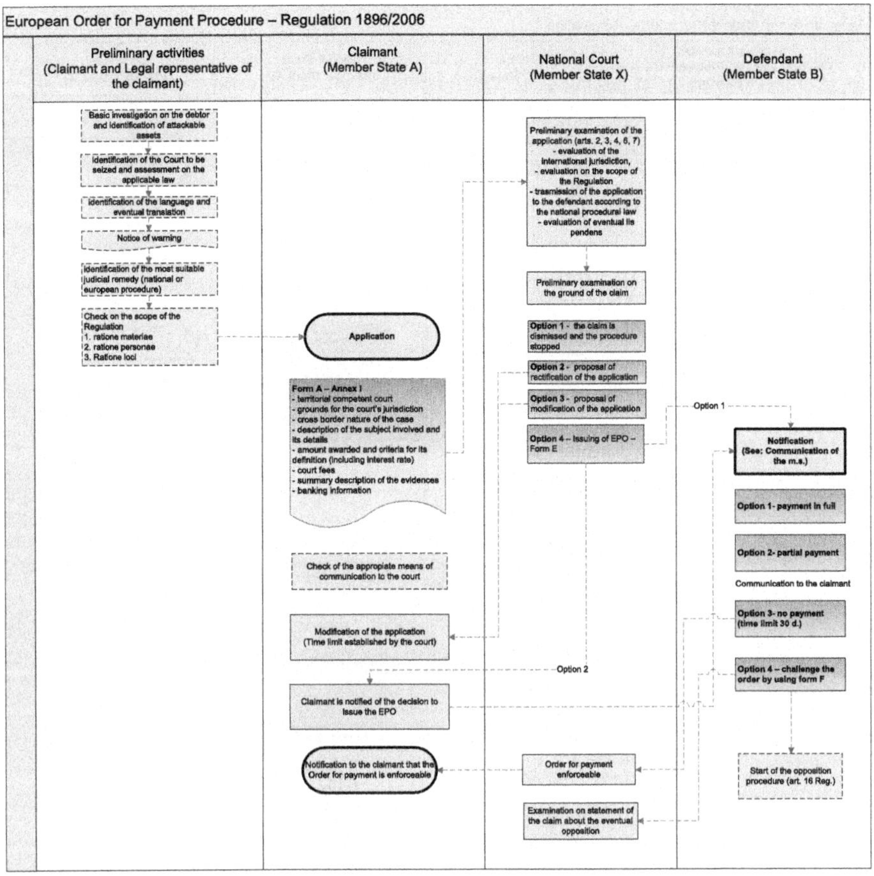

Fig. 11.1 European order for payment procedure

There were two parts to both simulations. One person follows the procedures as if making a claim under the EPO and ESCP. This required the person to fill out the forms online, following the instructions on the one hand and describing the process based on the flow chart on the other, while describing any obstacles or difficulties (or not) to filling out the forms.

The other person followed the procedure once the claims had arrived at the relevant court (in this case, the Justice of the Peace in Bologna).[4] In a similar way, this person had to follow the procedure in court. This required attendance in person at the Justice of the Peace in Bologna, to interview and ask how this procedure

[4]The author wishes to thank Ms. Battistina Fini, chief administrative officer of the Justice of the Peace Office in Bologna, for her valuable help in this part of the simulation.

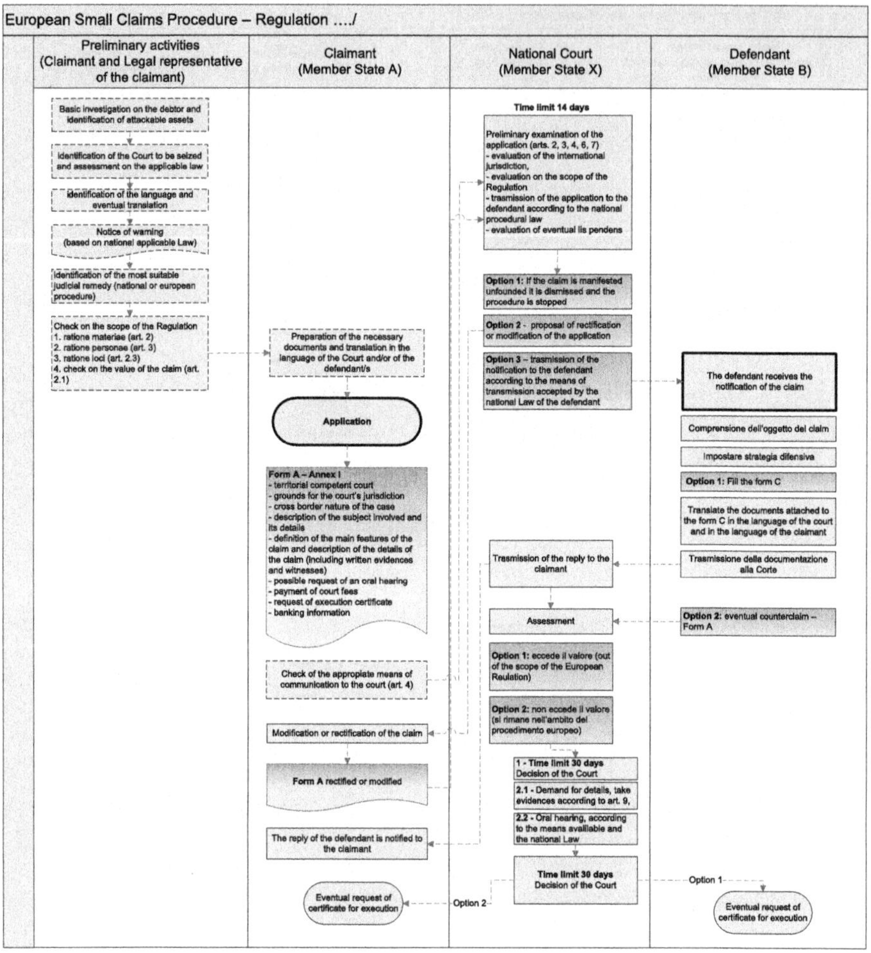

Fig. 11.2 European small claim procedure

was dealt with, in light of the steps laid out in the flow chart and according to the directive. This procedure was further described in the reports.

The conclusions explain the obstacles to the 'circulation of agency' found during the simulation. The obstacles for the EPO are a starting point for further discussion in light of the broader project. They also form the basis for this essay because they highlight the main difficulties for the claimant in this process. The reason for this focus is that these procedures are essentially there to serve claimants, rather than courts. In order to better advise on the further technical development of the ESCP and EPO, it is best that they be developed around claimants' needs. Furthermore, it has to be stated that, due to the methodology adopted, the findings of the simulation cannot be generalised, although they can be read in line with the results of the surveys by the ECC. They also highlight some of the difficulties that have to be considered when we design applications and infrastructure supporting such procedures.

The essay will look first at the problems for claimants with filling out the forms for both procedures, because the problems are common to both, and then with the problems after the claims are filed at court. The essay will not go in depth into either process, because they are described in initial reports for both simulations. Where the simulations showed similar problems for the same areas, they have been written about in one section; where the simulations showed different problems for same areas, I have given separate headings for the two different procedures.

11.2.1 Filing Claims Under EPO and ESCP

Firstly, there is a problem of expectations generated by this procedure. It is somewhat unclear from the e-Justice portal what the EPO consists of: whether it is only a summary proceeding to confirm a claim or if it includes enforcement. This is not a problem for the small claims procedure, where it is clear that you have a claim for a certain amount that falls within the ESCP. What may not be altogether clear is the difference between the two and how a claimant should choose the appropriate procedure, especially if the amount claimed falls under the ESCP but it would be faster under a summary proceeding such as the EPO. According to the experiences of the ECC-Net survey, claimants have been advised to use the EPO due to judges' ignorance of the ESCP (ECC-Net 2012, 18). Secondly, there is an issue related to the ease of filling out the form itself. The EPO site is more user-friendly than the ESCP site, based on the experience of the simulation. However, issues such as deciding jurisdiction if the user is not a lawyer, identifying attackable assets, calculating interest (if the user is not a banker), describing documents that the user has in support of a claim and any additional information in Italian are stumbling blocks for those attempting to proceed without legal representation. Users are faced with deciding when to give up and when to continue. It is easy to forget, whilst filling out this form in English, that at some point the user will have to write in Italian. Thirdly, whilst not a large problem by itself, there is a technical difficulty with the website, more so with the ESCP site than the EPO site. However, with the EPO site there were other, nontechnical problems.

Lastly, communication with the court appears to be a problem, in terms of connectivity, and what to do after the ESCP application has been received or the EPO has been issued. There appears to be little or no institutional support, although the EPO does not claim that you do not need a lawyer in the same way that the ESCP does. Technically, the EPO website could give a list of lawyers able and willing to offer a service for this procedure.

11.2.2 User's Expectations

The issue of expectations appears to be an EPO problem only. The opening page starts with an introduction to the EPO and outlines how the procedure works. What is interesting is that enforcement appears to be a separate procedure that requires further steps after the EPO has been issued.[5]

This is interesting because the claimant (not necessarily a lawyer) could expect this to be a 'one stop shop', given its name, and its nature as a 'summary proceeding' could lead users to believe that enforcement could be done at the same time. It is not assumed that users will need a separate proceeding because, according to the information on the e-Justice portal, users only need it if judgment has not been complied with.[6] This may serve as a warning to the user that the EPO may not be enough to claim their rights and that the process could go further. In another part of the e-Justice portal, it is clearly stated that a claimant will not have to take further steps to enforce the EPO abroad.[7]

With several clicks of the mouse, users may find conflicting information about what to expect from this procedure (i.e., whether they will be paid the amount under the judgment with or without enforcement, if they win the claim).[8]

11.2.3 Practical Problems in Filling Out the Form and Filing the Claim

To make a claim using either the EPO or the ESCP, the first form that must be filled out is Form A (ECC-NET 2011, 6). When users click on this, they are led to a map where they click on the country they wish to file the claim in.[9]

11.2.3.1 Initial Steps

The information given on both sites when users click on Italy explains how to communicate with the court, the language required and how long it will take (in

---

[5]https://e-justice.europa.eu/content_european_payment_order-41-en.do. Last accessed 4/16/2012.

[6]https://e-justice.europa.eu/content_enforcement_of_judgments-51-en.do. Last accessed 4/16/2012.

[7]http://ec.europa.eu/civiljustice/simplif_accelerat_procedures/simplif_accelerat_procedures_ec_en.htm. Last accessed 4/16/2012.

[8]During the simulation, this was indeed problematic for the claimant. However, because it is not within the scope of this essay to discuss enforcement proceedings outside the EPO proceedings, readers are directed to the report for more details on this issue.

[9]According to the ECC-NET report (page 20), the regulations require member states to offer assistance in filling out the forms.

this case, no more than 30 min). It also helpfully explains that data will be saved in case of inactivity for more than 30 min (which at the time of simulation was not true). From this point, there is a problem with language. If users do not read or write in Italian, they may have difficulty filing the claim. If the information required in this form is very basic, users may be able to use Internet translation tools to make the claim but if more information is required in clear legal language, problems may arise. This raises the issue of the target audience for this procedure. If it is aimed at repeat users with constant practice in cross-border transactions, it is possible that their knowledge of the local language will be sufficient to fill out the form. If, however, the user is someone who rarely conducts cross-border transactions, he/she may quickly reach the threshold of maximum manageable complexity (see Chap. 1).

11.2.3.2 Scope and Jurisdiction

There are two issues in this regard: what type of claims users can make (scope), and to which courts (jurisdiction). The ECC on these issues states that, 'In some cases identifying the court which has jurisdiction could turn out to be a significant problem' (ECC-Net 2012, 24). This is particularly true for countries in which jurisdiction is spread across a number of local courts, as in the Italian case, in contrast to simpler countries, such as Germany, where jurisdiction is entrusted to just one court.

On the types of claim you can make:

> There is actually no monetary cap or limit on the amount that can be claimed for the EPO (unlike with the ESCP, which has a limit of 2,000 euro). The only reference to monetary limitation relates to which court users choose to apply for the EPO; in Italy, for less than 5,000 euro users must go to the Justice of the Peace, whereas above that figure they must go to the ordinary tribunal. There is nothing here about rejecting complex or a variety of cases, and therefore probably no limitation on the types of evidence users may submit. This is an area that will require further research, however.[10]

It is possible to follow these rules quite easily. If a user's claim fits within one of these excluded areas, then the user is excluded from the scope of the EPO procedure. The EPO gives the user a choice of countries from the EU; the user chooses the appropriate country of residence, defendant's domicile and jurisdiction. Users who are unable to specify these are again excluded from scope of the EPO. This is somewhat different from the ESCP site, where users are provided with a box in which to describe the story of the relationship and the nature of the dispute, and thus why it is a cross-border case and a legitimate 'dispute' for the purposes of the ESCP.

[10]Not all types of claim will be accepted by the courts under these procedures, such as consumer contracts or cases concerning public administration. They also limit who can use these procedures to those who are in an actual cross-border dispute, defined as the parties having domiciles across two member states.

For the ESCP, the same regulation for types of cases applies as for the EPO but the form offers only one choice for scope and does not exclude any matters, unlike the EPO site. In describing the cross-border nature of the case, the claimant needs to show the cross-border nature of the transaction that took place, i.e., that he/she ordered goods and/or services from Italy.

The scope of the claims that can be made is not clear, however. For instance, it is unclear what would happen if the claimant was (living) in Italy when the goods/services were ordered but discovered a breach of contract/tort only after leaving Italy. This is an added complication and it is unclear from the site what solutions can be offered to the European trader.

Rules of jurisdiction: EPO The rules of jurisdiction leave the claimant to assume that the court seized is that of the defendant.[11] For the specific claim made in Italy during the simulation, a link exists to Italy's rules of jurisdiction, making a difference between 'magistrates court' and ordinary tribunals (for the non-lawyer, it will not be clear that 'Giudice di Pace' is the same as magistrates court). This has changed since the simulation took place in February 2012, and it is now called 'Justice of the Peace' instead of 'Giudice di Pace' (although it still may not be clear that this is the same as a court with limited jurisdiction).

Whilst this is dealt with in the preliminary activities of the flow chart, Section 3 of the form also asks for grounds for jurisdiction and gives a list of possible reasons for jurisdiction. This is a bit odd, given the information previously about using the defendants' domicile as the basis for jurisdiction (and indeed it is the first one on this list). However, if one is uncertain, one may choose five out of up to fourteen possibilities for grounds of jurisdiction.

Having identified the correct country and the correct type of court, users must then find the address of the court to which they must send their form. One problem identified during the filling out of the ESCP form (that was not encountered in the EPO) was that the address given of the court with jurisdiction over the simulated case was incorrect. We have learned that, in Italy at least, the post office will deliver a claim to the court even if it has the wrong address on it. Without correct addresses, however, there are no guarantees that a postal service will do the same in other member states participating in the project. Therefore, there may be no point in going further with the claim, let alone the project in general.

It is suggested that more guidance to select the appropriate jurisdiction may be helpful to the lay claimant. This could be in the form of an FAQ section instead of more detailed regulations and links, which may open up the user to more confusion. Given the report by ECC that claimants '. . . had a lot of problems with filling the claim forms due to the legal terminology therein' (ECC-Net 2012, 25) and the expectation of the ECC that member states will offer help in filling out forms, a more substantial project to guide claimants may be called for.

[11]http://europa.eu/legislation_summaries/justice_freedom_security/judicial_cooperation_in_civil_matters/l33054_en.htm#KeyTerms. Last accessed 4/16/2012.

Rules of jurisdiction: ESCP The court of the domicile of the defendant is the main criteria of jurisdiction but in some cases it could be incorrect. This happens, for instance, when the court is determined by the location of immovable property to be seized or when the court is agreed by the parties in the agreement.

Moreover, the criteria of jurisdiction's function on the ESCP form is to determine if an Italian court is competent rather than a French court, but in order to determine if the Italian court of Bologna or Modena is competent, other internal rules will apply. Whilst this is for Parliament to decide, and internal rules on territorial competence contain other criteria of connection that can cause complications, there is actually an explanation within the form itself to help users decide which court to direct their application to.

Furthermore, deciding jurisdiction is a bit trickier under the ESCP. Here, the claimant needs to explain why the forum he has chosen should capture jurisdiction. To a lawyer, these terms and criteria are quite clear, but anyone clicking on the links within the form to see the glossary for some of the legal terms employed will see that none of the terms have been explained and the other website on rules of jurisdiction for other types of cases is also unhelpful. Users are directed back to an index of proceedings for different types of claims and jurisdictions. This is not easy for a layperson to make sense of. Again, everything depends on the target audience and who would want this service, as well as their experience and connections. A layperson could quickly reach the threshold of maximum manageable complexity and have to hire a lawyer to finalise the claim.

Identifying attackable assets and representatives The first divergence from the guidelines of the EPO and ESCP from the flow chart appears in the preliminary activities of the debtor/claimant, in the 'basic investigation on the debtor and the identification of attackable assets'. The basic question here is whether or not it is reasonable and rational to check attackable assets under such a transborder procedure (or for the small amount of money at stake under the ESCP). Identification of attackable assets is not easy if the user is foreign and so does not know-how to investigate this. Foreign users would probably require a lawyer or court order to investigate private details of any possible assets. There are also issues of privacy involved, in terms of how far an individual citizen may investigate the assets of another citizen, especially of another country.

This step is logical from a procedural perspective—it means the claimant is not wasting time and money suing someone or an entity that is bankrupt or has no valuable assets to cover the claim should the claimant win. Whether or not a defendant has attackable assets should not detract from the fact that a claimant may have rights against him and may indeed be able to enforce claims in part and/or over time. Another problematic item within both flow charts is 'notice of warning'. This does not appear in any of the guidelines or the forms. This is apparently a basic courtesy to the alleged debtor that if he/she does not pay the debt owed within a certain amount of time, then the ESCP or EPO will be filed against him/her. One may wonder how many other such small steps have to be taken under domestic law that are not described in the procedures of either the ESCP or EPO.

Persons Both the EPO and ESCP require identification of actors in the proceedings, including claimant, defendant and representatives. Identifying the claimant and defendant is not a difficult process, but identifying representatives on the EPO form appears to be somewhat complicated. The ESCP form does not require this information in any special format, only a name and any other contact details if known (possibly because the ESCP claims that one does not need representation for this proceeding). The EPO requires more complex information, such as a special number that lawyers have in some member states to engage in electronic communication with courts, or registration numbers of companies or identification numbers.

If the user only fills out the parts for claimant and defendant, the process is quite easy. Otherwise, the user must ask their representative, as well as that of the defendant, for the details requested about them in this field. The form refers to identification codes but gives no link to sites where such codes may be found. Finding such codes can be difficult, and it is unclear how important this information is until the court responds to the form.

11.2.3.3 Court Fees

This is the first major obstacle for both procedures: How to pay. As in the ESCP simulation, the information on how to pay is in Italian (in recent changes to the EPO site, there is now a section in English as well, but it is not very useful). This is a problem of access to information in the relevant language as well as important information for the case to be processed. In the simulation, bank transfer was chosen as the means of payment, even though, at the time, we knew this to be impossible.

Further research has revealed that there is actually an option to pay court fees by paying into a specific postal account.[12] The court fees can be paid online through www.poste.it but the website requires registration and is available in Italian only. The registration procedure is not all that simple and a mobile phone is required to receive an SMS with the activation code. Further investigation uncovered the option of an official note from the Ministry of Justice[13] authorising the payment of court fees through a money order to a given bank account. Unfortunately, the note was not mentioned in the e-justice portal, nor was it known about by the court staff involved in the simulation.

Therefore, the payment process is quite problematic if users are claiming from abroad and do not know-how to pay court fees. It is also possible that the court will

---

[12]Versamento in conto corrente postale n. 57152043 intestato a Tesoreria Provinciale di Viterbo—Versamento contributo unificato spese atti giudiziari DPR 126/2001. See also http://www.contributounificato.it/esenzioni.html last accessed 4/16/2012.

[13]Nota 1°settembre 2010—Regolamento CE 1896/2006—Procedimento di ingiunzione di pagamento: http://www.giustizia.it/giustizia/it/mg_1_8_1.wp?previsiousPage=mg_16_1 andcontentId=SDC391384

send more information on court fees in further communication with the claimant if it identifies this as a problem with the form itself.[14]

One other common difficulty for both of these procedures is the guarantee of privacy of bank details once a claimant has submitted them. This is an interesting legal issue but easy to solve with a classical statement, such as 'the data provided with this form will be used exclusively for the procedure'. This is essential but has not been displayed since the site has been running. Privacy on bank data details is a real problem. According to the European legal framework, each court should expressly state the treatment applied to such data. The issue is, then, why they have not.

This issue was mentioned by the French ECC report, but mostly as an issue of communication between the claimant and the court (ECC-NET 2011, 6). The example given was that of a claimant looking to bring an ESCP claim to Germany who did not know-how to pay the fees. This was communicated to the claimant by the European Consumer Consortium instead of the court in Germany because the claimant did not speak any German and the court in Germany spoke no French.

11.2.3.4 Calculating Interest

During the simulation, random numbers were entered in order to move forward with filling out the form. This is an impossible task for anyone not versed in calculating legal interest (i.e., anyone but a lawyer/accountant/banker). Two options were randomly chosen but the guidelines, even though they were written in English, seemed somewhat unintelligible to the person conducting the simulation. This is another area in which more information or offers of guidance could be given by the website itself.[15]

[14]During the simulation, other problems with charging court fees were identified in terms of how to receive them without creating the danger of inappropriate behaviour, such as corruption or bribery. Please see report for more details, as this is also not a problem for the claimant per se.

[15]'If interest is demanded, this should be specified for each claim as identified in field [6] in accordance with the codes indicated on the form. The code must contain both the relevant number (first row of the codes) and the letter (second row of the codes). For instance, if the interest rate has been agreed by contract and covers annual periods, the code is 02A. If interest is demanded up to the decision by the court, the last box [to] should be left blank. Code 01 refers to an interest rate laid down by statute. Code 02 refers to an interest rate agreed by the parties. If you use Code 03 (capitalisation of interest), the amount indicated should be the basis for the remainder of the term to be covered. Capitalisation of interest refers to the situation where the accrued interest is added to the principal and is taken into account for purposes of calculating further interest. Please note that in commercial transactions as referred to in Directive 2000/35/EC of 29 June 2000 on combating late payments, the statutory interest rate is the sum of the interest rate applied by the European Central Bank to its most recent main refinancing operation carried out before the first calendar day of the half-year in question ("the reference rate"), plus at least seven percentage points. For a member state which is not participating in the third stage of economic and monetary union, the reference rate referred to above is the equivalent rate set at national level (e.g., by the national central bank). In both cases, the reference rate in force on the first calendar day of the half-year

The calculation of interest is a real problem outside of these complicated instructions. Firstly, there is a problem of applicable law: the citizen should assess which is the applicable law to the relationship, since the calculation of interest is a problem of 'substantial law' and not of 'procedural law'. Of course, the assessment of the applicable law is a difficult operation that is based on a specific EU regulation and on specific juridical criteria. Secondly, the material calculation can be difficult. Normally, an Italian lawyer calculates interest on the basis of specific software, which is also available on the Internet. I frankly doubt that the existence of this software is known to all citizens, let alone a foreign citizen.

The EU should facilitate the calculation of interest by providing common software containing all the data of the interest rates of each EU country. This should be feasible on the e-Justice website.

11.2.3.5 Calculating Costs

If reimbursement of costs is demanded, these must be described using the codes indicated on the form. These costs can include fees of a claimant's representative and pre-litigation costs. If the user requests reimbursement of the court fees but does not know the exact amount, it will be filled in by the court.

During the simulation, only 'court fees' were claimed. As with the ESCP, we assumed in this simulation that a lawyer was not needed. It says at the beginning that once the form is submitted, the procedure leads its own life, and the claimant is not required in court. Unlike the ESCP, however, the EPO does not tell users that they do not need a lawyer, or that they can have more than one. If it costs a fee to identify attackable assets at the beginning of this form, users may well be able to claim this as a pre-litigation cost. Claimants probably will not know that information on court fees and how to pay them is not available directly through the e-Justice portal.

This issue was very important in both ECC reports, especially in terms of the costs of translation. One thing that we did not come across in the simulation was the need to translate supporting documents. The English reports explain that quite a few member states (not all) require that supporting documents be translated into the language of the court (ECC-Net 2012, 21). For the types of case described by these reports (i.e., failed online purchase of goods, failed holidays, cancelled flights etc. (ECC-Net 2012, 8), it may not be worthwhile paying translation costs. The hidden costs represented by the possible need for translation was enough of a concern to be discussed in depth by both ECC reports.

---

in question will apply for the following 6 months (see Art. 3(1)(d) of Directive 2000/35/EC). The "base rate (ECB)" refers to the interest rate applied by the European Central Bank to its main refinancing operations.'

It has been asked whether, from a functional simplification perspective, all these details are needed (Kallinikos 2008), whether they need to be translated and whether the judge can accept all the requests as declared by the claimant.

11.2.3.6 Providing Evidence Available in Support of the Claim

This must specify the evidence available in support of each claim for both proceedings using the codes indicated on the form. One can assume a contract in this simulation. One should not forget to fill in this form in Italian. This is the only part in both forms (along with additional statements) that appears to require foreign language knowledge. Therefore, the linguistic semantic problems are limited to one specific question. This is a barrier to those who do not write Italian and have not hired an Italian lawyer to do this work. It maybe that the 1,000 euro claim assumed in this simulation is not enough incentive to pay a lawyer to fill this in for the user.

If the claimant can keep it simple, e.g., 'I ordered goods in Italy to the sum 1,000 euro and they were all faulty on arrival in England', this may be easily translatable within online translation tools. However, if the courts in Italy require more complex explanation, e.g., 'The defendant is in breach of contract, s. XYZ, clause ABC, in which he agreed etc.', with a whole page of legal explanation, then an Italian lawyer may be needed. It requires details of the claim in terms of the facts of the case. Again, if this can be kept simple, then maybe online translation tools would be sufficient. Evidence is simple enough if the user has a contract, a receipt or witnesses.

It can be added at this point that an Italian Justice of Peace applies the principle 'da mihi factum tibi dabo ius' ('you give me the facts, I will give you the law'), so before an Italian Justice of the Peace, a description of the facts is normally enough. However, the court may return the claim with Form B (for both procedures) for incompleteness, requiring either more details or more legibility.

This is a semantic problem, which may be solved if it is possible to identify ex ante a certain number of options to choose from, given that the complexity and variety of these claims are or appear to be quite limited. If there is a pre-established list of options, plus an 'open' class (to be filled in by the plaintiff), it may be possible to solve the main semantic problem.

11.2.3.7 Technical Problems

Given that it would be very difficult for any user to fill in this form in one sitting without all the available information, it should be possible to save this form. The website for both forms records the answers in the fields if users employ the same computer to fill out the form the second time around.

During the simulation, saving the ESCP appeared to be possible, but when attempted, it failed. This was also attempted for the EPO, which saved it as an xml document, but when an attempt was made to open it, it came out in code and many colours. We have no idea what went wrong. There is a feedback section of the website where users can complain about or report problems with the site. There have been recent attempts to fix this bug in order to save data, but similar problems were encountered on further attempts.

One detail that did surprise the researchers was that of signature. At some point in the guidelines to Form A, the user is reminded to date and sign the last page. This means that identification is provided by personal data entered in the form and by signature: copies of ID documents are not required. This is interesting within the broader project of interoperability, because there are problems in other similar cross-border projects relating to the acceptance of electronic identification, such as e-Codex.[16]

11.3 Findings from the Court

EPO Based on the rules of the EPO, once the form has been filled out and sent according to the rules of procedure, the whole thing should take on a life of its own without further steps from the claimant (unless the court requires more information). The Citizens' Guide to Cross-border Civil Litigation in the European Union, prepared by the Commission, states that, 'The court will examine your application and, if you have filled in the form correctly and replied to any requests for further information, the court should issue the EPO within 30 days. The EPO will now be served on the defendant by the court' (European Commission 2011, 11). Various problems with this were encountered in the second phase of the simulation, however, so an in-depth interview with the most experienced clerk to the Justice of the Peace court of Bologna was carried out to verify what steps were taken with regards to an EPO application.

We observed that there are mainly problems of communication between the court and the claimant, which would not be a problem if the claimant did not have to take further steps, but under the internal rules of the court, the claimant does have to take many further steps. The EPO is a default judgment against a defendant unless the defendant challenges the claim. Once the EPO has been issued, and once the foreign creditor acknowledges that a European order for payment has been issued, he/she has to serve it upon the debtor. This requires the claimant to know when the EPO has been issued. This is a major problem. Indeed, once the EPO has been issued, the Italian court does not inform the claimant nor serve the EPO upon the debtor or the claimant. This decision was taken by the Justice of the Peace office after a meeting with top judicial officials and has been endorsed by the Ministry of Justice.[17] Consequently, the claimant has to contact the court by phone or letter (in

[16] See http://www.e-codex.eu/.

[17] Nota 1 settembre 2010—Regolamento CE 1896/2006—Procedimento di ingiunzione di pagamento. In simple terms, once the judge has issued the EPO, the process follows the rules of the

Italian) because the court in Bologna will not inform the claimant. Unfortunately, this key piece of information is not provided on the e-Justice portal.

Furthermore, in order to serve the EPO upon the debtor, the creditor must obtain an original copy of the EPO and file a request for its service with the Italian judiciary service authority (*ufficiale giudiziario*). This normally entails the physical presence of the creditor or of a person acting on his behalf at the court building. It also requires further payment of court fees.[18]

Moreover, the request for the original copy, as well as the actual service of said EPO upon the debtor, should be carried out in the Italian language because the seized court normally competent to deal with requests does so in Italian.[19]

If the debtor has challenged the EPO within 30 days of receipt of the notice, then the creditor should be informed of this. If the creditor does not choose to stop the proceedings because of opposition from the debtor (within appendix 2 of the EPO forms), then a civil ordinary proceeding begins before the court seized. More information is unavailable about further proceedings at this stage from the European e-Justice portal.

The court in Bologna informs the creditor about any opposition by registered letter. Moreover, the court on its own motion fixes a hearing for the commencement of the ordinary proceedings: of course, the date of the hearing is also communicated to the debtor (unless the creditor has stopped proceedings). It would be extremely useful if these standard communications could be made available in letter form and translated into different languages. This is another area in which a case management system may help in providing a set of letters in different languages, as with e-Curia (See Chap. 9).

The communication is in the Italian language, which is not helpful for the (foreign) claimant who may not able to understand the content of the communication. Furthermore, it seems that the communication only informs the creditor about the date of the hearing; it does not provide any basic procedural information about Italian civil proceedings (i.e., his/her defensive rights, the facility/need to appoint a lawyer, etc.).

If the EPO is not challenged within 30 days, then the claimant may start enforcement proceedings.

ESCP Once the ESCP petition has been received, the court should process it. Council Regulation 861/2007 of 11 July 2007 establishes time limits for the parties

---

Italian Code of civil proceedings. Accordingly, the claimant has to go to the court to find out if the decree has been issued, to get an original copy and to serve it on the defendant.

[18]If the claimant has somehow made it this far, then it may mean that he/she has already successfully paid court fees once and will know-how to do it again at the various stages of the court proceedings if further fees are required.

[19]If the claimant has again made it to this point by filling out the original form in Italian, it may well be possible to apply for this in Italian again if necessary.

and for the court in order to speed up litigation. There is a summary in the regulation of time limits, but it is left up to the courts as to how to proceed.[20]

As concerns the 'timing' of the procedure, it must be remembered that time limits are compulsory for the parties but not for the courts. Time limits for the courts are just an 'indication', a suggestion for best practices, but no effects are provided in the case of non-fulfilment of the rules. This raises a question of possible breaches of article 6 rights, as well as the practicality of following a court case from abroad and the facilities for that.

Where the court has received a small claim that is incomplete because it is in the wrong language or because documents are missing, etc., the court will send the form back to be properly filled out. The only thing that is not specified here is the timeframe within in which this should take place.

Communication with the Justice of the Peace in Bologna is in Italian. There is no mention of translation software for the form on the e-Justice portal, or no desire to use it.

If the court returns Form B because of incompleteness, Form A can either be rectified or withdrawn. If it is rectified and then accepted by the court, notice will be given to the defendant. The key aspect at this time of the procedure is that it is always dependent on the claimant, whether the dispute is domestic or cross-border. It is for the claimant to start the claim and therefore to go to the trouble of doing the work and communicating with the court. There is a possible complication, however, if the defendant is not Italian, but only resides in Italy, which may be something worth considering, because Italians are not the only residents in Italy.

In terms of actual proceedings, the ESCP should be conducted using written procedures (these are not in breach of article 6 fair trial rights). If an oral hearing is demanded, then both parties must be available to attend.[21]

After final judgment is given, if the claimant wins, a copy of the European Small Claims (ESC) judgment will usually be enough to start the execution in Italy (that is to say, to proceed with the preliminary seizure of the defendant's assets). In practice, no bailiff will start the execution procedure if the local court does not declare the ESC judgment internally enforceable (there is a formula put on the ESC judgment called the *formula esecutiva*). This is a further step that implies the participation of a lawyer, because a normal citizen—especially a foreign citizen—will not be aware of so technical a step.

More generally, the Justice of the Peace of Bologna clarified that the small number of EPOs and the even smaller number of ESCPs represent small but tedious problems for the court. The low number of cases makes standardisation of the process problematic. Many times, non-Italian claimants have tried to get in touch with the court to find solutions to the problems highlighted above. Too many times, such problems have to be faced on an ad hoc basis and are therefore rather time

---

[20]http://europa.eu/legislation_summaries/consumers/protection_of_consumers/l16028_en.htm. Last accessed 04/17/2012.

[21]The steps the court can take are more variable under the ESCP than the EPO.

consuming. For the judges, the situation is even more complex. Indeed, the few cases are allocated to a high number of judges. Consequently, each judge has a very limited level of experience with these procedures and their peculiarities, giving the added risk of the application of Italian civil procedures when the procedures to be applied are European.

11.4 Discussion and Conclusions

In Chap. 1 of this book, Lanzara describes the need to explore the conditions (technical, institutional and organisational) for the circulation of legal agency. The circulation should be supported by interoperability through a well-built infrastructure that takes account of the domains in operation, such as technical, legal, semantic and institutional. He defines circulation of agency as, '... the capacity of an entity—human and nonhuman, material or symbolic—to produce effects upon a state of affairs. By circulation of agency, we mean the possibility for such capacity to be transmitted across multiple different media, national borders and functional domains' (see Chap. 1).

The domains are important to 'shape the circulation of agency in e-Justice'. It is therefore important to look, from the perspective of this simulation and of the various actors involved, at how agency circulates given the infrastructure, at the features that support and hinder circulation, and how complexity may affect both infrastructure and interoperability and, therefore, circulation.

As a basis for these procedures, EU policy is to offer '... citizens and businesses across the EU the means for quicker, more efficient resolution of cross-border cases, by making it easier to enforce a claim against a defendant in another member state' (European Commission 2011, 2).

To do this, certain requirements must be met in terms of cooperation, interoperability (communication, exchange of data) and adaptation to the needs of users, both end users and other actors, in terms of rules, technology and language, institutions and so forth. In order for such proceedings to be successful, domestic legal systems must firstly, 'Francesco, I remember you found this quote. Do you remember where from? The question at the end of this proof is about this.' (European Commission 2012, 8) They must also reduce complexity for all users, from the institutional to the end users. These conclusions will look at whether this has been done, from the perspective of the simulation itself.

11.4.1 Domains and Infrastructure of the EPO and ESCP

Concerning the technological domain, there would be problems with circulation of agency if data and documents were not exchanged due to any technological malfunctioning. From the website of the e-justice portal, where both procedures begin, it is clear that documents are not exchanged online, period. It is possible only to fill in the form online, which is awkward if users do not have all the necessary information available at their fingertips, because it is not possible to save inputted data whilst taking time to find other data. Recent improvements of the e-Justice portal appear to have solved the problem of saving data, however. Once the form has been filled in online, the application converts the form the claimant filled out to the language of the court, but not the answers inputted. Technologically, this is a rather limited function because all translation and semantic problems rest on the claimant and, to a lesser extent, on the seized court. Moreover, the form is not submitted online; rather, the claimant must print it out and then post it to the address that is provided by the e-Justice website (which, depressingly, may be an incorrect address). The fact that the court accepts the filing of the case without ID and with just a signature indicates that agency in this case circulates quite smoothly. This is surprising because in a normal Italian procedure the courts would not accept such a filing. This means that European institutions have been successful in simplifying a critical step in their procedures. It also means that the exchange of procedural documents certified by a hand-written signature is not under-performative. This is a lesson that should be kept in mind when designing information systems and infrastructures supporting the EPO and ESCP.

Concerning the semantic domain, there could be problems even though data has been exchanged properly if actors have not used the appropriate language, rendering the procedural requirements unfulfilled. The difficulty in terms of the simulation was that it was unclear from the outset how detailed the description of the heart of the lawsuit had to be and whether legal language was required. It turned out that a rather more detailed description with the use of legalese was required, and that the form that was submitted would have been returned by the court through Form B of the procedure for completion. This is problematic for the ESCP procedure because it is specified at the outset that no lawyer is needed. As discussed in the first chapter and earlier in this essay, matters could be simplified by providing users with options for identifying of problem they have (services rendered but unpaid for, paid-for services but no services rendered, etc.).

As regards the legal domain, a meaningful exchange of data could occur but the exchange is not performed according to relevant legal specifications. From the experience of the simulation, there were various problems with this, for both the claimant as well as the court. Part of the legal specifications for the submission of the small claim or the payment order was the payment of court fees. Lack of payment of court fees will not hinder circulation of agency but if the claimant decides to file the case without paying the court fees, the seized court, following Italian regulations, will file the case and invite the claimant to pay the court fees; if the claimant cannot pay the fees, the court is forced to file a case against the claimant. In theory, the EPO and ESCP can become claimants' traps.

Conversely, the court did not fulfil all legal requirements regarding these procedures, especially in terms of using the forms provided by the e-Justice portal for the ESCP, nor did the court fulfil timelines set out by the procedure, even though claimants were required to fulfil time requirements. For the EPO, once a claimant has submitted the form, the procedure should take on a life of its own, but as shown in the simulation, more steps had to be taken at the court. This shows that the court has not aligned its procedures in accordance with the legal requirements of the European procedure.

Concerning the institutional domain, it is clear that the national courts and the e-Justice portal are supposed to carry out administration and other processes to allow successful transborder submission of a legal claim. However, based on this simulation, it appears that the courts themselves are acting on an ad hoc basis, dealing with this procedure on a case-by-case basis. This may be because there are so few cases of this nature that they do not feel the need or the pressure to change institutionally or to standardise procedures. In addition, the aid and information provided by the e-Justice portal is negligent and often useless (such as the payment of court fees). Interestingly, it appears in both ECC reports that the ECC expects the courts to offer guidance to potential claimants, both in informing them about procedures and aiding them in filing the forms (ECC-Net 2012, 32). Courts and clerks are limited in the kind of advice they can give, however, because lawyers have the monopoly on giving legal advice and are very protective of that role.[22] The question now for member states is how they should organise help for claimants to fill out these forms with as little cost as possible.

These domains make up the infrastructure behind these cross-border online procedures. It can be seen that circulation of agency within this cross-border procedure is blocked by language issues, by administrative and procedural issues, such as the interpretation of European regulation by the national courts in this simulation, and not facilitated by the information and tools made available on the e-Justice portal. Even the simulation was a frustrating process. One can imagine how frustrating it would be for a real claimant and whether one would be motivated enough to continue using it if the system was so complicated to use and other information (such as how to pay court fees) so inaccessible. If one multiplies this by the number of possible courts to the number of possible users, one will have an unsustainable procedure.

11.4.2 Users' Concerns

The complexity of the procedure varies, depending on who is using it. In principle, this is an access to justice issue in order to support and develop the free market within the EU, so technically everyone should be able to use it. As seen here, however, European citizens without specific know-how will probably fail to file an EPO or an ESCP case. External support is needed in various stages of the procedure.

We can assume that people live in member states, not the EU, and rarely have cross-border experiences with businesses or administrations that would require a

[22] Such limits have been clearly pointed out by the head of Scottish court service during the project conference.

lawsuit afterwards. The majority of people will buy locally (although one can see from the experiences of the ECC that the Internet opens up cross-border purchasing possibilities). Only businesses and people with specific interests in buying goods/services (or travelling across borders) will have reason to sue. Moreover, consider that if you are a business or a repeat player in the market, you are likely to know the supplier you are suing and therefore also probably have knowledge of the language of the country you are dealing with or know someone who has such knowledge. Having said that, the ECC reports highlight that there are a growing number of consumers who purchase online from abroad, creating a lot of potential users of the ESCP and EPO. The English ECC report highlights that over a third of their organisations in EU member states recommend Alternative Dispute Resolution instead of the online procedures, but this may change in future if the procedure becomes more user-friendly (ECC-Net 2012, 30).

There should be technical support from the e-Justice portal itself or from other bodies if a claimant becomes stuck in one place or if there is a problem with the form, no matter what one enters into any given field. There is a feedback link at the bottom of the page of the e-Justice portal but further research should be done to see what type of assistance may be offered in the filing of the EPO.

From a fair trial rights perspective, the main issue that is truly problematic is that of the language of communication. In a domestic court trial (civil or criminal), the court will provide translation services to ensure that no rights of witnesses or parties are breached. If we apply this principle to written procedure, we can state that the burden/costs of the translation should be paid by the court itself, and by court fees, eventually.

From an accessibility point of view, there was no actual link to this procedure within the English courts, as far as we could see at the time of the simulation (it was under maintenance at that time), and Italian procedures did not even show up on Google during the simulation itself. The website of the Italian Ministry of Justice does not provide any advice on the EPO or ESCP. It was highlighted in both the English and French ECC reports that there is a general lack of information and knowledge in member states in general (ECC-NET 2011, 3; ECC-Net 2012, 17). This could indicate the irrelevance of these two procedures for European judiciaries, given their disconnected nature from national courts' websites and other information pertaining to domestic procedures. This may create serious problems of access to this service and this specific analysis should be further expanded. One can assume that if an ordinary citizen searches for a judicial remedy, he/she will look first to his/her own national judiciary (to check the possibility of suing the defendant in his/her national court) and then at the judiciary of the defendant. The expectation that, in order to solve a dispute or identify a judicial remedy, a person should look at the website of the European Commission seems to be unrealistic (although again this depends on the type of user the procedure is aimed at). Something for developers to consider is the identity of the real potential users of these proceedings and how to give them effective and efficient access.

11.4.3 Design

These proceedings attempt to simplify small claims across borders. However, because of the lack of legal interoperability in this area (i.e., not all countries have small claims procedures, countries that do have small claims procedures may have very different monetary ceilings for claims, some may have digital procedures and others may have conventional paper procedures), the result is a compromised procedure that hampers, in several instances, the circulation of agency. The EU has superimposed a procedure on participating states, and participating courts are left with no guidance as to how to proceed (let alone how to guide others) or which procedures take precedence—their own or the European—and the court in the simulation did not even consider priorities, but ease of use. This is an inaccessible procedure in which compromise rather than design was the end product.

User-friendly design implies that users and their capacity to handle judicial procedure are taken into account at the design stage, both for claimants/defendants and courts. The lack of consistent information, the difficult and sometimes misleading interface with the e-Justice portal and the fact that the digital part of the process ends with the printing of the form, which then becomes a conventional process, mean that these procedures fail in terms of user-friendly design.

Given the language, semantic and technical barriers that may be experienced during these procedures, from filling out the form to filing it at court, it is suggested that some form of greater institutional support than a generic 'feedback' link at the bottom of the e-Justice portal be developed. This should be done not only in light of the preliminary findings of the experiences of these simulations, but also in light of the likely customers for this service and what their linguistic, legal and financial skills will be. Further research is suggested to go deeper into the type of institutional support to be given at the member state level.

Lanzara further points out that interoperability, and therefore circulation of agency, should encompass the whole procedure and not merely end with the printing of the form and the exchange of data. There should also be the possibility of online communication that allows users to follow the life cycle of their cases and learn about any further steps they need to take. This would require further investment by EU and its member states.

At the end of the day, these procedures should function to hide complexity away from end users (again, both for claimant/defendants and courts) and create a smooth path to cross-border online claims.

References

ECC-Net, European Consumer Centre Network. 2012. European small claims procedure report.

ECC-Net, European Consumer Centres Network. 2011. Procédure de règlement des petits litiges et injonction de payer européenne. http://www.cec-zev.eu/fileadmin/user_upload/eu-consommateurs/PDFs/publications/etudes_et_rapports/4.4.3_procedure_de_reglement_des_petits_litiges.pdf. Accessed 29 Nov 2012.

European Commission. 2011. A citizens' guide to cross-border civil litigation in the European Union.

Kallinikos, J. 2008. Institutional complexity and functional simplification: The case of money claim online in England and Wales. In *ICT and innovation in the public sector: European perspectives in the making of e-government*, ed. F. Contini and G.F. Lanzara, 174–210. Basingstoke: Palgrave Macmillan.

Chapter 12
Building Semantic Interoperability for European Civil Proceedings Online

Marta Poblet, Josep Suquet, Antoni Roig, and Jorge González-Conejero

Abstract This chapter addresses the technological and semantic interoperability aspects relevant to the European Civil Proceedings Online, in particular to the European Small Claims Procedure and the European Order for Payment Procedure. It starts by offering an overview of the background of Semantic Web Technologies and presenting the concept of Semantic Interoperability. Secondly, it reviews ontologies as one of the most appropriate tools when it comes to addressing and solving a number of semantic issues, such as the existence of different legal terms and languages. Moreover, ontologies can be combined with other tools such as a XML mark-up language or a FAQ (Frequenly Asked Questions) list of terms. The chapter also identifies seven general semantic tools that can be relevant to solving some of the semantic issues identified so far. Finally, the chapter ends with some concluding remarks on semantic technologies and its role in assisting the parties of a process.

12.1 Introduction: Semantic Interoperability Issues for the European Small Claims Procedure (ESCP) and European Order for Payment Procedure (EPO)

The European Union Treaty solemnly enshrines the objective of maintaining and developing an area of freedom, security and justice that ensures the free movement of persons. To fulfil this objective, the European institutions have adopted different legal instruments in the field of judicial cooperation in civil matters having

M. Poblet (✉) • J. Suquet • A. Roig • J. González-Conejero
Institute of Law and Technology (IDT), Universitat Autònoma de Barcelona, Bellaterra (Cerdanyola del Vallès), Spain
e-mail: marta.poblet@uab.cat

F. Contini and G.F. Lanzara (eds.), *The Circulation of Agency in E-Justice*, Law, Governance and Technology Series 13, DOI 10.1007/978-94-007-7525-1_12,

cross-border implications.[1] In particular, Regulation (EC) 861/2007 of the European Parliament and of the Council of 11 July 2007, establishing a European Small Claims Procedure (hereinafter, ESCP), and Regulation (EC) No 1896/2006 of the European Parliament and of the Council of 12 December 2006, creating a European order for payment procedure (hereinafter, EPO), are two specific measures aimed at eliminating obstacles to the good functioning of civil proceedings.

Both regulations provide standard forms to be used by the courts and the parties, as well as some guidelines for filling in these forms properly. For instance, the ESCP Regulation provides a standard form and some guidelines for the claimant to fill in the claim (Annex I, Form A), a standard form for the court or tribunal to request the claimant to complete or rectify the claim form (Annex II, Form B) and a standard form for the defendant to answer the claimant with some guidelines for the defendant (Annex III, Part II of Form C). However, even if these standard forms are designed to support dialogue and avoid misunderstandings, daily practice has revealed that they are not clear enough. Both parties and courts may be led into confusion when dealing with them. Moreover, the claimant and the defendant do not engage in a direct dialogue; there are no horizontal mechanisms of cooperation between the parties, just vertical ones between the courts and the parties (Ng and Mellone 2011). In addition, their use requires cooperation among national tribunals rather than a European court.

In the European judicial cooperation area, where different languages and differently harmonised legal systems coexist, there are a number of semantic issues that need to be handled. For instance, Article 6 of the ESCP Regulation stipulates that the court may ask one of the parties to provide a translation of the documents into another language, even though legal terms, embedded in different legal traditions, remain largely a matter of a particular national system. An Italian court may assign a meaning other than that intended to something expressed by an English claimant in his claimant form. The European Judicial Atlas in Civil Matters provides online automatic translation of the application forms, but there is no translation available for the claimant's description of the nature of the issue and the object of the claim, aspects to be dealt with in ESCP Claim Form A (Number 8).[2] Particularly, Ng and Mellone have raised precisely some of those semantic issues in a simulation for a transborder small claim (ESCP) between the United Kingdom and Italy (Ng and M. Mellone 2011; Ng 2012; see Chap. 11). Moreover, Mellone (see Chap. 10) presents the legal framework of the EPO and ESCP procedures and provides a discussion from a legal point of view.

Indeed, the translation of the facts of a case has been reported as a possible problem. The same applies to related documents such as invoices or contracts. The option to appoint human translators to fill these significant gaps is exceedingly

[1]See article 67 and ss. of the Treaty on the Functioning of the European Union. Consolidated version available at http://eur-lex.europa.eu/en/treaties/index.htm (Last accessed 9 October 2012).

[2]Accessible at: http://ec.europa.eu/justice_home/judicialatlascivil/html/la_fillingforms_fr_en.htm. Last accessed 9 October 2012.

costly but state-of-the-art automatic translators do not appear to be accurate enough. In this regard, this paper will show how XML can be used to annotate the items of a structured text (e.g., in Form A or Form B) but not the content therein. The report has revealed additional problems, such as the determination of the addresses of the competent courts and the individualisation of the appropriate jurisdiction. In this regard, the European Judicial Atlas in Civil Matters may be of help for applicants.[3] For instance, after the end-user inserts a particular location, the application delivers the contact details of the territorially competent court.

In the pages that follow, we will pay attention to some of the semantic tools that may contribute to solving these particular issues. However, a precautionary principle will be added, for there are particular problems that semantic tools may not properly address, namely, the determination of legal interest by the applicants.

Ontology design is one of the most utilised strategies when it comes to semantic modelling. In this regard, legal ontologies have proved useful for the most part in modelling legal knowledge but may fall short of adequately representing complex legal or judicial decision-making as a stand-alone solution. To address such a task, the use of legal ontologies needs to be combined with the sequential modelling of the different steps of the process. Once the successive nodes are identified and represented, semantic tools can then enrich the decision-making model. Let us consider some practical issues that may happen in the ESCP process: the claimant initiates a claim by filling in a form; the court assesses the claim form in order to determine whether it is competent. Here, the court may determine that the claim is clearly unfounded or that the application is inadmissible and accordingly it may dismiss the application form. However, the court may give the claimant the opportunity to complete or rectify the claim to supply additional information or documents. Additionally, the court may transmit the claim form to the defendant, who will fill in the answer form and return it to the court or tribunal. Finally, the court may issue a certificate concerning a judgement in the ESCP. As a global decision process, it is clearly too broad to be solved by a single ontology. We will need to tackle such a complex process by transforming it into a succession of more specific problems to be dealt with, clearly determining the classification and the legal criteria involved in the decision-making process.

A number of European countries have already developed national e-justice systems. Notably, Money Claim Online in England and Wales,[4] CITIUS in Portugal[5] and COVL in Slovenia[6] aim at the same core objectives, namely, speeding up the judicial process, decreasing pending cases and thereby reducing the judicial backlog. Moreover, automated processes contribute to reducing costs and reassigning

[3] http://ec.europa.eu/justice_home/judicialatlascivil/html/sc_courtsjurisd_en.jsp?countrySession=3andtxtPostalCode=08008andtxtMunicipality=#statePage1. Last accessed 9 October 2012.

[4] https://www.moneyclaim.gov.uk/web/mcol/welcome. Last accessed 9 October 2012.

[5] http://www.dgpj.mj.pt/sections/english-version/legislative-policy/annexes/legal-projects/citius-dematerialization/citius-electronic4155/. Last accessed 9 October 2012.

[6] https://covl.sodisce.si/. Last accessed 9 October 2012.

resources to other types of requests. However, as with some cross-border systems, e-justice national systems may also raise some semantic issues: (i) claimants may find it difficult to express their will within a limited number of characters; (ii) courts are likely to interpret in legal terms what was simply conveyed in plain, non-legal language, so that claimants may need legal advice to properly draft their claims; and (iii) plaintiffs may encounter other issues, such as filling in certain details that may not be known (e.g., factual aspects, such as the defendant's domicile or postcode).

In the following pages, we will assess how semantic interoperability can contribute to organising and clarifying distributed knowledge regarding ESCP/EPO proceedings. The chapter is organised as follows: Sect. 12.2 focuses on the background of Semantic Web technologies; Sect. 12.3 addresses the semantic interoperability issue; and Sect. 12.4 provides an overview of ontologies, including features and capabilities. Section 12.5 discusses the suitability of the semantic interoperability toolbox that has been proposed to address some of the EPO and ESCP's semantic issues. Finally, Sect. 12.6 draws some conclusions.

12.2 Background: Semantic Web Technologies

In the foundational *Scientific American* article of 2001, Berners-Lee, Hendler and Lassila offered their vision of the future Semantic Web as 'not a separate Web but an extension of the current one, in which information is given well-defined meaning, better enabling computers and people to work in cooperation' (Berners-Lee et al. 2001, 29). The Semantic Web has come a long way since then, and even if the vision of it is not yet in full display, state-of-the-art Semantic Web technologies and languages today offer a new approach to managing information and processes, the fundamental principle of which is the creation and use of semantic metadata (Warren et al. 2006). Since metadata tell us about the content of a document, we may say that metadata are semantic tags that help to organise and find information based on meaning, not just text. By applying semantics, our systems can understand where words or phrases are equivalent or they can distinguish where the same word is used with different meanings. Moreover, semantics may improve the way information is presented and, instead of a search providing a linear list of results, the results can be clustered by meaning. In a typical pre-Web 2.0, people performed legal searches based on keywords or made up a concept believed to convey the core meaning of what was being looked for. There are also more complex queries, such as "Boolean searches" in which several keywords are combined with Boolean operators (AND, OR, etc.). Certain databases allow for the definition of several aspects of the search (e.g., date, type of court, etc.). However, these searches do not provide solutions or assistance when it comes to the interaction between symbols, terms and concepts. This is where the Semantic Web comes into the picture.

By applying metadata, semantics contribute to the merging of information in a meaningful way, removing redundancy and summarising where appropriate (Warren et al. 2006). The use of semantic metadata enhances the storage, search and

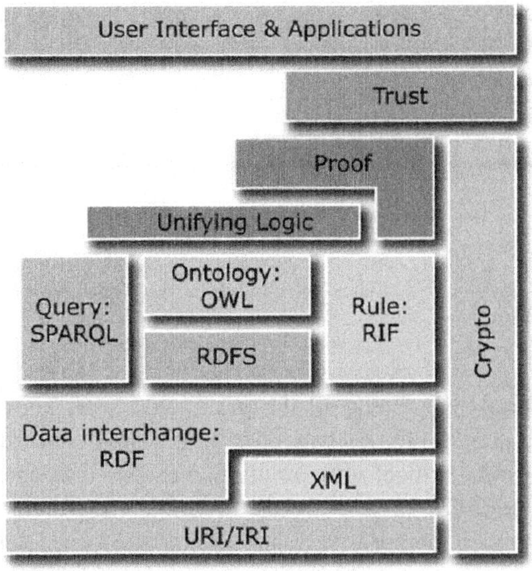

Fig. 12.1 Semantic Web layer cake (T. Berners-Lee), S. Bratt version (2007). (Source: http://www.w3.org/2007/03/layerCake.png. Last accessed 9 October 2012)

retrieval of information and human-computer interaction. From this perspective, the Semantic Web is a prolongation of Web 2.0, enriched with meaning.

The World Wide Web consortium (W3C) has been developing interoperable technologies, such as specifications, guidelines, software and tools, to fully develop the promise of the Semantic Web.[7] Berners-Lee's famous Semantic Web stack represents this growing level of complexity (more complex at the top) as higher layers depend on lower layers. The overall idea was to construct something (the Semantic Web) from the current work (the Web) so that the work done before was still of use (Fig. 12.1).

12.3 Semantic Interoperability

Broadly speaking, interoperability is the ability of two or more systems or components to exchange information and to use the information that has been exchanged. It is clear that several aspects related to this topic have to be considered in a previous stage of the exchange information process. Whenever a system is sending information, the receiver must know what type of information is being received to allow a correct interpretation. If the information is not interpreted correctly, it becomes useless. The Semantic Web has an important application in this field, for it is able to provide the abstraction layer needed to carry out a 'negotiation' or 'dialogue' between the participant systems to put in common concepts, vocabulary,

[7] http://www.w3.org/standards/semanticweb/. Last accessed 9 October 2012.

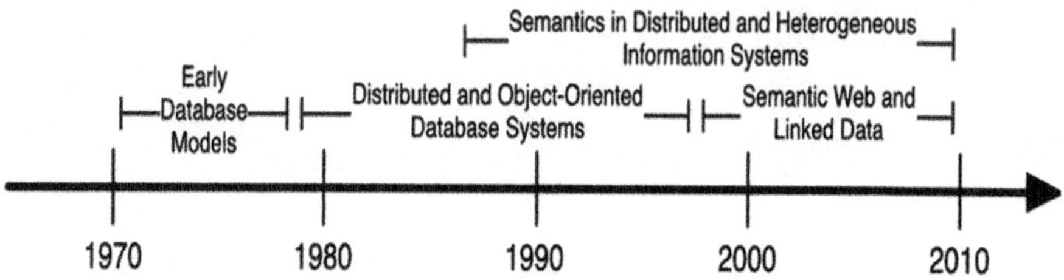

Fig. 12.2 Semantics and interoperability research in computer science (Halshofer and Neuhold 2011)

terms, etc. Thus, all the participants will know the meaning (not necessarily the content) of the exchanged information. Consequently, Semantic Interoperability (SI) is able to meet some requirements posed by interoperability affecting the EPO and the ESCP.

SI addresses the issue of knowledge representation independently from languages or cultural differences. Alongside other interoperability concerns, such as organisational interoperability and technical interoperability, SI (also referred to as Computable Semantic Interoperability) refers to the ability of computer systems to communicate information and have that information properly interpreted by the receiving system in the same sense as that intended by the transmitting system. As Halshofer and Neuhold have recently put it, 'the interoperability problem and the representation of semantics have been an active research topic for approximately four decades' (Halshofer and Neuhold 2011, 3). Figure 12.2 above shows the evolutionary path followed by research on semantics and interoperability from the early database models to the recent developments on Linked Data.

At the EU level, The European Interoperability Framework for pan-European e-Government Services establishes that SI 'is concerned with ensuring that the precise meaning of exchanged information is understandable by any other application that was not initially developed for this purpose. Semantic interoperability enables systems to combine received information with other information resources and to process it in a meaningful manner' (European Commission 2004, 16). SI requires that any two systems will derive the same inferences from the same information. Moreover, the core objective of SI is 'not only to allow information resources to be linked up but also to allow information to be automatically understandable, and, consequently, reusable by computer applications that were not involved in its creation' (European Commission 2004, 19). A further distinction deals with the difference between SI and syntactic interoperability. The former is understood as referring to data elements and the relationship between them (including vocabularies to describe data exchanges and ensuring that data elements are understood in the same way by communicating parties). The latter is understood as focusing on the exact form of the information to be exchanged, in terms of grammar, format and schemas.

The European Commission has devoted a sustained effort to SI policies. Pillar II of the Digital Agenda for Europe (2010–2020) deals with Interoperability and Standards. In this regard, the European Commission recognised in 2010 that action on interoperability is essential to maximise the social and economic potential of information and communication technology (ICT). In addition, it establishes that SI is jeopardised by different interpretations of the information exchanged between people, applications and administrations. SI, as well as interoperability at legal, organisational and technical levels 'should progressively lead to the creation of a sustainable ecosystem (...) which would facilitate the effective and efficient creation of new European public services' (European Commission 2010, 4).

The Semantic Interoperability Centre Europe (semic.eu)[8] is a participatory platform and a service by the European Commission that supports the sharing of assets of interoperability to be used in public administration and e-Government. Moreover, The Interoperability Solutions for European Public Administrations Programme (ISA Programme 2010–2015)[9] addresses this need by facilitating efficient and effective cross-border electronic collaboration between European public administrations. In the private sector, the activity of the Open Group is also devoted to SI.[10]

12.4 Information Management and Ontologies

12.4.1 Introduction

Information management has undergone a dramatic transformation in the last decade. Moreover, the Web has become the most important channel for sharing multimedia contents with the whole world: music, film, television, newspapers or books have been reshaped or redefined in the digital era. Web 2.0 tools and mobile technologies have lowered the barriers not just for people to access the Internet but to create and share content (Poblet and Casanovas 2012). In the social media context, 'mash up', 'like', 'follow' and 'tweet' are tinged with new, widely adopted meanings. The legal domain and its huge masses of textual and multimedia contents do not remain outside this movement.

Indeed, in the World Wide Web, there is a growing amount of unstructured legal information directly available to anyone. This is why there is an urgent need to construct conceptual structures for knowledge representation to share and manage intelligently all this information whilst making human-machine communication and understanding possible (Casellas 2008). As regards the legal information domain,

[8]http://www.semic.eu/semic. Last accessed 9 October 2012.

[9]http://ec.europa.eu/isa/index_en.htm. Last accessed 9 October 2012.

[10]http://www.opengroup.org. Last accessed 9 October 2012.

the production of legal rules has followed an inflationary path. Today, the main problems are how to handle the complexity of the different typologies of legal knowledge and which are the most adequate ways to store, retrieve and structure the ever-growing amount of legal information and data (Benjamins et al. 2005).

Ontologies are specific tools to organise and provide useful descriptions of heterogeneous content. From a human user perspective, ontologies enable better access to information and promote shared understanding while facilitating computers' comprehension of information and more extensive processing. In addition, the learning curve for ontology design has considerably lowered in the past few years with the availability of a considerable number of tools and applications to facilitate ontology editing and management.[11] For instance, Protégé[12] is a design tool that is specifically devised to develop ontologies from many kinds of fields, and reasoning algorithms such as Pellet (Sirin et al. 2005) provide reasoning capabilities.

In our scenario, we have to consider two main features that ontologies provide: (i) expert knowledge modelling and (ii) resilience to change. The first feature is related to ontology designers, because technical skills are not a sine qua non for developing an efficient model. By following a set of guidelines, experts in a particular field will be able to model their domain knowledge and interact directly with ontology design tools. The second feature is related to changes that could affect ontologies over time. By definition, ontologies are easily adaptable tools and maintenance tasks can be undertaken without significantly altering the overall architecture of the system. There are many desired extra features pointed out in Sect. 12.4.

In this chapter, we propose an SI framework to deal with the legal SI issue that concerns EPO and ESCP. This SI framework is composed of three different parts: (i) ontologies (knowledge representation); (ii) Protégé (design tool); and (iii) a reasoning algorithm (providing reasoning capabilities to ontologies). The parts of this framework are described in the next sections of this chapter.

12.4.2 Definitions

The term ontology has been borrowed from philosophy to be used in computer science and artificial intelligence in a technical sense. Nevertheless, there are many definitions of ontology in the computer sciences and AI domains, and such definitions have changed and evolved over the years. In 1991, Neches et al. defined ontologies as a 'top-level declarative abstraction hierarchies represented with enough information to lay down the ground rules for modelling a domain. An ontology defines the basic terms and relations comprising the vocabulary of a

[11] See, e.g., Suárez-Figueroa et al. (2011) for an updated overview of languages, methodologies and tools.

[12] Stanford University, Protégé, available online at: http://protege.standford.edu. Last accessed 9 October 2012.

topic area as well as the rules for combining terms and relations to define extensions to the vocabulary.' (40). Perhaps the most quoted definition of 'ontology' in the Semantic Web domain is the one that Tom Gruber provided back in 1993: 'An ontology is a formal specification of a shared conceptualisation' (Gruber 1993, 199). In a nutshell, an ontology describes the concepts and relationships that are important in a particular domain, providing a vocabulary for that domain as well as a computerised specification of the meaning of terms used in that vocabulary. These applications include natural language translations, medicine, standardisation of product knowledge and electronic commerce, among many others. Stemming from Gruber's influential definition, an extended version of it says that 'an ontology is a formal, explicit specification of a shared conceptualisation. Conceptualisation refers to an abstract model of some phenomenon in the world by having identified the relevant concepts of that phenomenon. Explicit means that the type of concepts used, and the constraints on their use are explicitly defined. Formal refers to the fact that the ontology should be machine-readable. Shared reflects the notion that an ontology captures consensual knowledge, that is, it is not private of some individual, but accepted by a group'. (Studer et al. 1998, 184).

One of the goals of ontologies is the construction of a catalogue of categories that exist in reality, connected with the classification and organisation of knowledge.

According to Guarino (1998), ontologies can be classified conceptually as:

- Representation ontologies or meta-ontologies. These capture the primitive representation used to formalise knowledge in a given knowledge representation.
- General or upper-level ontologies. These classify the different categories of entities existing in the world. Very general notions that are independent of a particular problem or domain are represented in these ontologies. The knowledge acquired is applicable across domains and includes vocabulary related to things, events, time and space.
- Domain ontologies. These are more specific ontologies. Knowledge represented is specific to a particular domain. They provide vocabularies about concepts in a domain and their relationships or about the theories governing the domain.
- Application ontologies. These describe knowledge pieces depending both on a particular domain and task.

In addition to ontologies, taxonomies represent a classification of the standardised terminology for all required and involved terms within a knowledge domain. In a taxonomy, all elements are grouped and categorised strictly hierarchically and are usually presented by a tree structure. In a taxonomy, the individual elements are required to reside within the same semantic scope, so that all elements are semantically related to each other to a certain degree.[13]

[13]See the Semic glossary at http://www.semic.eu/semic/view/smeta/Glossary.xhtml. Last accessed 9 October 2012.

12.4.3 Ontology Design Tools: Protégé

Protégé is a free, open source suite of tools for ontology development and use developed at Stanford University.[14] It is the main framework used at the Institute of Law and Technology of the Universitat Autònoma de Barcelona (IDT-UAB)[15] in those projects implementing ontologies. Protégé allows users to construct domain models and knowledge-based applications with ontologies but it also facilitates the implementation of a rich set of knowledge-modelling structures and actions that support the creation, visualisation and manipulation of ontologies in various representation formats. The Protégé framework supports two main ways of modelling ontologies via the Frames and OWL editors. The resulting ontologies can be exported into a variety of formats, including RDF(S), OWL and XML Schema.

Protégé is specifically designed to develop ontologies from many kinds of field. Due to its features and properties, it is ideal for the acquisition and management of knowledge in our scenarios. On the other hand, Pellet is an open source 'reasoner' that also provides powerful features to manage knowledge.

There are several ontology languages available in the literature (such as the OWL or WSMO families) with different levels of expressiveness and reasoning capabilities.[16] The main criteria for the selection of an ontology language are its knowledge representation mechanism and the inference support needed by an application. The high complexity required by the knowledge modelling requires a representation language with high semantic expressiveness. OWL combines the required expressiveness for ontologies and the compliance to W3C standards, which makes it the most appropriate language.

The Protégé platform is extensible and provides a plug-and-play environment that makes it a flexible base for rapid prototyping and application development. In the Protégé knowledge model, terminologies and ontologies are represented using 'frames' (classes, slots and facets). Classes are the entities and sometimes referred to as 'concepts' in terminologies. Slots describe properties or attributes of classes. Facets describe characteristics of slots. An ontology in Protégé consists of frames and axioms. Axioms specify additional constraints. An instance is a frame built from at least one class that carries particular values for the slots. A 'knowledge base' includes the ontology (classes, slots, facets and axioms) as well as instances of particular classes with specific values for slots (Fig. 12.3).

12.4.4 Ontology Applications

Ontologies are a critical tool when it comes to promoting interoperability services. The Institute of Law and Technology (IDT-UAB) has been involved in different

[14] http://protege.stanford.edu. Last accessed 9 October 2012.

[15] http://idt.uab.es. Last accessed 9 October 2012.

[16] See http://www.w3.org/standards/semanticweb/. Last accessed 9 October 2012.

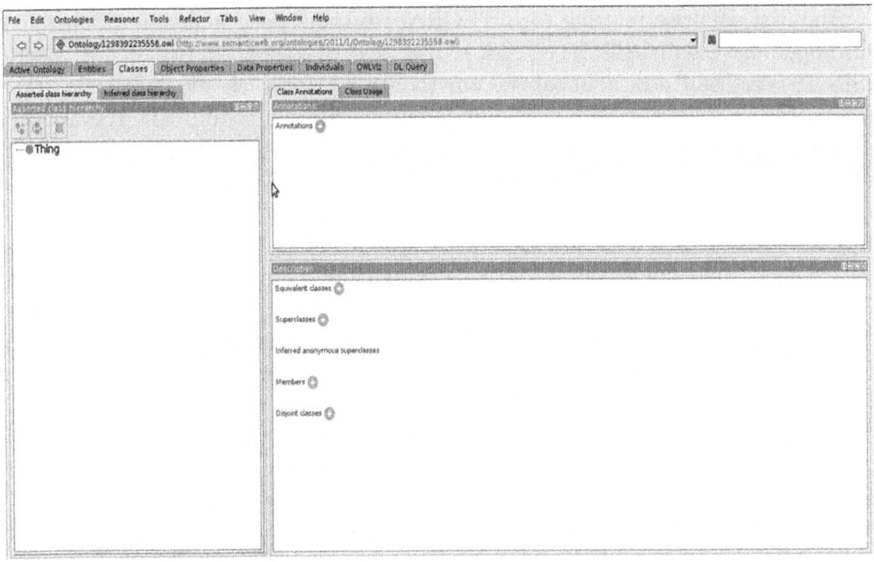

Fig. 12.3 Protégé framework in a GNU/Linux environment

projects in the field of SI, including information search, annotation and retrieval (e.g., IuriService, INTEGRA, ONTOMEDIA and CONSUMEDIA). For all of these projects, one of the core tasks has consisted of defining and implementing one or more legal ontologies.

12.4.4.1 Interoperability

The INTEGRA project (Research on Technologies for Decision Making in Immigration Policies) aimed at developing intelligent systems to manage migration flows in both regulated and non-regulated EU borders, with a global perspective of the problem and an approach to a European solution.[17] The growing differences in the development of the first and third world have caused migratory movements that have multiplied exponentially over the last decade. Migration is one of the most important challenges facing developed countries because of the effect it has on the demographic structure of both sending and receiving countries. As is well known, each EU country has different implementing legislation for EU Directives and subsequent regulations to regulate migration issues (Poblet and Vallbé 2011). In INTEGRA, ontologies were able to provide an abstract layer to represent the knowledge acquired from legislation and documentation from each country, making the exchange of information possible. The INTEGRA project also constitutes a good example of interoperability between different databases.

[17]INTEGRA (Research on Technologies for Decision Making in Immigration Policies); CDTI-Spanish Ministry of Industry, Tourism, and Commerce, Contract 15/02/2008.

The first database relevant to INTEGRA was the second generation Schengen Information System (SIS II).[18] SIS II had several elements: one main system (SIS II core) and one national system (N.SIS II) for each member state (that is, the national data systems that communicate with the central SIS II), as well as a communications infrastructure between the central system and the national systems providing a SIS II network and the data share between the national services responsible (SIRENE services). The second database was the Visa Information System (VIS). The VIS system was necessary for compliance with the common visa policy, cooperation among consulates and the requirements of the national institutions responsible for visas.[19] The third database was EURODAC, which contributed to the management of asylum requests, making it possible to compare fingerprints for the proper implementation of the Dublin Convention.[20] By checking EURODAC, member states could check whether a person who requested asylum in one country had already submitted a request in another member state. There was a central unity coordinated by the European Commission, a central database and electronic communication devices between member states and the core institution. The fourth database to take into account was TECS, an information system provided by the Europol Convention.[21] The Europol Information System (TECS) had three main elements: an indexing system, an information system (the Europol Information System) and an analysis system (the Europol Analysis System or OASIS).

The main interest of those database structures and systems of coordination lies in the fact that the central structure does not replace the national ones. Instead, it is added to them. Such a structure may also apply to EPO and EPSC, where no central procedure is considered, but rather a network and a coordination of national procedures.

The INTEGRA project produced two ontologies aimed at managing interoperability for countries within the Schengen treaty. The first one focused on document matching to provide interoperability among the different types of documents used

---

[18]Decision 2007/533/JAI of the Council, 12 June 2007, available at http://eur-lex.europa.eu/LexUriServ/LexUriServ.do?uri=OJ:L:2007:205:0063:01:EN:HTML. Regulation (CE) nº 1987/2006 of the European Parliament and of the Council, 20 December 2006, available at http://eur-lex.europa.eu/LexUriServ/LexUriServ.do?uri=OJ:L:2006:381:0004:01:EN:HTML. Last accessed 9 October 2012.

[19]Regulation (CE) nº 767/2008 of the European Parliament and the Council, 9 July 2008, on the Visa Information System (VIS) and the short term visa data sharing between member states (Regulation VIS) http://eur-lex.europa.eu/LexUriServ/LexUriServ.do?uri=OJ:L:2008:218:0060:01:EN:HTML. Decision of the Commission 2009/377/CE, 5 May 2009. Available at http://eur-lex.europa.eu/LexUriServ/LexUriServ.do?uri=OJ:L:2009:117:0003:01:EN:HTML. Last accessed 9 October 2012.

[20]Council Regulation (EC) No 2725/2000 of 11 December 2000, concerning the establishment of EURODAC for the comparison of fingerprints for the effective application of the Dublin Convention. Available at http://eur-lex.europa.eu/LexUriServ/LexUriServ.do?uri=CELEX:32000R2725:EN:HTML. Last accessed 9 October 2012.

[21]See the website of Europol at https://www.europol.europa.eu/content/page/about-europol-17. Last accessed 9 October 2012.

in the European Union to identify people (e.g., passports, ID cards, driving licenses, etc.). These documents are usually in the language of the country of issue. In this situation, the ontology provides a thesaurus that is able to help border agents to identify the documents they are handling. The second ontology was specifically designed to provide interoperability among different Law Enforcement Agencies (LEAs) within Europe. The main aim of this ontology was to identify the different permissions granted to agents in their country and their position within the LEAs.

12.4.4.2 Annotation

Files carry a meaning that can be very versatile. For a person, the meaning of a message is immediate, but for a computer that is far from true. This discrepancy is commonly referred to as the semantic gap. Semantic annotation is the process of automatically detecting the presence of a concept in a file. The annotation process aims at expressing the semantics of information, improving information seeking, retrieval, classification, understanding and use. With the emergence of the Semantic Web, ontology-based document annotation has been the focus of many projects and applications because the availability of annotated content is one of the key challenges to overcome in order to make the Semantic Web a reality. The ONTOMEDIA projects[22] are another example of the application of ontologies to annotate digital documents.

These projects were aimed at developing an ODR Web platform for users and professionals to meet in a community-driven portal where contents are provided by users and annotated by the platform. The ODR Web platform is tailored in the Business-to-Consumer (B2C) domain although later on it may be extended to other domains, such as family, health care, labour, environment, etc. (Poblet et al. 2010). Citizens (both professionals and users of mediation services) can use any kind of device to access the portal (computers, smart phones), and in any format suitable to their purposes (text, speech, video, pictures). Ontologies are used to annotate all kinds of content and to help analyse multimedia content. The multimedia analysis is devoted to enhancing the information a mediator possesses during a mediation session, capturing mood changes of the parties and any other psychological information inputs that can be useful for mediators, just as if they were in a room with the users of the mediation service. All types of metadata are automatically extracted and stored to be further used within the mediation process. ONTOMEDIA also foresaw the application of mediation services as tasks within a mediation process that could be formally described by means of both process ontologies and mediation ontologies.

[22]ONTOMEDIA (Semantic Web, Ontologies and Online Dispute Resolution); Spanish Ministry of Science and Innovation, CSO2008-005536/SOCI); ONTOMEDIA (Ontologies and Web Services for Online Mediation); Spanish Ministry of Industry, Tourism and Commerce) TSI-020501-2008-131.

12.4.4.3 Search and Retrieval

In the information era, the amount of digital documents stored by enterprises and people has been multiplied exponentially. In this scenario, the search and retrieval of this information has become an important challenge. Usually, the search by keyword or concrete string is inefficient due to the heterogeneous origin of the documents. In addition, the relevance of a document could be determined by the context and not only by the keyword or the string that performs the search. The use of ontologies to overcome the limitations of keyword-based searches has been put forward as one of the motivations behind the Semantic Web since its emergence in the late 1990s.

The IuriService application was designed to provide Spanish judges in their first appointment with online access to an intelligent Frequently Asked Questions system (iFAQ). The IuriService iFAQ consisted of a repository of practical questions (problems that newly recruited judges were likely to face), along with their corresponding answers.[23] The aim of the system was to discover the best semantic match between the users' input questions in natural language and the stored questions. The search engine was enhanced with a legal ontology—the Ontology of Professional Judicial Knowledge (OPJK)—and semantic distance calculation. The initial set of practical questions from newly recruited judges was extracted from previous interviews with incoming judges as part of an extended fieldwork in Spanish courts. The answers to these questions were left to senior judges from the Spanish School of the Judiciary (Casanovas et al. 2005). Eventually, these pairs of questions and answers comprised the initial repository of the system (Fig. 12.4).

The list of questions provided the input knowledge for the OPJK ontology, which ought to represent the relevant concepts related to the problems that take place during the on-call period, the knowledge contained in the list of questions. Thus, the conceptualisation process of the OPJK was based on the previous and careful knowledge-acquisition stage. This comprised the acquisition of the list of questions and the treatment of this corpus in order to obtain relevant terminology related to practical problems faced by judges in their first appointment, through term extraction from the corpus of questions faced by judges (Figs. 12.5 and 12.6).

12.4.5 Ontology Population

The manual performance of ontology development and population is both labour- and cost-intensive. If population of ontologies has to be done manually by humans,

[23]IURISERVICE has been developed within the framework of different national and international research projects: SEKT (Semantically Enabled Knowledge Technologies); UE (VI Framework Program, Information Society Technologies); EU-IST 2003-506826; IURISERVICE I (design of an online network to support newly recruited judges); Spanish Ministry of Science and Technology, FIT-150500-2002-562; IURISERVICE II (design of an online network to support newly recruited judges); Spanish Ministry of Science and Technology; FIT-150500-2003-198.

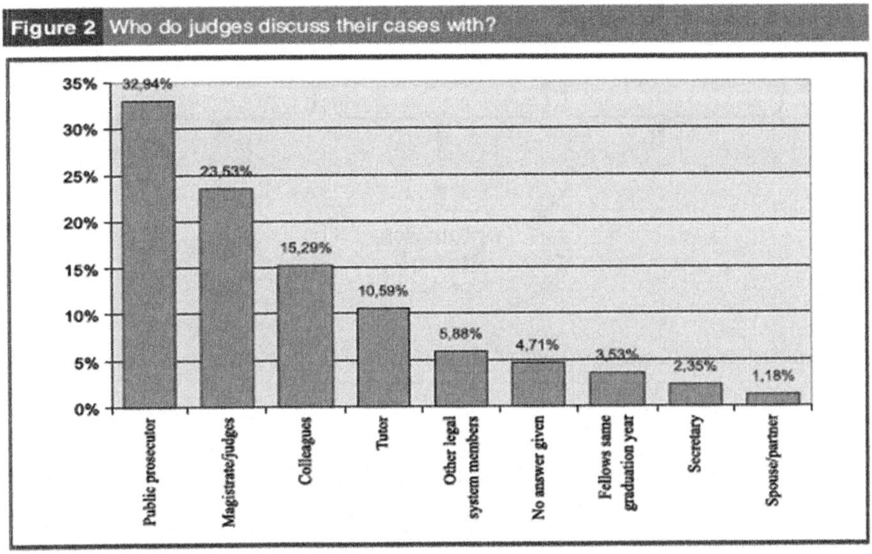

Fig. 12.4 Who judges discuss their cases with

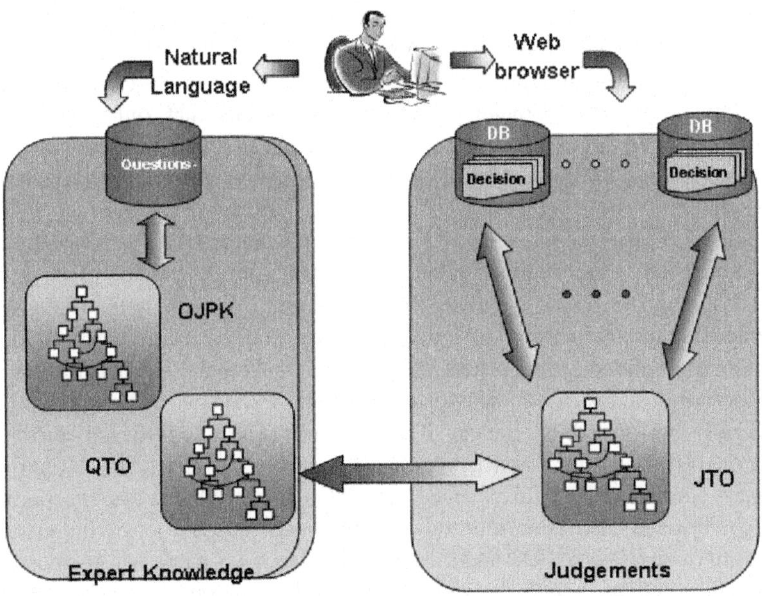

Fig. 12.5 Overall architecture for IuriService FAQ

the most cannot be got out of ontologies. It is therefore of paramount importance to develop the maximum level of automation for those tasks. For this purpose, the identification and extraction of terms that play an important role in the domain under consideration is a vital first step (Maynard et al. 2008). Semi-automatic knowledge

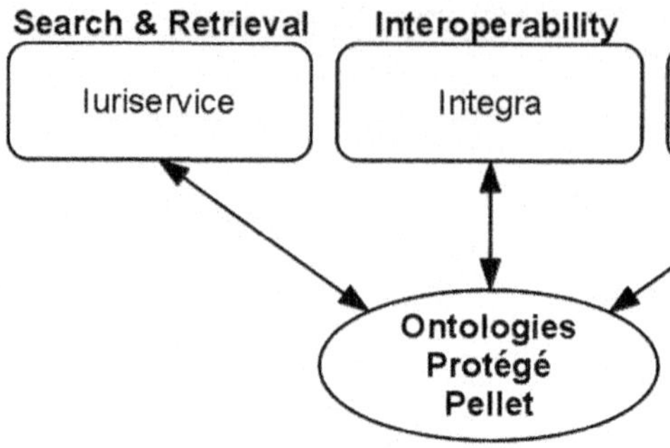

Fig. 12.6 Ontological applications in IDT research projects

acquisition has relied on the advancement of Natural Language Processing (NLP) techniques. This is a field of computer science and linguistics concerned with the interactions between computers and human—natural—languages and aimed at identifying the relevant terms of a corpus. The techniques are based on linguistic information, statistical methods or on hybrid approaches (Fernández-Barrera 2011).

Automatic term recognition (also known as term extraction) is a crucial component of many knowledge-based applications, such as automatic indexing, knowledge discovery, terminology mining and monitoring, knowledge management and so on. Term recognition has been performed on the basis of various criteria. The main distinction we can make is between algorithms that only take the distributional properties of terms into account, such as frequency, and extraction techniques that use the contextual information associated with terms (Maynard et al. 2008).

Ontology population is a crucial part of knowledge-based construction and maintenance that enables us to relate text to ontologies, providing, on the one hand, a customised ontology related to the data and domain with which we are concerned, and on the other hand, a richer ontology that can be used for a variety of Semantic Web-related tasks such as knowledge management, information retrieval, question answering, semantic desktop applications and so on. Ontology population is generally performed by means of some kind of ontology-based information extraction (OBIE). This consists of identifying the key terms in the text (such as named entities and technical terms) and then relating them to concepts in the ontology. Typically, the core information extraction is carried out by linguistic preprocessing (tokenisation, POS tagging, etc.), followed by a named entity recognition component, such as a gazetteer and rule-based grammar or machine learning techniques (Maynard et al. 2008).

12.5 Semantic Interoperability Toolbox for the European Payment Order and ESCP

12.5.1 A Combination of Tools for Semantic Interoperability

This chapter has reviewed ontologies as one of the most appropriate tools when it comes to addressing and solving a number of semantic issues, such as the existence of different legal terms and languages. As ontologies are also hard to build and maintain, they can be combined with other tools. For instance, XML markup language has proved useful to define document structures and translate standard forms. Assisted question-and-answer forms may also be useful for claimants. Moreover, an FAQ (Frequently Asked Questions) list of terms may be of assistance for users. A professional FAQ list based on expert knowledge is one of the user-friendly alternatives for sharing information. The potential users of this information system can be either lawyers or citizens with no legal expertise. The FAQs can be targeted in multiple directions, covering the most common problems that a user of EPO or EPSC can encounter during the procedure. Another advantage is that it can be adapted to national legal systems and can take into account specific procedures. We can provide thereby useful information for particular situations. Moreover, the system can evolve and be upgraded to address additional issues.

12.5.2 Specific Tools for EPO and ESCP

We have identified seven general semantic tools that can be relevant to solving some of the semantic problems identified so far.

12.5.2.1 Ontology for the Identification of the Court (EPO and ESCP)

One important issue raised by the experts is the identification of the court. The address indicated in Form A (Claim Form) should be used to determine the court that is supposed to solve the claim. To address this problem, we can easily conceive an ontology that automatically matches the domicile and the court that has to deal with the case. The ontology should have a list of the cities and their relevant court. Obviously, this could also be achieved with a general database or with a fixed set of rules, such as the European Judicial Atlas,[24] but opting for an ontology may be worthwhile in this case because it makes it easier to add, modify or reuse the links

[24] Available at http://ec.europa.eu/justice_home/judicialatlascivil//html/index_en.htm. Last accessed 9 October 2012.

between domiciles and court jurisdictions. We would only need to add, delete or modify the criteria. While a list of logic inferences is better for small challenges, an ontology is more useful in the cases of EPO and ESCP because it has to deal with different national rules of court competence attribution.

12.5.2.2 An FAQ for Practical Issues (EPO and ESCP)

The IuriService project reviewed above is an example of an FAQ and both coordination and management of decentralised expert knowledge. A project similar to this one, an intelligent tutorship system based on questions and practical answers, could be set up for the EPO/ESCP procedures. The goal of this FAQ system for EPO/ESCP would be to share the professional experience of both judges and lawyers. Moreover, parties could also report and look for similar experiences.

12.5.2.3 An FAQ for National Law Aspects (EPO and ESCP)

One of the main benefits of both ESCP and EPO procedures is that they provide uniform procedures at the European level. However, on some occasions the application of the procedural law of a particular member state may be required. That may be the case with regard to the determination of the costs of the proceedings (Recital 29 ESCP Regulation); moreover, when a claim is outside the scope of the ESCP Regulation, the court will proceed with it in accordance with its procedural law (Article 4.3 ESCP). In fewer cases, the substantive law of a member state will be required (e.g., the internal law of the seized court applies in order to determine whether the party is domiciled in that member state [Article 3.2 ESCP and Article 59 Regulation 44/2001]); moreover, the domestic rules apply for the calculation of interest (Recital 10 ESCP).

An FAQ list might therefore be useful. It could be oriented to be a guide for the most common cases and thus assist general users and foreign lawyers in identifying national requirements. As has been pointed out earlier, an FAQ can include expert knowledge and can be tailored to address practical issues. A general tutorship for users requiring quick and precise indications can be built. One of the advantages of an FAQ list is that the application can easily be customised, so it can assist both general users and legal experts. It can also be adapted to new situations, while a feedback mechanism from users can be set up to enlarge the FAQ list as necessary.

12.5.2.4 Ontology for Determining the Grounds of the Court's Jurisdiction (EPO and ESCP)

Both EPO and ESCP procedures clarify that the rules of Council Regulation (EC) 44/2001 on jurisdiction and the recognition and enforcement of judgements in civil and commercial matters apply. However, the application of those rules by citizens is far from being an easy matter. To solve some of these problems, there are various instruments that could be taken into account. On the one hand, the European Judicial Atlas[25] provides a database of national courts. Here, the end-user may insert his or her domicile or a particular postal code and the database would show which court would have jurisdiction to deal with the case. However, sometimes the database does not match certain postal codes with a particular court. Thus, it could be interesting to enrich such database with an ontology matching different villages or towns with particular courts. Additionally, the European Judicial Network in civil and commercial matters has a glossary that could assist some users.[26] However, the technical terms composing the glossary make this database primarily intended for experts. The ESCP and EPO procedures provide a standard form for the claimant to detail the grounds on which it is considered that the court has jurisdiction (ESCP, Form A, Number 4; EPO, Form A, Number 3). In any case, they refer to complex concepts such as the domicile of the defendant and the place of the harmful event or the place of performance of the obligation. It is difficult to see how a non-legal expert could complete these forms correctly; private international law scholars frequently discuss these connecting factors.

If a user wants to fill in the form correctly, he needs to know that a legal contract or situation is linked to a particular legal connecting factor: domicile of the defendant, domicile of the consumer, etc. Therefore, it would be advisable to formalise the expert knowledge of a private international law expert in such a way that most common situations could be managed. Obviously, this ontology will work better for easier cases and might not give any useful advice for complex ones. A disclaimer clause should also indicate that this tool does not pretend to substitute for a lawyer but merely to offer indications that the user may have to confirm.

12.5.2.5 Assisted Question-and-Answer Form for Discriminating What the Claim Relates to; Ontology for the Determination of Whether the Consumer Defendant Is Domiciled in the Same Member State Where the Court Is Seized (EPO, Form A, Number 6)

In order to ease the task of claimants as regards code discrimination in EPO Form A, Number 6, it could be possible to design an assisted question-and-answer form with the different categories and subcategories provided. This could be particularly suitable as regards code 1, regarding what the claim relates to (e.g., different types of contracts of service, types of rental agreements, etc.). Moreover, the same form (Number 6) includes a box that requires additional specifications for claims relating to consumer contracts. Here, an ontology would be able to set the answer to the

---

[25] Available at http://ec.europa.eu/justice_home/judicialatlascivil//html/index_en.htm. Last accessed 9 October 2012.

[26] Available at http://ec.europa.eu/civiljustice/glossary/glossary_en.htm. Last accessed 9 October 2012.

question of whether the consumer defendant is domiciled in the member state where the court is seized. This would be performed through the information introduced in Number 2 of the same form.

12.5.2.6 An Ontology of Legal Concepts (EPO and ESCP)

A general legal translator is not yet in sight, but a list of the most relevant concepts could be built in order to improve the interoperability of different legal systems, with its equivalent in different countries. An ontology of legal concepts could be built up with the legal equivalent of the more commonly used legal concepts in the different national judicial systems. This semantic tool could help general users and legal advisers in finding equivalent legal terms or better understanding facts under discussion.

12.5.2.7 Annotation Using XML (EPO and ESCP)

As can be seen, one general issue with interoperability in Europe is related to the use of multiple languages. Some legal mandates of translation are indeed provided but when there is no translation, the semantic annotation of the structure of the document may be of help. The European Judicial Atlas provides for such a translation for EPO/ESCP application forms. According to this, XML permits the annotation of particular items on the application forms, such as names, addresses, etc. After translation, the structure of the application form is translated into another language. However, a further step may be to extend the XML annotation from the structure of the application form to its content. For instance, this could apply to the details the claimant may write in Form A. There is a general limit to what can be solved with this tool, however; we cannot translate all the descriptions of the facts provided by the parties. A human translator would be needed in this case.

The European Eurovocs multilingual thesaurus (a comparative multilingual vocabulary compilation) also has an XML version that could be useful,[27] but it is mainly focused on formal language and therefore a complement of NLP should be added to it.

12.6 Conclusions

In the shift from the current human-readable Web to the machine-readable Semantic Web, the use of knowledge representation languages and tools such as ontologies (Casellas 2011) is of paramount importance. In the legal field, different efforts are

[27] Accessible at http://eurovoc.europa.eu/drupal/. Last accessed 9 October 2012.

being made (Francesconi et al. 2010) toward this end. Ontologies and FAQs can be very useful to formalise and manage expert knowledge in a way that general users or experts can take benefit of it, but ontologies may be improved a great deal. For instance, some efforts are being put towards the intelligent processing of non-expert-generated content. This will certainly improve the capabilities of existing tools, such as in the search and retrieval area. Ontologies are being proposed today by a community of experts who agree on the representation of a particular domain while non-expert content by unknown producers is being produced in a distributive way, delivering content that lacks conceptual harmonisation. The idea of emergent semantics throws the autonomy of engineered ontologies into question and emphasises the value of meaning emerging from distributed communities working collaboratively through the Web (Fernández-Barrera 2011). Therefore, some literature is focusing on a way to map formal ontologies expressed in RDF or OWL with implicit ontologies emerging from user-generated content. One of the research activities consists in making ontologies (top-down metadata structures) compatible with bottom-up tagging mechanisms such as folksonomies (Fernández-Barrera 2011). There are several possibilities under consideration, from transforming folksonomies into lightly formalised semantic resources to mapping folksonomy tags to the concepts and the instances of available formal ontologies.

The approach to creating a new tool should preferably be bottom-up, first identifying the problem and then trying to offer a possible solution. We also believe that it might not be necessary to substitute the whole procedure and create an e-justice procedure. This is not the case for ESCP and EPO, where national procedures are fully preserved and there is only a coordination and alternative procedure built upon national rules.

Semantic tools are also evolving and can broaden the range of possibilities in the near future. Indeed, IT may help and assist both parties. Given the current state of semantic tools, however, IT does not fully substitute for the general advice of an expert. We have to be humble and honest enough not to create added problems instead of solving them. Once this is conceded, we can nonetheless affirm that real benefits can be obtained from semantic tools. We have mentioned some of them, and the list may grow thanks to problems yet to be detected.

References

Benjamins, V.R., P. Casanovas, J. Breuker, and A. Gangemi. 2005. Law and the semantic web: An introduction. In *Law and the semantic web: Legal ontologies, methodologies, legal information retrieval, and applications*, eds. V.R. Benjamins, P. Casanovas, J. Breuker, and A. Gangemi. LNCS 3369: 1–17.

Berners-Lee, T., J. Hendler, and O. Lassila. 2001. The semantic web. *Scientific American* 284(5): 29–37.

Casanovas, P., M. Poblet, N. Casellas, J. Contreras, R. Benjamins, and M. Blazquez. 2005. Supporting newly-appointed judges: A legal knowledge management case study. *Journal of Knowledge Management* 5(9): 7–27.

Casellas, N. 2008. Modelling legal knowledge through ontologies. OPJK: The ontology of professional judicial knowledge. Doctoral thesis. Universitat Autònoma de Barcelona.

Casellas, N. 2011. *Legal ontology engineering: Methodologies, modelling trends, and the ontology of professional judicial knowledge*. Heidelberg: Springer.

European Commission. 2004. European interoperability framework for Pan-Europeane-Government services version 1.0. http://ec.europa.eu/idabc/servlets/Docd552.pdf?id=19529.

European Commission. 2010. Communication from the European commission to the European parliament, the council, the European economic and social committee and the committee of the regions towards interoperability for European public services 744 final.

Fernández-Barrera, M. 2011. User-generated knowledge through legal ontologies: How to bring the law into the semantic web 2.0. Doctoral thesis. European University Institute.

Francesconi, E., S. Montemagni, P. Rossi, and D. Tiscornia (eds.). 2010. *Proceedings of the 4th workshop on legal ontologies and artificial intelligence techniques*. Fiesole (Florence): European University Institute.

Gruber, T.R. 1993. A translation approach to portable ontology specifications. *Knowledge Acquisition* 5(2): 199–220.

Guarino, N. 1998. Formal ontology and information systems. In *Formal ontology in information systems*, ed. N. Guarino. Proceedings of FOIS'98, Trento, 6–8 June 1998. 3–15. Amsterdam: IOS Press.

Halshofer, B., and E.J. Neuhold. 2011. A retrospective on semantics and interoperability research. In *Foundations for the web of information and services: A review of 20 years of semantic web research*, ed. D. Fensel, 3–27. Heidelberg: Springer.

Maynard, D., Y. Li, and W. Peters. 2008. NLP techniques for term extraction and ontology population. In *Ontology learning and population: Bridging the gap between text and knowledge*, ed. P. Buitelaar and P. Cimiano, 107–127. Amsterdam: IOS Press.

Neches, R., R. Fikes, T. Finin, T. Gruber, R. Patil, T. Senator, and W.R. Swartout. 1991. Enabling technology for knowledge sharing. *AI Magazine* 12(3): 36–56.

Ng, G.Y. 2012. EPO and ESCP simulation UK—Italy claim: Regulations (EC) No. 1896/2006 and 861/2007. Paper presented for the 'building interoperability for European civil proceedings' online conference, 14 June 2012, Bologna.

Ng, G.Y., and M. Mellone. 2011. The legal interoperability and the European Small Claims Procedure. Report presented at the meeting of the research project 'building interoperability for European civil proceedings online', 1–2 Dec 2011, Bologna.

Poblet, M., P. Casanovas, J.M. López-Cobo, A. Cabrerizo, and J.A. Prieto. 2010. The ontomedia project: ODR, relational justice, and multimedia. In *Intelligent multimedia: Managing creative works in a digital world*, ed. D. Bourcier, P. Casanovas, M.D. de Rosnay, and C. Maracke, 349–364. Florence: European Press Academic Publishing.

Poblet, M., and P. Casanovas. 2012. Crowdsourced crisis mapping: How it works and why it matters. The conversation, 16 May 2012.http://theconversation.edu.au/crowdsourced-crisis-mapping-how-it-works-and-why-it-matters-7014.

Poblet, M., and J.J. Vallbe. 2011. Children immigration in the Catalan parliamentary debate: The empty set. *Culture, Language, and Representation* 9: 135–171.

Sirin, E., B. Parsia, B.C. Grau, A. Kalyanpur, and Y. Katz. 2005. Pellet: A practical owl-dl reasoner. UMIACS technical report 2005–68.

Studer, R., V.R. Benjamins, and D. Fensel. 1998. Knowledge engineering: Principles and methods. *Data and Knowledge Engineering* 25(1–2): 161–197.

Suárez-Figueroa, M.C., R. García-Castro, B. Villazón-Terrazas, and A. Gómez-Pérez. 2011. Essentials in ontology engineering: Methodologies, languages, and tools. In *EEBuilding data models: Proceedings of the 2nd workshop organised by EEB data models community*, 9–21. Luxembourg: Publications Office of the European Union.

Warren, P., R. Studer, and J. Davies. 2006. Introduction. In *Semantic web technologies: Trends and research in ontology-based systems*, ed. J. Davies, R. Studer, and P. Warren, 1–8. New York: Wiley.

Chapter 13
Coming to Terms with Complexity Overload in Transborder e-Justice: The e-CODEX Platform

Marco Velicogna

Abstract What does the making of a trans-national information infrastructure in the Justice domain entail? How is it designed? How is it implemented? The analysis of the e-CODEX, a large-scale pilot project to improve cross-border legal communication in the EU, sheds some light upon these questions. The purpose of e-CODEX is not just creating a technical system supporting transborder data exchange, but developing a functioning infrastructure that supports a legally valid, electronically mediated judicial communication system that can produce legal effects across different EU national jurisdictions. The e-CODEX case provides a flavour of the complexity entailed by such endeavour. It illustrates the clash between the attempt to organize and assemble the technological components on the one hand, and, on the other hand, the attempt to cope with the unexpected events and drifts that occur as the project progresses. It shows how the multi-layered legal and organizational dimensions (at the national and European level) become ever more relevant, and how cultivation strategies must be enacted to successfully implement the platform.

13.1 Introduction

This chapter deals with the initial stage of the making of an information infrastructure through an analysis of the e-CODEX project.[1] The e-Justice Communication via Online Data Exchange (e-CODEX) is a Large Scale Pilot project co-funded

[1]The observation and investigation of the e-CODEX project were carried out by the author while he was involved in it as IRSIG-CNR research team scientific coordinator and while he was supporting the Italian Ministry of Justice in the e-CODEX work package 7 (Architecture) coordination. The author wishes to thank Giulio Borsari, e-CODEX work package 7 coordinator

M. Velicogna (✉)
Research Institute on Judicial Systems, National Research Council of Italy (IRSIG-CNR), Bologna, Italy
e-mail: marco.velicogna@irsig.cnr.it

F. Contini and G.F. Lanzara (eds.), *The Circulation of Agency in E-Justice*, Law, Governance and Technology Series 13, DOI 10.1007/978-94-007-7525-1_13,

by the EU Commission.[2] The goal of this project is to improve 'the cross-border exchange of information in legal proceedings—where citizens, businesses and governments are involved—in a safe, accessible and sustainable way'.[3]

The e-CODEX project is coordinated by Germany's Justizministerium des Landes Nordrhein-Westfalen (Jm Nrw). It was initially carried out by 18 partners either being or representing the national Ministries of Justice of 15 European countries, plus the Council of Bars and Law Societies of Europe (CCBE) and the Conseil des Notariats de l'Union Européenne (CNUE).[4] Within the first year, the National Research Council of Italy (through two of its institutes—IRSIG-CNR and ITTIG-CNR) joined the project. The project started in December 2010 and was expected to end in December 2013. An extension of the project is at present under negotiation with the Commission. To give a better idea of the project scale, we can give some figures: its overall budget is over €14 million and about 1,400 person-months are committed to it. With the extension phase the budget should be increased by an additional €10 million, the number of partners should rise to 29 (representing 24 countries) and the end of the project should be postponed until February 2015.

Infrastructures typically form when multiple and heterogeneous systems merge, 'in a process of consolidation characterised by gateways that allow dissimilar systems to be linked into networks' (Edwards et al. 2007, i). In this instance, e-CODEX is developing and will soon be testing a set of technological components

for his fundamental role and the many insightful conversations. The author also wishes to thank all e-CODEX participants who are fighting to make e-CODEX happen, and without whom this chapter could not have been written. The opinions expressed in this chapter are those of the author and do not necessarily reflect the positions of the aforementioned persons and institutions.

[2]e-CODEX is an EU co-funded project (Ref. CIP-ICT PSP 2010 no 270968). The e-CODEX project is the first European Large Scale Pilot of the Information and Communication Technologies Policy Support Programme (ICT PSP) in the domain of e-Justice. Within the Competitiveness and Innovation Framework Programme (CIP), the ICT PSP is part of the European Union effort to exploit the potential of the new information and communication technologies.

[3]http://www.e-codex.eu.

[4]In addition to the Justizministerium des Landes Nordrhein-Westfalen (JM NRW) GERMANY, the project sees the participation of: Bundesministerium für Justiz Österreich (BMJ Austria) AUSTRIA; Federal Public Service Justice (MoJ Belgium) BELGIUM; Fedict Belgium (Fedict Belgium) BELGIUM; Ministry of Justice of the Czech Republic (MoJ Czech Republic) CZECH REPUBLIC; Ministry of Justice (MoJ Estonia) ESTONIA; Ministry of Justice France (MoJ France) FRANCE; Aristotelio Panepistimio Thessalonikis (AUTH Greece) GREECE; Italian Ministry of Justice—Directorate General for IT (MoJ Italy) ITALY; Malta Information Technology Agency (MJHA/MITA Malta) MALTA; Ministerie van Justitie (MoJ Netherlands) NETHERLANDS; Instituto das Tecnologias de Informação na Justiça (MJ—ITIJ Portugal) Portugal; Ministry of Communications and Information Society (MCSI Romania) ROMANIA; Spanish Ministry of Justice—Directorate General for Modernisation of Justice Administration (MJU Spain) SPAIN; Ministry of Public Administration and Justice (KIM Hungary) HUNGARY; IT Department of the Ministry of Justice of Turkey (MoJ Turkey) TURKEY; Council of Bars and Law Societies of Europe (CCBE) BELGIUM; Conseil des Notariats de l'Union Européenne (CNUE) BELGIUM; the National Research Council of Italy (CNR) ITALY.

which constitute a platform connecting existing national e-justice systems[5] and the European e-Justice Portal, thus contributing to the development of a 'pan-European interoperability layer for electronic exchanges in Europe in the field of Justice' (e-CODEX 2010, 9). The e-CODEX technological platform is intended to support data and document communication through the creation of an interoperability layer. According to the e-CODEX Technical Annex (2010), the concept of interoperability 'must be understood considering its different dimensions: organisational, semantic and technical. In practice, interoperability works through inter-administrative agreements, standards' definition and use' (e-CODEX 2010, 19), as well as existing Public Administration infrastructures, systems, applications and services. In addition, interoperability must take into consideration the temporal dimension in the sense that it should provide access to information to its users at any time (e-CODEX 2010, 19). Furthermore, the interoperability layer must be sustainable. Not much thought, though, is given to the critical aspect of evolvability in the analysis of information infrastructures (see Chaps. 1 and 2).

At the same time, the purpose of e-CODEX is not limited to the creation of a technical system (which comprises an organisational and a semantic dimension) allowing for the transborder transmission of bits, data, information or even documents between national e-justice systems or with the European e-Justice Portal. Its purpose is to build a functioning infrastructure that supports a legally valid, electronically mediated judicial communication capable of producing legal effects across different EU national jurisdictions. In other words, this exchange of bits and information must not be limited to a descriptive connotation but must produce changes of legal status: it must be legally performative. Indeed, 'legal processes and the utterances [statements] that constitute them are made up of performatives, intended to institute specific changes to the social order and to re-establish relations between citizens within a legal order' (Mohr and Contini 2011, 999). Authority and recognition of justice systems and their procedures are rooted in the material, social, spatial and temporal dimensions of the communication through which the parties interact, in which their statements are recorded and decisions are taken and made known. The creation of a technological platform that mediates the procedure and components affects not only the material components of the communications (documents, receipts, etc.) and their social and legal value, but also the material and institutional settings of judicial proceedings.

It should not be surprising, then, that part of the project is dedicated to test if the new system will be capable of maintaining the performative efficacy of the procedure. According to Edwards et al., 'the initial stage in infrastructure formation is system-building, characterised by the deliberate and successful design of technology-based services' (Edwards et al. 2007, i). Indeed, the project commitment includes running a live pilot of cross-border e-justice services, managing real users and real cases for 12 months. The electronic services that have been selected in

[5]For analysis of European e-justice systems see Fabri and Contini (2001), Fabri (2007), Velicogna (2007, 2008), Reiling (2012).

the first part of the project are the European Payment Order (EPO), the European Small Claim Procedure (ESCP), the European Arrest Warrant (EAW) and the Secure cross-border exchange of sensitive data. The extension phase plans to include two additional services: Synchronous Communication and Financial Penalties.

The performativity of the cross-border communication carried out through the e-CODEX platform should therefore be well tested. The initial idea was to start the experimentation of the services with real cases as soon as the technological components were ready and the technical interoperability layer tested. This idea is being reconsidered, though. The emerging legal and organisational issues suggest a more gradual approach. As a consequence, at present the possibility is being discussed to initially test and monitor the procedures with mock actors and mock cases, followed by testing with real (voluntary) actors and mock cases, and only in the final stage move to real actors and real cases. Through practical experimentation in a 'safe environment', this process is intended to bring to surface technical, organisational and legal problems that may hamper performativity and would otherwise be discovered only by users trying to solve real cases, to their own cost.

It should be noted that the project is still in the phase of developing the technological components of the e-CODEX infrastructure and that the pilots are not running yet, even though, as we will see, the on-going development process is itself producing effects and bringing to light likely consequences.

The rest of the chapter is organised as follows: the first section provides a description of the organisational setting established with the purpose of coordinating the actions of the large number of ministries, public bodies and international organisations required to develop a shared pan-European e-justice communication platform. Section 13.2 provides a description of the technological platform itself. An account follows of some of the sources of complexity that the project participants are starting to face when they move from the development of a technological platform for the exchange of legally valid documents to the attempt to make such exchange performative in situations of practice, with real cases and real users. Some conclusions are then drawn that reflect on the difficulty of striking a balance between planning and emergent complexity.

13.2 The Project's Internal Organisation

The project is formally structured in seven core work packages (WPs) covering technical, organisational, legal, policy and communication aspects. Accordingly, the work is divided between technical, non-technical (general coordination and communication) and the actual piloting (implementation and operation in real live systems). The technical work is structured into three main areas of development of the core technical interoperability components. These three WPs are complemented by a horizontal architecture work package responsible for the alignment of their work areas as well as the incorporation of technical components from other areas (e-CODEX 2010).

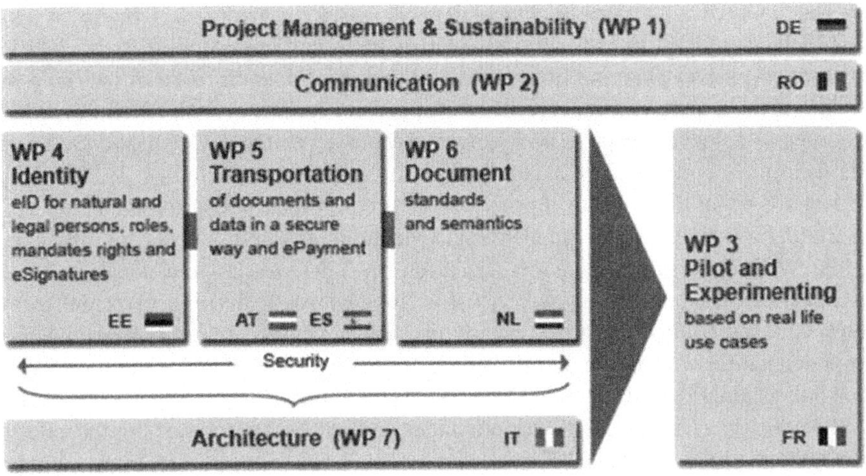

Fig. 13.1 e-CODEX work packages (Source: http://www.e-codex.eu)

As graphically summarised in Fig. 13.1, the WPs are as follows:

- WP1 Project administration and sustainability—includes project progress monitoring and quality assurance, budget monitoring and Community funds allocation, and maintenance of contacts with the European Council and Commission.
- WP2 Communication—aims at engaging the stakeholders who do not directly participate in the project.
- WP3 Pilot and experimenting—tasked with selecting, implementing and testing e-justice services based on the components developed in the 'technical' WPs (WP4, WP5 and WP6).
- WP4 Identity for natural and legal persons, roles, mandates and rights/e-Signatures—addresses issues such as user authentication and authorisation, as well as verification and implementation of e-Signatures when necessary to ensure authenticity and integrity of documents or to provide trusted timestamps when required by a procedure.
- WP5 Exchange of documents and data and e-payment—interface descriptions (standards, concepts) as well as conception and a base implementation of an interoperable exchange mechanism for the pilot implementations.
- WP6 Document standards—deals with the contents and semantics of the documents and metadata involved.
- WP7 Architecture—focuses on high-level architectural issues such as the identification of high-level and common functional requirements (what the system is supposed to do) and non-functional requirements (how the system is supposed to be) and high-level decisions (e.g., which pre-existing components does e-CODEX reuse? What needs to be done at a national level and what by e-CODEX? Who builds what?) in order to support the coordination of WPs 4, 5 and 6 activities.

The e-CODEX project Technical Annex (2010) provided a complex workflow detailing tasks, milestones, deliverables and interdependencies for each WP. 'Thorough project planning, rationalisation and prioritisation of tasks will help in obtaining the appropriate resources at the opportune moment' (e-CODEX 2010, 38) in order to achieve the project objective. According to the e-CODEX e-Delivery platform development plan, as soon as pilots have been selected (in WP3), WPs 4, 5 and 6 begin the high-level processes and requirements description. This leads to the definition of assets, standards and technological components in WPs 4–6, while WP3 starts describing test scenarios. In WP7, meanwhile, the high-level architecture has been described. All this, together with the above results from WPs 4, 5 and 6, feeds into the specific process and 'use case'[6] requirements, the implementation conception and the inputs for technical reviews for the three WPs that build standards and reusable assets. At the same time, the piloting work package (WP3) will have finalised the development and test infrastructure for the pilots. Next, the modules and technological components are developed. The integration of these components into the pilots leads to the completed implementation. Both this and the testing that follows are subject to technical reviews, which are coordinated by WP7. After a stable running environment has been set up in WP3, the closing and final documentation phase starts in WPs 3 and 4–6. The task of external architectural coordination in WP7 is, of course, on-going throughout the whole course of the project and responsible for bringing the different building blocks together (e-CODEX 2010, 39).

In line with this plan, all partners have allocated a number of person-months to each WP with the exception of WP1, which is entirely under the competence of the project coordinator. At the same time, the involvement of the various partners in the WPs vary quite a bit, in relation to formal human resource allocations agreed within the grant agreement, available competences and needs, and actual interests of the partners once the project has actually started.

Two other bodies play a very relevant role in the organisation and governance of the project: the Management Board and the General Assembly. The Management Board, which includes, among other people, the project coordinator and the WP leaders, monitors the effective and efficient implementation of the project, supports the project coordinator in preparing meetings with the European Commission and makes proposals to the General Assembly in relation to relevant topics such as rearranging tasks and budgets; it is also responsible for the proper execution and implementation of the decisions of the General Assembly, to which it is accountable. The Management Board has played a very active role in managing a number of problems that could not be solved at WP level.

The General Assembly is composed of one representative per partner with each country having one vote. While it is the ultimate decision-making body on the day-to-day conduct of the project, it meets only twice a year and plays more of a role

[6] A 'use case' is a cross-border procedure selected for the piloting of the e-Codex e-Delivery platform.

in ratifying decisions and proposals from WP and Management Board level than an active strategic orientation and driving force of the project as envisioned in the grant agreement.

The complexity of the organisational structure devised to carry out the project is a reflection of the complexity of the task at hand. At the same time, even this organisational complexity has not been adequate enough to confront all the multiple issues that emerged during project implementation. Interdependencies between WPs soon led to a deformation of the formal structure, not only to cope with local delays but also to allow the finding of shared solutions. In this, a key role was played initially by WP7 (architecture) and, as the piloting phase came nearer, by WP3 (piloting). Sub-groups and special ad hoc units were created. So, for example, in addition to the bodies that have been formally established from the beginning, an additional unit is playing an increasingly relevant role: the e-CODEX Legal Sub-Group. As the WPs' structure shows, while the final objective is to provide services to the users through the creation of a platform, the focus, at least initially, has been on the technological components. With time, though, the participants have become increasingly aware of the complexity of the normative component involved in creating a platform that supports the exchange of performative utterances in and across different national legal domains. For quite a long time, the normative layer was discounted as a set of well-known rules (many of which have a legal background). Therefore, it was thought it could have been easily dealt with by the technical WPs as a set of plain and clear functional requirements to be inscribed (Czarniawska and Joerges 1998) into the technological components. As the participants began investigating and discussing the legal dimension, and the results of another research project[7] were shared with some key members of the e-CODEX working group, a number of unexpected findings emerged:

- The mapping of all the EU and national norms that are relevant for the circulation of legal agency across member states is a daunting task and requires very specific competence.
- Even apparently homogeneous EU Regulations are interpreted and implemented in different ways by the various member states, thereby introducing complexity into the overall system.
- Given the complex net of norms, different interpretations and implementation practices pursued by the participants or by member states, the need emerged to find shared agreements on what could be done and how. What was a purely technical project became a political endeavour and an exercise of European integration.

[7]In particular, the Building Interoperability for European Civil Proceedings Online project (BIECPO). The project is a research project co-funded by the European Commission and coordinated by the IRSIG-CNR. The project objective was to contribute to e-justice development in transborder cases with research findings coming from in-depth case studies of national and European e-justice applications, and with an analysis of the legal, institutional, organisational and technical conditions in which e-justice can successfully support and handle national and transborder civil cases. The participation of IRSIG-CNR researchers in the e-CODEX project was useful for cross-fertilisation between BIECPO and e-CODEX.

This has led to the creation of a Legal Sub-Group composed of legal experts from within the project but also from outside, with experience in EU law and in (some) member states' law.

13.3 The e-CODEX Technological Platform

The main focus of e-CODEX is upon the cross-border electronic data and documents exchange. As we will see, one of the consequences of the switch from paper to the digital medium is the change of some key properties of the techno-legal objects supporting data and document exchange. So, for example, the content of a paper form sent by the claimant to the court maintains its structure and format once the envelope is opened at the court. This is not necessarily true for an electronic document, whose visualisation may depend on the application used to open it. A typical example is the opening of a Word document using Microsoft Word or OpenOffice Writer, or an HTML or XML document by two different browsers. Furthermore, while the 'original' of a paper document can be submitted by postal service, its digital version is necessarily a copy. It is important to remember that in the justice domain, it is not just the content of a document that is of importance. The form, including the presentation of the content and the way in which the information is packaged, can be relevant for it to perform its purpose. To face these challenges, e-CODEX has to find viable techno-legal solutions.

For example, the EPO and the ESCP Regulations require the claimant to sign the claim form. The electronic version requires an advanced electronic signature, as defined by Directive 1999/93/EC of the European Parliament and of the Council of 13 December 1999 on a Community framework for electronic signatures (which guarantees the integrity of the text, as well as the authentication). While a paper signature can be easily done by any claimant and, it is assumed, can be verified by any reader (although the validity of this assumption could be easily questioned), this is not so in the case of an advanced electronic signature. In the case of an advanced electronic signature, both signature and signature verification require the litigant to have access to specific and typically not interoperable technologies. So, for example, an Italian claimant may be able to electronically sign a document in a way that is adequate and can be verified by an Italian court, but if the document is sent to a court of another EU member state, this court cannot verify the Italian signature even if it has its own (national) e-filing infrastructure. This happens because the various judiciaries have developed solutions that are not technically interoperable.

For this reason, the e-CODEX infrastructure is being built by taking into account not just the specific procedures it will support, but also the ICT solutions that member states have already adopted in the justice domain. Despite pre-existing European Regulations such as the ones mentioned above, the specific solutions found by member states respond to specific requirements of national legal systems. Their development meant considerable investments in terms of financial and human resources, and they are now a constitutive part of the way in which justice is administered in member states. Furthermore, an important principle that needs to be considered when acting at EU level is a general principle of EU law, namely, subsidiarity. According to this principle, the EU may act only if an objective cannot be sufficiently achieved by the member states.

Recognising that 'national solutions ... cannot simply be replaced in favour of new, centralised approaches' (e-CODEX 2010, 11), e-CODEX aims to create an interoperability layer for the electronic exchange of data and documents between the existing European national information systems and infrastructures. Accordingly, 'e-CODEX ... should not be a new centralised approach or duplication of any national solution at the European level' (Klar et al. 2012, 14).

Furthermore, given the size, complexity, cost and independent evolution of such national systems, feasibility and evolvability reasons recommend avoiding, wherever possible, any attempt at modification in order to fit e-CODEX needs (Borsari and Velicogna 2011, 10). What e-CODEX wants to create, therefore, is an e-Delivery platform based on a multilateral solution in which all parties agree to common e-CODEX interoperability standards.[8] The choice of a multilateral solution should avoid the need to implement bilateral arrangements because this would 'create the need for the maintenance of a multitude of solutions and agreements' (Boersma 2011, 30) and increase complexity. In practice, the e-Delivery platform exchanges data and documents that are translated from sending national format to e-CODEX format and then again to receiving national format (for legal purposes, the transmission of 'original electronic versions' of the documents that are exchanged may be required).

In order to develop the e-CODEX delivery platform it was used a methodology (e-CODEX 2012a) based on:

- Identification of building blocks (a conceptual map of the main building blocks is provided in Fig. 13.2.
- Analysis of the existing building blocks in other EU Large Scale Pilots (PEPPOL, SPOCS, STORK, though STORK LSP uses the same e-Delivery solution as SPOCS for its pilots) and the ebMS standard, which had been adopted by another European project (European Cross border Filing—e-Filing). A scheme of the reusable transportation building blocks of the analysed e-Delivery solutions is provided in Fig. 13.3.
- Selection of reusable building blocks (considering elements such as technology maturity, maintenance needs, degree of coupling with other building blocks).
- Identification of missing building blocks to be implemented within e-CODEX.

e-CODEX relation with the existing LSP was not limited to that of a 're-user' of various components. During the first year of implementation of the project, the

[8]e-CODEX Standards and Architectural Guidelines are based on the European Interoperability Framework for European public services (EIF version 16.12.2010 COM(2010) 744 final) and the Architecture Guidelines for Trans-European Telematics Networks for Administrations (IDABC Version 7.1) (Borsari and Velicogna 2011, 10).

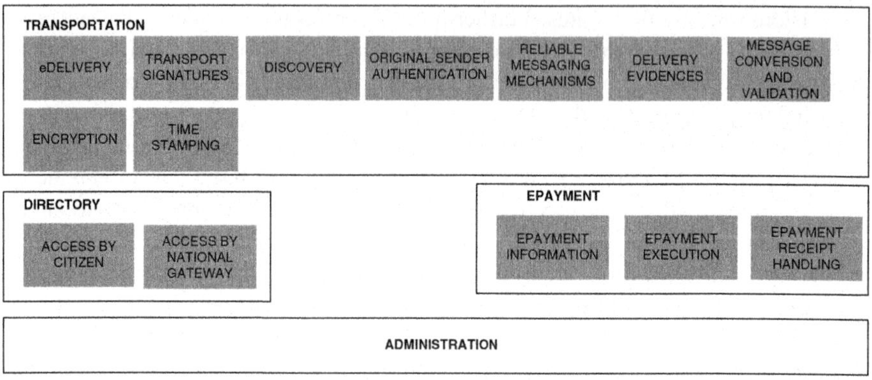

Fig. 13.2 e-Delivery technological building blocks conceptual map from e-CODEX WP5 perspective (Source: e-CODEX 2012a)

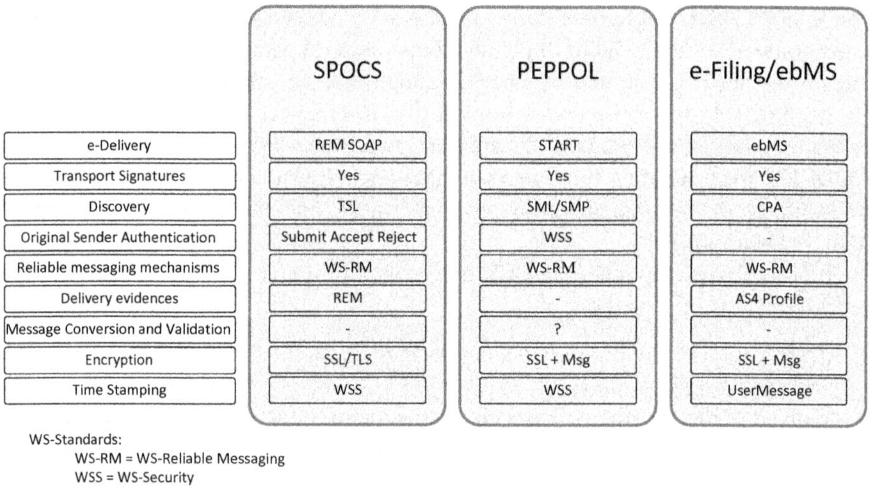

Fig. 13.3 Reusable transportation building blocks (Adapted from e-CODEX 2012a)

European Commission outlined the importance of the transport infrastructures of the existing Large Scale Pilots converging towards a common solution (e-CODEX 2012a, 80). Consequently, an effort was undertaken by the participants of the Large Scale Pilots, the member states and the European Commission to define a roadmap towards a common e-Delivery protocol. A first kick-off meeting to work on the convergence was held in July 2011, with the participation of experts presenting their visions from all LSPs as well as from the standardisation organisations ETSI and OASIS. As a result of the meeting it was decided to write a 'Scenario for the Convergence of LSP e-Delivery Solutions' document, which provided a first definition of what a convergent scenario could look like (Widgard and Rödlich 2011, 8). Within this convergence strategy the e-CODEX project has been tasked with piloting a first version of this common solution, while specifications are extended to ascertain that the needs of all Large Scale Pilots are met; the goal is for the other platforms to converge over time towards this infrastructure. The European Commission also stressed how the acceptance and the support coming from the industry were to be considered as very important success factors, and that the 'e-Delivery solution should also include industry standards' (e-CODEX 2012b, 18). As a result, the chosen building blocks for the "converged" solution were: the OASIS ebMS protocol for the transport layer, the ETSI REM standard supporting e-Delivery evidences for non-repudiation (where needed), and the PEPPOL approach for dynamic routing/capability discovery.[9]

One of the key concepts adopted by e-CODEX to reduce the technological complexity and the users requirements is the creation of a 'circle of trust' between the judicial authorities involved. This circle of trust should provide the basis for the judicial authorities to trust the information provided through e-CODEX, allowing for mutual recognition between member states of an electronic document within the existing legal framework. In other words, e-CODEX relies on each member state's trust of other member states on issues such as confidentiality, e-identification,[10] e-signature, e-documents, e-payment and transport (Borsari and Velicogna 2011, 10). So, for example, 'through the use of the "circle of trust" the responsibility of verifying the signature lies with the sending country. The process does not have to be repeated in the receiving country' (Weber and Nikkarinen 2012, 25). As e-CODEX analysis has shown, without such a circle of trust the complexity of the task would be too high to be managed in order to produce a working solution. At the same time, the circle of trust is not a technological component, but a multilateral agreement about who is entitled to check the identity and the signature: not the judicial authority receiving the document, such as the seized court, but the member states that agreed to belong to the circle of trust.

The circle of trust, therefore, also requires a formal agreement between the States and in some cases the introduction of national norms in order to make it performative in the national justice domains.

Since e-CODEX is an exchange platform, it is not designed for the storage of data and documents, but only for the transport of messages. As a consequence, after a successful message transmission, the message is deleted and only the log information is stored for statistical and security purposes (Weber and Nikkarinen 2012, 22).

The technological and semantic requirements for the e-Delivery platform to support the four initial use cases (the EPO, the ESCP, the EAW, and the Secure cross-border exchange of sensitive data) were identified in three business-process

---

[9] http://www.e-codex.eu/?id=132

[10] Typically, e-service users need to identify and authenticate themselves in order to be recognised by the system and use the services, i.e., signing in to an email account through user name and password.

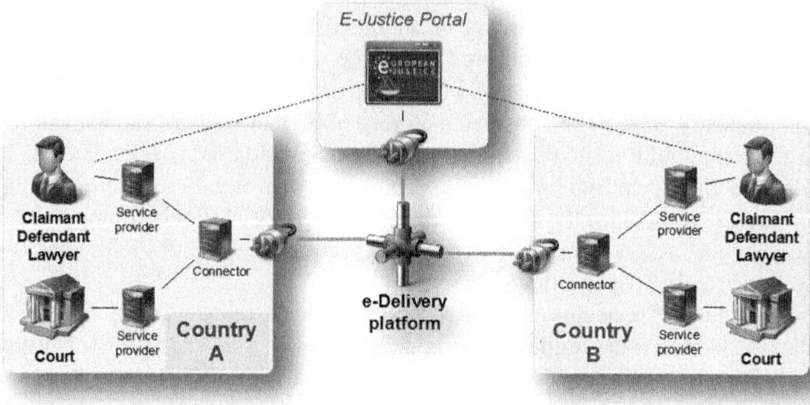

Fig. 13.4 e-CODEX technological components from the EU member state perspective (Source: e-CODEX D7.3 v1.0)

modelling meetings.[11] In such meetings, the objectives behind each use case, the procedural steps involved, the supporting elements and the solutions required for their implementation were analysed. The modelling of each use case was based on the related European regulation or decision, as the use cases themselves were selected on the basis of the existence of an EU legal framework. Where any uncertainties existed in the EU framework about the steps of the procedure, the modelling was based on indications provided by the e-CODEX legal experts (Velicogna 2012, 12). The combined effort of WP3 and WP7 facilitated the creation of an apparently robust map of the formal requirements for the exchange of legally valid documents across national borders. Fig. 13.4.

Let us now look in more detail at the e-CODEX platform in action. An e-CODEX user creates, submits and receives his/her files through national e-justice system already used for e-filing of national cases (e.g., the Austrian WebERV), an ad hoc national solution or through the e-Justice Portal. Such systems and the secure transport infrastructures used to connect it to the e-CODEX connector and gateway act as e-CODEX service providers. Data collected in the preparation of the piloting showed that countries are planning to use a variety of architectures.

- Some countries will use a secure national identification and transport infrastructure, such as the Austrian WebERV, the German EGVP and the Italian PEC, to send messages from the gateway to the court.
- Some countries plan to directly connect a national portal to the connector and gateway.

[11]Small Claims and EPO: Dusseldorf, 7 July 2011; EAW: The Hague, 20–21 September 2011; Secure cross-border exchange of sensitive data: The Hague, 12 December 2011.

- Some countries will directly connect one single court to the connector and gateway (i.e., if a court has national jurisdiction over the concerned matters).
- Some countries plan to use an Enterprise Service Bus to connect the court systems to the connector and gateway.

In order to be an e-CODEX service provider, the system must be able to deliver a service in conformity with e-CODEX standards (e.g., security standards, privacy). An e-CODEX Service Provider may be a governmental solution (e.g., the Italian Trial OnLine infrastructure) or a private solution (e.g., an application and transport infrastructure used by the lawyers). In other words, depending on the use case, or on the role of the user, the e-CODEX service provider can be a national application maintained by the participating country's government, the European e-Justice Portal or another application used, for example, by legal professionals (Hvillum et al. 2012, 14).

In any case, the 'e-CODEX service provider' consists not only of the application but also of the secure transport infrastructure used to connect that application to the e-CODEX connector.

While in theory no change should be required if the application respects e-CODEX minimum requirements, in practice both technological and normative changes are required, sometimes involving national authorities outside e-CODEX. The Italian online procedure, for example, requires the sender to have, amongst other things, the possession of an Italian Fiscal Identification Number to enter a claim that will be accepted by the system. The reason for this is fiscal and the solution to this issue requires the involvement of the Italian Ministry of Finance. In addition, the XML of the documents sent by the Italian courts to the parties is being modified in order to enrich it with data not required by the national infrastructure but requested by e-CODEX.

The technical interoperability between the national e-justice applications allowed by the e-CODEX e-Delivery platform is based on two main components: a national connector and a national gateway. Overall, the e-Delivery platform is responsible for the secure and reliable transport of data and files from one e-CODEX gateway to the other. A decentralised architecture was chosen. If a technical need emerges in the future, a central hub will then be considered. To allow access to all potential users, the system will use the Internet with encryption to ensure a secure connection. In principle, the e-CODEX e-Delivery platform will be 'content agnostic' (e-CODEX 2012a, 25).

The e-CODEX connector (see Fig. 13.5) is a piece of software that implements the interface between the national e-justice communication infrastructure and the gateway of that nation. It performs two main functions:

1. It transforms the outgoing message received from the national e-justice application from the national to the e-CODEX standard and adds a 'Trust-OK' token to the documents. The Trust-OK token is generated both in a human-readable PDF and in a machine-readable XML form, and provides the results of electronic

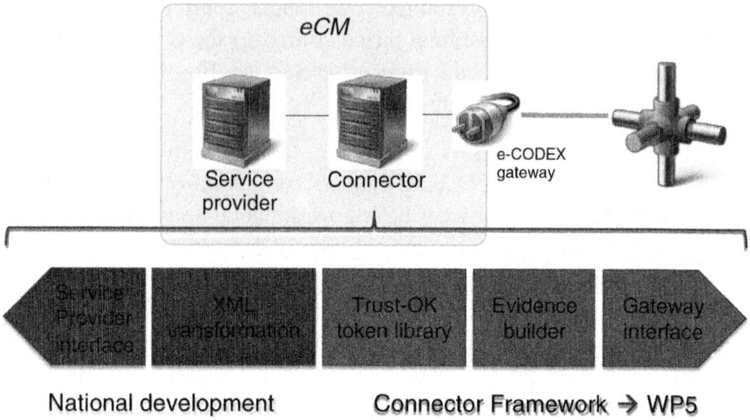

Fig. 13.5 Connector components (Source: Borsari 2012)

signature verification[12] or a statement guaranteeing that the document was issued by an advanced electronic system.[13] The Trust-OK token therefore indicates whether the document is considered trustworthy or untrustworthy (in the relevant country). All documents of the message and PDF Trust-OK token are placed in an ASiC-S container, which is signed (with a detached XAdES signature[14]) to ensure data integrity (Klar et al. 2012). In line with the circle of trust agreement, responsibility for the implementation and control of those characteristics lies with the member state whose party to a procedure uses the system (Hvillum et al. 2012, 18). The receiving country can then trust the documents and is not required to validate them again (e-CODEX 2012b).

2. It transforms the incoming message received by the e-CODEX gateway from the e-CODEX standard to the national standard and verifies the Trust-OK token (both XML and PDF versions) and that no data has been changed (Teschner and Hommik 2013, 15). The receiving member state has no obligation to carry out a verification of the authenticity and integrity of the document(s) and may rely on the information provided by the Trust-OK token.

---

[12]Indicating also whether a Qualified Electronic Signature or an Advanced Electronic Signature is used.

[13]An advanced electronic system is defined as an electronic system that meets the following requirements: the created document is uniquely linked to the user; the system is capable of identifying the user; the document is created using means that the user can maintain under his control; any subsequent change to the data of a created document is detectable.

[14]'DG Market's Digital Signature Services (DSS) Tool provides a solution to create and validate signatures that follow the ETSI standards and thereby should be accepted across Europe. The close collaboration with ETSI is reflected in both signature creation and signature verification. WP4 decided, together with the e-Justice portal, that DSS offers the most appropriate solution for e-CODEX needs. This decision is based on the results of the comparison of DG Market DSS and PEPPOL' (Klar et al. 2012, 18).

The e-CODEX connector might also perform protocol and 'semantic translations'. Member states' are free to decide at what stage in their infrastructure they will perform these actions if they are necessary at all. As the figure below highlights, part of the connector development, the one 'looking' at the national system, is within the competence of each member state, while the part 'looking' at the e-CODEX gateway is within the competence of WP5. To complicate the picture, the Trust-OK token library was to be developed by WP4, which was discovered not to have all the required competences and did not manage to find them within the e-CODEX resources, forcing the outsourcing of the Trust-OK token library design. This process of contracting generated a delay because of administrative complexities.

The e-CODEX gateway is the technical and organisational infrastructure provided and managed by an e-CODEX member state for routing incoming and outgoing electronic communication with that member state within the e-CODEX System. The gateways are required to fulfil specific security requirements within their operation and for communication with others. The gateways perform different functionalities, such as establishing a connection to other gateways, formatting the content of a message to be sent to the e-CODEX standard (ebMS3.0) and extracting the content of a received e-CODEX message (Klar et al. 2012). For outgoing messages, the gateway provides a transport signature and a timestamp, while for incoming messages it checks the transport signature, providing a timestamp and sending an acknowledgment of receipt. ebMS supports signature and encryption of messages according to Web Services Security 1.0 and 1.1 (based on the XML Signature standard and XML Encryption standard), and the Web Services Security X.509 Certificate Token Profile (e-CODEX 2012b, 34).

An e-CODEX message sent or received by a gateway via the e-CODEX system consists, therefore, of at least one or more documents, accompanied by a Trust-OK token. From a technical perspective, the project is using Holodeck open-source ebMS-based b2b messaging software. Holodeck is not taken off the shelf but is being extended according to e-CODEX needs with regard to logging and message reliability. More in detail, WP 5 identified and developed some components not available in Holodeck: the *REM ETSI evidence generator*, the *enhanced logging* system, and the *web service interface* that supersedes the file system based approach. Fig. 13.6.

The *back end web service* and *logging module* were introduced in the gateway itself, while the *evidence generator* is part of the National Connector (e-CODEX 2013, 11). The logging module is 'based on the standard log4j implementation, recording the logged activity to a data-base instead of a variety of flat text files. The back end web service is an additional interface to the ebMS gateway. It enables a way to send messages from the web services perspective without access to the gateway file system, reinforcing the security of the system and enabling a way to generate the initial Sub Mission Acceptance Rejection evidence. The "REM ETSI evidence generator" is a module integrated as part of the National Connector and it is responsible for the generation of the selected evidences and its release through the gateway connection or the national system' (ibidem). For a graphical representation of e-CODEX gateway components, see Fig. 13.7

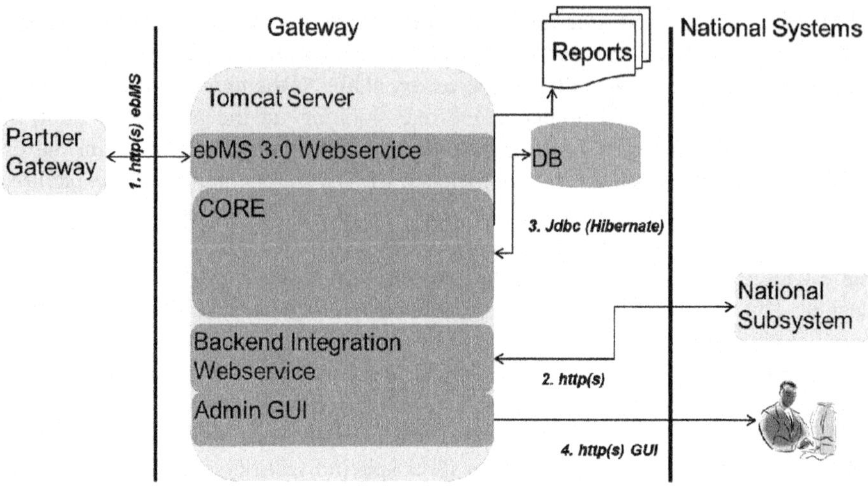

Fig. 13.6 e-CODEX Gateway architecture (Source: e-CODEX 2012b)

As payment of court or other fees can be required by the procedure, e-CODEX addresses the issue. While apparently simple, this aspect is also a source of complexity because the various member states have different ways of handling e-payment (when they have one). To cope with this complexity, pilot solutions will 'vary from direct debit handling outside the e-CODEX process to online payment done with a national system parallel to the e-CODEX process and handing over the payment receipt to the e-CODEX process' (e-CODEX 2012b, 14). A representation of the electronic cross-border judicial communication exchange process supported by e-CODEX is provided in the swim lane diagram in Fig. 13.7.

13.3.1 Non-technological Components of the Platform

In addition to the technological components, a number of non-technological components have emerged as relevant. As anticipated, in order to allow the proper exchange of cross-border documents, a formal agreement on the circle of trust has been required. The need for this formalised agreement was fully recognised only after the Legal Sub-Group was created and strengthened with the needed competences and the time to begin the piloting came closer. It then became evident that when exchanging information across borders, piloting partners in the e-CODEX project lacked a legal basis to recognise the exchanged information. The agreement of the circle of trust will form the legal basis for the recognition of information exchanged across borders between piloting partners. At the same time, the agreement has no effect on existing European or national legislations and binds only the signatories.

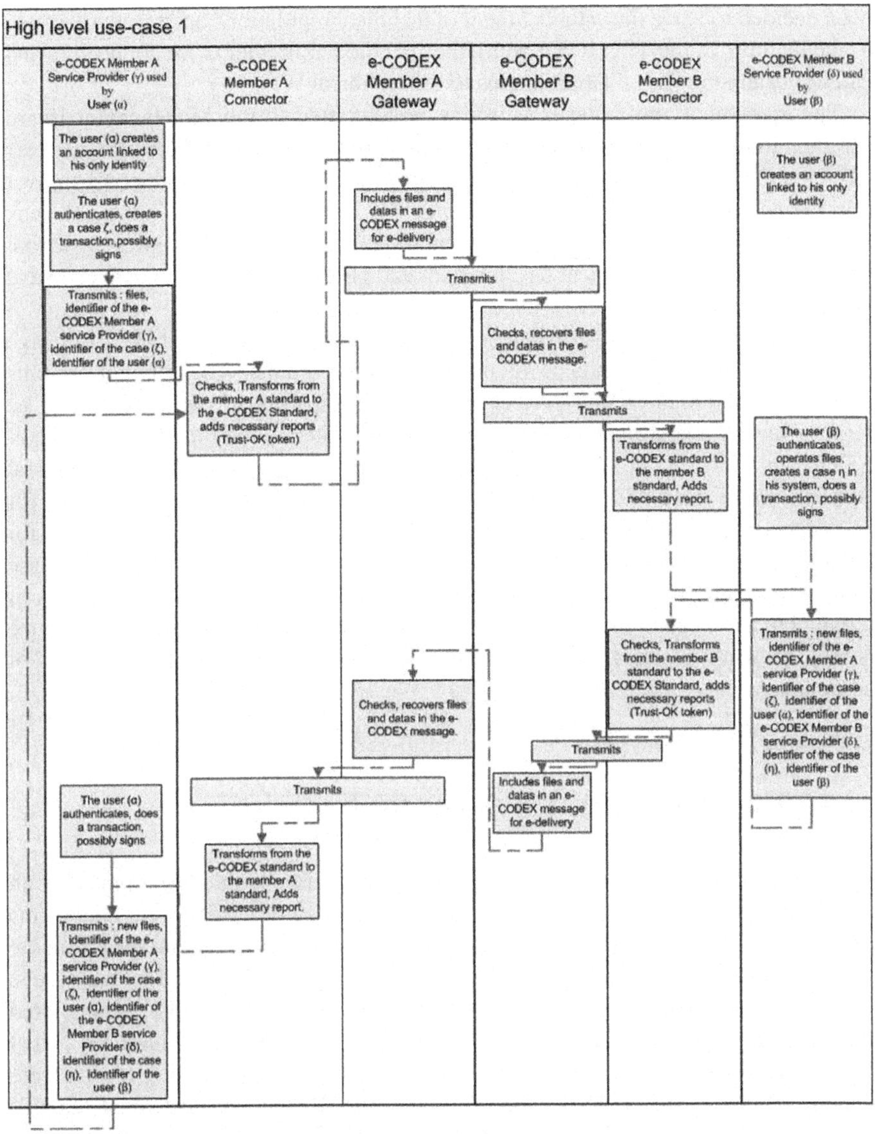

Fig. 13.7 High-level use cases scenario (Source: e-CODEX D7.3 v1.0)

The agreement, which is written by the Legal Sub-Group, defines not only the principle of a circle of trust but also the responsibilities of the subjects involved, data protection and security issues, legal effects of the Trust-OK token and the general requirements of the components (such as reliability and availability). The agreement also regulates the termination of a project partner's participation in the piloting of one or more services. While the agreement provides a general framework, it has been decided to leave the establishment of technical regulations and standards (such as the features of the Trust-OK token), the specific requirements for connectors and gateways, and the list of Time Stamps to the technical WPs.

The agreement and annexes will first be submitted to the Management Board and then to the General Assembly for approval, before being signed by the partners participating in the piloting. While the agreement is being introduced to cover piloting activities, it is foreseen that it may be extended in time and that it may have an impact on future e-justice regulation. If so, it would represent a first example of how technological development and procedural regulation can coevolve at transborder level.

Another non-technical component that emerged as crucial for the exchange of information is the presence of national contact points. These contact points should be appointed by the project partners participating in the piloting and be responsible for operational and technical matters related to the functioning of the e-CODEX platform at national level. Once again, the initial focus on the technological components of the e-CODEX platform delayed the discussion about the need for an organisational component to support and be responsible (and accountable) for the functioning of the platform until a very late stage. As in the national case studies presented in this book, e-justice development requires additional layers of regulation and organisational structure. Rather than de-bureaucratising, e-justice is reconfiguring justice administration through the creation of additional layers of complexity.

13.4 The Complexity of Building the E-services

The previous section discussed the complexity that arises in the development of an e-Delivery platform capable of supporting the exchange of legally valid documents across national borders. This section analyses the complexity that emerges from the attempt to make such exchanges performative in real cases handled by real users. This additional complexity came to light when the first two 'use cases' to be piloted (the EPO and ESCP) were analysed (e-CODEX 2012c). By looking at the actual procedures taking place in the courts in more detail, some surprising results were obtained. Luckily, thanks to the contribution of the BIECPO project (see Chaps. 1, 10, 11 and 14), the discovery of unexpected sources of complexity took place before any real-life experimentation was undertaken.

Both the EPO and ESCP procedures are based on Regulations where 'for the first time the European Union legislator not only regulated certain aspects related to civil proceedings in cross-border cases (e.g. the jurisdiction, the serving of documents, the gathering of evidences etc.), but also tried to propose an autonomous model of rules governing civil proceedings' (see Chap. 10).

Both procedures should allow EU citizens to autonomously file a cross-border case without having to resort to legal assistance or at least reducing its need. The procedures do not require the presence of the parties before the court and the communication exchange between the actors of the procedure (parties and seized court) is supported through structured forms provided by the Regulations, which are available in all official languages of the EU. Furthermore, the e-Justice Portal provides a step-by-step guide to the procedure and multilingual online forms.

While simple in theory, the mere filling out and submitting of the claim raise at least four main problems from the claimant's perspective: identifying the competent court, filling out the claim in one of the languages accepted by the seized court, paying the court fees (if applicable) and submitting the claim (see Chaps. 10 and 11).

Most of these problems, which the potential user of the EPO and ESCP services must confront, are not tackled by the e-CODEX platform because they remain outside the formal scope of the project. At the same time, they are key to the users' participation in the piloting and for future uptake of the system.

Complexity also emerges at the receiving end of the filing. Rather than a uniform interpretation and application of the same EU Regulations in the various countries, a preliminary analysis of courts' offline processing of the EPO and ESCP showed a number of different organisational solutions and practices. The implications of such complexity are only now being uncovered and addressed through a more systematic analysis of the current practices adopted for the EPO and ESCP in member states. Analysis of the regulative framework is not enough, and interviews are required with qualified experts, such as lawyers, judges and administrative personnel, with concrete EPO and ESCP case experience. The risk is that the huge effort carried out to build the e-CODEX platform to support the electronic delivery of procedural documents will not be able to provide real benefits to potential users or support the cross-border circulation of legal agency.

13.5 Concluding Remarks: The Drift from Planning to Cultivation

Hanseth and Monteiro highlight the fact that 'Establishing a working information infrastructure is a highly complex socio-technical task' (1997, 183). The e-CODEX case provides a flavour of the complexity that must be confronted not only when building a technological interoperability layer capable of supporting the cross-border exchange of data and documents, but also when making such exchange performative in the justice domain. The project is characterised by the clash between, on the one hand, the attempt to plan, organise and assemble the technological components and, on the other hand, the attempt to cope with the drifts and the unexpected events that take place as the project advances (Ciborra 2000; Contini and Lanzara 2009; 2012). Indeed, 'tensions inherent to infrastructure growth present imperatives to develop navigation strategies that recognise the likelihood of unforeseen (and potentially negative) path dependence and/or institutional or cultural barriers to adoption' (Edwards et al. 2007, ii). At the same time, much of the e-CODEX actions are still consistent with the notion of 'infrastructure building as a planned, orderly, and mechanical act' (Edwards et al. 2007, i). Objectives are fixed, schedules are created, deadlines are set and programmes are implemented, but then, in spite of that, the unforeseen and unexpected frequently occur (Czarniawska 2012; Velicogna and Contini 2009).

As this case study shows, multiple drifts have influenced the implementation process. Firstly, the identification of the technological requirements of the system revealed the complexity of the multiple legal requirements imposed by the national techno-legal systems. The attempts of EU law to bring homogeneity are not very successful; rather, being interpreted in different ways in each member states, such efforts tend to feed heterogeneity and complexity. Legally valid electronic documents have different features in the different judicial domains. The way in which a document is transmitted and the events happening during the transmission have implications for the validity of the document, and the implications vary. Some of the complexity stemming from the need to build a legal interoperability layer was expected from the project. Nevertheless, the knowledge available to the Ministries of justice involved and to the other partners was often focused on national experiences, each one assuming that the national interpretation of the procedure was *the* interpretation. A legal group was created and its role became more and more relevant with time as the legal complexity continued to unfold. Whether such complexity can and will be managed (including through the circle of trust agreement) remains to be seen. The tackling of the legal layer resulted in the increased relevance of a further layer of complexity, namely, the organisational one. While some of the partners pointed out that the infrastructure being created would require an organisation to manage it, the organisational problem was silenced by the decision to adopt a decentralised architecture, in which each partner was going to be in charge of its part of the infrastructure. As a result of the discussion over the circle of trust agreement, however, it was pointed out that the organisational issue could not be avoided: someone had to be responsible (and accountable) for the functioning (or otherwise) of the system. Hence, the establishment of the national contact points. Furthermore, progress in the e-Delivery system development revealed that in many cases changes to national systems and their legal regulations were required, with the need to resort to specialised actors (e.g., software houses, offices different from those involved in the project within the Ministries of Justice, etc.) other than the project partners. A number of the original assumptions guiding the project have therefore been challenged by the project's implementation itself.

Another aspect of the organisational problem emerged when the partners set off to prepare the pilot and courts and other organisations had to be taken on-board, thereby generating the organisational complexity needed to make the system actually performative and usable. This layer of complexity is only now being exposed and explored, and will probably lead to other sources of complexity that will have to be dealt with in the near future.

The story thus portrays a track in which several unexpected events gradually led the unaware project partners from the planned design and implementation of a technological e-Delivery platform toward the cultivation of an information infrastructure (Hanseth 2010). This gradual drift did not and is not taking place intentionally, however, but occurring bit by bit through sequential problem-solving and changes in layers not considered in the original plan. The emergent drifts, changes and problem-solving that lead to the information infrastructure turn out to be necessary to make the system performative and allow the circulation of agency. So far only the buds of the infrastructure are visible. The pilot will tell us if they will take root and evolve.

References

Boersma, R. 2011. Standards and guidelines. In *e-CODEX deliverable 7.1 governance and guidelines definition v.1*, eds. Borsari et al., 21–32. http://www.e-codex.eu/news-and-media/media/deliverables.html. Accessed 28 Jan 2013.

Borsari, G. 2012. e-CODEX: E-justice communication via online data exchange WP7 presentation. Working document.

Borsari, G., and M. Velicogna. 2011. Executive summary. In *e-CODEX deliverable 7.1 governance and guidelines definition v.1*, eds. Borsari et al., 10–12. http://www.e-codex.eu/news-and-media/media/deliverables.html. Accessed 28 Jan 2013.

Ciborra, C.U. (ed.). 2000. *From control to drift: The dynamics of corporate information infrastructures*. Oxford: Oxford University Press.

Contini, F., and G.F. Lanzara. 2012. Beyond interoperability: Designing systems for European civil proceedings online. Paper for the 'Building interoperability for European civil proceedings online' research conference, Bologna, 15–16 June 2012.

Contini, F., and G.F. Lanzara (eds.). 2009. *ICT and innovation in the public sector: European studies in the making of e-government*. Basingstoke: Palgrave Macmillan.

Czarniawska, B. 2012. Does planning belong to the politics of the past? *Contemporary Economics* 6(4): 36–48.

Czarniawska, B., and B. Joerges. 1998. The question of technology, or how organizations inscribe the world. *Organization Studies* 19(3): 363–385.

e-CODEX. 2010. Technical annex v.1.1.

e-CODEX. 2012a. Deliverable 5.2 reusable assets v.1.0. http://www.e-codex.eu/news-and-media/media/deliverables.html. Accessed 28 Jan 2013.

e-CODEX. 2012b. Deliverable 5.3 concept of implementation v.1.0. http://www.e-codex.eu/news-and-media/media/deliverables.html. Accessed 28 Jan 2013.

e-CODEX. 2012c. Newsletter: 2/2012.

e-CODEX. 2013. Deliverable 5.4 developed modules v1.0.

Edwards, P.N., S.J. Jackson, G.C. Bowker, and C.P. Knobel. 2007. Understanding infrastructure: Dynamics, tensions, and design. http://pne.people.si.umich.edu/PDF/ui.pdf. Accessed 28 Jan 2013.

Fabri, M. 2007. *Information and communication technology for the Public Prosecutor's Office*. Bologna: Clueb.

Fabri, M., and F. Contini (eds.). 2001. *Justice and technology in Europe: How ICT is changing the judicial business*. The Hague: Kluwer Law International.

Hanseth, O. 2010. From systems and tools to networks and infrastructures—from design to cultivation: towards a design theory of information infrastructures. In *Industrial informatics design, use and innovation*, ed. J. Holmstrøm, 122–156. London: IGI Global.

Hanseth, O., and E. Monteiro. 1997. Inscribing behaviour in information infrastructure standards. *Accounting, Management and Information Technologies* 7(4): 183–211.

Hvillum D.B., C. Murie, L. Ferrand, and J.M. Pellet. 2012. e-CODEX deliverable 3.3 documented system requirements and specifications v.1. http://www.e-codex.eu/news-and-media/media/deliverables.html. Accessed 28 Jan 2013.

Klar, A., V. Viljar, C. Murie, and L. Hommik. 2012. e-CODEX deliverable 4.2 concept for implementation of WP4, v.1. http://www.e-codex.eu/news-and-media/media/deliverables.html. Accessed 28 Jan 2013.

Mohr, R., and F. Contini. 2011. Reassembling the legal: The wonders of modern science in court-related proceedings. *Griffith Law Review* 4: 994–1019.

Reiling, D. 2012. Technology in courts in Europe: Opinions, practices and innovations. *International Journal for Court Administration* 4(2): 11–20.

Teschner, Rudi and Lesli Hommik. 2013. e-CODEX deliverable 4.3 developed modules and building blocks v1.0.

Velicogna, M. 2007. Justice systems and ICT: What can be learned from Europe? *Utrecht Law Review* 3(1): 129–147.

Velicogna, M. 2008. Use of information and communication technologies (ICT) in European judicial systems. CEPEJ Studies No. 7. Council of Europe. http://www.coe.int/t/dghl/cooperation/cepej/series/Etudes7TIC_en.pdf. Accessed 28 Jan 2013.

Velicogna, M. 2012. Introduction. In *e-CODEX deliverable 7.2 requirements finalisation and deliverable 3.2 described test scenarios v.1.1rev*, eds. Borsari et al., 11–17. http://www.e-codex.eu/news-and-media/media/deliverables.html. Accessed 28 Jan 2013.

Velicogna, M., and F. Contini. 2009. Assemblage-in-the-making: Developing the e-services for the justice of the peace office in Italy. In *ICT and innovation in the public sector: European studies in the making of e-government*, ed. F. Contini and G.F. Lanzara, 211–243. Basingstoke: Palgrave Macmillan.

Weber, A., and L. Nikkarinen. 2012. Architectural decisions. In *e-CODEX deliverable 7.3 high level architecture definition v.1*, eds. Borsari et al., 17–32. http://www.e-codex.eu/news-and-media/media/deliverables.html. Accessed 28 Jan 2013.

Wigard, S., and F. Rödlich. 2011. e-CODEX deliverable 5.2 reusable assets, appendix I, scenario for the convergence of LSP e-Delivery solutions, v.0.5. http://www.e-codex.eu/fileadmin/user_upload/media/deliverables/e-CODEX%20D5.2%20Annex%20I%20Scenario%20for%20the%20Convergence%20of%20LSP%20e-Delivery%20solutions%20v1.pdf. Accessed 22 June 2013.

Chapter 14
Let Agency Circulate: Architectures and Strategies for Pan-European e-Justice

Francesco Contini

Abstract The development of a pan-European e-justice platform supporting transborder proceedings requires shared infrastructures supporting interoperability at legal, semantic, technological and institutional level. The challenge may quickly reach high level of complexity hindering the development and use of the system. Moving from the theoretical framework developed in the book, and from the findings of six case studies, the chapter pinpoints design principles addressed to ease the design and development of an e-justice platform supporting the circulation of agency in transborder judicial proceedings. Principles are meant to keep the development and use of the system below the threshold of maximum manageable complexity, without impinging the requirements of legal and social performativity needed by judicial proceedings. The design principles, being relevant for e-justice application at national and pan-European level, are used to identify alternative techno-institutional architectures supporting the circulation of agency in the Payment Order and Small Claims Proceedings recently introduced by the European law. Architectures are assessed considering their impact on complexity and the effects on the circulation of agency. Finally, the chapter suggests a strategy based on the cultivation of the installed base and on the decupling of European and national e-Justice platforms to cope with the multiple and contradictory requirements of e-justice development in transborder proceedings.

F. Contini (✉)
Research Institute on Judicial Systems, National Research Council of Italy (IRSIG-CNR), Bologna, Italy
e-mail: francesco.contini@irsig.cnr.it

F. Contini and G.F. Lanzara (eds.), *The Circulation of Agency in E Justice*, Law, Governance and Technology Series 13, DOI 10.1007/978-94-007-7525-1_14,

14.1 E-Justice, Circulation of Agency and Performative Utterances

In the long run, e-justice will change the landscape of the justice systems, but the switch from conventional or paper-based procedures to digital ones is not just a change of the tools used to access information and exchange procedural data and documents, nor just a way to make justice more efficient and effective. Rather, it involves a reconfiguration of the established structure of legal agency built by our forebears (Lanzara 2009).

In e-justice, agency must be able to flow across different media (oral, digital and paper), regulative regimes (law and technology) and forms of governance (market and bureaucracy). The simple migration of the signature from conventional to digital proceedings may transform the simplest 'ready to hand' gesture into the most intricate procedure based on a manifold techno-legal assemblage (Contini 2009, see also Sect. 3.4).

Adapting the World Bank definition of e-government (2003) to our case studies, we can define e-justice as the use of information technologies to transform the relations of judiciaries with citizens, businesses and other arms of government. Thus, e-justice may entail the use of various technological applications: websites providing a range of information and forms required to handle judicial proceedings; e-services that make case-related information (i.e., public access) available to targeted groups of users; and the exchange of procedural documents (filing, petitions, judicial decisions) in electronic format (Reiling 2009). While European judicial systems have largely taken advantage of the first two types of technological application, the results achieved in the electronic exchange of procedural documents lag behind (Velicogna 2008). Only in the last few years have a growing number of European judiciaries made some improvement in this sector. The design of our research project has been affected by this state of affairs.[1]

For a better understanding of the present situation, we have introduced the concept of 'performative utterance', i.e., a sentence that changes the state of the world it refers to into a different state. It can be easily understood that actions such as filing a case, exchanging petitions and publishing a sentence change the status and relationships between people, and between people and things (Mohr and Contini 2011, further developed in Sect. 3.2). The 'filing of a lawsuit' establishes a relation and a new peculiar status between two subjects (claimant and defendant) before a court of justice. The entire judicial proceedings can be conceived as regulated exchanges of performative utterances. As a consequence, the case studies and design problems we confront can be analysed in terms of the transmission of performative utterances across different media and jurisdictions. Indeed, the European Payment

[1] Indeed, the choice made in 2010 concerning the national case studies to be analysed in the research was influenced by the absence of a running system in other European jurisdictions, with the remarkable exceptions of Austria, Finland and, as far as injunctive orders are concerned, Germany.

Order (EPO) and the European Small Claims Procedure (ESCP) require not just accurate and reliable information about 'how to' use the procedures, but also mechanisms to support the preparation/drafting of the performative utterances and their transmission to the competent judicial authority. This entails the identification of suitable mechanisms, architectures and strategies enabling and easing the circulation of agency across different domains (in our case, conventional and digital) and jurisdictions.

In order to proceed to such identification, after focusing on the concept of performative utterance, we will draw some lessons from the e-justice case studies discussed in the book. Subsequently, we will briefly consider the current functioning of the EPO and ESCP to ascertain in which circumstances and through which procedural steps agency circulates, as well as those in which it is prevented from doing so. Finally, after having introduced a set of new design principle, we assess some alternative architectures based on the design principles and on the imperatives of keeping the complexity to be faced by the actors (users or developers) below the threshold of maximum manageable complexity while at the same time pursuing the goal of maximum feasible simplicity (see Sect. 1.8).

We must emphasise, though, that e-justice development is not just a matter of building architectures; it also entails process strategies and the careful cultivation of the infrastructure (Chap. 2), and of smart regulation of technology (Chap. 3). The findings of these chapters are the foundations upon which we build this concluding chapter.

The concept of performative utterance drives us to focus on the peculiar nature of what is transmitted to whatever media. In the case of e-justice, at the machine level, the Internet or wide area network essentially allow for the exchange of bits among different systems. At a higher level, computer systems codify the bits exchanged into data. Users can transform such raw data into information, i.e., interpreted data. To do this, they must give a meaning to the raw data, and thus the semantic problem arises (see Chap. 12). In transborder proceedings, data interpretation is made difficult by the different languages and the different judicial systems, but bits, data and information have shown themselves to flow easily and smoothly in a digital environment. The problem arises when performative utterances have to be produced, formatted and then transmitted through digital channels.

To be performative (i.e., to be able to change the state of affairs, the relationship or the status), the utterances and the way in which they are exchanged must be submitted to regulation. The ESCP and EPO can be filed only by using the forms prescribed by the EU regulations, made available on the e-Justice portal and delivered to the competent court using the means prescribed by the regulations.

Email is not considered an adequate way to file a case, exchange pleadings or summon case parties in a significant majority of EU member states, Finland being a notable exception (Fabri 2009). The authorities of the member states have established a set of formal rules specifying which technology has to be used to accomplish these operations. As a consequence, the operations are performative only if they are carried out according to specific technological requirements or using the systems made available by courts and ministries of justice.

Digitisation procedure is not, then, just a matter of inscribing existing procedural rules into technologies. The technology to be used has to be established by law as well. Identity, signature, non-repudiation and authenticity are some common features usually regulated in the effort to move the exchange of performative utterances from paper-based to digital. The introduction of technologies into judicial proceedings therefore also requires the introduction of legal regulations. Law and technology, two distinct regulative regimes (Kallinikos 2009b), have to come to terms with one another, and this often leads to levels of complexity that are unmanageable for users, and sometimes even for systems developers (see Sect. 7.4).

14.2 A Summary of Case Findings

14.2.1 National and European Findings

The six case studies tell different stories about complexity, interoperability and circulation of agency. Indeed, having to pursue different goals and being related to different procedures, they faced different levels of complexity: two cases deal with 'simple' injunctive (or money) orders (MCOL and COVL), two with broader and more complex sets of civil proceedings (CITIUS and TOL) and two with cross-border cases (e-Curia and EAW-SIS).

They therefore offer a good variety of scenarios in which e-justice has been successfully developed.

They illustrate how simplicity has been pursued, how complexity can be controlled and how complexity can go out of control, delaying the development process or hindering the circulation of agency.

Money Claims OnLine (MCOL) enables the e-filing and handling of money claims online through a web-based platform open to any English and Welsh citizen (Chap. 4). Complexity has been reduced through the establishment of an ad hoc streamlined and functionally simplified procedure. Legal changes have been implemented to grant procedural simplification so that, to cite an example, signature is not needed. The system has also benefitted from pre-existing technological and organisational components. The digitally enabled procedures are handled by just one court through pre-existing back office technological and organisational facilities. On the one hand, this has contributed to black-box complexity in a centralised and specialised organisation. On the other hand, this has freed county courts from repetitive paper-based work linked to money claims. Law and technology have been kept decoupled: the law does not regulate in detail the functioning technological application but simply makes its use legal (see Sect. 3.5.2). At the same time, the adoption of e-government technological standards has made possible a system that is both evolvable and compatible with other e-government initiatives.

COVL, the Central Department for Enforcement on the basis of Authentic Documents (Chap. 5), has been developed by the Slovenian Supreme Court to speed up and make more efficient the handling of enforcement procedures. Unlike MCOL, the Slovenian case made scarce use of the installed base, which was outdated and difficult to update. Consequently, COVL system development required the transition from a decentralised installed base to a centralised one. Accordingly, the jurisdiction was also centralised in just one office with the advantage, already noted in MCOL, of the black-boxing of procedural complexity. In addition, a number of tasks previously handled by judges have been transferred to clerks. Radical procedural simplification has been used as a design principle in various instances, starting with the decision to substitute the signature on petitions with a declaration of the veracity of the claim and identification based on registration on the website. The existing e-government technological standards and guidelines have been adopted in this case.

CITIUS is a long-term project carried out by the Portuguese Ministry of Justice to reduce the average length of civil proceedings and to ease access to procedural data and information through digitisation (Chap. 6). Unlike the other two cases, it is not just an e-justice application supporting one specific procedure but a set of technological developments covering different areas of court proceedings.

The technological and procedural complexity faced by CITIUS is therefore greater than in the previous cases. It has been faced by a mix of organisational changes addressed to the centralisation of some of the services provided through the digital channel, as well as a number of legal changes introduced to host technological innovation and make it performative. Only when applications proved to be functioning properly were regulations introduced to formalise the new proceedings. It thus represents an example of cultivation of the installed base through piecemeal development based on progressive and mutual adjustments between the regulatory framework, the technological implements and court organisation. This mutual and recursive adaptation can be a useful development strategy effective in keeping the level of complexity at a manageable level while bootstrapping and growing the e-justice platform.

Italy's Trial OnLine (TOL) national e-justice project is the most ambitious among those we have studied (Chap. 6). It was developed for the complete digitisation of the entire range of civil proceedings without any form of ex ante procedural simplification. System architecture was imposed by legislation that prescribed advanced digital signatures. Further complexity was introduced by identification mechanisms requiring the involvement of all 165 local bar associations spread across the country. Civil procedures were not simplified or made more suitable for digitisation for a long time, however. As a consequence, complexity became unmanageable from the design stage forward. After years of struggling, the Ministry of Justice first decided to downsize the project, moving from the digitisation of the whole body of civil proceedings to the simpler money orders (like COVL or MCOL), and then to switch the identification and access components from an ad hoc technology to a more accessible one. These two sources of simplification have been effective in making TOL more accessible and facilitate the bootstrapping of the information infrastructure.

The Court of Justice of the European Union handles complex and high profile cross-border cases in all the official languages of the EU (Chap. 9). In such a complex environment, the development of an e-justice application (e-Curia) has been driven by the search of maximum feasible simplicity. This has been pursued by establishing simple access requirements for potential users based on username, password and web. The regulatory framework does not prescribe the technical features of the application but, as in the case of MCOL, it does authorise the court to use the e-justice application once it has been successfully tested. At the organisational level, the court is effective in black-boxing procedural complexity: the General Directorate of translation handles the linguistic complexity and the registries black-box procedural complexity, guiding users in a predictable way. All this procedural complexity has been inscribed into e-Curia so that it can provide better guidance to users.

The electronic transmission of the European Arrest Warrant from an issuing judicial authority to the judicial authority of another member state has been facilitated by exploiting the pre-existing Schengen Information System (Chap. 8). It thus represents a case of smart exploitation of the pre-existing technological installed base. This has been made possible by a number of legal instruments authorising and regulating the use of SIS, but also by organisational components effective in backing up agency and black-boxing complexity. The creation of the SIRENE bureaus in each member state, the 'human interface of the SIS, designed as 'the single point of contact for each Schengen State in respect of SIS Alerts and post-hit procedure' (Sect. 8.2.3), makes clear how qualified organisational units may be essential to securing the smooth transmission of information and performative utterances in the digital domain.

Despite accurate planning, the ways in which agency circulates and performative utterances are transmitted often suggest improvisation, path dependency, ad hoc problem-solving and even some randomness. Mediations between legal optimal requirements, technological applications and organisational arrangements are often critical to granting the transmission of performative utterances, and the judiciaries of the member states found different answers.

Such assemblages are arranged neither in a self-contained and coherent system nor in a clear multi-layered structure. Legal, technological or organisational components are present in any of the assemblages in different configurations, but the different ways in which they enable the transborder circulation of legal agency or the transfer of agency from conventional to digital point to a regular pattern, which leads to singling out design principles for the architectures that could better support the circulation of legal agency. Before doing this, however, we must briefly assess the circulation of agency in the EPO and ESCP.

14.2.2 The EPO and ESCP

Our study found that the identification and transmission of paper-based procedural acts are easy and swift for both users and courts, and that the delivery of the filing through the normal postal service does not constitute a problem.

Surprisingly, in the current functioning of the system, identification, security, non-repudiation and authenticity, i.e., the most critical steps in the transmission of performative utterances, are not problematic at all. Circulation of agency is hampered by a number of factors, however. Since more detailed analysis is provided in Chaps. 10 and 11, and in Sect. 1.4, we will simply summarise their findings. The e-Justice portal provides information that is not always clear and sometimes outdated.[2] It was impossible to pay court fees online, and in some cases it is necessary to go to court to do this. It is difficult to calculate the legal interest and it may be difficult to write some sections of the form in a foreign language. In some member states, too many courts are handling the procedures with the result that procedures are not well standardised, forms prescribed by the regulations and available in the e-Justice portal not always used and the single cases are treated on an ad hoc basis. Scant experience cannot lead to the consolidation of skills in dealing with procedures. Rather than the EU guideline and regulations (European Judicial Network in Civil and Commercial Matter 2011), the Italian courts adopted the procedure prescribed by the Italian code of civil procedure and officially endorsed by the Ministry of Justice. Consequently, the payment order issued by the judge is simply made available to the court counter; it is neither delivered to the plaintiff nor served to the defendant. This contributes to procedural complexity that can interrupt the circulation of agency; the plaintiff must first understand what is going on and then find a way to collect the paper copy of the order at the seized court. The procedure also works this way in other member states. Finally, no statistical data are collected at EU level about the two procedures and, with some exceptions, national judicial systems do not collect statistical data. The impression we received from the court we visited was that very few EPO claims are filed and even fewer ESCP claims. This perception is confirmed by the recent ECC-Net study stating that 'there are still courts in some member states who have never even heard about the European Small Claims Procedure' (ECC-Net 2012, 3).

14.3 Design Principles

Our starting point is the idea that information infrastructures, such as those analysed in the case studies, cannot be designed from scratch (Ciborra 2002; Hanseth 2003). Rather, they evolve and the design process is meant to address their evolution towards the desired outcome (Sect. 2.5). Design is consequently encountered in terms of information infrastructure and installed base cultivation (Design Principle 1, Chap. 2). While cultivating information infrastructures, other factors have to be considered, starting with the 'dynamic design space' encompassed by the threshold of maximum feasible simplicity and maximum manageable complexity (Sect. 1.8). Two further principles have been identified: the need to design systems pursuing the principle of maximum feasible simplicity while maintaining the performativity

[2] For example, the postal address of the court that carried out the simulation had not been updated 10 years after the court had moved to a different building.

of the information and documents exchanged (Design Principle 2; Sects. 1.7 and 3.5.4); and the need to avoid reaching the upper threshold of maximum manageable complexity because it may hinder the circulation of agency and delay the growth of the infrastructure (Design Principle 3, Sect. 1.7). Since these high-level design principles have been spelled out in detail in the first two chapters of the book, we do not need to go into further detail explaining how they work. Instead, we want to supplement them with other principles aimed at clarifying how legal, technological, organisational and institutional components comprising the architecture absorb or generate complexity. Here, the focus is on the architectural components and on their relationships rather than strategy and dynamics.

We must not forget that our aim is to outline a legal framework appropriate for e-justice development (Design Principle 4). Too often, e-justice is dealt with as just a problem of technological development in which the legal framework is something fixed and unchangeable. However, all the case studies point to the fact that e-justice always requires legal amendments that are powerful means of functional, administrative, technological and infrastructural simplification. Legal changes are needed to better host ICT development, outline a simpler architecture, set up a proper organisational support and avoid some of the intricacies associated with building information infrastructures. Before considering how technological implements can transform the administration of justice, then, it is necessary to check whether the current legal framework is appropriate for e-justice development and to identify the changes required to avoid an unmanageable level of complexity. The development of MCOL and COVL was fast and smooth thanks to the implementation of legal changes aimed at functionally simplifying the procedures to make them more suitable for digitisation. CITIUS followed a different approach, in which law and technology were updated in a iterative fashion to render the technological component developed by the Ministry of Justice performative.

The next principle is to keep law and technology decoupled as much as possible in order to avoid unmanageable complexity (Design Principle 5). While an appropriate legal framework is needed to simplify e-justice development and make the electronic exchange of information and performative utterances legal, legal changes can also generate complexity. This happens especially when the law prescribes the kind of technology that must be developed and adopted and how applications should work, as in the case of TOL (Sect. 3.5.2). Law and technology are two distinct regulative regimes, and intrusions of the law into the field of technology are risky. E-Curia provides a good example of how the law works well when it simply gives the green light to a given technology once its functioning and effectiveness have been tested (Sect. 9.6).

Design Principle 6 is the reduction of complexity through functional, technological and administrative simplification (Kallinikos 2009a). As noted when analysing the case studies, simplification is often a prerequisite of e-justice development. Legal changes are a powerful means of simplification, as we have already noted in this chapter. The best example is that following legal changes, a signature is no longer needed in petitions or procedural documents filed or exchanged through MCOL, COVL or e-Curia (Sect. 3.5.1). In addition, the EPO and ESCP benefitted from some procedural simplification (Chap. 11). Simplification can also be pursued without legal changes, however, simply by streamlining administrative and procedural steps, as in the case of MCOL, a paradigmatic example of how complexity can be reduced through administrative simplification. Simplification can also become necessary during the technological development, such as when TOL developers decided to focus their efforts on the digitisation of the money order instead of the entire set of civil proceedings (Sect. 7.4.2).

Design Principle 7 involves the black-boxing of complexity through tailored organisational arrangements. Many case studies provide examples of the centralisation and specialisation of organisational units in charge of handling or easing digitised procedures. The SIRENE bureaus and General Directorate of Translation at the Court of Justice and the national boards in charge of dealing with injunctive orders in COVL, MCOL and CITIUS all provide good examples of how tailored organisational arrangements can handle complexity that is offloaded by other courts. So far, the unique exception in this trend is TOL, in which digitally enabled procedures are not handled by a specialised or centralised board but are supposed to be handled by the entire Italian court system. As noticed in Sect. 7.6, this has delayed development and deployment of the system.

Design Principle 8 suggests to black-box complexity through procedural standardisation. The Court of Justice, COVL and MCOL provide clear examples of how standardisation facilitates the inscription of procedural steps and action components into the computerised systems. In these cases, having just one organisation in charge of handling the procedures eases standardisation and then inscription of the procedure into the technological system. The standardisation of procedures in the case of the EPO and ESCP is particularly difficult, amongst other reasons, because of the number of different courts adopting the procedures and the low effectiveness of the means available at European level for promoting standardisation in this area.

Enabling the transmission of data, information and performative utterances through the channels or media that better support it is Design Principle 9. In pursuing this goal, switches and gateways to allow the circulation of agency from digital to conventional (and vice versa) have to be provided. The 'one stop shop' and paperless offices (or procedures) are fascinating goals (Abdulaziz and Druke 2003) but they often trigger the need for highly sophisticated technological and infrastructural components, thereby introducing complexity into the system. A cursory glance at the case studies highlights how performative utterances are always transmitted through a web of digital and conventional channels. Going to the post office to send a procedural document to court may not be the best option but the document's digitisation and online transmission may require legal changes or expensive technological implements. More generally, some types of agency may circulate easily in the digital environment (for instance, access to general procedural information) whereas others may circulate easily in both media or not at all in the digital domain. Therefore, the architecture should facilitate the circulation of agency in the media that best supports it, and interfaces and switches allowing the circulation of agency in the various media should be provided to that end (Sect. 3.5.3).

Design Principle 10 entails the use of information infrastructures to absorb complexity. Information infrastructure development, may suffer from unmanageable complexity (Hanseth and Ciborra 2007; see also Sect. 2.4.3.1 in this book). As noticed in Chap. 7, the story of TOL is one of painstaking development of components of the information infrastructure that do not happen to be shared by prospective users. Similarly, for reasons that are not totally clear yet, SIS II is still stuck in a never-ending development stage (Sect. 8.3.1). In some cases, however, information infrastructure may absorb complexity. This is the case when e-justice systems and services are built with and upon components that are already available and shared by the prospective users, as demonstrated by some of our case studies. In MCOL, identification has been based for a long time on the payment of court fee through debit or credit card because other technologies were not available. In e-Curia, identification is based on simple registration and access requires nothing more than a valid email address and a web connection. In addition, information infrastructures embed knowledge about 'how to do' given sets of operations, such as e-banking, e-commerce and a number of other operations in the digital domain, and make such knowledge available to service providers and users. The more the new e-justice application resembles established digital practices, the more it will take advantage of the knowledge pool and technological components embedded in the infrastructure. This is particularly important in the case of occasional users, as it should be in the EPO and ESCP, while learning costs are more sustainable for frequent users. At the same time, performativity requires that the context of judicial procedure has to be well signalled and consequences of the actions made in the digital environment well understood by users (Sect. 3.5.4).

Balancing the type and the amount of agency delegated or assigned to each technological and organisational component to provide smooth circulation of agency is Design Principle 11. The circulation of agency is blocked every time one of the components gets overloaded and reaches the threshold of maximum manageable complexity. Too much complexity to be handled by an agent (be it the plaintiff, the local court or the defendant) may block the action or the transmission of performative utterances, or may require the involvement and support of third parties such as lawyers and translators. In the case of the EPO and ESCP, this happened a number of times. Moreover, at the design and development stage, too much procedural complexity inscribed or to be inscribed into a given technological application results in serious delays or in difficult evolution, as happened in the case of SIS II (Sect. 2.3.1).

14.4 Making It Simple: Assessing Alternative Architectures

We can now proceed to introduce some alternative institutional and organisational architectures and synthetically assess to what extent each of them meets the design criteria discussed in the previous section. Architectures are not just made of technological components: they are a combination of legal frameworks, institutional arrangements and technological implements that affects the circulation of agency and the transmission of performative utterances. Each of the architectures has different effects on the overall complexity of the system and provides a different way of handling it. The main goal of the architectures envisaged in the following is to keep procedural and architectural complexity below the upper threshold of maximum manageable complexity. At the same time, they have to respect the principle of maximum feasible simplicity by maintaining procedural and legal fairness and by allowing effective transborder proceedings (Sect. 1.7).

As we have seen in analysing the EPO and ESCP, in many cases the complexity to be handled by citizens or companies to file a case and carry out a procedure becomes too high (in spite of deliberate efforts at simplification). As a consequence, the plaintiff may make various mistakes, such as filing the case to the wrong court or filling out the form with the wrong information, or major difficulties may arise when paying court fees or trying to get a copy of the Court Order. These and other obstacles of various kinds interrupt the circulation of legal agency (that is, the capacity of a plaintiff resident in one country to file a case to a court of another country, or else the capacity of a court to effectively respond to citizens of a different country). Hiring a lawyer could help to solve the problem, but the EPO and ESCP have been designed to empower citizens and business, not to make them more dependent on legal intermediaries.

The new architectures always comprise an assemblage of institutional, legal and technological components. So, as a first step, we will identify a set of institutional and organisational architectures that may better support the circulation of agency. We will then identify some procedural improvements, and finally focus on the role that can be played by technological components. Some of the changes envisaged would require some kind of legal adaptation, whereas others can be implemented without any legal change.

14.4.1 Institutional and Organisational Architectures

The previous sections (and, in more detail, Chaps. 1, 10 and 11) clearly point out that the current regulations at the national and European levels are not effective in providing organisational frameworks that can effectively black-box complexity, and that a number of ad hoc interventions are needed to keep it at a manageable level; also that local courts have the same problem. In short, the analysis points out that the current organisational architecture is not effective in black-boxing complexity (Design Principle 7). Moreover, we observe an uneven allocation of complexity, with too much complexity to be faced by citizens and local courts and very limited support at central (EU) level.[3] The EU acts as a regulative body and

[3]See below for a discussion of the role of central national authorities (Ministries of Justice and Judicial Councils).

clearinghouse by providing standard information and downloadable forms but this may not be sufficient.[4] A strategy that introduces European procedures with very limited European support runs the risks of being self-defeating.

Institutional architectures should therefore be designed that reduce the overall amount of complexity to be handled. The goal of maximum feasible simplicity can be achieved through procedural standardisation, an improved organisational framework and a more balanced allocation of complexity across the human and nonhuman components of the service delivery system.

At the European level, three alternative architectures can be considered:

- The establishment of an ad hoc European Court,
- The establishment of a virtual European Court,
- The establishment of European Agency for transborder civil litigation.

From a functional perspective (i.e., providing functionalities and getting the work done regardless of costs and political wills), the best option would be to establish a European Court for transborder civil proceedings with judges and clerks hired by the EU to handle transborder cases. To understand the advantages of this institutional solution in terms of procedural simplification and capacity to manage the complexity, it is sufficient to examine the case of the European Court of Justice (see Chap. 9). However, because of the high costs associated with it and the strong political support needed to set it up, we think that at present this is not a viable solution.

Alternatively, less demanding solutions are available, such as the establishment of a virtual European Court, i.e., a virtual organisation in which national courts (or justice systems) assign some of their resources (judges and clerks) and which operate primarily through electronics means. The European virtual court should be composed by national judges appointed and trained to deal with transborder civil litigation such as the EPO and ESCP. Judges would work in their own national courts, keeping their role, status and wage, but would operate in the name of the European Court. This arrangement would not lead to relevant additional costs. Selected judges would handle the EPO and ESCP as part of their 'ordinary' judicial duties, but they would work in a coordinated way with colleagues handling the same cases in other countries. ICT can support such distributed organisation in various ways through groupware technology and dedicated case management system (on this point, see Sect. 14.5.3). This solution would not establish a new European Court with judges and staff employed by the EU; instead, it would

[4]The e-Justice portal aims to be a 'one-stop (electronic) shop for information on European justice and access to European judicial procedures. The Portal is targeted at citizens, businesses, legal practitioners and the judiciary. Citizens shall enjoy the same access to justice in other member states as they would in their own and the European e-Justice Portal contributes in a practical way to the removal of barriers, such as providing information in 22 languages and a wealth of links to relevant websites and documents.' e-justice.europa.eu/contentMaximisation.do?plang=enandamp;legalnotice=1. Last visited 30 December 2012.

be a light organisational arrangement, network-based, intentionally designed to create a community of practice and shared standard procedures that black-box complexity (Design Principles 7 and 8). On the one hand, it would buffer the national courts from the complexity involved in handling the EPO and ESCP. On the other hand, it would enhance the capacity of organisational actors to manage the complexity associated with such procedures, thereby raising the threshold of maximum manageable complexity. In addition, effective procedural standardisation would reduce the uncertainty associated with the different application of the EPO and ESCP procedures at national level, so it would pursue the goal of maximum feasible simplicity more effectively without hampering the legal safeguards.

A third option would be the establishment of a European Office in charge of handling selected administrative or quasi-judicial activities that could be better managed in a centralised European body. Unlike the two architectures discussed above, it would not provide any judicial function and the competent courts would remain those established by the EU or member state legislation. The primary function of the Office would be to ease the circulation of agency in selected areas. It could facilitate the identification of the competent court and the routing of the procedural documents. It might ease the payment of court fees and keep updated the registry of the courts with the jurisdiction over the EPO and ESCP in each member state. It might also provide various kinds of support to the procedure, such as advising both case parties and local (or national) courts about the steps to be followed, including the organisation of training for judges of the member states. The Office could also be responsible for the maintenance of the technological systems (case management or e-filing application) that support the EPO and the ESCP, such as the e-Justice portal, the e-filing application currently piloted by e-Codex and the case management system that will be considered below. Some of these functions have been performed by the European Judicial Network in civil and commercial matters and are now mediated by the e-Justice portal. However, while we have noticed some improvement, a lot of work still has to be done, since a service like this, to be effective, cannot be just a collection of general information more or less updated. It must be supported by a back office in charge of providing case-related information and other functions. With such functions, the Office would absorb a relevant share of the complexity currently handled by courts, plaintiffs and defendants, thus enabling pro se litigation for citizens and businesses, supporting national courts and reducing uncertainty, complexity and costs associated with this kind of litigation.

The establishment of an organisational structure capable of black-boxing procedural, organisational and semantic complexity (Design Principle 7) and of simplifying functional activities (Design Principle 6) to ease the circulation of transborder agency is the minimum necessary requirement to transform the EPO and ESCP into procedures really accessible to EU citizens and businesses. Such a central office could operate by supporting the 'European virtual court' or the 'national courts', and provide the required organisational and technical support to the technological applications described below.

The institutional and organisational architecture can also be improved with changes at the level of member states. In several European countries, the EPO and ESCP have to be handled by the ordinary local court with territorial jurisdiction. This raises complexity for both sides: for the claimant, who may have serious problems identifying the jurisdiction, and for the local court, which, handling few cases, may have serious problems identifying the right procedure.

This institutional arrangement could be improved by identifying one (or a few) specific national court(s) with jurisdiction on transborder cases. This solution has been successfully implemented in various countries. Here, the most important change would be to establish a specialised national jurisdiction for transborder procedures in any member state (Design Principle 7), as is the case of EPO in Germany and Austria. This change in the current architecture has the effect of offloading complexity from local courts, thus concentrating the handling of the cases in a single specialised unit. The identification of the jurisdiction is also made easier because all EPO or ESCP claims must be filed at one national court and not at local courts, helping to solve one of the problems for the plaintiffs and increasing the simplicity of the system. The greater advantage of a unified national jurisdiction is to have a specialised court handling the procedures on a regular base, thus avoiding the need for local courts to handle a few cases per year and improving the capacity of the central court to black-box complexity through effective procedural standardisation (Design Principle 8). Indeed, this centralised solution would ease the establishment of standard procedures and facilitate the debugging of problems and misapplications of the regulation as identified by the simulation. It may also make the linguistic barriers less critical because it would be easier to concentrate the staff with foreign-language skills in the court with national jurisdiction, provide multilingual documentation services and, more generally, support learning processes.

In passing, it is also worth mentioning a further scenario that could by-pass the EPO and ESCP. Indeed, if the problem is to facilitate transborder litigation within the EU, the possibility should be seriously considered of opening the existing national e-justice services for small claims (such as MCOL, COVL, TOL and CITIUS) to all European citizens, business and lawyers. This is currently allowed only by Slovenia's COVL, while the other systems are open only to citizens or lawyers of the respective member states. Since these applications, in most cases, are already providing good services at the national level, the possibility to extend their accessibility to transborder users should be explored. In this scenario, any EU citizen could file a case in any of the e-justice services provided by the national jurisdictions. However, since this option bypasses the EPO and ESCP, it will not be discussed further here.

14.4.2 Simplifying the Procedural Framework

Independent of the changes envisaged at the architectural level, some improvements should also be considered at the procedural level to make procedures more suitable for e-justice development (Design Principle 4) and functionally simplified (Design Principle 6).

First, some of the semantic problems affecting the access to the EPO and ESCP could be solved by the use of one or a few standard languages. Even though this choice will create asymmetries between the citizens of the European Union, the reduction of the complexity associated with semantic issues would make access to transborder remedies much simpler for a larger number of prospective users.

Second, it may be helpful to increase the ceiling for filing ESCP claims because the current limit of €2,000 is too low to attract prospective users. Without releasing this excessively tight constraint, it will be rather difficult to reach a critical mass of users for the ESCP and produce self-reinforcing cycles (see Chaps. 1 and 2) and ensure the long-term sustainability of the application (see below).

Third, it is strongly advisable to decouple law and technology (Design Principle 5), especially when EU regulation prescribes the use of a given technology (advanced electronic signature) for the identification and signature of electronic documents in the EPO. With this constraint, it is almost impossible for the largest majority of European citizens to file a case electronically because it prescribes the use of a technological component that is not sufficiently diffused, and this contingency makes the development of interoperable procedures at the European level extremely difficult and complex as emerged in Chap. 13.

Some legal changes (or better implementation of the current regulations) may be required also at member states level to facilitate the black-boxing of complexity through effective procedural standardisation. In particular, each member state should implement the appropriate measures to have legislation (and technology) supporting electronic payment of court fees, since it is not clear if this is legally allowed in each member states. In addition, the court fees for such specific procedures should be all inclusive lump sum, to avoid the need of paying additional fees to get the copies of the order or of the judgement issued by the court, as emerged during the simulation. While they may look as minor changes, the removal of such procedural oddities in the transborder circulation will be extremely beneficial to establish an effective legal and administrative interoperability and promote a more effective implementation of EPO and ESCP regulations.

14.4.3 Technological Interoperability and the Cultivation of the Installed Base

Technological, procedural and institutional components of the architecture are entangled in various ways. Sometimes they cancel one another out and sometimes they reinforce each other. It may happen that technological artefacts inscribe and absorb critical organisational functionalities, thus curbing organisational complexity, but it may also happen that new organisational components are required to manage technology, thus adding to organisational complexity (Sect. 1.6). Moving from this understanding, we have identified a set of minimal procedural changes needed to establish the organisational and procedural preconditions required for e-justice development.

We have also introduced different institutional architectures designed to offload the complexity faced by users and local courts handling the EPO and ESCP: a full-fledged EU Court, a virtual EU Court and, at the national level, the identification of just one court in charge of such procedures in each member state.

We also maintain that an EU Office with some capacity to support circulation of agency at EU level is a functional need. This is currently carried out by the Commission and single member states through the management of the e-Justice portal, but should be further improved in different ways (see below).

E-justice applications can support each of the three envisaged architectures in different ways. A full-fledged EU Court, being a relatively autonomous institution (like the European Court of Justice), would require a very limited degree of interoperability with the ICT systems of the judiciaries of the member states. The Court could build its own systems decoupled from those of the member states. A virtual European Court would benefit from groupware technologies and from a shared platform with case management facilities for handling cases. Sadly, such architectures will not be implemented in the short term. We can therefore discuss in more detail how e-justice can support the current architecture, within which cases are dealt with by member states (with local courts, or with courts with national jurisdiction) while the e-Justice portal provides some information and guidance for prospective users.

Within this framework, our final design question is: Which features should an e-justice application have in order to effectively support the EPO and ESCP without being too complex to be developed, too interoperable to be evolvable and too expensive to be sustainable in the long run? In this case, too, we should identify a solution by considering the twin design principles of maximum manageable complexity and maximum feasible simplicity.

At present, the technology supports the EPO and ESCP through dynamic web forms available at the e-Justice portal, and through the information provided by the European Judicial Atlas in Civil Matters. The forms can be downloaded or filled out online, printed and sent by post to the competent court. As the simulation showed, they provide inadequate support to prospective users; consequently, the circulation of agency is hindered in various ways. For instance, based on the current level of technological support it is difficult, if not impossible, to pay the court fee, to get a copy of the payment order or to serve the court decision to the defendant through the bailiffs of another country.

These difficulties are to be taken as the starting point for cultivation of the installed base that is currently represented by the e-Justice portal, with the purpose of easing the circulation of agency. The system should provide an effective procedural support to users and courts, black-boxing the complexity they have to face.

As with MCOL or COVL, the new system should work as a web-based interface for both courts (judges and clerks) and external users (plaintiffs and defendants). It should also work as a case management system that black-boxes complexity through strict procedural guidance and standardisation (Design Principle 8) and by providing additional services to judges and clerks.

To be more precise, the system must provide case and workflow management functions for both users and courts, which currently are not provided. A case management technology for the EPO and ESCP, made available to the courts of the member states, can enhance procedural standardisation and reduce complexity (Design Principles 8 and 10). In addition, a case management technology entails functional simplification and closure and would enforce a standard procedure across European jurisdictions (Design Principles 6 and 9). The ways in which this can occur is discussed below in the analysis of how the digitally supported procedure works.

The cultivation of the e-Justice portal should benefit from the semantic technologies as outlined in Sect. 12.5. The toolbox is composed of various instruments such as an ontology for the identification of the court, FAQs for practical issues and for questions about national law, ontologies and question-and-answer forms for determining key legal issues such as the ground of the court's jurisdiction (a wizard providing this function has recently been added to the e-Justice portal). All these technological implements are aimed at inscribing procedural complexity (Czarniawska and Joerges 1998) into the e-justice platform. The inscription is not cost-free or something that can be done in one shot: the cultivation of the e-Justice portal would require some organisational development to support operations. A back office in charge of monitoring, maintaining and updating the platform must be established, and the 'EU Office' introduced above should take care of such functions that require a mix of technical, legal and administrative know-how.

Going back to the results of our studies, the simulation has shown how agency circulates smoothly in two critical areas: the identification of the parties (the simple hand signature is accepted without any problem even in Italy) and the transmission of the form to the court via normal postal service. A logical consequence is that the e-Justice portal should exploit the advantages offered by the introduction of smart switches between digital and conventional agency (Design Principle 9), to pursue the goal of letting agency circulate across national borders and across different media. As a matter of fact, in some cases agency circulates more smoothly offline than online. The system should therefore provide digital channels for communication between all the actors involved but also support offline paper-based procedures to by-pass problems emerging in the digital domain, such as digital signature or digital identification (Design Principle 9).

In both our research and in the e-Codex project, emphasis has been placed on access, identification and transmission of performative utterances or procedural documents. At this level, the transborder circulation of agency based on conventional procedures is working smoothly. Therefore all users unable to satisfy the current technological requirements prescribed by the EU regulation, in particular advanced electronic signature, can use the conventional channels (hand-written signature and post) without having or creating particular problems. This observation explains the difference between the solution we envisage and that being pursued by the pilot of e-Codex. Indeed, e-Codex is trying to establish interoperability between the digital identification systems of the member states in order to sign the forms with advanced electronic signature and transmit them to the competent authorities through secure digital channels. As we have noted, our study found that this is not what creates problems for the transborder circulation of agency; the problems are elsewhere. So, while waiting for the successful piloting of the e-Codex technologies and for the planned 'citizens entry point' placed at the e-Justice portal, conventional access will remain open and will work trouble free (see Chap. 13).

While waiting for the "citizens entry point" to be opened at the e-Justice portal, and for the interoperability between national eIdentity and signature solutions as with the pilots developed by STORK, other options could be considered. Here we can observe, again, that in order to insure the reaching of a critical mass of users, access must and could be provided also through existing technological solutions. Identity federations already in place, such as those developed in the pan-European research network, could make European trans border proceedings easily accessible to a first bulk of potential users. For example EduGAIN,[5] the identity inter-federation of the research and education domain, provides eIdentity to about 16 millions users spread all over Europe.[6] Other European projects, like SEMIRAMIS,[7] are suggesting the use of identity federations to grant identification and ease the access to pan-european e-Services (Neinert 2010).

14.5 A Design Proposal for a Digitally Enabled Procedure

We now have the components required to show how the system could function from the user's perspective.

14.5.1 Claimant: Registration

- The new user registers his/her credentials into the web application supporting the EPO and ESCP and accepts the terms of use of the system (as with e-Curia or other services based on the user's registration). The procedure should be similar to those of common e-commerce services.

[5] http://www.geant.net/service/eduGAIN/Pages/home.aspx. Last visited 20 June 2012.

[6] See https://www.idem.garr.it/it/fatti-e-cifre/cifre-edugain. Last visited 20 June 2012.

[7] See http://joinup.ec.europa.eu/software/semiramis/description

14.5.2 Claimant: Preparation of the Claim

- Once the registered user has received a username and password, he/she can log in to the system and, through a secure website, enter the data into a web form, similar to those already developed in the new release of the 'e-Justice portal'.
- The web-based system should offer strict procedural guidance, supporting the user in critical areas such as the identification of the competent court and the payment of the court fee. The last release of the e-Justice portal already provides this kind of guidance.
- The semantic toolbox described above can further support the preparation of the case.
- In addition, the website should provide a procedure for granting the online payment of the court fee, one of the main obstacles in the current functioning of the procedures.

14.5.3 Claimant: Delivery of the Case to the Competent Court (Switch Online–Offline)

- At this stage, the form must be delivered to the competent court. If the user has a digital identity recognised by EU regulation and supported by the system currently developed by e-Codex, he/she should be entitled to sign the form and send it digitally to the competent court. In this case, electronic filing has to be considered adequate. The solution developed by e-Curia to avoid changes to the procedural document, such as unique identification number and hash tag, can be used also in this case.
- We believe that electronic filing will be accessible to a very limited number of prospective users so, following the Design Principle 9, the system should provide a handy switch to go offline. The user can save and print the form, sign it and deliver it to the competent court through normal post. As in the previous case, a unique ID number and a hashtag are attached to the form to ensure that the document delivered by post is identical to the one saved in the e-justice platform. The data entered in the form (and the documents) are also submitted to the competent court in digital format. Not being digitally signed, the filing can be considered complete only once the court has received the paper copy duly signed. The court uploads the digital file together with paper filing and can take advantage of these data for its operation. All the data are saved into the e-Justice portal.
- The claimant (and, at a later stage, the defendant) could use the e-Justice portal as a tool to stay informed about procedural developments of his/her case.

14.5.4 Court: Case Processing

- In both cases, the competent court receives an alert that a case has been filed with a communication that can be sent by the official email address of the court. The email informs the court that the case must (or can) be processed by taking advantage of the e-justice platform for the EPO and ESCP. From a court perspective, this e-justice platform should work as a case management system, providing guidance about what has to be done (expected procedural steps, etc.) and collecting all the data about the procedure.
- Court users must have user names and passwords. The web-based application should ease data entry in the forms to be completed by the court and should allow procedural checks, such as control of the court fees. As we have seen, it is critical to provide strict procedural support to the courts to avoid mistakes.
- The system should offer the options of printing off the payment order and sending it by post or delivering it by electronic means. Checks should be provided to push courts to serve the orders as indicated by the regulation. Following the MCOL experience, the court should serve not just the court order but also a 'claim pack', with all the data and information required to reply through the e-justice platform for the EPO and ESCP or on paper. The documentation should be served by post but also delivered digitally for the parties that have accepted the terms of use (as in e-Curia).

14.5.5 Defendant

- Once the defendant has received the claim pack, he/she can access the e-justice EPO and ESCP platform and use it to acknowledge the debt, file an opposition or take any procedural step prescribed by the regulation. In addition, the defendant must have the option to use the medium he/she prefers.

We do not anticipate that this use of the platform would require legal changes. Indeed, the use of the forms provided by the e-Justice portal is already prescribed by the legislation and therefore can be extended to the forms made available on the case management system provided by the e-Justice portal. In addition, national courts should be encouraged to use the platform because it would provide guidance and services tailored to the needs of the transborder procedures, procedural checks and deadlines, statistical data collection, etc. Even in this case, the development of technological implements and the cultivation of the information infrastructure require a joint intervention at the organisational level.

As we have noted, different types and levels of interoperability are needed to allow the circulation of agency. The institutional architectures have major effects on institutional interoperability, the semantic toolbox improves semantic interoperability and procedural changes ease legal interoperability, but what kind of interoperability is needed at the technological level between the system we have outlined and the computerised systems of national judiciaries?

To find the answer to this we need to know the number of users, which, in the absence of any statistical data, appears to be rather limited. At this stage, there are no good reasons to build interoperability between the envisaged technological platform enabled by the e-Justice portal and those of national justice systems. To set up a system supporting the circulation of bits and data for a very limited number of cases would raise technical and organisational complexity with minimal returns. At the same time, the platform should be developed with the possibility in mind of making it interoperable with other applications, but only if the number of users grows significantly.

14.6 Building Interoperability for European Civil Proceedings Online: Some Final Remarks

The original goal of the research project has been to establish interoperability at legal, technological, semantic and institutional levels. The result has been the discovery of the huge amount of complexity to be faced to achieve interoperability. It was clear from our studies that complexity represents a major obstacle to the circulation of agency across media and national justice systems. Hence, we started to explore how to design for simplicity and learned how to avoid some of the complexity traps affecting e-justice development and the transmission of performative utterances. The result is an unconventional approach to e-justice in which technological system-to-system interoperability is kept to a minimum and various interventions are identified and proposed to reduce or black-box complexity through various means. The outcome is, on the one hand, a technological and organisational architecture in which the smooth circulation of agency in transborder civil proceedings is secured by a number of measures at organisational, semantic and procedural level, but, on the other hand, limited interoperability between the e-justice applications of member states. Indeed, as we have noted, the system can work without establishing system-to-system interoperability between national digital identification platforms: it does not have to be interoperable with national case management systems or national e-justice platforms. It is simply a web-based platform designed to work as a self-contained system, even if the possibility of building gateways and interfaces with national systems should also be considered.

The loose coupling between the e-justice platform supporting the EPO and ESCP and the national e-justice systems keeps infrastructural complexity low while increasing the level of service provided to users. Indeed, we believe that the threshold of maximum manageable complexity would be quickly reached if the judiciaries of the member states built and maintained gateways between their own systems and the European one. The loose coupling also facilitates evolvability: the web application could change without imposing modifications on the national systems, and vice versa. Indeed, the development of interoperability among national systems is everything but easy and inexpensive. It requires high development, maintenance and evolution costs. Any time a national system has to be updated, the connections with the European gateways allowing interoperability between member states has to be re-established. Is it worthwhile? If we follow the theory of information infrastructures (Chap. 2), we ought to say yes, but only if we expect to have a high and growing number of cases. Expecting a limited number of EPO and ESCP claims, simpler solutions are needed, and so less agency has to be delegated to computer systems and more to organisation and humans. At the same time, when the system is eventually used by a growing number of citizens and companies, the e-justice platform supporting the EPO and ESCP can be integrated with the e-justice systems of the member states. In this manner, we claim, agency will be able to circulate across media and national jurisdictions without reaching the threshold of maximum manageable complexity and maintaining the legal, functional and semantic standards required by judicial proceedings.

At the same time, we have identified a set of interventions at institutional, semantic and procedural levels to increase interoperability at these levels and ease the circulation of agency without the direct involvement of technology. We have learned that the design and adoption of technological solutions to solve problems that belong to other domains (institutional, legal or semantic) are among the key reasons for complexity growth.

References

Abdulaziz, M.K., and W.E Druke. 2003. Building the "paperless" court. Paper presented at the CTC8, Kansas City, 27–30 Oct 2003.

Ciborra, C. 2002. *The labyrints of information. Challanging the wisdom of the system*. Oxford: Oxford University Press.

Contini, F. 2009. ICT, assemblages and institutional contexts: Understanding multiple development paths. In *ICT and innovation in the public sector. European studies in the making of e-government*. ed. F. Contini and G.F. Lanzara, 244–271. Basingstoke: Palgrave.

Czarniawska, B., and B. Joerges. 1998. The question of technology, or how organizations inscribe the world. *Organisation Studies* 19(3): 363–385.

ECC-Net. 2012. *European small claims procedure report*. Bruxelles: European Consumer Centers Network.

European Judicial Network in Civil and Commercial Matter. 2011. A citizens' guide to cross-border civil litigation in the European Union. European Commission, Bruxelles. doi: 10.2838/13991.

Fabri, M. 2009. E-justice in Finland and in Italy: Enabling versus constraining models. In *ICT and innovation in the public sector European perspectives in the making of e-government*, ed. F. Contini and G.F. Lanzara, 115–145. Basingstoke: Palgrave.

Hanseth, O. 2003. Design as bootstrapping. On the evolution of ICT networks in health care. *Methods of Information in Medicine* 42(4): 385–391.

Hanseth, O., and C. Ciborra (eds.). 2007. *Risk, complexity and ICT*. Bodmin: Edward Elgar.

Kallinikos, J. 2009a. Institutional complexities and functional simplification. The case of money claims online. In *ICT and innovation in the public sector. European studies in the making of e-government*, ed. F. Contini and G.F. Lanzara, 174–210. Basingstoke: Palgrave Macmillan.

Kallinikos, J. 2009b. The regulative regime of technology. In *ICT and innovation in the public sector*, ed. C. Francesco and L. Giovan Francesco, 66–87. Basingstoke: Palgrave.

Lanzara, G.F. 2009. Building digital institutions: ICT and the rise of assemblages in government. In *ICT and innovation in the public sector*, ed. F. Contini and G.F. Lanzara, 9–48. Houndsmill: Palgrave.

Mohr, R., and F. Contini. 2011. Reassembling the legal. 'the wonders of modern science' in court-related proceedings. *Griffith Law Review—Special Symposium: The Laws of Technology and the Technology of Law* 20(3): 994–1019.

Neinert, S. 2010. Semiramis. Copenhagen. http://www.terena.org/activities/tf-emc2/meetings/16/semiramis_at_tfemc2_copenhagen_2010-09-22.pdf.

Reiling, D. 2009. *Technology for justice. How information technology can support judicial reform.* Leiden: Leiden University Press.

The World Bank. 2003. A definition of E*Government. The world bank. http://www1.worldbank.org/publicsector/egov/index.htm. Accessed 12 Dec 2003.

Velicogna, M. 2008. Use of information and communication technologies (ICT) in European judicial systems. CEPEJ Studies N. 7. European commission for the efficiency of justice (CEPEJ), Strasbourg.

About the Authors

Davide Carnevali researcher at the Research Institute on Judicial Systems of the National Research Council of Italy (IRSIG-CNR). His research interest and publications deal with areas of judicial reform, judicial administration, ICT management and organizational change in justice systems, improvement and assessment of the quality of justice. Consultant in the above mentioned research fields and lecturer in related training programme, he served also as Organisational Analyst at the Italian Ministry of Justice, IT General Directorate.

Francesco Contini senior researcher at the Research Institute on Judicial Systems of the National Research Council of Italy. He studies technological and organisational transformations of European judiciaries. He has coordinated the project 'Building Interoperability for European Civil Proceedings on Line', which findings are publish in this book, and has worked as advisor in various areas of judicial reform. His last book on e-justice is 'ICT and innovation in the public sector', edited with Giovan Francesco Lanzara (Palgrave 2009).

Diana Fernandes research assistant at the Centre for Social Studies of the University of Coimbra and of the Permanent Observatory on Portuguese Justice. Her current research interests concern mental illness and law, sociology of family law, and methodology of comparative law.

Paula Fernando researcher at Centre for Social Studies of the University of Coimbra and of the Permanent Observatory on Portuguese Justice. Her current research interests focus on the domains of the legal professions, sociological characterization of the judiciary and judicial reforms.

Conceição Gomes researcher at Centre for Social Studies of the University of Coimbra, Executive Coordinator of the Permanent Observatory on Portuguese Justice and Coordinator of the Unit for Legal and Judiciary Training. Her current research interests focus on the domains of the sociology of law and sociology of the administration of justice, State and judiciary, and justice reforms.

F. Contini and G.F. Lanzara (eds.), *The Circulation of Agency in E-Justice*, Law, Governance and Technology Series 13, DOI 10.1007/978-94-007-7525-1,

Jorge González-Conejero Ph.D. in Information and Communications Engineering (2009). He is currently a researcher at the IDT-UAB. His research interests are focused on Image and Video Processing, Legal Knowledge Representation, and Compliance and Risk Management. He has authored and coauthored 20 contributions to international conferences and two on international journals.

Ole Hanseth professor of Information Systems at the department of informatics, University of Oslo. His research interests concentrate on the socio-technical complexity of large-scale information systems and infrastructures: how such systems and infrastructures are evolving and strategies and approaches to their development.

Giovan Francesco Lanzara professor of Organization Studies and Political Science at the University of Bologna, Department of Political and Social Sciences., and visiting professor at the London School of Economics and Political Science (2006–2012). He has given broadly published contributions to three major disciplines – organization studies, information systems research, and political science. His focal research interest is the processes of ICT-based innovation in organizations, institutions and professional practices.

Giampiero Lupo researcher at the IRSIG –CNR (Research Institute on Judicial Systems – National Research Centre). His interests are the use of ICT in the Justice Systems, quality of the Justice Systems, quality of democracy, quality of deliberative democracy, social capital and migrations.

Marco Mellone Ph.D. European Union Law and researcher at Research Institute on Judicial Systems of the National Research Council of Italy (IRSIG-CNR). His main fields of research are private international law, rules on civil proceedings and European Union law.

Richard Mohr sociologist who has worked in universities, and the public and private sectors. He is director of Social Research, Policy and Planning (an Australian consultancy) and is a visiting professorial fellow in the Legal Intersections Research Centre at the University of Wollongong, Australia. He has published widely in socio-legal and semiotic journals. His most recent book is Law and Religion in Public Life: The Contemporary Debate, edited with Nadirsyah Hosen (Routledge 2011).

Gar Yein Ng assistant professor at the Legal Studies Department of Central European University, Budapest, Hungary. Her research interests are comparative constitutional law, especially focusing on judicial power, court organisation and management, and legal proceedings.

Marta Poblet researcher on law and technology and the current director of the UAB Institute of Law and Technology. She lectures at the International Master on Conflict Resolution of the Universitat Oberta de Catalunya (UOC). Her research areas cover legal organisations, judicial systems, conflict management and resolution, ADR-ODR, mobile technologies for development, and crisis mapping.

Andrea Resca Post-Doc at LUISS "Guido Carli" University, Rome, Centre of Research on Information Systems (Ce.R.S.I.) is continuing to collaborate with The Research Institute on Judicial Systems (IRSIG-CNR) on e-Justice. His publications range from the Organisation Theory discipline to Information Systems discipline including e-government and e-participation as his current research domains.

Antoni Roig professor of constitutional law at the UAB Law School. He has been a researcher of national and European projects. He has published in the areas of the sources of Law, European Law, databases, e-Government, free speech and technology, and citizens' and workers' privacy. His recent publications deal with privacy and social networks. He holds a doctorate in law at the UAB and has conducted post doctorate research at the universities of Cattolica di Milano (Milano 1996–1997) and Università degli Studi di Firenze (Firenze 1997). He is currently enrolled in a Computer Science Technical Engineering degree at the Open University of Catalonia.

Gregor Strojin Master of International and Comparative Law, a Specialisation in Information Technology and Intellectual Property Law and a Bar qualification. Since 2002, he has worked at the Supreme Court of Slovenia on a number of ICT related projects in the judiciary. His main work and research topics are optimisation of legal procedures and perception of law in society.

Josep Suquet researcher at the UAB Institute of Law and Technology. He participates in both European and national research projects. His areas of research cover Online Dispute Resolution, Alternative Dispute Resolution, Online Consumer Mediation and Semantic and Legal Interoperability.

Marco Velicogna researcher at the Research Institute on Judicial Systems of the National Research Council of Italy. His research interests are in the areas of judicial administration, comparative judicial systems, court technology, information infrastructures, evaluation and the management of innovation. He has participated in a number of national and international research projects; served as consultant and collaborated with the Italian Ministry of Justice and several international institutions.

Index

F. Contini and G.F. Lanzara (eds.), *The Circulation of Agency in E-Justice*, Law, Governance and Technology Series 13, DOI 10.1007/978-94-007-7525-1,

CPSIA information can be obtained
at www.ICGtesting.com
Printed in the USA
LVOW04*2003260516
490139LV00010B/79/P

9 789400 775244